The Career Guarantee

The Career Guarantee

Take Control of Your Future!

by Christopher J. Kusellas

Career T.E.A.M., LLC

The Career Guarantee
Take Control of Your Future!

by Christopher J. Kuselias

Career T.E.A.M., LLC
P.O.Box 185160
Hamden, Connecticut 06518
info@careerteam.com
www.careerteam.com
(203) 407-8800

ISBN: 978-0-615-28386-9

Printed in the United States of America

First printing

Cover design: TLC Graphics, www.tlcgraphics.com
Typography and composition: www.dmargulis.com

To all those, present and future, who through this publication find their true calling, establish their unique and compelling contribution and attain the most critical measure of success—balance. I salute you!

Contents

Before You Begin

"Your career will have a profound effect on your health, family, relationships, purchases and peace of mind. Knowing this, why would anyone possibly leave their happiness and success to chance? With all the inventions, mergers, innovations and opportunities in this new global economy, anyone willing to explore their true motivations can find a career they love."

—Chris Kuselias

I WOULD PERSONALLY LIKE TO thank you for making the decision to read *The Career Guarantee,* an exciting career management-training system. This book is a healthy mix of idealism and realism and is complemented by www.thecareerguarantee.com, the most exciting career website available.

The purpose is *to help you maximize your career potential.* If you fully dedicate yourself to this process, I am confident you will acquire the competitive edge needed to obtain your career calling and succeed in today's highly specialized and competitive job markets. Remember, my objective is your success!

> The unique aspect of my work is to package you as a product ... a problem solving energizer to be marketed efficiently and effectively in the 21st century workplace.

While you and I may never actually meet personally, I know you better than you think. What you're looking for is what we are all looking for ... happiness, recognition, security and benefits, an opportunity to meet new and exciting people and, of course, maximum compensation for your professional contributions!

To prepare you, I have spent my life researching and analyzing the process of career happiness. The company I created, *Career* T.E.A.M., LLC, is founded on the principle that individuals should take a proactive role in designing and managing their career. I believe that when you truly enjoy what you do, work feels like play. Our firm has been recognized nationally for innovative and inspirational methods with thousands of clients on welfare to corporate executives earning over $1,000,000 per year.

After 25 years, I know what separates those who have passion and purpose in their career from those who remain unfulfilled. Most people today are seeking a career path where they feel like they matter ... where their contributions are making a difference ... where they can be happy to their very core!

Why *The Career Guarantee*?

I MADE THE DECISION TO launch www.thecareerguarantee.com and author this book because of dire economic conditions and because I see a lot of unhappy people who have no place to go for beneficial career advice. Consider this ...

- Where do you go when in need of a physical or when you have an ailment? Answer ... you go to a doctor.
- Where do you go with a financial question or in need of tax advice? Answer ... you go to an accountant.
- Where do you go when you are in need of legal advice? Answer ... you go to a lawyer.

Where do you go when you need career management advice? Answer ... (Jeopardy theme heard in the background). Bingo! There was no reliable source ... until now!

As a media personality paid to deliver speeches, write books and appear on television and radio, I have an agent who manages my career. What does an agent do? An agent provides advice and counsel. Think of me as your *career agent*, because I am here to help match your skills, interests and abilities with the best opportunity for you. My career calling is to help you find yours! It's time to get your career in gear and recapture your passion!

3 Reasons to Read This Book

H ERE ARE 3 REASONS why you should read this book:

1. You will learn a proven formula (the 5P's) for finding your career calling with the challenge, recognition and emotional rewards you want and *deserve.*
2. You will learn the secrets of mastering the 21st century workplace and establishing a competitive edge for prosperity and lifelong career success.

3. www.thecareerguarantee.com will become the most valuable website resource in your personal learning library as your needs change over time and you are challenged to keep up with an ever evolving job market.

The 21st century workplace continues to undergo massive changes right before our very eyes! Today the average person changes jobs over 15 times in their life, with each job lasting about 3–4 years. My role is to be a positive resource and help you make sound decisions as your needs, values, and interests change. And believe me, they will change!

The fact remains that only about 20% of the careering process requires mastery of the *mechanics* of finding a job. *Mechanics* refers to the resume, cover letter, interviewing, employment applications, creating a thank-you letter, salary negotiation, etc. 80% of the process of obtaining your true calling is mastering your own *psychology.* What makes you unique? What do you want to do? What is holding you back? What do you fear? What are your strengths? What do you value? Who are you really? Answering these questions in a fun and interesting format is why these methods have been so successful.

How This Book Is Organized

"Realizing your career calling is like building a model. If you have a clearly defined set of instructions and can work at your own pace … the process becomes easy!"
—Chris Kuselias

I HAVE ORGANIZED THIS BOOK by starting with the chapters about the psychology of your success, presenting the *why* first, followed by the *how.*

1. *The Career Guarantee* is divided into 10 easy to follow chapters (steps); each a building-block to help you achieve your ultimate calling.
2. Chapters contain practical exercises and quotes from noted authors and industry experts to enhance each important phase of the process.
3. Each chapter is summarized by major points for ease of use, while success tips are highlighted to reinforce key concepts.

On www.thecareerguarantee.com, you can join our mission and access valuable resources for you to enhance your knowledge. It is my goal for every family to establish a personal learning library in their home, a library that contains best practices for living a life of contribution, balance and prosperity. The user friendly information will hopefully become part of your *wellness* collection.

I subscribe to the theory that many people need to hear a message a minimum of 8 times before it truly sinks in and becomes a habit. Here is the formula:

Repetition (make a conscious change)

    ↘

        Routine (create a subconscious change)

           ↘

                Ritual (develop an emotional attachment)

                    ↘

                        Rhythm (create incredible momentum)

                            ↘

                                Results (a great career!)

How to Apply What You Learn in This Book

HERE ARE 3 STRATEGIES you can use in applying what you learn in this book:

1. Simply read the book straight through, from beginning to end.
2. Read through the entire book with a highlighter; then go back and read your highlighted sections.
3. Adopt it as a part of your daily learning routine. Read and apply a new chapter every week, every 2 weeks, every 2 months, or in whatever time frame works for your schedule.

The more open and honest you are with yourself in regards to your answers, the more accurate you will be in obtaining a terrific career. Keep in mind that attaining true career happiness involves reflection and self-analysis.

To help you avoid procrastination, I have divided *the process of finding your calling into a series of 10 manageable chapters* to be completed in a systematic, step-by-step approach. Building momentum with these small steps will help you resist the temptation to make excuses for not achieving everything you want in your life. You will *learn to associate your decision to pursue your career calling with fun and enjoyment. Together,* we will inventory your achievements, you probably have more to be proud of than you think!

Want results? Together, we will *decide as quickly as possible exactly what path you want to follow.* After you have formulated a career objective and assessed the qualifications needed to obtain the position, we will assign priorities to your list of action steps, which you will need to complete in order to reach your ultimate goal.

Model the actions of people who have achieved career success and happiness in the fields that interest you; and *imitate their behaviors.* This simple technique will separate the career dreamers from the career achievers and save you years of frustration. Career success is not due to luck or fate, but rather to quality mentors, a specific focus and a strong commitment to finding your calling.

You will create affirmations and learn to *visualize yourself already performing in your calling.* Consider the positive feelings you would have if you obtained your ideal job. What are the differences between what you do now and what you would ideally like to be doing? Think in terms of emotions, feeling, monetary rewards, and spiritual benefits. By identifying with the proper incentives, you will have the motivation to reach your target.

Most people make a myriad of excuses for not fulfilling their true career potential. These are created to justify our natural tendency as human beings to be lazy and to avoid risk at any cost. I am confident that by incorporating the Master Career Formula 5 P's (*Passion, Purpose, Power, Profit* and *Peace of Mind*) as your compass, you will experience newfound wealth, happiness, and career satisfaction.

So, relax, take a deep breath, and get ready to change your life forever … for the better! And please don't be nervous! For the duration of these exercises, I will be here to serve as your personal career coach, a friend and mentor who can help you unlock your hidden career potential. Our website, www.thecareerguarantee.com provides continuous assistance and timely updates; I suggest you participate. As you go on to achieve your calling, please stay in touch by writing to tell of your good fortune. Thanks again for your participation and best of luck in your quest for career happiness. Enjoy the journey!

Acknowledgments

L IKE ANYTHING WORTHWHILE AND meaningful in my life, this book is the result of a well-orchestrated team effort.

I offer my most sincere gratitude and appreciation to my wife and family for their unconditional love, support and guidance.

I would like to thank the incredibly talented staff at *Career* T.E.A.M., LLC, who dedicate their time and energies to making the career dreams of our clients and customers become daily realities.

Special thanks to: my marketing agent Brian Jud for his support and guidance, Brian's production team—my patient editor, Beth Bruno; cover designer Monica Thomas; and typographer Dick Margulis—John Atashian of John Atashian Photography, and Chris Walsh for the creation of the informative website.

Finally, my heartfelt thanks go to the numerous mentors who have graciously contributed their wisdom and knowledge to help me on the path to serving others and to understanding that contribution is our ultimate reason for being.

Chris Kuselias
2009

The Career Guarantee

The 21st Century Workplace

KEY QUESTION

WHAT ARE THE NEW *RULES* IN CAREERING?

In the introduction, you will learn:

KEY TOPIC
- 10 Trends for the 21st Century Workplace
- Going Green Is Now a Reality

KEY MESSAGES
- Job security is a thing of the past.
- Americans are working harder and longer.
- Taking control of your career is essential.
- Baby Boomers are taking over.
- Employers will change the way they manage employees.
- Where the future jobs are.
- Home-based businesses expand.
- Entrepreneurship will continue to flourish.
- Franchising remains a great calling option.
- Innovation and technology will continue to expand at an incredible pace.

"Have an understanding so you don't have a misunder-standing."

—Charles Blair

10 Trends for the 21st Century Workplace

"Self-education is, I firmly believe, the only kind of educa-tion there is."

—Isaac Asimov

T O EDUCATE YOU ON the rules of 21st century careering, I have includ-ed the following trends, which may influence your thinking or assist you in your decisions. The information may appear bleak in some cases, but there is opportunity everywhere.

Trend 1: Job Security Is a Thing of the Past

The U.S. Department of Labor estimates that 50% of avail-able jobs found over the next 6 years ... have yet to be created!

Looking back from the 1920s to the mid 1980s, large companies dominated the hiring market with the dream of most Americans being to get a job with a big company with good benefits and a pension. Training was plenti-ful, as were internal promotion and upward mobility with the same em-ployer. This all changed suddenly in the mid to late 1980s.

What happened? The simple answer is: Technology. Mechanical en-hancements began to rapidly displace the need for manual labor and inno-vations that used to take 25 years to develop now took only 3 to 4 years, and sometimes, only months. The net result is that approximately 20 million blue-collar workers were laid off. Obsolescence became a major concern to those who failed to keep up with the incredible pace of change. The para-digm shift of workers without enhanced (state of the art) skills becoming "surplus" will continue.

Baby Boomers (those workers born between 1946 and 1964) will also affect the makeup of the workplace. According to AARP, over ⅔ of work-ers between 50 and 70 plan to work in some fashion during retirement, or never retire at all. Companies like Home Depot now offer "snowbird" programs where certain staff can work in a warm weather store location (for example, Florida) during winter months and transition back to their hometown for the balance of the year.

The other change is the emergence of a new workforce to replace the Baby Boomers. Generation X (those born in 1965–1977), who total 46 mil-lion members, and the 78 million members of the Entitlement Generation (those born after 1978) are now essential to avoid an impending labor crunch in the labor supply. This group desires flexible work schedules, variation, recognition and feedback, and continuous training. These groups will establish the trends for staffing and will have tremendous leverage as employers struggle to fill important positions.

The net result? There will be enough total workers but a shortfall of experienced, skilled workers to keep up with the demands created by the exodus of Baby Boomers.

> The United States could see a workforce shortfall of up to 10 million workers by 2010 ...

Job security is a thing of the past. There, I said it! Recall the words of General Douglas MacArthur, who said, "Security is your ability to produce." Said another way, the mantra today seems to be: We do not pay for effort but only pay for results! In my opinion, the only true security can be found in a complete and thorough understanding of who you are, what you want, what you do well, and where you can be compensated for performing these contributions.

It is increasingly important to be able to articulate your competence, that is, your unique and compelling contributions. This is the secret to your long-term stability and success. Your strategy must focus on mastering the changes brought about by innovation and the ability to transform these changes to your benefit. "Keep up or be discarded," sounds callous, but some of you reading this have personally experienced this harsh reality.

Here are the facts we must all accept before creating a game plan to live and work in the 21st century workplace:

- There are millions of unemployed Americans, and *it is estimated that at any given time, 40% of the working population is actively seeking a new job.*
- Employers will soon face a critical labor shortage due to the impending Baby Boomer retirement development. Baby Boomers will exit the workforce at unprecedented rates.
- We are experiencing 20 years of documented decline in birthrate, which creates a negative effect on the supply of qualified workers.
- Employers continue to out-source more functions to subcontractors and other less costly options than full time workers.

Fast Fact

At our company, *Career* T.E.A.M., we have a motto: "Leaner, meaner, faster, smarter ... "

- Technology will create jobs for upward mobility of middle class. There will be fewer but better jobs available
- Employers strive to upgrade technology skills of low-wage workers to accommodate need. Training, education and awareness of technology are the centerpiece of this paradigm shift
- The number of native-born workers obtaining higher education degrees is declining. Due to the global economy, skilled immigrants are finding quality positions in their home nations. A shortage is occurring as employers today seek more skilled workers ... and cannot find them.
- Self-promotion and marketing become mandatory skills as competition for jobs intensifies

This is the order of the day; it is time for each one of us to take control!

"50% of economists were optimistic, 45% were pessimistic and the other 5% didn't have a coin to flip."

Trend 2: Americans Are Working Harder and Longer

"Despite longer hours and advances in education, technology, service, product innovation and the global economy, the majority of individuals are still underachieving in the organizations they work for."

—Chris Kuselias

Our workaholic culture is legendary. We have seen a gradual increase in the required commitment to our jobs, which is having a negative effect on our family life. I have observed a disconcerting development where workers seem to categorize how many hours they work as a badge of honor. "I put in 80 hours this week, yeah, baby!" is a common boast as workers today struggle to get ahead and claim their rightful place in the corporate world. We are becoming richer with regard to our material possessions (bigger house, SUV, etc.) but losing more of our most precious resource ... our time.

In her book, *The Overworked American,* Harvard economist Juliet B. Schor states, "The shrinkage of leisure, experienced by nearly all types of Americans, has created a profound structural crisis in time."

In 1990, Japanese workers averaged 2,031 hours per year while Americans averaged 1,861, almost 10% less. Today, the average American works 36 hours more than the Japanese (1,825 vs. 1,789). According to the Organization for Economic Co-operation and Development, South Koreans lead the world with an average 2,394 hours per year while Norway's average worker spends only 1,364 hours on the job.

According to the Families and Work Institute, as of 2002, dual income households with children under 18, were putting in 91 hours per week (up from 81 hours per week 2 years earlier). Consider these facts:

- According to the U.S. Department of Health and Human Services, 1/3 of American workers feel they will experience burnout within the next 2 years
- According to the National Center for Disease Control and Prevention, more people die on Monday at 9 AM than any other time of day or any other day of the week!

At the risk of pointing out the obvious, working harder does not necessarily translate into greater productivity and a faster promotion. Working *too hard* is often symptomatic of a lack of balance in one area of life (for example, health, financial, relationship, spirituality) and is often an unconscious attempt to mask boredom, loneliness, loss or pain created in another area of a person's life. In unhappy marriages we often see an inability to create or maintain a healthy social calendar or a lack of hobbies and non-professional outlets. Hello! People, we all need to let loose and let off a little steam on a regular basis or we become dull and uninteresting.

Individuals that are consumed with work, promotion and conduct themselves in an overly ambitious manner, often burn out and "hit the wall" before those who pace themselves and live a life of balance. When interviewing new staff, we, as an organization, target candidates who demonstrate a healthy balance in their personal and professional lives because we know from experience that those candidates stay longer, have less sick time and are better role models to their peers.

There is no definitive formula for how hard to work, but the easiest measure is your own personal thermostat, where you can feel when you have invested too much time and energy in your professional career at the expense of your personal life. I have had the privilege and pleasure to meet some of our nation's most successful entrepreneurs, managers and builders of quality organizations who all share a similar view. Focus, commitment to excellence and good old-fashioned hard work are essential ingredients to upward mobility (promotion) but no amount of dedication can make up for the challenges associated with an unhealthy professional life caused by overwork.

The pursuit of a career calling requires a tremendous amount of energy and perseverance, but not at the expense of your health, fitness, family, hobbies or spiritual pursuits. It is only 1 of 5 key areas in my wheel of balance (career, financial, health & fitness, relationships, spirituality) and should be treated as such.

Fast Fact

According to the Families and Work Institute, more than 25% of all American families do not use their vacation time because they were afraid there job would not be there when they got back. Did you know that the average Italian worker averages 42 vacation days per year?

Trend 3: Taking Control of Your Career Is Essential!

"Indecision is the greatest thief of opportunity."
—Jim Rohn, *Facing the Enemies Within*

Considering these sobering developments, it is absolutely essential that you immediately take control of your career and become proactive in formulating a plan for long-term survival and prosperity. Think of yourself as a company for hire and not as an employee looking for their next place to camp out until you are either laid off or the company folds.

More realities ...

- As of this writing, the Bureau of Labor Statistics forecasts 50 million new jobs; the challenge is that due to the incredible pace of change, they are unsure what 50% of those jobs will actually be
- 20 Million Americans are now telecommuting, that is, earning a living from a location other than the company headquarters
- Health care benefits are gradually being eliminated, so an increasing number of Americans will need to keep working, solely to cover the ongoing cost of health care

Chart of the Pre–21st Century and Post–21st Century Workplace

Pre–21st Century	Post–21st Century
Work hard, structure	Work smart, flexibility
Loyalty is valued	Loyalty less prevalent
Company responsible for training	Individual responsible for own training
React to company directives	Proactive gun for hire
Gold watch for 30 years valued service	No such thing
Job security	No job security, average job tenure 3–4 years
Career confined to single industry	Career involves multiple industries
Long term employment	More than 15 jobs per person
Retirement benefits	Disappearing, focus on funding own retirement
Work at the plant or office	60% Telecommute, mobile workforce
Full time employees	Contract staff, consultants
Clearly identified career path	Uncertain future, 50% of jobs not yet invented
Little or no home based businesses	60% of homes have a business
Lucky to have a job	Work resembles play
Working for the money	Work is a "calling" ... Would do for free

I strongly urge you to explore available personality type assessments and tests, which are often helpful in narrowing your focus and serve to identify your unique characteristics and values. Here are some basic keys for taking control of your career in the complex 21st century workplace:

Think Service!   We are and will remain a Service Economy. Focus on the value of your contributions and choose service over salary. Remember the words of Thomas Watson, Sr. (IBM) who said, "Don't worry about profits, worry about service." My personal belief is that customer service in this country has declined to the point of being downright embarrassing. Management guru Tom Peters agrees: "Customer service in America stinks." Want to get ahead? Commit yourself to being a service guru in whatever field or endeavor you choose and you will go far. Prove you have excellent customer relations skills and you have an immediate advantage, regardless of industry.

Keep Your Promises   Build your integrity by establishing a reputation as a person who makes and keeps their promises. Background checks have become sophisticated to the point of being almost invasive. Employers are more leery about hiring candidates because the investment in their training can be significant. Never lie to a potential employer or business associate. I remember the story of a college football coach who after years of building his credentials, finally realized his lifelong dream to be the head coach at a major university, only to be fired because he lied on his resume about a relatively obscure position he once held several years ago. Sam Walton, founder of Wal-Mart, had this to say, "Always remember, a promise we make is a promise we keep."

Be Persistent   We are in a global economy, which means that there is more competition today than ever before. To succeed, you must be persistent and never back down from adversity or quit in your pursuit of your calling. I love the quote from Josh Billings who said, "Be like a postage stamp. Stick to something until you get there."

Be Innovative   Following the traditional path and doing what everyone else is doing will get you ... well, to be honest, what everybody else is getting (which based on the statistics I am sharing, is pretty discouraging). Seek a competitive edge to differentiate yourself from the competition. Remember to be clever but not obvious.

There is the story of a man who attempted to cross the Canadian border on his motorcycle. He carried 2 saddlebags strapped across his seat. The border guards questioned, "What is in your saddle bags?" "Rocks," the man replied. The guards proceeded to empty the bags and inspect them. Finding nothing but rocks, they let the man go ahead with his bags full of rocks. A couple weeks later, the same situation occurred and continued for every 2 or 3 weeks for several months. The border patrol guards endured the cyclist's entry over the border with saddlebags full of rocks. Finally, one day, the guards could no longer take it. "Listen, we know you are smuggling something across the border but every time we inspect your saddle bags, we find nothing but rocks. It is driving us crazy. Tell us what you are doing and we promise not to turn you in." "It is simple, really," the man said with a smile." I am smuggling motorcycles."

More trends you should be following and responding to:

- The average job tenure is getting shorter, now only 3–4 years
- Job seekers need to know their competitive edge as they transition from industry to industry
- The current job search averages multiple months; an industry rule of thumb is that for the experienced job seeker, it takes 1 month for every $10,000 in salary
- 80% of the U.S. population can be classified as being "underemployed"
- Many college students graduate without a job and accept roles unrelated to their field of study or degree
- 80% of all job vacancies are never advertised; they are filled through the hidden job market
- The majority of all current job vacancies exist with employers who have less than 100 employees ... small business is where

Where People Work

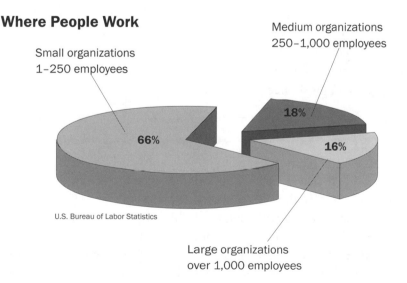

Small organizations
1–250 employees

Medium organizations
250–1,000 employees

66%

18%

16%

U.S. Bureau of Labor Statistics

Large organizations
over 1,000 employees

Learn the techniques to target small businesses!

the majority of jobs are! (Remember, every large Fortune 500 Company was once a small company.)

- Job posting (Internet) boards list jobs, but often provide them in an impersonal way and offer no guidance on strategies to attain these positions. They are also increasingly acting as a screening tool through unreliable questionnaires or evaluations.

Trend 4: Baby Boomers Are Taking Over!

One Baby Boomer is turning 50 years old every 8 seconds ... more than 12,000 per day!

Between 1946 and 1964, the Baby Boomer generation was born (no pun intended!) It was a post-war era and people returned home and, well ... got downright busy in the bedroom and expressed their affection!

Today, this historic event represents 84 million North Americans who comprise ⅓ of the continent's population. *The wants and needs of this massive generation should be a major concern for each of us, and will factor significantly in available employment opportunities.* Beginning this year in America, every 8 seconds another Boomer will turn 60! That equates to 4½ million each year!

Industry executives are aware of this paradigm shift and know that your work life and future career options are affected every day by this development. What will they eat? What do they wear? Where do they live? What do they watch or read? What are their technology needs and capabilities? Where do they spend their money? What services are important to them? The informed career seeker sees this as opportunity to marry this need with their passion for service.

The federal government saw half of its employees become eligible to retire in 2007 ...

Consider this: In 1800, the average life expectancy was less than 40 years. By 1900, this figure had increased, but only to 47 years. Today, the average life expectancy (for modernized nations) is 74 years (the U.S. life expectancy is 77 years). Where will it be by 2100? My guess is that it will rise significantly. What is my point? The point is that we are not only living longer, we are also enjoying ourselves more and are participating in more activities previously reserved for younger individuals. Today, people are working longer but not necessarily in the same job or industry.

Consider these examples:

- Warren Buffett is still considered the world's greatest investor into his 7th decade!
- Sean Connery (in my opinion he is the real James Bond) was voted the sexiest man alive by People Magazine (1989) at 59 years of age!
- Mick Jagger and Paul McCartney are still rocking to sold-out stadiums at over 60!
- John Glenn went back into space when most people his age were reading their AARP magazines!
- Galileo created *Dialogue Concerning The Two New Sciences* at 74!
- Mahatma Gandhi successfully completed negotiations with Britain for India's independence at 72!
- Groucho Marx (one of my favorite funny men) began his career as a TV host at age 69!
- Ichijirou Araya successfully climbed Mount Fiji at age 100!

The message: It is never too late to start! Opportunity is created not only for those who are Boomers and choose to continue working or start a business later in life, but to entrepreneurial minded passion seekers who create or design solutions for this group.

These folks are all sexagenarians (over age 60!):

- Cher (Her farewell concert tour grossed $190 million)
- Connie Chung (CBS Evening News)
- Sally Field (2-time Oscar winner ...)
- Goldie Hawn (still ravishing)
- Tommie Lee Jones (actor, former Al Gore college roommate)
- Barry Manilow (he writes the songs ...)
- Bette Midler (singer, actress ...)
- Dolly Parton (currently still touring ...)
- Linda Ronstadt (pop star)
- Pat Sajack (still spinning that wheel ...)
- Diane Sawyer (host of *Good Morning America*)
- Suzanne Somers (*Three's Company* & the Thighmaster)
- Sylvester Stallone (Can it be possible? He looks 40!)
- Donald Trump (the tycoon)

Boomer Alert! *Beware of the Social Security Crisis* ... With the impending Social security crisis, you would be smart to establish your own plan for retirement and prosperity vs. hoping your employer or the U.S. government will handle your golden years. Entrepreneurship often creates a self-sufficient strategy for ensuring you have enough money as we all live longer. Here is the challenge in a nutshell ...

The first Social Security check was made in the Depression era, when there were nearly 42 workers for each Social Security beneficiary. As people began to live longer, due to advances in health and wellness, the system became taxed. Instead of 42 workers for every beneficiary as we had in 1940, today there are 3.4 workers. By 2050, this figure is expected to decline to a ratio of 2 to 1. This will create an impossible burden on workers at today's benefit levels.

In his book, The Power Years, author Ken Dychtwald, Ph.D, points out, "Beginning in 2008, the first Boomers will be eligible for early retirement, and the following 2 decades will see a rapid rise in the cost of delivering Social Security benefits, from about 11% of all taxable earnings to more than 17% when the final Boomers reach normal retirement age in 2031. To convert Social Security and run it like a traditional pension would require $12 trillion, a staggering amount that exceeds America's total economic output for a year. It just won't happen."

We must learn to fund our own retirement!

Scared yet? A colleague recently informed me that the Bureau of Labor Statistics says that out of 100 people that start working at the age of 25, by the age of 65:

- Only 1 will be considered wealthy
- Only 4 will have enough money to retire
- 63 will depend on a shrinking Social Security system or require charity to get by
- 29 will be deceased
- What's disturbing about these statistics is that ... *95% of people who live to age 65 cannot afford to retire ... many will be forced to work until they die!*

Retired Americans Are Moving South!

A 90-year-old man and woman who recently met decided to get married. Shortly after the ceremony, the elderly pair was getting ready for bed when the husband noticed his wife taking a pill and swallowing it down with water. "I wasn't aware you were taking medication," he said. "Oh, its not medication," said the wife, "it is just a pill I take daily that makes me feel more youthful in the morning when I wake up." Not wanting to have his wife appear more youthful looking than he, the husband waited until she went to sleep and proceeded to swallow half the entire bottle of pills before going to bed. The next morning the wife awoke and could not find her husband anywhere. Finally, after searching the house to no avail, she looked out the front window and spotted her husband sitting on the front curb, with his head buried in his hands. "What is the matter?" she questioned. The husband looked up with tears in his eyes and said, "I think I missed my school bus."

This is a cute story, but on some level it is probably fair to say that we all seek to reclaim our youth or delay the aging process. While there is certainly nothing wrong with seeking strategies to increase vigor and energy, I perceive my golden years as a phase in my life to be filled with reflection, wisdom and the opportunity to share the value of my collective experience with others. I have no plans to slow down, and neither should you!

Retirement has often been positioned as the final chapter in life, during which an individual has "paid their dues" and can "lapse into a meaningless routine of waiting to die." On this subject, I suggest that we never adopt the belief system where we hope to stop working or stop contributing so we can fade off into a meaningless retirement mode. Contribution, often achieved through one's work, does not have to stop at 65 or even 95; contribution should continue to the day we meet our maker. The best is yet to come!

For many, the period of retirement means choices ... specifically the opportunity to select the ideal climate in which to live. When considering opportunities to fulfill your passion and purpose, do not overlook the trend as to where the U.S. population, particularly retired Americans, is migrating. It is obvious to anyone who has recently traveled to Southern cities and been stuck in traffic due to major congestion, that people want warm weather and are packing up and heading south.

To support this claim, a Del Webb survey indicated that nearly 60% of all retirees relocate after leaving their career. Here are the top 5 current choices of retirement relocation in the U.S.:

1. Florida (21%)
2. Arizona (18%)
3. North Carolina (10%)
4. South Carolina (10%)
5. Tennessee (9%)

Florida is hot (and I don't mean the outside temperature!) According to the U.S. Census, there is a net migration of more than 1,000 people arriving daily! This does not include the one million snowbirds, part timers who head south every winter. Florida is on target to exceed New York's population.

These trends should provide insight into what goods and services these Baby Boomers will require, and where they will require them. *Theme Communities* appear to be a hot trend as developers create vast complexes for people with common interests, complete with schools, libraries, entertainment, malls, etc. Convenience and companionship are the primary benefits of this growing trend in housing.

This information is valuable to you as a career seeker if you have a passion for warm weather and decide to fulfill your dream job in a warmer climate. Don't forget your sun block!

Trend 5: Employers Will Change the Way They Manage Employees

Fast Fact

The prime age workforce (25–54), which grew by 54% between 1980–2000, is expected to grow by only 3% from 2000–2020 …

When considering your calling, become educated on how employers are adapting to changes in the economy, societal values and, of course, Baby Boomers. Employers face a severe shortage of experienced, qualified workers as Baby Boomers exit the workforce in record numbers. The new Generation, called Generation X, does not have the knowledge, savvy or experience needed to effectively fill these key positions. As a result of these developments, employers are forced to adjust strategies for managing personnel. Many have begun establishing creative employment packages, benefits and even schedules designed to lessen this mass exodus and retain some of these critical skills. I was amazed to learn that currently, nearly 40% of all American employers not only allow employees to work from home, but in many cases, encourage this paradigm shift. This figure has doubled over the past 5 years and is expected to rise even further.

This paradigm shift is occurring not because working from home yields better performance, but because employers have no choice! I have friends and associates that work for established companies like Home Depot, Pitney-Bowes, Wal-Mart and IBM who report their firms are becoming more proactive in retaining older talent. Employees are often re-hired as consultants or allowed to create their own flexible hours plan to accommodate personal issues or family concerns. Job sharing, where multiple part-timers fill the role of a traditional full time position, is on the rise.

Ever the optimist, I believe there is tremendous economic vitality in American businesses, and this should continue. Other trends include:

- Companies are reinvesting in their businesses and gaining appreciation for their most valued employees
- Regarding job creation, most employers remain cautiously optimistic but are less hopeful than in prior years
- Job creation is more prevalent for part time workers and consultants, than full time workers
- International trade continues to increase and businesses cite increases due to an ever-evolving global marketplace
- The loss of U.S. jobs remains a concern to most employers
- Significant increases in health-benefit costs remain a major concern to most businesses

Bottom line: Although employers are open minded to new styles of management and becoming more flexible to accommodate these changes, you have to become absolutely 100% responsible for managing your career and life choices. With the advent of newer and faster technology, many will see an increase in discretionary time. We will have more choices to make: Which industry, which employer, entrepreneur, full time employee or subcontractor, what country, what city, home office or corporate office, benefits or monetary compensation and self-managed retirement plans … if you are even offered one. If not, you will need to initiate a fiscal plan that will last into your 90s and hopefully beyond. This will lead to another range of choices: where to invest, with whom, domestic or international, fixed income or growth?

The list of choices will overwhelm us if we are not carefully prepared and have not spent time on critical reflection assessing and analyzing our life and choices. Consider the following from one of our era's greatest business thinkers:

> *"In a few hundred years, when the history of our time is written from a long-term perspective, it is likely that the most important event those historians will see is not technology, not the Internet, not e-commerce. It is an unprecedented change in the human condition. For the first time— literally—substantial and rapidly growing numbers of people have choices. For the first time they will have to manage themselves. And society is totally unprepared for it."*
> —Peter Drucker, management consultant

Trend 6: Where the Future Jobs Are

According to the Bureau of Labor Statistics, 17.5 million new jobs will be created over the next 5 years. Service-producing industries will grow at an amazing 30% and account for virtually all job growth, with service and retail industries accounting for 14.8 million of these new jobs. The population is aging and we are living longer. An increase in Baby Boomers will mean an increase in services needed. *Health services, social services, business services, engineering, management and other related services are projected to account for nearly 1 of every 2, salaried jobs.* It is no surprise that 9 out of the 10 fastest growing industries can be found in one of these groupings. That being said, there is tremendous value in looking to those industries (and job titles), which present exciting future opportunities and which can be married to your passions. For your benefit, here is an overview of the 21st century workplace and what experts predict will be in most demand in the future.

Regarding the development of technology, the fastest growing occupations between 1998–2006 (Bureau of Labor Statistics-*Monthly Labor*

10 Industries with the Highest Projected Growth Rate	
Computer & Data Processing	108%
Health Services	68%
Management and Public Relations	60%
Transportation Services	60%
Residential Care	59%
Personnel Supply Services	53%
Water and Sanitation	51%
Social Services	50%
Offices of Health Practitioners	47%
Amusement and recreation Services	41%
10 Fastest Growing Occupations	
Computer Engineers	109%
Systems Analysts	103%
Personal and Home Care Aides	85%
Physical and Corrective Therapy	79%
Home Health Aides	77%
Medical Assistants	74%
Physical Therapists	71%
Occupational Therapists/Assistants	69%
Paralegal Personnel	68%
Special Education Teachers	59%

Review, "Occupational Employment Projections to 2006") are database administrators, computer specialists, computer engineers and systems analysts. The Internet is here to stay and design, research and web management remain strong.

Trend 7: Home Based Businesses Expand …
Direct Selling Is a Viable Option!

"Home based businesses are one of the fastest growing segments in our economy, and that trend will only continue as the Age of the Corporation, which began barely a century ago, now gives way to the Age of the Entrepreneur."
—Paul Zane Pilner, world-renowned economist

A famous singer once wrote, "The times, they are a changing." When my dad worked, the mantra was go to school, get a job with a big company, work hard, and you would be protected and rewarded with a healthy retirement. As companies continue to downsize or move production offshore (taking jobs with them), small business and, specifically, direct selling have evolved as a more prevalent option in the 21st century workplace.

Direct selling (sometimes referred to as network marketing, multi level marketing, pyramid marketing) is not for everyone but certainly is a credible option, despite some negative perceptions. Many people perceive direct selling to be a scam, where you are required to attack your friends and family with useless products or services in some diabolical pyramid scheme.

The fact is that today, one of every 8 households in America is involved in a home-based business, many of them in direct selling. Worldwide, 55 million people have found value in direct selling, many of whom began with the thought of generating supplemental income but were successful enough to transition to full time. Direct selling has sales of $30 billion in this country and over $100 billion worldwide. It is one of business's best kept secrets.

Why has this option grown so substantially? Direct selling offers the benefits of working for oneself and the freedom to create one's own schedule. Often done from home, direct selling eliminates long distance commuting, capped salary or compensation, and demanding bosses. Participants choose what they market, when they market and to whom. Family responsibilities can be attended to more easily with a set work schedule, and the power and reach of the Internet make it easier than ever before.

Paul Zane Pilzer, world class renowned economist, was quoted as saying, "The impact of the Internet, which is even now only in its infancy, can only be compared to the invention of writing, which created the birth of civilization, and the printing press, which created industrialization."

If you have an interest in direct selling or a home-based business, I strongly urge you to do your homework on the industry and any particular companies you are considering working with. As is the case in any endeavor, there are good entities and those who are lacking. I strongly suggest you interview at least 3 current direct sellers of any product or service before you commit. Do your homework!

Equally important is to choose a product or service that you can be passionate about: one where money is not the sole or primary motivator. Does the product offer customers a benefit that you feel good about representing? Are the messages ethical and credible? Do your peers or associates share a high level of integrity?

Another benefit of direct selling is that there is less of a start up fee (investment capital) and your business plan and support system are already in place. Plus, you don't have to manufacture or create the products or services; you merely need to become a solid distributor and offer customers value for their dollar. Large companies like Time Warner and Citigroup have launched direct selling companies because they see the unprecedented opportunity to earn huge quantities of income. It is here to stay!

In addition to earning potential, another advantage of direct selling is the ability to choose a product or service that allows you to make a difference to your customers: one that you have a passion about. International author and speaker Stephen Covey states, "Direct selling helps affirm people's worth and potential, and can open up a whole new alternative income stream that can make a huge difference in their life. It is an entrepreneurial opportunity where people can use their talent and passion toward a greater good."

Bottom line: In the 21st century workplace, direct selling presents a viable option to either supplemental or full time income. The key is to select an organization whose philosophy mirrors your own and a product that you feel allows you to utilize your 5P's (passion, purpose, power, profit and peace of mind) and attain your career calling.

Trend 8: Entrepreneurship Will Continue to Flourish

Fast Fact

According to the National Federation of Independent Business (NFIB), a business venture can now be found in 60% of American homes ... this number is growing.

Another paradigm shift is the dramatic increase in entrepreneurship and consulting based on training obtained from previous employers. This occurs for 4 key reasons:

1. A desire to pursue their calling and establish their independence from corporate America
2. The increase in the number of Baby Boomers who may have accumulated funds to start their own business or who are going through a mid-life crisis
3. Corporate downsizing and the need to cut costs by reducing or climinating employee benefits
4. Modern day technology and Internet access makes it easier than ever before to start your own venture

Have a great idea? Do not be afraid to pursue it! You never know! Everett M. Rogers is quoted as saying, "When 5% of society accepts an idea, it becomes imbedded in the population. When 20% agrees, it is unstoppable." Despite this philosophy, starting a successful venture will always have its critics.

Consider these comments:

"Watches without hands? You're crazy!"

"You can't put music on a roll of tape."

"Mr. Bell, please remove this silly toy from my office. There is no room in the market for a telephone."

"You cannot put a crocodile on a shirt to replace the pocket. Nobody will buy them!"

"People will never accept a zipper on the front of their pants; they prefer buttons."

Did You Know?

If the founder of a new business venture is over 55 years of age, the venture has a 73% better chance of being successful ...

One other comment: I remember Warren Avis, the great businessman and rental car mogul, who when asked about the secret to entrepreneurial success had this to say: "Anyone who thinks that earning 5 million dollars is enough is not the kind of person who can earn 5 million dollars in the first place." The message is that the pursuit of autonomy and individuality through entrepreneurship means constant and never ending improvement. Work is not a means to an end, but rather, an opportunity to contribute through a product or service. From this philosophy, greatness is achieved!

Speaking of millionaires ...

In 1980 there were only 1.5 million millionaires in America. By the year 2000, this number increased to 7 million. By the year 2020, this figure is expected to become a whopping 50 million! Today, every 4 minutes someone in America becomes a millionaire. Maybe you will join this elite group. Chances are that most of them are individuals who have found their calling, see work as play and are living their dream!

If you are considering starting your own venture, I highly suggest that you contact the Service Corps of Retired Executives (SCORE), which works closely with the U.S. Small Business Administration. SCORE has a national network (please consult www.score.org for the chapter nearest you) of over 10,000 advisors who can guide you to entrepreneurial success. Small Business Development Centers (www.sba.gov/sbdc) is another useful source with multiple offices across the country.

Trend 9: Franchising Remains a Great Calling Option

Is it my imagination, or is there a coffee shop on every corner? Starting your own business is at best a difficult undertaking and we all know the failure rate for startups. Franchising can reduce this challenge by providing proven systems and support for products and services that have demonstrated consistent sales. It can give you a chance to do something different, but with guidance and support from an established entity.

Franchising is also on the rise. There are approximately 4 million Americans between the ages of 40 and 60 who are deemed "dislocated workers," a term designated for middle managers who have lost their positions in typically larger companies. Because it is often difficult to replace their significant salary level, many are turning towards franchising. Many today and in the future will trade conventional work paths for a chance to be their own boss. There are more than 600,000 franchise units in the U.S., which accounts for $800 billion in annual sales, over 40% of all retail sales.

Which franchise should you choose? It is estimated that less than 20 organizations have franchised as many as 5,000 units. The challenge is that the more established a franchise is (for example, McDonald's, Blockbuster, Starbucks) the larger the investment required to purchase that franchise. Research indicates that as of this writing, the minimum investment to open a McDonald's franchise is $540,000.00! Most people do not have that kind of capital so they settle for a $50,000.00 to $100,000.00 franchise, which involves greater risk, as the parent company may have less to invest in national advertising, brand building and innovation.

In any event, do your homework and talk to owners who were successful and others who were not. Often, you will get a better perspective from those who failed or sold their franchise. Franchising can represent an opportunity to own your own business and realize your passions while serving others. My strong suggestion is not to select a franchise solely on the financial potential, but rather to explore whether or not the nature of the work will provide purpose and passion. Oversight of a franchise means you are leasing an established brand and the true boss is the trademarked entity, not you. If you are a person with a lot of creative ideas and do not like to follow procedure or established systems, than franchising may not be for you.

Bottom line: Consumer demand and convenience will continue to make franchising an attractive career option.

To begin, contact the International Franchise Association (www.franchise .org) the longest tenured franchise trade group in the world. Members include franchisors, franchisees, and suppliers. Benefits of joining include strategies and techniques and a free online Franchising Basics course, which details the pros and cons of franchising, common questions and answers, and applicable laws and regulations that govern the franchise industry. Also included is a helpful list of lawyers and consultants who specialize in franchise-related work. There is even a program entitled VetFran, which offers unique financial incentives for veterans.

If you want more information on franchising, I would suggest that you start your search with a review of www.franchise.com and www.franchise-handbook.com/index.asp.) I also suggest the inc.com home page (*Inc. Magazine*); look for "Franchise Inc."

Trend 10: Innovation and Technology
Will Continue to Expand at an Incredible Pace

> *"There is nothing so powerful as an idea whose time has come."*
>
> —Victor Hugo

Things are moving so fast it is almost overwhelming. I recently made the honest mistake of informing my 16-year old nephew that he "sounded like a broken record." His puzzled reply was, "Uncle Chris, what is a broken record?" (Perhaps I should have said he sounded like a mini-DVD!)

To put into perspective the power of information technology, consider the following:

Media	# Years To Build An Audience of 50 Million
Radio	38
Television	13
Internet	4

Consider these once remarkable advances that today we take for granted:

- Today, in nearly every country on earth, you can casually walk up to an automated machine, insert a plastic card, type in 4 digits, have this mysterious machine validate your identity, establish your credit balance, deduct money and have it translated into the correct currency, rebalance your account and even tell you to have a nice day ... all in 11 seconds!
- You can send an important package overnight anywhere in the free world and be able to access a worldwide Internet system and determine at any given moment precisely where your package is en route to its final destination. With a few keystrokes, you can learn the country, city, truck number, etc., where your precious cargo currently resides. You can literally monitor the step-by-step delivery of a pair of socks to your cousin overseas and feel confident it will arrive as promised.
- You can now purchase telephones, cell phones, radios and even televisions that, via smart acoustic systems, have the ability to customize signals to match your unique auditory range. Watching a sporting event, you now have the ability to select the camera angle to watch the game.

- We now have anti-aging spas, therapeutically cloned livers, kidneys, hearts, lungs and bones for replacement, and high-tech exercise equipment that can be customized and programmed to your individual body type and chemistry. These advances are available to make you stronger, healthier and more youthful.

I believe we are living in the greatest time in history because the list of incredible inventions, innovations and advances creating unique career opportunities is endless and coming to market at lightening speed. Who is behind these inventions? People just like you and I. The reality is that someone is going to find their career niche, their calling, and it's not always going to be the most academically gifted person or the individual who has the best credentials. It all starts with a big idea and we all have at least one. Here are some other inventions creating more opportunities to pursue a calling:

- Tired of pesky stickers on your fruit? Distributors are now experimenting with natural light labeling or fruit tattoos, which include an expiration date
- Want taste without the calories? Flavor sprays with no fat or carbohydrates are in development which mimic the taste of BBQ, chocolate, and even bacon and can quell your desire for these foods, resulting in weight loss
- Japanese scientists are developing a robotic exoskeleton, which can learn to duplicate one's walking pattern to help the disabled or elderly walk better as bioelectric sensors actually pick up brain signals to the muscles
- Want to knock 10 strokes off your golf game? A manufacturer has unveiled a new line of sport shades … contact lenses that for golfers provide an edge by enhancing the dips and curves of a putting green. Of course they also filter ultraviolet rays
- Overtired in the morning? A new alarm clock that doubles as a watch is equipped with a built-in motion detector, which measures your sleep patterns and will wake you up when you are in a light sleep
- Fond of animals? Cloning continues with sheep, dogs, … (I must admit I have mixed feelings on this subject!)
- 2 left feet? A robot is in production that not only teaches you how to dance but also has the technology to sense your foot patterns to predict your next steps

The list of innovations is endless and is creating fascinating career opportunities. Keep up with these trends as they affect your life and they could represent your calling. In summary, I am not suggesting that you have to invent the next hot product or even invent anything at all, but you should be aware that this energy, this pursuit of progress, and the incredible power of the human mind is alive and well and creating opportunities for exciting careers like never before in the history of our planet.

The bottom line: These trends should be factored into your plan for establishing and living your career calling. Information is power and the more educated you are on trends and the opportunities they create, the greater the likelihood of you attaching your career objective with an opportunity. As the saying goes, when preparation meets opportunity, watch out!

You are probably thinking, *Boy, that sure was a lot of information to absorb. I can see that the process of obtaining my calling is not as simple as spending an afternoon on line or in the library doing research.* I told you that great accomplishments require an investment of time and energy, but I promise you in the long run it will be worth it!

Is technology changing? Consider this: During my very first year as a communications consultant, I once traveled to Xerox Headquarters in Stamford, Connecticut, in the early 80s to discuss recommendations for enhanced communications. I remember an entire floor dedicated to their computer system, which involved huge main frames, etc. Fast forward 25 years to my 5-year old daughter playing state of the art video learning games on her own desktop computer, which has more speed, power and functionality than the entire Xerox Corporation had when I 1st visited their site! Today, I watch my son get ready for the gym with the iPod, a credit card sized audio device that holds 10,000 songs! The speed of new and faster technology has accelerated to almost unfathomable proportions. My message: "Keep up or else!"

I hope you found these emerging trends both educational and informative. It is my wish that the enclosed will serve as the spark or impetus for you to make the unquestionable decision to take complete control of and responsibility for your career and understand, that from this day forward, it must be managed and nurtured with proper care and attention to detail.

It is no longer a question of doing so to make a few extra dollars or enjoy the work more, but rather as a matter of survival in the ever changing, constantly evolving 21st century workplace.

Greening Your Career

I WOULD BE REMISS IF I did not include information on "going green" and how it will profoundly affect your career. The news is consumed with green, as in environmental friendliness, job opportunities and profits. The green industry has expanded to several billions and is here to stay. More environmentaly conscious products and services are introduced every day, and consumers are spending money and investing consistently with a belief in the need for a greener world. The challenges we face are well documented: global warming, depletion of natural resources, hazardous chemicals and waste, deforestation, water and air pollution, acid rain, habitat loss, human poverty. These challenges are as significant as the opportunities. Becoming a green ambassador is not only good for our current and future environment, but is a smart career move.

Our government has begun to pour hundreds of millions of dollars into this emerging industry, even as many key questions remain unanswered. Who qualifies as a green worker? Will schools create new certification programs for green jobs? What incentives are available for maintaining a green work environment? Can companies create working prototypes of a product or service to obtain seed money? In these current economic times, is it risky to target a green occupation at a startup over a more traditional career path?

One thing is certain, and that is that the majority of businesses in the world today (about 90%) can be classified as small or medium sized. In America, 60% of our approximate 6 million businesses (that's 3.6 million!) have fewer than 5 employees while 90%, or 5.4 million, have 20 or fewer employees. These organizations have received little or no guidance on the process of greening and may have few resources to explore the merits. Venture capital investment in green startup companies is up significantly. The belief is that green companies are a good investment and will continue to thrive in the 21st century. Eco-entrepreneurs are establishing themselves as a viable force for greening the balance of the economy. Is the green industry a source to contribute your unique and compelling passion and purpose? I am of the belief that for millions it will be. A report by the American Solar Energy Society predicts that by 2030, jobs related to energy efficiency and renewable energy will employ 16 million people. I believe that if the current government continues its aggressive policies this number could easily double.

Because going green is evolving rapidly, I suggest you monitor its evolution and career opportunities on www.thecareerguarantee.com. Posted are resources to educate and inform you. Regardless of what direction your personal or professional greening experience takes you, know that by being green conscious, you are having a positive impact on our planet. No action is too small (from turning off a light bulb to purchasing a hybrid vehicle) as we collectively take steps to heal our environment and protect our future.

CHAPTER 1

The Master Career Formula
(5 P's to Success)

KEY QUESTION:
HOW DO I FIND MY CALLING AND BECOME
SOMEONE WHO TRULY LOVES THEIR WORK?

In this chapter you will learn:

KEY TOPICS

- We Are in the Midst of a Paradigm Shift!
- The 5 P's to Success
- An Overview of the 21st Century Workplace

KEY MESSAGES

- Finding your career calling will create balance in your life in 5 critical areas: career, financial, health and fitness, relationships, and spiritual enlightenment.
- 3 questions to help you realize your passion ...
- 3 questions to help you realize your purpose ...
- 3 questions to realize your power ...
- 3 questions to help you maximize profit ...
- 3 questions to help you find peace of mind ...
- Remember that approximately ⅓ of your life will be spent at your career; make sure what you "do for a living" is something you are intensely passionate about!
- Life is not a dress rehearsal; there are no 2nd chances!
- Find a *measurable*, quantifiable difference between where you are and where you would like to be; then let your desire be the catalyst for change!
- Model and monitor the actions of successful achievers employed in your ideal career.
- The more specific you are on your career direction, the faster you will attain your career calling.
- A strong desire and positive outlook can overcome a lack of education or experience.
- Be proactive, not reactive in your quest to find and maintain your career calling.
- Begin the careering process by looking internally at your needs, wants and values.
- Successful people continually revisit their desired career outcome and reasons for wanting it.
- It is essential to formulate a competitive career edge and cost-justify your position to any potential employer or new business partner.

- Associate positive feelings with obtaining your passionate career and negative emotions with your current function; identify what is lacking or missing.
- Are you living off old memories or creating new ones?
- It is never too late to obtain your ideal career; today is a new career starting point; forget the past.

"If you love what you do, you will never work another day in your life."

—Confucius

We Are in the Midst of a Paradigm Shift!

HERE IS A PROMISE: If you implement the strategies in this book as they are described, you will obtain the career you always dreamed of. When you do, you will be so energized, so empowered, so completely infused with joy and happiness that you will jump straight up in the air, pump your fists and yell, "Yeah!"

Here is the deal: 80% of working people are unhappy and unfulfilled at work while only about 20% truly love their work. *No worries, you will soon be one of the 20%!* These enlightened individuals have learned the secret to greater happiness, more money and peace of mind. They know, like you soon will, that it is not luck, fate, education, race, gender or location that determines true success. It is a mindset, a proven formula and you can learn it! This book is designed to put you into this elite group, *those who live their lives filled with passion and purpose.*

Your desire for more meaning and purpose is not unique. Can you feel it? Change is in the air! There is a paradigm shift occurring in this country. It has been building for a few years and is now ready to erupt! After the tragic events of 9/11 and more recent world events, our perspectives are changing.

More than ever before, you and I want to make a difference; we want to matter. We want to be inspired and no longer wish to view our career as simply a way to consume our precious time, pay our bills or purchase more stuff. We want passion, purpose, recognition! We want to find our career calling and we want it now!

There has never been nor will there ever be another individual exactly like you ... you are unique and compelling. Your talents, experiences, thoughts, ideas, beliefs, desires, preferences and contributions can never be duplicated. It is time to put your self-marketing plan into action. It is time to stake your claim!

The Career Guarantee is about exploring the *unique and compelling you*, the person you are today and the incredible one you have the potential to be tomorrow.

It is not about directing you to "high growth" career opportunities that do not feed your passion, but rather about creating an effective game plan for realizing *your* life's work (your reason for being). It is, in essence, a system for assisting you to re-claim your passion and purpose and maximize your power, profit and peace of mind. As your personal career coach, I will introduce the process of self-exploration and how to get in touch with the real you or as I call it, your *authentic* self.

This is not a "how to" book or one like the numerous career books you will find on the shelves of your local library or bookstore. Most of these publications, while well intentioned, miss the mark because they focus on the *mechanics* of the careering process like (finding a job, resume, dress, interviewing, etc.) with little or no attention given to the reader's mindset of innermost wants, needs and desires. Little has changed over the past 50 years in terms of linking ones unique contributions to a compelling vocation ... until now!

Today we know that your mindset matters and, together, we can explore and harness the amazing power of your mind to ensure you find and obtain your unique career calling! Studies show people only use about 10% of their brain capacity. Together, we will explore techniques to maximize your potential.

I have dedicated my life's work to helping people just like you obtain their career calling because I understand how central work life is to the happiness of the individual, their family and the character of any society. If you think about it, work consumes the majority of our time, defines our values and creates our future. If time is indeed our most valuable asset, then our choice of work has a profound effect on our health, mindset, happiness, legacy and reason for being. Those of you who have been made physically or mentally sick by an unhappy career know exactly what I am talking about.

> *"Every day, I observe that an unhealthy ambition for career success and focus on keeping up with the Joneses has eroded the quality of family life."*
>
> —Chris Kuselias

In the 21st century, there is a growing movement toward changing the perception of work from the traditional, "another day, another dollar" mentality to that of working as a "platform for service to others." Work is not a necessary evil and does not serve merely to obtain monetary reward or social status; it is an opportunity to celebrate and contribute your unique and compelling talents, skills and gifts. It is an opportunity to create a connection between your contribution and reward.

Malcolm Gladwell, #1 bestselling author of *The Tipping Point* and *Blink*, is a man I have tremendous respect for. In his recent book, *Outliers—The Story of Success*, he points out, " … those 3 things—autonomy, complexity, and a connection between effort and reward—are, most people agree, the 3 qualities that work has to have if it is to be satisfying. It is not how much money we make that ultimately makes us happy between 9 and 5. It's whether our work fulfills us. If I offered you a choice between being an architect for $75,000 a year and working in a tollbooth every day for the rest of your life for $100,000 a year, which would you take? … Work that fulfills those 3 criteria is meaningful."

It is often dangerous to attempt to separate one's professional life from their personal life; there is simply too much overlap to create a distinction. A thank God it's Friday (TGIF) mantra results in an incomplete, often unfulfilled life leaving many with an "is this all there is" outlook. Ever feel that way? Finding your career calling means you enjoy the work product and view this time spent as pleasure, as a chance to unleash your unique contribution.

Gladwell further points out, "Hard work is a prison sentence only if does not have meaning. Once it does, it becomes the kind of thing that makes you grab your wife around the waist and dance a jig."

Career Success Is Predictable

Having spent the better part of my lifetime studying successful authors, speakers, coaches, business people, athletes and families, I have concluded that career success is entirely predictable and can ultimately be defined by mastering a single word … *contribution*. The more you give … the more you get! What makes us truly happy is when we are needed and part of a solution to a challenge. You probably feel the most fulfilled when you are doing something to help another. When you lose sight of how your current work contributes to a greater purpose, you feel bored, lazy and tired.

This book was designed as a practical guide to help you find your *career calling* and to help you recognize your unique and compelling contribution; your *Career DNA*. The text and corresponding exercises also serve as reinforcement and encouragement when you get off course, as we all inevitably do.

"Be yourself; everyone else is already taken."

—Dr. Seuss

In my own career, I have helped a range of folks find happiness and prosperity, some of whom were interested in the bare necessities while others struggled with the deeper search for meaning. You see, we are all on a continuum, constantly seeking improvement and the ability to contribute while being recognized and appreciated for our value. When we are acknowledged, we feel empowered and inspired to give even more. Absent this approval, we can become distant, confused and even apathetic. Stress soon sets in and we seek constant relief in distraction or escape to numb our unhappiness.

"I am too blessed to be stressed."

—Chris Kuselias

It is said that awareness (recognition of your circumstances) is the first step to genuine progress. To educate you on this process, there exists a series of events as we progress through the cycle of "survival to significance." In talking with those who love their careers and are excited about their futures, here is an interesting pattern: These folks have considered the following questions in an effort to pursue "a higher calling" rather than viewing work as a resource for paying the bills.

Those just starting out begin in this phase:

Survival Phase: People often think . . .

I can eat today . . .
My kids (if applicable) have clothes to wear . . .
The lights are on because the bill is paid . . .

When this phase is achieved, we often move to the next phase, which we call:

Success Phase: People often think . . .

I have an important job title . . .
I own a home and buy designer clothes . . .
I save for retirement . . .

After a measure of wealth and success has been achieved, the final phase is targeted and the vocabulary changes:

Significance: People often think …

> I make a difference …
> I contribute to others by …
> My legacy will be …

It is at this stage, "significance," that the magic occurs! And aren't we all significant in some way? I know we are!

Speaking of magic, Earvin Magic Johnson, former NBA Hall of Famer turned Entrepreneur and Community Leader (and author of the book, *32 Ways To Be A Champion In Business*), states, "Doing business and giving back really go hand in hand. It's the best way to truly create a win-win situation for everyone."

Magic created a new legacy once his basketball days ended; it is never too late to start if you have the passion. Please keep in mind that we can consider our legacy or contribution at any stage of the process. Age or experience is not a prerequisite to being a person of *significance*.

Survival to Significance:

1. *Survival:* Work is for Survival/Money: 60% of people see a job as a source of income to pay bills with financial compensation as the primary motivator
2. *Success:* Work is for Acceptance/Status: 30% percent of people see their work life not as a job but as a career where progress, promotion, advancement and awards are the measure of success and value
3. *Significance:* Work is for Passion/Contribution: Only 10% of people see their career as an outlet for talent, where their contributions fuel their personal passions and benefit society in a measurable, meaningful way

If you find yourself in categories 1 or 2, I suggest we get busy with helping you change your perception of work so you can move to category 3! This is the ideal way!

It is more likely that people merely looking to eat that day or not have the heat turned off are in a mindset of *survival* and not *significance*. They typically have a short term view of the world; long term planning is not a luxury they consider.

Those fortunate enough to "graduate" to the level of *success*, often remain there forever, trapped in a "keeping up with the Joneses" mentality with little or no peace of mind. Advertisers are quick to target this group with the latest gadget, style or product. Success is often a "thing" like the size of a house, a car make or model or a certain neighborhood and not necessarily a feeling. Often, chaos or a life changing event may create a desire for deeper meaning.

The desired phase, what we call being *significance*, is a blessing that is not decided by education, race, gender, wealth or any other finite characteristic. It is more of a mindset and a decision as to how to live one's life and how to pursue one's contributions. People of *significance* have found the formula for true career happiness; they are not apathetic, restless, anxious, stressed out or burned out.

True, they have challenges, but they view each day as an opportunity to assist in the bigger picture. These folks have found the secret; they look to serve others in a major way and thus create a larger contribution. *I want you determine your unique and compelling contribution and to be significant!*

Consider this interesting dialogue ...

"I understand you are applying for the job of railroad switchman. To get hired, I need to ask you a few questions. Number one, what would you do if you saw 2 trains approaching each other on the same track?"

"I would activate the lever and switch one train onto another track."

"And if the lever and signals jammed on you?"

"I would grab a red flag and sprint out onto the track."

"And suppose the train engineer did not see you?"

"Then, I would call my little boy."

"Your little boy? What could he do?"

"Nothing, he just loves to watch train wrecks."

Perhaps you have felt like your career thus far is analogous to a "train wreck!" Most likely it was because it lacked meaning and purpose and was not creating the passion you require. Life without meaning and contribution leads to unhappiness.

It is not the "stuff" or "status," it is the emotional peace of mind achieved through contribution. Still not convinced? According to recent statistics, we as a nation, despite more choices than ever, are stumbling.

- 80% of American workers feel they are *under-employed* and over 40% are actively looking for a new job
- Only 3% of Americans have written goals, 97% do not
- 70% of American families have no discretionary income with the lottery their hope of financial security
- The average American family is only 2 months away from potential homelessness
- Over 50% of Americans are overweight
- Over 50% of all marriages now end in divorce
- Everyday, more and more people become morally and spiritually bankrupt

When we are not clear on our contribution (in large part made through our work) problems occur, stress develops and we often seek relief from unhealthy sources to distract or divert our attention. The 1st step is to make a commitment to yourself and your loved ones that you will become a student of career success.

This commitment includes 3 aspects:

1. Possess a sincere desire to improve
2. Have faith in the process
3. Take decisive action

Bouncing Back from Job Loss

> *Every year, more than 2.5 million people lose their jobs ... Approximately 20 million Americans will change jobs this year!*

Maybe you are reading this book because you were laid off or are out of work. If you get caught up in losing your job or if you are fired, the first thing to remember is that nobody is free of failure or is an untouchable. Many people, after the initial shock of a loss, are shattered but recover relatively quickly. Some of us take a much longer time to recover, particularly if losing your job has a profound effect on your lifestyle or if you have people who are dependent upon your income.

Career change can often motivate a person to take on risks that he or she may not have otherwise taken. The old saying is that when you're at rock bottom, there's really no place to go but up. Just because you lose your job or are fired, don't feel that you're alone. Most of us have lost a job at one point or another; learn to view it as a temporary setback.

Think back to a time when you were involved in a relationship and you broke up. Just because the relationship didn't work out doesn't mean you're a failure for future relationships. I'm sure you left the relationship having learned a lot about either yourself or about the other person.

Look at job loss as an opportunity to gain and learn from your mistakes. Maybe the job you were in was just a bad fit. Maybe you are better suited to having your own business than working within an organization. For many, this process is a blessing in disguise. Maybe you'd rather work with a group than an isolated role … Maybe your values weren't being fulfilled and it was affecting your self-esteem. And as a result, you weren't truly committed to your career and weren't performing at your peak.

Remember that you cannot always control every aspect of your life or your career. Everybody has setbacks in their careers. I know of one woman who was turned down after 15 straight interviews. After finally getting a job that she wanted, she calmly said, "Hey, I didn't fail 15 times. I just learned 15 new ways not to conduct an interview." Be optimistic.

For many people, setbacks were the result of their unclear or unrealistic objectives. People often find difficulties in their middle years, like their mid-50s, when they come to terms with the fact that when they were younger, they had envisioned themselves doing wonderful things with their career and they realize at this point in their life that they never will achieve their dreams. It is never too late to realize your career calling but you need to "inconvenience" yourself a bit if you seek greatness. You need to push yourself!

> *"Never throughout history has a man who lived a life of ease left a name worth remembering."*
>
> —Teddy Roosevelt

I've worked with many successful people who started new careers well into their 40s. I think it's important to remember that at 40 years of age, over half of your working life is still ahead of you! Many people today are still working while in their 80s. It may not be so unrealistic to want to change your career and experience a totally different shift of strategy after age 40.

Satchel Paige, a Hall of Fame Major League Baseball player who pitched until he was 50 years of age, is credited with this thought: "How old would you be if you did not know how old you were?"

Maybe your career aspirations are misguided because you never really knew how to determine your passion and purpose, and were just working for the money or following the crowd to the plant. Anyone can get displaced, but the fact is that people who understand their own internal *wants* and *whys* bounce back more quickly.

Being displaced is not to be taken lightly. It hurts! Be aware that there is an 8-step process associated with being laid off or displaced, which includes:

1. *Shock:* You were unprepared for the news, you have no alternative plan, you were caught up in making a living instead of designing your life
2. *Denial:* This cannot be happening to me!, refusal to accept the truth, procrastination
3. *Anger:* You become stubborn, assign blame, complain to anyone who will listen
4. *Reality:* Fear, uncertainty and doubt set in, you question your professional worth, financial challenges
5. *Confusion:* No strategy, disorganized, listen to anyone, unsure what to do next
6. *Depression:* Overwhelmed, physically and mentally ill, rut!
7. *Acceptance:* Begin to get organized, consider options, create a viable plan
8. *Action:* Create a routine, more positive outlook, visualize future success

Sound familiar? If you are reading this book because you have recently lost your job, you most likely now find yourself involved somewhere in this process. Seeing this should provide some relief that you are not alone! The key is to understand that support and guidance are available.

A job loss is surpassed only by the death of a spouse, divorce, jail or a major illness, when it comes to comparing life's major stressors.

So how do you deal with career unhappiness or the feelings that come with being fired or laid off? How do you learn to transition failure into a positive occurrence and learning experience? I think by first realizing that getting fired or laid off or not feeling passion in your career is a part of life. It's a natural thing. You have never been taught!

3 Keys for Treating Career Stress

1. Allow sufficient time to heal (most people take 2 months to complete the cycle)

2. Practice stress relieving exercises and meditation
3. Try not to make important decisions until the process is complete and you get mentors to help you!

Resolve yourself to the fact that at certain times in your career you're going to experience anger along with the highs and lows that go with any job. If you are laid off, fired or lose a job and are unhappy, let yourself *feel* the unhappiness because it's that same unhappiness that will motivate you to want to feel good again about yourself. Don't just say, "Well, that's life," and move on. Take some time to sit back and really experience what it feels like. But be wary of getting too far into a rut and blaming other people because, as I mentioned, there is only one person to blame for your career dissatisfaction. And that's you. You control your own destiny. You have such a wide variety of opportunities to consider today and so many exciting occupations to match your passion, there are no excuses for not finding your career calling.

I have failed many times; who hasn't? I have trained myself to look inward before assessing blame elsewhere. I am accountable! Whenever I find myself in a situation where I failed at something, I immediately look inside myself. I conduct my own self-analysis. I ask myself what drove me to fail or not meet my objectives in this particular area. Was it an unrealistic goal I had set for myself or was it something that really wasn't within my means? I immediately jot down what I learned from the experience and press on!

If you go on an interview and are rejected, don't feel defeated. Take the positive things you learned from it, whether it be friendship, experience, or the knowledge needed not to make the same mistake twice. By doing so, you will slowly gain confidence and momentum, which will provide you with success the next time you compete.

> *"Most times people are rejected because they lack enthusiasm and passion for the opportunity. They may have internally felt it, but were unsuccessful in communicating their desire to the person across the desk."*
>
> —Chris Kuselias

Finding your passion and purpose will help you gain momentum! If you have ever watched a sporting event, especially a sport like basketball, you may have noticed that all of a sudden one team will grow confident and you sense the confidence rising in the way they run up and down the court and the way they pass the ball to each other. When one player goes up for a shot, you can just look in his eyes and know that he's going to make that shot. They are in the zone!

All of you have had that same experience in some area of your life, that feeling of being "hot," as I like to call it, where you just know you can't miss. Things are going to go your way that day. Career seekers who discover their passion and purpose and possess this momentum get hired faster! Everyone wants to be associated with momentum, which is derived from passion.

Bottom line: Failure and success are to be expected. It is the mature career seeker who realizes that highs and lows are part of life. Use the loss of a job as a chance to start anew. It is a clean slate. So, if you lose your job, don't panic or procrastinate. Assess your position, plan for your next objective and take action. More often than not, with proper planning, it may turn out to be a blessing in disguise.

You Are Not Alone ... Career Coaching Is Exploding!

The number of executive coaches has soared from 2,000 in 1996 to over 10,000 today.

While these pages contain a unique and compelling approach to obtaining your career calling, you may decide to incorporate an additional level of support, guidance and accountability once you have completed this book. Career coaching is exploding as a profession. Visit www.thecareerguarantee.com for a list of suggested career coaches.

Time is your most precious asset. High achievers use it wisely. Last time I checked, there are only 24 hours in every day. If you spend 8 of them working, average an hour to get ready for work and another hour in commuting to and from work; that means you are investing 10 hours per weekday of your valuable time in activities associated with your occupation. That is 10 hours out of the 24 precious hours you are afforded each day.

My question to you is: Do these 10 hours inspire, invigorate, empower and energize you or are they wasted hours spent engaged in unfulfilling activities? Many individuals are turning to coaches to ensure they fulfill and maintain their potential.

As a nation, we are facing major challenges regarding the future of our workforce. Certain articles even refer to our current economic downward spiral and loss of jobs overseas as a "race to the bottom." In America today, we have millions unemployed. Add to this figure the number of *underemployed* Americans, those that dislike their job, which is in the millions, and we have an epidemic … an epidemic of unfulfilled workers losing faith in the employment system and their ability to sustain an acceptable level of career happiness. My conclusion: It is impossible to lead a healthy life when you are unhappy or unfulfilled at work. Find your contribution!

As the CEO and Founder of my own company, *Career* T.E.A.M., a nationally recognized workforce solutions provider, I am afforded the opportunity to help people compete in the 21ˢᵗ century workplace. My incredible staff and I create solutions to solving the opportunity divide that exists between the *"haves and have nots."* I often observe generational unemployment and a hopelessness attached to what was once the American dream. A large part of my life's work is to bridge this gap and help every American realize their special gifts, and teach them to apply these unique and compelling talents to find their calling in life.

The sad reality is we are a nation of dissatisfied workers with a growing number without health insurance. How did this happen to our once proud nation? While it is convenient and partially accurate to blame corporate leadership or the federal government for our woes, *the real problem lies in misguided priorities and values by our own people.* Why should we care about this issue and not just worry about ourselves? Whether you realize it or not, we all own this unemployment and cynicism; this is our country.

> *"Hourly workers make up 70% of America's workforce."*
> —*The Enterprise Talent Management Benchmark Report:*
> *Hiring Right, Hiring Smart*, Aberdeen Group
> and Human Capital Institute, March 2005

As a country, we appear to be losing our edge. Need proof? According to the Kaiser Foundation, there are at least *45 million Americans today without health insurance* and this number is growing. From a social policy viewpoint, these folks avoid medical attention until their problem is so severe that it is often too late or results in expensive treatments.

As a nation, we are getting lazier, fatter and more complacent as a result of modern conveniences and misguided perceptions created by television. Americans are driving huge gas guzzling SUVs to discount superstores so we can save a few bucks on products made in another country, by workers willing to work for less than our people!

The 21st century global economy certainly provides numerous efficiencies, but for many, this has resulted in a pace too fast to keep up with and a mentality focused on material possessions and a culture devoid of sacrifice to attainment. Many people have lost track of their values and have chosen to follow the *"show me the money"* movement. Disturbing studies point out that college students who used to have a vision to change or improve society now select majors or courses of study that promise the highest initial salary, regardless of whether the actual job duties are fulfilling.

The concept of corporate social responsibility is all too often absent from our nation's largest employers. Corporate scandals became everyday news as financial staff succumbed to greed and faced tremendous pressure from shareholders to exceed quarterly projections or lose their jobs. And since the beginning of this century, CEO's have sent over 3 million jobs overseas where labor was cheaper but not necessarily better.

Those of us who seek to obtain their career calling are an elite force! Like the marines, *we are the few, the proud and the brave*! By elite, I don't mean to sound condescending but rather elite in that we are willing to pay the price to seek and find answers. We don't expect handouts, we don't blame the system, and we do possess a strong moral compass. We don't need to be monitored or controlled; we know what is right and wrong.

While the workplace continues to change and evolve, you will be faced with opportunities that never before existed ... and your decisions will dictate your happiness and quality of life. *Take comfort in knowing that within the pages of this book there is a plan!*

I promise you that each and every strategy, tip or suggestion in this program is one that I personally use to bring me closer to the balanced life I strive to live, each and every day. They say the hardest step in any journey is the first one. By reading these words, you have begun a journey, which will activate feelings, emotions, pride, and peace of mind that you may have thought was beyond your scope or reserved for others. Your potential is astounding and through this process, you will begin to truly realize it. Life is now in session; let us begin!

What Is a Career Calling?

Question: Have you have reached a point in your life where you have lost your job or desire to change your position and are no longer willing to tolerate an unfulfilling professional life that provides financial compensation but little else in the way of reward? It is no longer good enough to simply have a job; we want more and we want it now!

You have heard *it* called many things. Some refer to it as your purpose; others refer to it as your vision or mission in life. Still others call it your ultimate goal or dream. Whatever title you attach to it, recognizing your calling, and answering that call, is the key to experiencing *true* happiness.

If you have not found your career calling, you feel incomplete. Is there a yearning for more? Is there a hole in your soul? Is something gnawing at your gut that suggests you have not done all that you can or should? Do you worry about regret and wasted talent? When did your dream die? When was it consumed by the realities of bills, responsibilities and dead-lines? When did complacency, procrastination and apathy creep into your life? When did you allow yourself to be consumed with daily routine and ignore the importance of taking time each day for self-awareness and personal career planning?

For me, I would define the feeling as a *restless aching*, a relentless feeling that simply cannot be suppressed or ignored. Maybe you can relate to what I am talking about but lack a definitive plan to master this yearning to *feel significant*.

Many people lack the vocabulary to define this "restlessness" but can articulate their strong desire for a "career with more meaning." What they (you) are ultimately seeking is the key to this entire book ... *the need to obtain happiness and peace of mind that comes from making a positive contribution to others through meaningful work.*

So the question is: *What do you really want?* Here is how many describe their ultimate career desire:

- I don't know what to call it, but I want to help other people
- I want to wake up every morning and look forward to my job
- I want to come home from work every night and know in my heart that I made a difference
- I want to be memorable and make my family proud
- I know I have a special gift; I just have not found the right outlet for it yet
- I want to be like the small percentage of people I have met who actually love their job
- I want to take pride in describing what I do for a living
- I want to know that I mattered!

What is your career calling? Why is it important to acknowledge and respond to this emotional pull at your heartstrings? The answers to these critical questions will become clearer as we explore this subject in more detail.

What Is This Enigma Called Work?

"Where the spirit does not work with the hand there is no art."

—Leonardo da Vinci

"All right, Chris," you may say, "you have my attention but I have never stopped to analyze the concept of work that deeply or intensely." That is OK! Most people who are unfulfilled have not. They exist in a state of numbness to their internal selves and become absorbed in daily tasks or obligations. Occasionally, they may have a desire to find out if there is more, but often retreat back into the process of making a living instead of designing their life. Sounds pretty depressing, doesn't it?

From this day forward, be prepared to work hard on understanding your own professional needs, wants and values. There are no shortcuts!

Cutting Corners ...

3 young boys were comparing notes about their father's abilities. With an air of pride, the 1st boy said, "My dad is so fast he can shoot an arrow at a target and catch the arrow before it reaches the target."

"That's pretty good," the 2nd boy responded, "but my dad is so fast that he can shoot a deer and tackle the deer before the bullet gets there."

Listening quietly, the 3rd boy could restrain himself no longer. "Oh yeah? Well, my dad is faster than both of yours. He can get off work at 5:00 and be home by 4:15!"

The Movie Game Exercise

To make progress, you must begin with an accurate appraisal of where you are today. Where are you right now? How would you describe your own career? Here is a fun exercise to help you assign a brand to yourself and associate your education, skills and work history with a motion picture, which is in essence a story or set of experiences. *Make sure to itemize the reasons, themes or even specific scenes or characters you relate to and why!* Which movie title (not necessarily the content) would you say best describes your work life? Feel free to choose from the list below or make up your own!

1. *Apocalypse Now*
2. *Back to the Future*
3. *Catch Me If You Can*
4. *Gone With The Wind*
5. *Home Alone*
6. *Liar, Liar*
7. *Mission Impossible*
8. *National Lampoons Animal House*
9. *One Flew Over the Cuckoo's Nest*
10. *Planet of the Apes*
11. *Psycho*
12. *Superman*
13. *Terminator*
14. *The Addams Family*
15. *The Fugitive*
16. *The Sixth Sense*
17. *The Sound of Music*
18. *Titanic*
19. *Top Gun*
20. *Towering Inferno*

Now that we have had a little fun (at your expense!), let me ask you a basic question: What is work? Work, which Webster's dictionary defines as "bodily or mental effort exerted to do or make something: purposeful activity" is supposed to be the outlet for our passions, personality traits and future dreams. *Can you honestly say you are currently engaged in a "purposeful activity?"* Unfortunately, for many, work has become something much different.

Consider these common responses to the question: What is work?

- Work is a way to pay the bills
- Work is what allows me to enjoy the weekends
- Work is what keeps my (spouse or parents) off my back
- Work is what you are supposed to do to feel responsible
- Work is an alternative to boredom
- Work is what you do for 40 years so you can retire and die in peace

- Work is the opposite of play
- Work is same %#@*+, different day

Wow, if those aren't an eye opener! It seems for most, the concept of working is a dirty word often filled with negative connotations. How about this abbreviation ...

JOB = Just Over Broke!

I have found that people who view their occupation as a job, barely get by, while career planners like you are creating a life of abundance! Show me a person who complains about the boss, the hours or the daily grind, and I will predict they are struggling each month to pay their bills.

Be aware that there is a huge difference between a JOB and a career.

> A career is the lifelong plan of how you will use your unique and compelling talents to contribute. A job is simply a step in the process. A useful analogy: your career is the whole ladder; a job is merely a rung on the ladder.

People who focus on jobs and not the careering process will find frustration and barely make ends meet. From this day forward, we focus on careers, not jobs!

If you live in the western world, you can agree that we are often defined by our job ... what we *do*. Think about when you first meet someone, one of the 1st questions asked is, "*So what do you do for a living?*" The words "what do you do for a living" are telling ... Paraphrased, the question is seeking information on your quality of life based on your choice of career. I am amazed at how many people sheepishly answer the question as if they are embarrassed by their livelihood. If it is accurate that we are defined by our occupation, then far too many people are spending their lives engaged in a constant state of fear, uncertainty and doubt.

Work, for most, has become a daily grind instead of an expression of our unique and compelling skills and attributes. As of this moment, let us both agree that this unacceptable! I wrote this book to help you identify and obtain the career of your dreams, the one that you want and the one that, more importantly, you deserve. *Why not you?*

I propose that 80% of your success will be a result of getting in touch with your authentic self (understanding who you really are and what you truly want) and that the remaining 20% is simply a function of tools; teaching you how to get there by either empowering you to get off your butt and start your own venture, join a new organization or simply improve your status with your existing employer.

Regardless of your career goal, I am delighted you accepted the challenge to improve your status and I'd like to congratulate you on making the best investment you can make … an investment in yourself. You have now begun a process that will change the scope of your life forever, for the better. In the information to follow, *you are going to learn the formula for what separates those who have found their career calling from those that remain professionally unfulfilled.* And believe me, career success stories leave clues!

Let me pose to you 3 important questions:

1. Are you unemployed or seeking to re-enter the current work force?
2. If you are working, are you disenchanted with your current job? By disenchanted, I mean are you bored, tired, underpaid, unhappy or some combination of all of these? Are you working for a paycheck?
3. Do you lack passion for your work and find your enthusiasm to find a role where you can make a difference dulled by the daily grind of an unfulfilled career?

If you answered yes to any of these, here is my promise … If you follow the guidance and suggestions contained within this book, I am confident that you can change your perception of work, improve the quality of your work life, obtain a career that fills your innermost calling and leave a profound legacy.

If You Make Finding a Great Career a Craps Shoot … You Wind Up with Crap!

A famous tight rope artist was once asked the secret of successfully walking on a tightrope between 2 extremely tall buildings on a skinny beam, where a slip or mistake would cost him his life. He responded that the key to success on the tightrope trapeze is exactly the same as the key to life … One must focus on where he or she is going and look straight ahead with intense focus. Not down, not behind you, but merely where you are going without hesitation or fear. Be decisive. If you follow these instructions you will emerge victorious!

If you make finding a great career a craps shoot, you will wind up with crap. The key to finding your career calling is to focus on your values, that is, what is important to you personally and professionally. Be sure that you focus on your values and not the expectations or belief systems of others.

> *"Most people are trapped in an ongoing psychological wrestling contest between their own identity (who they truly are), societal pressures to conform (what society, friends or family say they should do), and internal limiting beliefs (what they believe they can or cannot do)."*
>
> —Chris Kuselias

When you find your career calling, you will know it because it your work life feeds the most important aspects of your personality. In the right career, you are making use of your best attributes and not forced to struggle with skills that don't come as naturally. You are in a flow where you are doing what comes naturally and work does not feel like work. I would like to make clear that there is no one ideal job to which we can all aspire, but rather there exist many different paths to many different jobs, which can match your unique and compelling personality, values and skills. In short, there is no magical role for everyone, but there is an ideal career for you!

Radio Station WIIFM! *What's In It For Me?*

> *"When work, commitment and pleasure all become one, and you reach that deep well where passion lives, nothing is impossible"*
>
> —Anonymous

As crazy as it may sound, I am granting you permission to be selfish! You will need to be if you are to experience real career progress. You must be willing to prioritize your thoughts, feelings and emotions and find the time to dedicate yourself to uncovering your passion and purpose. This will involve changing your current routines and, in some cases, acquaintances.

> Whenever you move ahead, you must leave some behaviors, habits and people behind ...

So far, you know that obtaining your career calling begins with a commitment to self-understanding, which is achieved through *critical reflection.*

This is a fancy term for simply taking time to explore your own wants, needs and desires.

My 1ˢᵗ objective is to ignite your hidden passion and uncover your unique and compelling contributions (ideally at as young an age as possible) and then provide a specific plan to show you how to make a living doing it. Once your career purpose is determined, your job is to write it down and read it aloud every day, which will secure this belief in your subconscious mind. This sounds deep, but it really isn't!

If you have not yet achieved what you want, I would guess it is because you have not identified exactly *what* you want. *Most people who fail to make a change have not identified a strong enough why.* While you may have a general idea of success and happiness, you most likely have not defined your needs, wants and values in clear and compelling, vivid detail.

How do I know? I have dedicated my life's work to understanding the process and have created a formula based upon analyzing thousands of people who are living and working their dream. I work with individuals, corporations and governments every day who have the same challenge as yours. My conclusion: People who take the time to discover what they truly want from life usually obtain it, and people who do not spend the time and do not know exactly what they want, rarely if ever do. You have been presented with another choice!

One of my primary objectives is to ignite your inner flame regarding the incredible benefits of *critical reflection*. Simply defined, this means to get in touch with your *authentic* self, the real person beneath the layers of societal conditioning, kids, designer clothes and life roles. This holistic process of reflecting is not what you might initially think; it is not like the process of burning incense, engaging in primal screaming or chanting at the stars. I take a more practical approach.

What I profess is carving out a specific time each and every day to quietly consider your place in society, the value of your contributions and if you are on target toward fulfilling your ideal calling; *to truly reflect on your purpose.* It is time to turn to station WIIFM, *what's in it for me!*

Making the Time to Be Great

"Honesty is the first chapter in the Book of Wisdom."
—Thomas Jefferson

Taking an honest and sincere appraisal of your worth and inventorying your accomplishments are often not a priority and are therefore ignored. The fact is that to obtain your calling or purpose, a change is required. That change may be emotional, physical, spiritual or some combination of all 3. Let go of your inhibitions or conditioning. Trust in yourself, as there is greatness in you! Consider the words of Ernest Holmes who said, "The thing we surrender to becomes our power."

How can you possibly expect meaningful progress or positive change in your life if you are not willing to put the brakes on, get off the treadmill of life, take a deep breath and establish an honest plan for your professional future? I am not interested in your social mask, the one you put on for others, but instead, your true inner self.

In my experience, most people spend more time applying makeup, selecting the right designer clothes and creating the appropriate external persona (for the world to see) than they do in getting in touch with their inner talents, skills and desires or what I call, their authentic self. Let me ask you a question. Do you spend more time preparing your external self (creating a professional exterior of hair, makeup, wardrobe, accessories, etc.) or more time reflecting on your internal development (skills, unique value, true desires, likes and dislikes, goals, etc.)? I suspect it is time you make a decision to dedicate the proper time on your authentic self by engaging in the regular daily practice of critical reflection. If you do, you will exceed even your most ambitious objectives and amaze yourself!

But Chris, you might be thinking, *in today's information age, who really has the time to reflect? I am so busy with career, family, clicking through my 500 TV channels, paying bills, drinking $5 latte's, managing my finances and shrinking 401K plan, trying to lose that last 10 pounds, parenting and trying to keep up with the rush of life that I can barely find a minute to call my mother and tell her I love her.* Who has the time to reflect? You do!

I would be willing to wager a large sum of money that if they created a new reality television show entitled, *"Chris Kuselias moves in with you and analyzes your non-productive time,"* that within one day I would provide you with a more constructive daily schedule, eliminate many of your useless and non productive activities, prioritize your essential issues, coach you to avoid negative influences and create a lifestyle designed to allow for daily *critical reflection*. I would also be willing to bet that if you utilized this newfound free time to plan your life, without the common distractions of television, music or kids, you would begin to realize your enormous potential and begin to live the life you were destined to live! You would be in a position to effectively design and achieve your legacy.

Now, as much as I would like to be a reality TV star (not!) and move in with you for a day or 2 … this is not going to happen. The alternative to this far-fetched scenario is to communicate with you through these words and exercises and coach you to establish the discipline to implement the enclosed proven strategies. If you do so, I am confident you will achieve your true purpose, also known as your *career calling*. As an author, speaker and consultant, I have had the privilege to meet and befriend some of the nation's most successful people, individuals who have achieved true balance and harmony in their personal and professional lives. These are folks who embrace change and look forward to the future.

A common theme is that each of these people consistently practices the regular art of reflection; they carve out time each day to design their life instead of being directed by external forces. Certainly they experience unforeseen challenges, but their foundation is so solid that these curve balls become mere distractions that do not derail their ultimate focus. This is my wish for you!

I will get into greater detail on the process of reflecting, determining your unique and compelling interests, skills and qualities, but for now, I want you to think back to 3 instances in your life when you felt the greatest sense of joy and happiness. When did you last feel completely alive and vibrant? What were the common elements to these incredibly positive occurrences? Can you observe a common theme in your selections (for example, you were recognized, praised, creative, assisted another person or group, closed a deal, overcame an obstacle, saved an animal, or cooked a tremendous meal)?

> My key question for you is: Can you identify a way to earn a living engaged in these highly desirable activities or ones that allow you to utilize these skills or experience these amazing feelings on a consistent basis?

I have found that people who have found their career calling and truly love their work *think* differently than those who have not. A breakthrough for me was learning that if you analyzed their thought process and modeled their actions, similar results could be achieved. I learned that studying their mindset and becoming aware of how my own thoughts and conditioning were holding me back was the key ingredient to success. I learned to program my mind for career success, the same way truly happy people had done. From this, a career success formula was born!

Great Performers Start with the End in Mind!

> *Close your eyes ... Fast forward in time and imagine you are 90 years old and are sitting in a comfortable rocking chair on a beautiful summer day. As you sip a cool drink, a peaceful breeze refreshes your face and you hear a soothing musical wind chime in the distance. At ease, you begin to reflect on the decisions, associations and events that comprise your life. While you may have forgotten the details about people, places or things, a certain collection of memories and events resonate and evoke strong emotions within you. As you reflect over the course of your life, is the end result a smile or a frown?*

Anticipating the inevitable reflection we all face, the key questions are these: What will you remember? Will it be your relationships and those you loved and who loved you? Will you take pride in your material possessions or the inheritance you leave to your heirs? Will you recall your career achievements and relish thoughts of using your creativity and overcoming challenges? Will you have made peace with your maker? Will you experience the pleasant glow of a life fulfilled with joy, hope, risk, reward, love and passion, or will you have regrets such as wishing you had spent more time with your children, taken more risks, traveled more, or enjoyed your work?

An increasing number of people today are making important changes in anticipation of this day and taking decisive action to ensure they live each day with zest! Their comments:

"I was so busy and consumed with daily tasks, I never had the time to consider my true feelings. Now after losing my job, I finally found my purpose ... At last!"

"My kids think I do more than just make money and after years of boredom, I am showing them by example that working is not a dirty word."

"Can you believe it? At 51, I finally found my reason for being. I always felt I was a good teacher, but I finally got the courage to explore *The Career Guarantee* 5P's and my potential. You are never too old to change!"

"Starting my dream career was risky, but worth it. Every day I answer to myself!"

"Well, I don't make the money I once did and now look at prices on a menu before ordering, but my health is great, I am happier than ever and every day I wake up with a smile. This is awesome!"

"Goodbye 90 minute commute, hello personal life!"

"I feel like I have been paroled. I never realized how dull and boring I had become until I found *The Career Guarantee* Master Career Formula (5 P's) and attained my calling."

You and I are given one chance to savor this life and extract the incredible joy available to us. And because we happen to live in the most exciting time in history, where modern day innovations and technology create incredible opportunities and more free time, you and I have more choices than ever before. The enlightened few know that the ultimate tragedy is a life filled with regret and unfulfilled potential. What will you do with these choices?

The older I become the more I realize that day in the rocking chair is approaching faster than any of us want to admit or believe. There is no dress rehearsal or do over … Life is in session!

3 Important Questions:

1. How will others talk about you when you are gone?
2. Will you have mattered?
3. What will be your legacy?

A never ending list of books, seminars, workshops, webinars and coaching programs exists to remind us how to be organized, set goals, and get motivated, along with a seemingly endless array of strategies and tools to lead a more effective life. On line or in your favorite bookstore are hundreds of "How To" publications about getting a job, writing a resume, interviewing, etc. Most are well intentioned but don't produce the results you seek.

With the speed of technology and rush of life, I find most people have trouble getting through the day, much less taking the time to design their life or find their career calling. Without a solid game plan, obtaining a great career is stressful, especially if you are unemployed, have been laid off, feel burned out, are worried about the economy, have financial responsibilities, and also need a retirement plan.

The Career Guarantee is a simple yet effective model for the careering process – that is, uncovering your unique and compelling contribution and providing a blueprint to achieve your professional legacy. It is not a "How to" book, but more of a "Why" book. The solution to career happiness is between your ears and in your heart and soul. You are unique and there will never be another human being exactly like you, with your vision, ideas, creativity, talents and mindset.

By now you may be thinking, "OK, Chris, I get it! I need to determine who I am, what I want, and why I want it!" But how do I do this and find my unique career calling? By applying the *Master Career Success Formula*, you can enjoy a life filled with zest and vigor, and love what you do … any day and every day! What is this Magical Process? I call it …

The 5 P's to Success

Passion
Purpose
Power
Profit
Peace of mind

In chronological order, the 5 P's formula includes …

1. Discovering your **P**assion, leads to …
2. Finding your **P**urpose, which assists you in …
3. Expanding your **P**ower, which accelerates …
4. Gaining your **P**rofit, which results in …
5. Achieving **P**eace of mind, which equals happiness, the ultimate goal!

Do the 5P's Work? Yes!

Scott Adams had a passion for drawing but found himself working in a job that was not his true career calling. So every day before work, he got up early and drew cartoons until he had 50 samples; he then mailed the samples to various syndicates. United Features saw his work, offered him a contract and the rest (Dilbert creator) is history …

PERSONALLY, I STUMBLED ACROSS this incredible formula while going through one of my, "Is this all there is?" moments. I was working in corporate America, successful by most standards (nice car, nice house, etc.) and had a daily routine (coffee, decent co-workers, occasional feel goods) but something was missing! When I was truly honest with myself, there was a huge void in my professional life (no passion!) and looking back, this often negatively affected my health and personal life. *I had a hole in my soul!*

Sometimes we need a defining moment or 'aha' moment, as some call it. It was my father's diagnosis of terminal cancer that finally had enough shock value for me to realize that life is short and there are no 2nd chances. You will hear more about this event later (my dad overcame incredible medical odds and is alive and well!). A conversation on his "supposed" deathbed about "finding one's true identity and contribution" and my growing restlessness that my life was passing me by were enough incentive to immerse myself into studying the secrets to career success and happiness. This resulted in my life's calling and this book, so you don't have to wait for similar extreme circumstances to create a breakthrough to pursue your passion!

Within a short time of adopting this *Master Career Formula* in my life, I began to experience incredible levels of success. I pursued my passion of helping others in their careers, quit my high paying but unfulfilling corporate job, assembled my limited finances to pursue my dream and went for it! I put passion and purpose ahead of short-term income or opportunity.

With a passion for helping others find passion and purpose, I formed my own company, *Career T.E.A.M.,* LLC, and began helping people find their career calling. After a short time I was hired by the Federal government to assist 10,000 former welfare recipients find jobs.

With *passion* and *purpose* in my corner, I began to expand my reputation and expertise, gained *power* and was invited to the White House to meet with the President and several *Fortune* 500 CEOs. *Career* T.E.A.M., LLC was named one of *Inc.* Magazine's 500 fastest growing, privately held companies. In line with the *Master Career Formula*, I quickly became a multi-millionaire (*profit*) and I experienced more *peace of mind* than I ever imagined, knowing I had found my reason for being, my career calling.

When I combined the power of my mind with this proven success formula, my career skyrocketed. You can do the same! Today, I conduct seminars worldwide and now have a goal to help 1 million people leave unfulfilling jobs and find their unique and compelling career calling.

The funny thing is, I had always wanted to be wealthy and spent a lot of time thinking about how to make more money. When I adopted this newfound philosophy, it was never about the money, it was about finding that feeling in my gut that told me I was doing what was right for me. The anxiety and stress disappeared, and the money came in faster than when I focused solely on making it! I learned that when you do what you love, big money follows.

Think of this *Master Career Formula* as a blueprint, which, if followed, will lead to your unique career calling. The formula works because outcomes are in accordance with your *true* identity, that is, what is in your heart, mind and soul. It is a formula for helping you discover the *real* you and the contribution *you* were born to make!

When you really think about it, the challenge for each of us is that we enter this lifelong project without the benefit of an instruction manual. Certainly, many profound authors or consultants have attempted to provide solutions to the pursuit of passion and purpose. Few, however, have succeeded in creating a universal approach to the eternal question regarding our search for career purpose or meaning.

Regardless of gender, race, religion, education level, work experience or personality type, we are all unique and compelling creatures with individual belief systems. There are several versions of what constitutes happiness, the obvious outcome of achieving one's career calling. Happiness is a personal feeling within the people who consistently achieve this state of mind, and the actions they take leave clues.

Systems do work and I am a believer in such. According to Michael Gerber, author of one of my favorite books, *E-Myth Mastery,* "Systems [formulas] permit ordinary people to achieve extraordinary results, predictably." My system will assist you to find your way to where you are supposed to be, where true happiness lies.

There is one distinct difference between a highly successful person and one who is not, and that is that highly successful people develop good habits and make choices that others do not like to make. By having the courage to exercise their right to choose, they achieve greatness.

> *"You are free to choose, but the choices you make today will determine what you will have, be and do in the tomorrow of your life."*
> —Zig Ziglar

You have made the choice to pursue career greatness. Let us begin your journey to career success and happiness with a review of the. *Master Career Formula* ...

1st P—Finding Your *Passion*

> *"Now, here is my secret, a very simple secret. It is only with the heart that one can see rightly: what is essential is invisible to the eye."*
> —Antoine De Saint-Exupéry, *The Little Prince*

Your first choice if you truly seek to be highly successful is to identify and pursue *your* passion. Not mine, not your parents', not your significant other's but yours! *In order for you to achieve your potential, you must make a firm decision to restructure your life around your passion.*

   Finding your passion involves getting in touch with your heart and identifying your dreams. The process has to start here, because only your heart will reveal what really matters to you and what truly brings you happiness. What is it that you crave, and what fills you with energy and excitement? What is that one thing that gets you up in the morning, and keeps you awake at night? When you answer these questions, you will have found your passion.

"Bob from Accounting … Damn glad to meet you!"

Passion is not a privilege of the fortunate few; it is a right and a power that you possess. If you get in touch with the passion that defines you, I promise you will have an amazing life. In your quest to find your passion, there are a few areas you can explore that will assist you on the road to discovery, such as:

1. Brainstorm and identify what you daydream about, what gets you excited, what you consider fun, what you like to do, or what you would get a kick out of doing.

2. Peer into your childhood and think about anything that you may have had an affinity for growing up. Is there something that you were good at as a child that you would like to do again?

3. Evaluate your talents and skills. Take a piece of paper and write down the things that you do well or that come naturally to you, without any effort on your part. These talents should be viewed as your unique and compelling gifts … special gifts that have been passed on to you genetically.

4. Test yourself and your passion. One way to validate your passion is to put it to the test, and you can accomplish this by revisiting your feelings 2 or 3 weeks after you have identified it. Do you still get that fire in your belly when you think about it? Are you willing to sacrifice everything to fulfill it, or take risks for it? Your responses will separate your true passion from mere interest.

Once you begin to experience passion in your life's work, your passion will create a personal intensity, which will uplift and inspire you. It will heighten your performance and enable you to achieve things that you may never have dreamed possible. Finding passion is the key to happiness in your career, and in every other area of your life.

If you have uncovered your passion, but are finding it difficult to take the next step, you may need to break down the barriers that are preventing you from turning your passion into reality. When you make decisions based on your heart's desires, and not on societal dictates, you open up an assortment of challenges, and will have to allow yourself to move beyond the fear or paralysis that grips you and, perhaps, is preventing you from answering your calling.

> *"Find your passion and follow it. That is all the career advice you will ever need."*
> — John C. Maxwell, management guru

Barriers to Living Your Passion

1. *Fear:* Passion is a mystery, and often you do not know exactly where it will lead you. You may wonder what life would be like if you followed your heart and decided to change careers. If fear creeps in, your thoughts may become distorted and create elaborate scenarios of failure. There is no greater barrier to fulfilling your passion than fear of the unknown.

2. *Self-doubt:* Self-doubt is an extension of your fear, and focuses on your perceived personal inadequacies. This self-doubt causes you to question your own abilities and potential, and can lead you to imagining yourself as a failure, rather than a success.

3. *Paralysis or numbness:* When faced with confusion or uncertainty, you may find yourself locked into an emotional paralysis. While you may want to change your life and career, you are unable to harness the power to do so. You may become so accustomed to the demands and stresses of life that you move beyond paralysis into numbness. You may not even realize that you are unhappy and unfulfilled, and that you have become emotionally disconnected.

4. *Limited scope:* When you identify yourself by stereotype (that is, white-collar or blue-collar, baby-boomer, etc.), you limit your potential. Labeling yourself this way causes you to accept an identity that probably has nothing to do with who you really are or what your passion is.

5. *Procrastination:* "One day, some day ... " is an excuse for putting off what could be the most important step in your life. Your passion will never become a reality as long as you keep putting off pursuit of it.

6. *Caution:* Your fears may prevent you from acting on faith and belief. You may pursue your dreams in a very controlled and calculated manner, leaving little room for your passion to take over. While you may never know failure, you may also never know the success that comes from unleashing your passion.

Here are 3 questions to uncover your passion ...

1. I am happiest when I am ...
2. I feel energized when I am ...
3. I would work for free doing ...

Moving forward, trust your heart and listen to your inner voice. Acknowledge your passion and nurture it. Incorporate it into your existence, and your life will become an accurate reflection of your true identity and who you aspire to become. Once accomplished, you will graduate to the next step: Acquiring a sense of purpose!

2nd P—*Purpose* Is Obtained from the Fuel of Passion

> *Hans Selye, the pioneer in the understanding of human stress, often asked the following question: What is the most stressful condition a person can face? His unexpected response ... "Not having something to believe in."*

What do you believe in? Why are you here? What contribution were you born to make? Were you meant to sit in a cubicle day after day without a clue as to whether you were impacting your company? Maybe yes, but most likely no!

After you have found your passion, by answering your calling you will begin to answer these questions and acquire a *sense of purpose*. Purpose springs from belief and the fact that you are doing what you love and desire. Your dreams and hopes are becoming a reality, and you have moved outside of the norm. You are engaged in tasks and activities that feel like play; working is a labor of love.

You have fought off conventional wisdom to work for the money or prestige. You are empowered and committed to continue on this path. You believe whole-heartedly in your cause. Your sense of purpose is evident in everything you do—the way you act, speak, look and think. You are contagious! This sense of purpose will continue to flourish as you completely immerse yourself in pursuing your passion.

Determining your higher purpose starts with defining the word *success*, because that is the paradigm with which most people identify. Later on, we will discuss this further but for now:

1. Which direction are you moving and where is your passion and purpose leading you?
2. Are you prospering toward the next achievement by building new mentors and learning from your missteps, or are you trying to avoid the prospect of failure by not competing for your career calling at all?

At this stage, the key question is: *What is important to me about being successful?* Success is a deeply personal issue. One needs more than persistence, ambition or motivation. You need to be inspired to the very core of your being. If you cannot verbalize your contribution, it will not last. Your true purpose is: *Your sincere, deepest desire and motivation for action!* When you discover your true purpose, you will feel yourself gaining confidence and power.

Without a true purpose you will:

1. Experience more stress
2. Be prone to suffer burnout
3. Often feel overwhelmed
4. Have difficulty making decisions
5. Feel anxious and restless

Here are 3 questions to help you realize your purpose ...

I was meant to ...
My place in this world is as a ...
I feel most meaningful when I ...

3rd P—*Power* and Confidence Are Realized When Purpose Is Allowed to Flow

> *"Being powerful is like being a lady; if you have to tell people you are ... you aren't."*
>
> —Margaret Thatcher

It makes sense that once you acquire a sense of purpose you become more powerful. By taking the steps that lead to fulfilling your passion, you begin to feel as though you are in control of your life and your destiny. You are on a path that provides the greatest rewards one can experience. You are not working by others standards; you are working because it is what you *choose* to do. You are in command!

Like your sense of purpose, *gaining power* in your life evidences itself through every orifice of your being. You experience more energy and you walk with an air of confidence. This newly obtained power is also a result of attacking your fears and increasing your level of courage and confidence.

Another contributor to your feeling of power is your attitude. Your positive attitude makes you happier, more productive, and more successful, which, in turn, also makes you more powerful. Other people will gravitate toward your energy, which will become infectious. Those who are trapped in the fog of apathy, lethargy and even depression will crave your new-found enthusiasm and confidence. They will want to associate with you because you project an image of congruence, a trait that we all admire and aspire to obtain. You are positively contagious!

Here are 3 questions to realize your power ...

People recognize me for my expertise in ...

I know more than most on the subject of ...

I can best assist others by ...

4th P—*Profit* Inevitably Follows Those Who Contribute

"Explore and understand your authentic self, learn to do what you love and are passionate about and the money will follow."

—Chris Kuselias

If nothing else, you are already gaining *wealth* by the benefits you are enjoying up to this point (finding your passion, acquiring a sense of purpose, and gaining power).

Not only is your profit centered on financial gain, but also on your emotional, spiritual, physical, interpersonal, and professional experiences. J. Paul Getty's brother, (who wasn't nearly as financially well off as his famous tycoon brother) used to send him notes, which began, "from the richest man in the world to the wealthiest." Riches are not measured solely by the size of your wallet.

In working with numerous highly compensated executives, who often experience severe depression when laid off, it is apparent to me that many people fill voids in their emotional lives by basing their self-worth on money and material possessions. When you take away their "toys" as I like to call them, very often there is an emotional void and a lack of true identity. How sad!

When you have found your passion, purpose and power, interestingly, you become the center of attention, and people begin to seek you out. They want to know what you have that they do not and why you feel so good.

Hiring authorities are willing to compensate you for your knowledge. You become in demand because you had the courage to pursue your passion. You are a leader!

We can all agree that leaders in any organization are typically recipients of the highest praise and most lucrative compensation. At my company, *Career* T.E.A.M., we have a saying for our leaders, which is, "If the light ain't on at the top, it is dim all the way down." In my experience, society ultimately rewards those who find their unique contribution and exhibit these qualities. This is how big money is made. I know very few people, if any, who are wildly wealthy and aren't passionate about their work.

In your career, if you master the first 3 P's (passion, purpose and power), enhanced compensation (profit) will inevitably follow. Advancement opportunity and increased salary become more readily available due to your changed attitude and level of energy. People will gravitate to your knowledge and begin feeding off your passion. Having followers will increase your responsibility, which inevitably increases your earnings.

Here are 3 statements to help you maximize profit ...

I define professional success as ...
With more money I would ...
What I want that I don't have now is ...

5th P—*Peace of Mind* Is Achieved When We Have Found Our True Calling

> *"I have lived long enough to learn how much there is I can really do without ... He is nearest to God who needs the fewest things."*
>
> —Socrates

The 5th P is the most precious asset—*peace of mind*. This state of mind comes from the realization that you are contributing to others in a passionate and purposeful way. When we are contributing, that is, truly helping others through our work, we feel a tremendous sense of internal joy and happiness. We adopt the belief system that we matter. We develop a legacy that outlives our physical body. People all over the world would give their last dollar to experience true peace of mind, and for many of them, the lack thereof is the direct result of living their lives according to someone else's standard, and not their own.

To avoid societal conditioning and to forge your own path requires a great deal of courage and honesty. We must be true to ourselves, live in sync with our established identity and be congruent in our internal belief systems. Peace of mind comes from learning the skill to become your *authentic self*.

> *According to Gallup, "The percentage of Americans who voiced the need to experience spiritual growth has increased from 58% in 1994 to 82% today."*

Like you, I have always craved peace of mind but was often restless. Today, I understand that until I lived my life in accordance with these 5P's; and spent my time engaged in activities consistent with my identity, I would never be truly content. Stress was my enemy and relaxation was a skill I had not mastered.

I have become a believer in meditation, not the unfavorable view of a person in some bizarre robe with mushroom-scented incense but rather a more personalized experience where one shuts out the problems and distractions of the world and contemplates their authentic self and true aspirations. The process should provide critical benefits and that is, to learn, recognize and *listen* to the sound of your inner voice, what I call your higher self.

For me, this process creates a mindset that has allowed my most outstanding ideas and visions to penetrate the confusion and distractions of my hectic life. It challenged me to ask myself life's most pressing questions, those that cannot be addressed or answered with the television playing, music blasting, children crying or business looming. Take 10 minutes and just sit quietly and reflect on what you really want, what you are great at and what brings you joy.

Here are 3 questions to help you find peace of mind ...

I want to look back on my life and feel ...
When people think of my life, they will think ...
I will feel my life was worth living if I ...

The End Result

B Y MASTERING THE 5 P's, you will begin to understand what it truly means to be content, at peace, and happy. Having applied this *Master*

Career Formula in your life, you will promote balance in what I view as the 5 areas that dictate life balance: career, financial, health and fitness, relationships, and spiritual enlightenment. Top performers, such as you, recognize that total happiness in life can only occur by mastering these 5 key areas.

When you get to this final stage of development, you are experiencing success on your own terms, and enjoying life. Your existence is validated, and you matter! Your life is in harmony with your being, and you feel whole and complete. You are basking in the glow of looking into your innermost desires and contributing your unique and compelling gifts to others in the form of your career calling. This is the essence of becoming happy and self-actualized!

> *"The best way to cheer yourself up is to cheer everybody else up"*
>
> —Mark Twain

By remaining true to your passion, and incorporating the *Master Career Formula* into your life, you will reap rewards you never anticipated, because finding your calling (passion) and answering that call will take you to another level of living. *The Career Guarantee* serves to provide exercises, examples and reminders of how you can achieve this standard of living. Let's begin!

An Overview of the 21st Century Workplace

> *"The best way to predict your future is to create it."*
>
> —Stephen Covey

WE CAN ALL AGREE that, more than ever in our history, the future is filled with so many unanswered questions regarding what employment will look like. Industries are being consolidated and in some cases even eliminated, seemingly overnight. International competition and the new global economy have made the world a much smaller place when it comes to marketing or producing goods and services.

With so much uncertainty, you may be looking for a set of guiding principles to help you navigate through these uncertain workplace waters. Many feel like they have been thrown into the rapids without a paddle, life jacket, map or the proper equipment! This is our collective challenge as strategies and techniques that may have worked in the past are now as obsolete as an 8-track player.

Today, You Are What You Do ...

The 21st century workplace promises more change and dramatic industry fluctuations. In my experience, there are very few things as challenging as changing career and few life experiences as demoralizing as the loss of one's job. Here is why. Many people *define* themselves by their job title or job description. Their job is their *identity*.

I recently attended an open house at my daughters' elementary school; it was a meet and greet for parents and teachers. It was interesting to observe parents with small kids (in this case 1st grade) in today's competitive world jockey for position with the teacher, the principal and even the teacher's aides!

We all convened in the cafeteria and were served juice and crackers and after we listened to the teacher speak about the curriculum and objectives, we were left to mingle with the other parents. Earlier that evening, I had told my wife that I was going to keep a formal record of how many people asked me what I do for a living and when the question of my occupational status came up in conversation with other parents. She said she would help (as long as I did not do anything to embarrass her).

During the course of the evening, which lasted 2 hours, I met a total of 54 sets of kindergarten parents. Of these, 46 (85%!) asked me what I did for a living within their 1st 3 questions. After requesting my name, the curiosity as to my occupational status was the 2nd most asked question.

Do you find this to be the case in your life? We can all agree that "what do you do for a living" is a universally accepted phrase. Consider those words, which associate your job or career with a "living," that is, how you exist ... Clearly, your career is more than just a way to pay the bills.

> Some people identify so strongly with their job title that if they are laid off or lose their job, they feel as if their identity has been surgically removed from their body.

People have different value systems; some actually develop a self-concept based on their occupation, or even the amount of money they earn. Have you ever heard of the 6-figure club? One of my friend's wives had to remind him (in a not so pleasant manner!) that he may be the boss at work, but at home she was not his secretary and that the kids were not employees. It is often difficult to separate our work persona from our personal persona. My friend had the common challenge of making sure his identity was not defined by his job title or duties, but rather by a variety of personal and professional characteristics.

So what is the solution to competing and winning in the 21st century workplace? To begin, I am an advocate that while understanding the global landscape is important and necessary, *your chosen career path should be based on your passions and internal beliefs rather than on availability or what jobs pay the most at any given moment.*

I am not naïve to practical concerns or being pragmatic when it comes to formulating a decision, but I strongly believe that before falling prey to the trappings of a job and lifestyle that does not provide passion and purpose, one should explore their goals and objectives in detail.

The good news is that you are living in an exciting era with incredible advances and innovations. America remains the greatest nation on Earth; we simply have more opportunities and better resources. Next time you find yourself complaining, consider this to help gain some perspective ...

Fast Fact

USA Today Snapshots ran a profile from the National Park Service that cited Americans flush down toilets 6.8 billion gallons of water per DAY ... while there are 1.2 billion people worldwide who do not even have access to clean water!

Becoming "Me, Inc." Is a Must!

> *Avoid the single-minded danger that Abraham Maslow observed: "He that is good with the hammer tends to think everything is a nail."*

It is time to expand your horizons and take the blinders off. The 21st century global economy has created a paradigm shift where borders no longer exist and the perception of one's career identity must shift from the finite title on a business card to that of a *solutions oriented resource. You are a problem solver or you are obsolete!* Although the world is more complex, simple is still powerful.

Here is a profound message as to how you should perceive your career from this day forward ... *ME, INC.* You are your own personal services corporation responsible for your own research, marketing, human resources, financial and quality control. There is no employer or company looking out for your best interests; this is ultimately your job.

It is time to broaden your horizons and adopt a single-minded approach to your livelihood. There is an ocean of opportunity created by this new global economy. Those who decide to put away the trappings of conformity and pursue their unique destiny are creating fortunes every day. A sample:

- Billionaire media mogul Oprah was only 19 when she started her career as a news anchor at Nashville's WTVF-TV; her show is now seen in over 100 countries by an estimated 46 million weekly viewers
- Billionaire Michael Dell founded Dell Computer at 19 with $1,000 from his dorm room at the University of Texas; by age 27 he was the youngest CEO ever to earn a ranking on the Fortune 500
- At 40, Harland "Colonel" Sanders began cooking chicken for his customers from his service station and sold his Kentucky Fried Chicken company in 1964 with over 600 outlets nationwide
- At 52, Ray Kroc stopped selling milk shakes, purchased a restaurant and turned it into the planet's most successful fast food enterprise, McDonald's.

Is there an exciting idea or 2 in you? Maybe you are reading this book because you have recently faced a life-altering event like a layoff or illness, or maybe you are simply tired of living an uninspired existence. Often the will is there but the knowledge of specific strategies and techniques to realize this new ambition is lacking.

Maybe, like millions of workers, you have looked at recent world events and have decided to marry your skills and talents with a more rewarding occupation. Maybe you have confronted your own mortality and have a new perspective on what is truly important and what is not. Every day, I hear more and more people say, "I am willing to work for less money if I feel I am making a difference in my job." Or they will say, "I want some meaning in my life and a career that makes me feel good about myself."

Sound familiar? I am of the belief that there is a paradigm shift occurring where people in record numbers are searching for the emotional benefits associated with a career that provides a measurable benefit to society. We want to know that we matter; we do not wish to be deemed insignificant.

"I know this now. Every man gives his life to what he believes.
Every woman gives her life for what she believes. Sometimes

THE CAREER GUARANTEE

*people believe in little or nothing, and so they give their lives
to little or nothing."*

—Joan of Arc

To support this more concentrated search for purpose and this growing trend towards integrating religious beliefs with our career, in his book, *How To Find Your Mission In Life*, well known career author Richard N. Bolles points out, "According to 50 years of opinion polls by the Gallup Organization, 94% of us pray, 88% of us believe in God, and 33% of us report we have had a life changing experience" ("The People's Religion: American Faith in the 90s").

It is evident that an increasing number of people seek to realize a similar level of empowerment from their career that they experience from their spiritual undertakings. Finding your calling is a process, which combines your intellectual, physical, spiritual and emotional capabilities to create a feeling of positive contribution and the peace of mind associated with serving others.

Please keep in mind that attaining your career calling, like following your religious pursuits, is an ongoing process that one never masters, but gets closer to the ideal.

Employer downsizing is a constant reality and is creating a need to plan one's career differently than in the past. Perhaps you have recently lost your job. There is a whole set of vocabulary for this evolving trend towards fewer full time workers with paid benefits to more part time workers or contracted employees. Have you ever heard these words?

**Let go, Fired, Downsized, Displaced,
Right sized, Reorganized, Reengineered**

Maybe you were just "surplus" and part of a "cost reduction exercise." Whatever you call it, the process of losing your job is no fun and can be, for some, emotionally crippling. Consider Paul's story . . .

Paul lost his job as a tool and die maker after 32 years of valued service (he never missed a day for being sick in 32 years!) and described the loss of his job as a loss of his *identity*. In fact, Paul, the displaced worker in this example, stated that he felt like someone had, "surgically removed my identity." Without his job, Paul did not know who he was anymore or what to do with his time. His company-provided outplacement program offered information on the mechanics of finding a new job (his resume, cover letter, etc.) but spent little time on what Paul desperately needed, which was, coaching him through his emotional loss and the step by step re-building of his self-esteem. What Paul needed most was not a resume and a handshake, but the re-establishment of his confidence and a plan for determining where his passions and contributions could be utilized.

Paul identified with his role as a tool and die worker so strongly that he had confused his own self-concept and he literally felt like a part of him had died when told he could no longer work in his former capacity. His value system was completely imbalanced and because he had been conditioned this way for so many years, I prescribed a serious career makeover. Paul was initially resistant to the process; it seems he had not been on an interview for nearly 30 years!

My solution was obvious: I helped him with the process of transition while simultaneously assisting him to appreciate and recognize his non-work related aspects and joys, which also (even Paul did not initially realize or appreciate) shaped his sense of self and purpose. His work life was only a fraction of his total identity. Paul needed to be reminded that he was a grandfather, a husband and a "dad." He was a member of the local Knights of Columbus, which spearheaded several community-based contributions and was active in his local church. Paul was an extremely tough case; he was angry and resistant to letting go of his resentment towards his former employer for "ruining his life." He had trouble sleeping and was often short with his loved ones.

After much support to gain perspective on the importance of his non-work identity, Paul began to soften and eliminate the hate in his heart. He became a member of the local Senior Business Leaders group and even took a course at the local community college. Today, Paul has lost most of his bitterness and is re-inventing and re-building his identity, on his way to finding a new calling and the next great chapter in his life. Paul now has a plan; and it involves not just finding another job, but seeking his passion and purpose. He is leading with his heart; he knows the rewards will follow.

What can we learn from this story? To begin, never let your work consume your identity to the point where your value is dictated by your job title or role. Duties are fleeting and can be taken away or eliminated at a moment's notice. Do not let yourself get to the point where your entire life revolves around your work, meaning if work is going great you are happy and when things are not so great, your personality reflects this as well. Be mindful to not let yourself invest your entire identity and reason for being into a work related function. You are much more than that, but in today's fast paced, win at all cost, bottom line global economy, this takes a constant effort and daily reminder.

In sum, what is important is to focus on the essence of your contributions and the positive feelings generated rather than on the title or trappings of work, such as title, or the prestige of a position. If you lose your title or role with one employer, you can feel confident that you can replace or re-channel your contributions in a modified way, because you have taken the time to recognize your unique and compelling skills.

The world is changing ... often faster and more rapidly than any of us are comfortable with. Although many people yearn for the simplicity and traditions of yesterday, a simpler time when human capital dominated the workplace, the reality is that technology and innovation are here to stay. You can try to fight it and protest by keeping your old handwritten Rolodex, refusing to buy a cell phone, printing your brochures vs. accessing the Internet, and sending out mass mailings as opposed to applying online, but you will inevitably lose that battle. Technology is increasing, any way you look at it, but people still are the lifeblood of the workplace.

Exercise: Your Current Perception Versus Your Ideal Perception

Step 1   Define your current view of work (if you get stuck, select 3 words that accurately describe your current situation).

Step 2   Define how you would ideally like to perceive work (if you get stuck, select 3 words that would describe how you would most like work to be).

Step 3   Identify what 3 words or phrases are missing from your current situation as opposed to your ideal situation.

See the difference? For most people, there is a decided (and measurable) difference between their current view of work as opposed to their ideal vision of what work could or should be for them.

> *"I will not be satisfied until you are in that select group of 20% of the country who view work and play ... as the same thing!"*
>
> —Chris Kusclias

The process of finding your unique niche begins with your thoughts and what you ultimately want from your career. Your "career identity" consists primarily of the conditioning you have received in the past. Your thoughts were formed, which led to feelings about your career, which led to actions (or non-actions), which lead to your results. Where you are today in your career is a function of how you have been conditioned or "programmed" to think about what work is and how far you are entitled to progress. My question for you is this: Who has shaped your career identity?

The "Kick the Cat" Syndrome

> *Your current perception of working was formed when you were young and remains in your subconscious mind. To a large degree, this conditioning controls your career thermostat (career potential and level of success). For example, many young people were introduced to working as a necessary but unfulfilling part of life, while others were taught to believe that money is the root of all evil. Simply put, you have been programmed by parents, friends, teachers, religious leaders and the media as to how much you can and should accomplish. These teachings become your personality and automatic responses. Only 10%–20% of people will explore these limitations and formulate their own set of beliefs, which often catapult them to greatness and career happiness. That is what these principles are about!*

You see, most people are conditioned from birth to view work as an obligation, something responsible people in society do to maintain their existence. Perhaps you observed your parents or caretakers walk in the door after a long day, tired, bored and drained of energy to do much else. As a child, maybe you were the unlucky recipient of an underserved lecture or worse because of work related frustration by your parent(s). I call this common occurrence the "kick the cat" syndrome.

> *"There is nothing wrong with me. I simply learned that I had my father's career blueprint imbedded in my head and that was my biggest problem and barrier to success."*
> —Robert, from Buffalo, N.Y.

For example, let's say your father was chastised at work for some innocuous event and came home upset and angry without an outlet to release his frustration. So when he walked in the door after fighting the traffic and harboring resentment for his boss, you received the brunt of his frustration because your room "which really wasn't that messy" was not clean. He, in essence, projected his anger toward his boss onto you. Feeling picked on but not fully understanding why, you as a child had nowhere else to turn so you channeled your anger to your younger sibling, the next in line. The pecking order continued as your younger sibling channeled their hostility and anger at the only family member with lower position in the pecking order ... poor old "Fluffy" the cat who got a swift kick for no reason other than the fact that your father's boss had a bad day and the anger ran down-hill! (I always wondered how "Fluffy" took out her frustration ... maybe there are a few abused mice somewhere....)

When you observe this behavior at a young age, you can see how it could shape a child's perception of working. Perhaps, your perception of work may have been shaped at a young age by a similar story.

How First Jobs Often Taint Our Perception of Work

Another challenge is that most of our initial experiences with working (that is, our first jobs) were most likely not in roles or functions that allowed for self-expression or creativity. It was most likely an entry-level, hourly wage position (mine was in fast food, I was the fry cook extraordinaire!) following specific orders with little room for innovation. You were most likely unskilled, underpaid and overworked, which is negative way to be initially exposed to the concept of working.

For most, the concept of working is synonymous with obligation and a means to make money ... period. Most likely, you followed the crowd (and the want ads or Internet listings) to your first exposure to what would evolve into a component of your life that would consume more of your precious time than any other undertaking. The scary part is that most people spend almost the same amount of time and pursue their occupation in the same way they did for their very first job! Is it any wonder that most people are not fulfilled and inspired by their work?

Be Careful of Others' Perceptions

Far too few individuals I counsel recall a parent walking in the door grateful and exuberant for their unique contribution with positive family dialogue about the virtues of having found their calling. More likely, they present the ingrained thoughts from an early age concept of "being lucky to have a job," which often extinguishes any hope or thought of finding a position they might actually enjoy.

Like you, I have held unfulfilling jobs, been extremely frustrated at times in my career and, at my core, felt that I was meant to do something that made a difference. I wanted a noble occupation, one that touched my heart! Like you, I am challenged on a daily basis to maintain balance in my individual, married and professional life. With 3 children, numerous family obligations and a thriving business, finding time for reflection, fitness, career planning and social activities is no easy task!

Life issues like responsibility and aging often cloud the pursuit of your career calling and become an easy excuse for accepting professional mediocrity. Many people are in this vicious cycle of wanting to plan but having no time. In the past, many people looking for jobs sought a secure profession. And you observed people at the company until they retired and received a gold watch or some reward for 30 years of loyal service. No matter what level of disenchantment or unhappiness, they stayed in the same occupation with the same employer. Today, the average job tenure is only 3–4 years (the average person will hold over 15 jobs in their life!) and people are forced to take a more proactive role in how they will sustain their livelihood. We call this development a *paradigm shift*, which has led to the necessity of mastering your ability to transition between jobs and often between industries.

I would also caution you to be aware that most of us identify with one or both of our parents regarding our career. Simply put, we act and behave in accordance with *their* belief systems. These may be handed down from generation to generation and seem like "tradition" but can be extremely damaging. Their belief systems, while comfortable, may not be in sync with yours.

Consider this tale of the woman who prepares a ham for holiday dinner by cutting off both ends. Her confused husband asks her why she does this. "That is how my mom prepared ham." During the holiday dinner, the husband asked his mother-in-law why she cut off both ends. She replied, "That is how my mom cooked it." When the great-grandma showed up, the husband asked her why she cut off both ends and started this tradition. Thinking there was some hidden meaning, you can imagine his surprise when great-grandma replied, "Because my pan was too small."

CHAPTER 2

Taking Inventory

KEY QUESTION: WHERE AM I *RIGHT* NOW?

In this chapter, you will learn:

KEY TOPICS

- Where Are You Now?
- Will The Real You Please Stand Up!
- How Can You Tell If You Are in the Right Occupation?
- Critical Reflection: What Is Truly Most Important to You?
- Habit Management
- The Power of ANTICIPATION
- Standards and Their Amazing Effect
- The Quest to Outserve!

KEY MESSAGES

- Someday is not a day of the week ... Start now!
- Great performers start with the end in mind!
- Your identity is tied to your career.
- Evaluating your childhood perceptions and beliefs about working.
- Be certain to get in touch with WHY you want a better career.
- Understanding your personal and professional values.
- Determine 3 things you want to have, do or become as a legacy.
- Internalize the emotional benefits of finding your career calling.
- Find a defining moment, an event so significant that you must change!
- While many people crave more money, making a *difference* is the real need.
- Figuring out how to make a greater contribution is the key ingredient to increasing wealth.
- Don't wait for your employer or the economy to make you happy; it is your responsibility.

"You do not want to get to the top of the ladder and find out you were climbing the wrong wall."

—Anonymous

Where Are You Now?

ARE YOU *REALLY* READY to find your career calling? This is a simple but effective exercise to measure your optimism ... What do you see when you read the letters below?

OPPORTUNITYNOWHERE

Some see the words *opportunity no where*. Others read the same letters but instead see the words *opportunity now here*. I think you will agree that there is a significant difference! Whether you realize it or not, you have been conditioned to see the good or bad, to focus on the positive or negative. You can decide what type of outlook you want to have, how you earn a living and how you choose to see the world.

My guess is if you are reading this book, it is because you are not where you want to be and have a strong desire to improve your career and life. Your commitment is to complete this book, while mine is to help you maximize your talents. Together, we will re-shape your outlook and adopt new behaviors, tools and strategies to find *opportunities galore*!

Opportunity in any endeavor, one's career included, is often a function of proper evaluation, preparation and then action! Highly successful people, those who love their work, all seem to follow the same basic approach, which I will introduce to you through a series of carefully planned exercises and examples. They may call it something different, but most likely they take inventory of where they are and want to be, and then follow this progression:

Phase 1   *Evaluation Phase* (Who Am I?)
      Explore your passions, interests, job aptitudes and marketable talents to determine your specific job and career objectives
Phase 2   *Planning Phase* (How Do I Stand Out?)
      Learn how to market yourself to employers as a product and employ useful job search strategies and techniques to determine your competitive edge
Phase 3   *Implementation Phase* (How Do I Obtain and Maintain My Great Career?)
      Use your new job search skills to obtain your chosen career while constantly monitoring your progress for retention and upward mobility

Who you are and what you truly want will be recurrent themes throughout this book. While at times I may become a royal pain, my intention is to help you see the vision and attain the dream. It is waiting for you!

Will the Real You Please Stand Up!

"Everyone thinks that the principal thing to the tree is the fruit, but the point of fact is the principal thing to it is the seed."
　　　　　　　　—Friedrich Wilhelm Nietzsche (1844–1900).

YOU MAY NOT RECOGNIZE or believe yet that you possess the *seeds* of greatness. The fact is we all do. The objective is to determine where this greatness lies within your body, mind and soul and then, once discovered, to dedicate your talents in a way that contributes to society.

The essential question is: Who are you? Before you begin rattling off your educational background or the professional jobs that comprise your resume, stop for a moment and answer my question. Who are you *really*? What passions lie deep within your soul? What makes you unique and

"Yeah, I took one of those aptitude tests.
It showed my ideal career path was retirement!"

compelling? To lend further clarity to the question, consider this classic formula:

Who Who are you and what makes you unique and compelling?

What What do you really want? I suggest that the only true objective is the attainment of your inner happiness achieved through the process of making a positive contribution to others.

Where Where are you in the process of finding your ideal career or career calling? Are you unemployed, working but unfulfilled, working and somewhat content, wanting to start your own business or somewhere else altogether?

When When do you want to make a change to obtain your calling? Is the timing right for you and are you fully committed in spirit, mind and body? Remember, there is a difference between being interested in success and being fully committed to its attainment.

Why Why do you want to find your calling? This is the most important question you can ask yourself! If you do not have a compelling reason and emotional investment in changing your current path and re-inventing yourself, you will most likely never live the life you deserve and find the career you are uniquely qualified to contribute.

How How will you achieve the goal to find your calling? I am of the belief that 80% of your career success is comprised of your belief in wanting the calling, while only 20% involves the mechanics of actually getting hired (that is, interviewing, resume, follow-up).

> After following *The Career Guarantee* philosophy of looking inside my heart and soul for my passion and purpose, I came to the conclusion that while my job had prestige and was envied by my peers, being a big shot vice president in my old firm was not what I really wanted to do with the rest of my life.

Each question or exercise is systematically designed to move you closer to understanding your true values and motivations. Unless you are extremely fortuitous, if you do not expend the effort to deeply understand yourself and obtain clarity with regard to your concept of career satisfaction, you will most likely never find your calling. By making a conscious choice to uncover the "real you," you will learn to channel your inherent strengths into a career that provides incredible happiness.

Paul Tieger, who many refer to as the world's Personality Type expert, is a friend, colleague and man whose work I greatly respect and admire. Mr. Tieger professes that each of us is born with one of 16 distinct personality types and that there is a science to matching your personality type to a list of potential jobs in which others with your type have found success. This is an exciting and interesting analysis and I highly recommend that you research your options and consider these tools to move closer to your calling.

On page 9 of his book, *Do What You Are*, Paul D. Tieger and Barbara Barron-Tieger state, "Since the right job flows directly out of all the elements of your personality type, you need to spend some time trying to figure out what makes you tick. By making a conscious effort to discover the "real you," you can learn how to focus on your natural strengths and inclinations into a career you can love as long as you choose to work."

Regarding the challenge to finding ones calling, the authors summarize, "The solution? To achieve as great a degree of self-awareness as you can before making any decision with long lasting career consequences."

The 3 Types of Career Seekers

With this in mind, I want you to consider these simple, yet complex questions: What motivates your achievements? Why do you work? Is it the money, the recognition or the challenge? Did you choose your job or did it choose you? My father taught me to understand that there are basically 3 classes of people:

1. Those who make things happen (a.k.a. the doers)
2. Those who watch things happen (a.k.a. the drifters)
3. Those who wonder, "What happened?" (a.k.a. the dreamers)

Regardless of your self-assessment, learn to associate positive emotions with your future, regardless of what has occurred in the past. Your past does not equate to your future. View work as an expression or outlet for your unique talents.

For the most part, career status can be summed up in 3 basic groups:

Group I: "Same %*@#^, Different Day!"
(60% of Workers)
Here, we find the individual who is not really motivated by anything, and just mulls along taking each day as it comes. They spend a lot of time doing things that they really do not want to do, because they feel they have to.

They tend to be complacent and unenthusiastic. They are unhappy in their career, and often unhappy in other areas of their life as well. Bottom line: It is a paycheck, and it pays the bills! Can you say "dead end job"?

Group II: "I Have a Job, It Is Prestigious (Want to See My Fancy Business Card?)" (20%–30% of workers)

Within this category lies the individual that has what most people will consider a good job. It provides the things that are important to the average working person: an important title, recognition, benefits, great pay, and excellent rewards. There is job satisfaction, and the individual derives certain benefits from what they do. However, deep within this person's soul, there is a nagging feeling that it still is not enough. Something is missing. There is no emotional attachment, and he or she lacks a sense of completeness.

Although they have "a good job" by most standards, they are plagued with the feeling they are not accomplishing all that they should and that true fulfillment has eluded them. Ask yourself:

- Are you failing to reach your full potential in your life?
- Have you given up on a dream that lies dormant in the back of your mind, and haunts you day and night?
- Is there a yearning within you to make a greater and more lasting impact on society?
- Do you feel that your life is out of sync, and you just cannot put your finger on what it is that is missing?
- If you lost your job, would you feel like you lost a big part of your identity?
- Do you feel that your contributions are often meaningless and unappreciated, which leaves you feeling incomplete and, at times, insignificant?

If you answered yes to any of these questions, my strong suspicion is that these feelings have surfaced because you have not yet identified your calling and answered it! Fear not, help is on the way!

Group III: "Work? … This Isn't Work, It Feels Like Play!" (Only 10%–20% of workers)

Reaching this place is what distinguishes those who are living their dreams from those who are not. If you are in this category you are empowered beyond belief, and motivated by your own actions. You are not married to the clock, and you look forward to what each day will bring. Your success is not measured by money, status, or society; rather, your success is the result of applying yourself to what is important in your life, every day, and fulfilling your potential.

> *"When you engage in work that taps your talent and fuels your passion—-that rises out of a great need in the world that you feel drawn by conscience to meet—-therein lies your voice, your calling, your soul's code. There is a deep, innate almost inexpressible yearning within each of us to find our voice in life."*
> —Steven Covey, *The 8ᵗʰ Habit*

You enjoy balance in those key areas of your life: financial, relationships, spiritual, health and fitness, and, of course, career. The harmony, sense of comfort, and rewards you experience are all derived from one simple action: answering your calling!

What does this person have that others lack? What are the characteristics of an individual who reaches this point of self-actualization and contentment in life? How does a person go about identifying and answering their calling, and what are the steps they must follow along the way? The answers to these questions lie ahead, and my goal is to help you find your purpose in life by guiding you through carefully structured activities and exercises to help you live your dreams!

The 5 Career Hurdles

The good news is that you will always have opportunities, but there are obstacles. Take a look at this list that I use in my seminars. For more information, see www.thecareerguarantee.com and discover where you fit in:

Hurdle 1   *Right Industry or Employer, Wrong Attitude*
Stay at your current job. You like your industry and duties; you simply have developed a poor attitude. Take initiative and become proactive, not passive, so you can achieve greater passion and purpose. Sometimes there is greatness right in front of you!

Hurdle 2   *Right Industry or Employer, Wrong Job Title*
Move laterally. If you determine your current industry provides opportunity, passion and purpose but you are in the wrong job, move laterally within the same organization.

Hurdle 3   *Right Career, Wrong Employer*
Sometimes the culture of one employer in your field of choice offers more variety, challenge, money or freedom. Maybe it's time to change the name or logo on your team uniform!

Hurdle 4   *Right Attitude, Wrong Career*
Leave your current occupation. A change of scenery is needed. Start a new venture; find a career or a new position that allows you to experience passion and purpose.

Hurdle 5   *Wrong Attitude, Uncertain Career*
Here, you need to re-invent yourself and discover what I call your *authentic* career self. Until you take the time to understand your wants, needs and desires, you will bounce from job to job and remain frustrated.

Regardless of how you rated yourself, the exercises and examples serve to clarify your thinking and create a plan tailored to your unique needs. Keep in mind that most careers last nearly 50 years and go through many changes. Careering is not a destination, it is a process to be savored and enjoyed!

How Can You Tell If You Are in the Right Occupation?

Sophia from the West Coast contacted me and shared that she was working in an IT position that simply wasn't her true calling. She felt anxious, unsettled, nervous, up tight, stressed out and, worst of all, like she was wasting her valuable time. This went on for more than a few years until she followed the strategy of pursuing her true passion, finding her purpose, gaining credibility and power, increasing her income and profit and realizing the peace of mind that accompanies working at what you were meant to do. She had reached a breakthrough!

She commented that making the decision to pursue her calling was scary at first, but she realized that there are millions who had made a successful transition who were no more educated or experienced than she; they simply summoned the courage to take action! It was never a case of her credentials, but rather one of her internal self-imposed limitations. She thought that the worst case scenario would be to become a cynic, not take any action and settle for mediocrity; she concluded that a life filled with regret was the ultimate failure.

Comparing her newfound calling (working at an animal shelter) to her prior IT job, she commented that it was like a light went on in her brain and the fog that had clouded her ambition and enthusiasm had lifted. Each day, she experiences (Passion) and (Purpose) in working with, caring for and saving animals, has developed a following of assistants who seek her wisdom (Power), has been promoted since her transition (Profit) and goes to bed each night satisfied she is doing what she was meant to do (Peace of Mind).

Is It Time for a Career Change?

Are you in the right job? Have you found your calling? While sometimes it is relatively easy to tell if you like your role, *few people discover that the formula for finding your career calling is to contribute in an area that you enjoy the most.* For many, the process is not obvious and requires taking a look inward to find what you truly enjoy doing.

As odd as it sounds, many people cannot verbalize what they actually enjoy doing. They can state what they DON'T like (overbearing bosses, long commutes, low wages, mundane jobs, etc.) but have never stopped to articulate what they DO want. Here is a list of factors to think about before you make a career change.

1. *You feel stagnant in your current role.* Before making a change, make absolutely certain that your current role, employer or industry does not offer you a chance to demonstrate your unique talents. Remember, it is YOUR responsibility to explore and promote yourself. Often, just asking for more responsibility or joining an internal task force to solve a critical challenge can re-energize your career. Stop blaming your boss, the employer, the industry or the economy and take control. If you are not moving forward, you are falling behind!

2. *You often feel physically or mentally ill.* If you have reached the point where you dread going to work, it is time to reassess. Do the people, environment or culture of your current scenario fill you with uncertainty or unhappiness? Before you find yourself taking medication for physical ailments like headaches, stomach problems or acid reflux, consider the cause of your discomfort. Is there excessive pressure, deadlines and stress causing these problems or have you simply lost enthusiasm for the day to day functions you perform? There is an old saying that "when the mind hurts, the body suffers." Often, a change of scenery can eliminate these symptoms overnight!

3. *You feel excluded from important decisions.* If you have reached a point where you no longer feel like you have a say in the future direction of your job and the company, and you perceive that you are being excluded from important meetings or decisions, it may be time to move on. It is a lonely feeling to be "on the outside looking in" and to observe others getting raises and promotions ahead of you. Honestly assess whether you have the passion to

remain competitive or if there is a good reason why you are being overlooked. Do you need to work harder, smarter, or acquire
some new skills?

4. *Your purpose and work functions are going in opposite directions.*
    Sometimes people find themselves in a situation where their job
    duties begin to change and move away from their goals. If you
    are having trouble linking your passion and purpose to what you
    do each day, it is clearly time to assess your employment situa-
    tion. As we often do not notice these subtle changes, a regular
    monthly check-in with yourself may help you chart what is going
    on. Changes occur gradually until one day a person wakes up and
    realizes they are working in a position that does not fulfill their
    internal needs.

5. *You have lost pride in sharing what you do for a living.* If you get to
    the point where you are ashamed, embarrassed or no longer take
    pride in your position, title, employer or industry, it is time to
    reconsider your career choice. When you love what you do, you'll
    want to shout it from the rooftops!

Should I Stay or Should I Go?

Take this quiz to determine if it is time for a career change.

Below are 15 questions to assist you in deciding if you are in the right occupation. For many participants, simply reviewing the questions, regardless of the answers can be a real eye opener and result in a change in habits
or beliefs! Consider this an entertaining and informative exercise to propel
you closer to your individual career calling and help you capture true passion at work!

1. How often do you find yourself daydreaming about another role?
    A. Never
    B. Sometimes
    C. Often
    D. Always

2. Has your current position caused or contributed to any physi-
    cal ailments such as headaches, stomach problems (that is, acid
    reflux, constipation, ulcers)?
    A. Never
    B. Sometimes

    C. Often

    D. Always

3. Does your current role allow you to utilize your favorite skills and strengths (for example, artistic, managerial, organizational)?

    A. Always

    B. Often

    C. Sometimes

    D. Never

4. Does your current profession allow you to enjoy your most important values? (for example, travel, challenge, creativity, problem solving, variety)

    A. Always

    B. Often

    C. Sometimes

    D. Never

5. For the same salary and benefits, is there another position or set of duties you would rather have?

    A. No

    B. Almost

    C. Likely

    D. Definitely

6. Do you take pride in telling others what "you do for a living"?

    A. Always

    B. Often

    C. Sometimes

    D. Never

7. Do you enjoy reading up on or researching your current field or industry during non-work hours?

    A. Always

    B. Often

    C. Sometimes

    D. Never

8. Do you have a clear and focused career path or do you simply get the work done on a day to day basis with little regard for the future?

    A. Highly focused career plan

    B. Solid plan with little variation

    C. I used to have a plan

    D. Day to day tasks

9. How much time do you spend on career planning?
   A. Extensive
   B. Some
   C. Very little
   D. None
10. On Fridays do you feel elated, relieved, ambivalent, or sad?
    A. Elated
    B. Relieved
    C. Ambivalent
    D. Sad
11. Have you ever uttered the phrase: "take this job and #$@^% it!,"
    "life sucks and then you die!" or "another day another dollar"?
    A. Never
    B. Sometimes
    C. Often
    D. Always
12. If your current job was eliminated tomorrow, would you feel
    elated, relieved, ambivalent or sad?
    A. Sad
    B. Ambivalent
    C. Relieved
    D. Elated
13. If you won a lottery worth $10 million, would you remain in-
    volved in your current job or field?
    A. Yes
    B. Stay for a while
    C. Wait till my replacement was trained
    D. Job? What job?
14. How much time do you spend during work hours daydreaming,
    surfing the net on non-work activities or engaged in gossip?
    A. Never
    B. Sometimes
    C. Often
    D. Always
15. Do you feel your best professional days are ahead of you or be-
    hind you?
    A. Ahead
    B. Right now
    C. Behind
    D. There will never be "best days"

How did you score?

Mostly A's: You are in a field that suits you with an employer with whom you have a mutually beneficial and respectful relationship.

Mostly B's: Your work relationship is a good one. Keep working at what you enjoy doing.

Mostly C's: Something is up here. Take some time to assess what is going on. Would you ever have had more A answers? If so, what has changed that you no longer feel the spark?

Mostly D's: It is time for you to do a serious assessment of yourself and your work goals. Think about what it is that YOU truly want to be doing and what steps you will need to take to get there.

Creating Enough Leverage: Where is Your Pain?

To make a change, you need to establish *leverage* or what I call a strong enough *Why*. Without enough motivation, you will simply stay in your current pattern. Usually, it is a desire to gain more pleasure from work (passion, more money, freedom) or a desire to eliminate pain (boredom, unhappiness, low wage) that causes a person to take action!

For this 1st exercise, write down the top 3 reasons you want to make a career change. I do not want you to list what is wrong with your current scenario (for example, I hate my boss, I am underpaid, etc.) but rather what you *do* want from a change (to feel part of a team, positive culture, assist others, greater recognition, flexible work hours, etc.)

Next, write down 3 things that you are no longer willing to tolerate in your career (for example, a 2-hour commute, marketing a product I do not believe in, lack of recognition, underpaid, no voice in major decisions, lack of interaction with customers, etc.)

Take some time to analyze your answers and how you will feel if you can add the new items and eliminate or reduce the items you will no longer tolerate.

Why Finding Your Calling Is Not a Should ... But a Must!

> *"All of us can consciously decide to leave behind a life of mediocrity and to live a life of greatness—at home, at work and in the community. No matter how long we've walked life's pathway to mediocrity, we can always choose to switch paths. Always. It's never too late."*
>
> —Steven Covey, *The 8th Habit*

Though he may not know it, Dr. Steven Covey has served as a mentor to me and is a man whose work I respect tremendously. His quote should reinforce that no matter where you are in the career cycle, it is never too late to find your calling.

As an example, my father worked in advertising for 40 years, starting right out of college and concluding with a forced early retirement when he was asked to leave the only employer he ever knew. Some reward for 40 years of loyal service! As you might expect, he quickly became my favorite new client and we immediately employed the same process for him that you have and will continue to experience in this book. My dad had always had a fascination with building and architecture, but the rush of life, family obligations (there are 5 of us Kuselias kids!) and a rigorous work schedule restricted him from exploring this passion more deeply. Plus, his 2nd oldest son, Christopher, had not developed his formula for helping others (including himself) find their calling!

Upon his forced early retirement, we quickly established a game plan for my dad's new career as a builder, and soon he was off and running, starting with a simple porch and patio in a neighbor's backyard and progressing to building my sister and her husband a brand new 4,000 square foot customized house from scratch!

He was skeptical at first and initially doubted his own abilities; after all, he had worked in the same field for his whole adult life, and architecture was a pipe dream ... right? Wrong! Today, his firm employs subcontractors and has built several new customized houses for families. He has found a brand new passion and cannot wait to get up every morning and expand his new career. His only wish is that he had stepped off the treadmill of life and done it sooner. His daily activities give him a sense of pleasure, challenge and accomplishment. Oh, one small detail I didn't mention ... my dad is over 75 years of age! While others his age are busy complaining about physical ailments, politics, the weather, the price of gasoline or how their life has passed them by, he is embarking on the next chapter of his life and looks and feels 20 years younger. He is no different than you are! He simply made a decision to pursue his calling.

Like my dad, we spend an enormous amount of time engaged in our work, sometimes too much. Those of you who are workaholics know what I mean. The key is to continually evaluate your challenges and your motives.

Key Question

Who is to blame for you not being in exactly the right career for you, earning the money you deserve, using your unique and compelling skills, working with inspiring people with a positive outlook for your future?

Your parents?

Your teachers?

The government?

The economy?

Your boss?

Your co-workers?

Your spouse?

Your kids?

Are you getting my message? These are influencers but it is YOUR responsibility … you take the credit when you are on top and should be responsible if you are not where you want and deserve to be!

> *"Seize the day and accept responsibility for your future."*
> —Starbucks CEO Howard Shultz

Another trend appears to be a growing number of people who seem resolved to a life of regret. Have you ever noticed that some people seem to delight in being unhappy, and appear to enjoy commiserating with others for their inability to find their calling? There is no honor in complaining about how unhappy you are in your work life.

> *"As miserable as some people might be, for many there is a kind of perverse pleasure in the self-righteous indignation one feels when one is treated unfairly. We hold on to our pain, wear it like a badge, it becomes part of us and we are reluctant to give it up. Letting go of our customary responses, as destructive as they may be, may seem frightening, and often fear abides on a deeply ingrained subconscious level. And added to this, of course, are the secondary gains to holding on to our grudges, jealousy, and dissatisfaction, as our constant complaints serve to elicit sympathy and understanding from others."*
>
> —His Holiness the Dalai Lama
> and Howard C. Cutler, M.D.,
> *The Art of Happiness at Work*

If you are in a bad place emotionally, mentally or attitudinally, to change your current momentum you must become a proactive career-seeker by first assessing your passions. Regardless of your educational level, whether it be GED or Ph.D., you must be willing to say *Yes* to possibility, *Yes* to change in order to be successful, and be willing to do some soul searching to target what talents and skills you have, and what makes you unique. That's the 1st step on the journey to achieving your calling. Take inventory.

Throughout this book, I will challenge you to understand the "why behind the want," which is the key to meaningful change. *Remember that 80% of finding your career calling lies in the psychology (that is, understanding your motivations, finding your passion) and only 20% of your success is based on the mechanics of the job search process (that is, resume creation, interviewing strategy, etc.).* I want to challenge you with specific questions like: Why do you want to change your job? When do you want this to happen? Do you want it to happen today, right now, or in 3 years, 5 years, 10 years? Do you have a specific date in mind? Do you have a specific amount of money that you want to earn? How long do you think it's going to take you to achieve the next benchmark ... a day, a month, one year, 5 years?"

You may at times feel frustrated for being asked such pointed questions, but believe me, this is for your own good! One of my jobs is to help you notice how unhappy and unfulfilled you are, so that making a change is no longer a *should*, but an absolute *must*!

> Here is a secret ... You will only change careers when the pain or boredom of your current situation is replaced by the belief that pleasure will be the result of a new pursuit or venture.

Critical Reflection: What Is Truly Most Important to You?

> *"I have always wanted to be somebody. I should have been more specific."*
>
> —Lily Tomlin

BEING PRECISE IN YOUR needs, wants and values is essential to obtaining them. Most people who get discouraged or who fail in their quest to find true career happiness and life balance, do so because they are unclear about what they want. They have a general idea and seek happiness—most people do—but beyond that they fall short of defining a *specific* outcome. To help you avoid this, I have created a simple exercise to help narrow your focus and identify what is truly important to you.

I want you to make a list of:

- 3 things you really want to have
- 3 things you truly want to do
- 3 things you absolutely want to be or become before you leave this earth

This may sound easy at first but once you start writing you will see how rusty your "wants" truly are. The more you do this, the clearer your goals will become. Do this now ... See, you are critically reflecting already!

Success Tip

If you ever get stuck determining what you want, try asking yourself, Wouldn't it be great If ...

A consistent theme among individuals who have found their ideal is that they know exactly what they want to *have*, to *do* and to *be* or *become*. This is a common theme among all high achievers. And I assume if you reading this book, you seek achievement! Many even develop a scrapbook so they can continuously visualize and reinforce each *want*. They are mentally rehearsing their success and anticipating great things.

This is fun! At this stage I do not want you to stress out or worry about quickly converting your interests and desires into an occupation. This is a process. Together, we will systematically follow a proven step by step plan. I simply want to begin to revive your inner spirit and get you to associate the process of internal analysis (critical reflection) with fun. It is exhilarating to learn about yourself and it creates an amazing level of confidence and peace of mind when one feels connected at their core! It is like going to a health club after neglecting your physical fitness, or actually working out but achieving inferior results; we have to build your endurance and confidence so you won't quit the process out of frustration!

Please do not be afraid to dream! Avoid the common tendency to make excuses or blame the outside world when the real answers lie inside your heart and soul! Gender, race, education, the economy, lack of training, housing, family life, geography, abuse: all make the list of reasons why many of my clients feel they have not achieved their calling and may never reach that goal. While certainly these may provide obstacles, we can all name numerous individuals who have overcome greater obstacles than you face who, despite these challenges, went on to achieve their career calling. It is not where you start; it is how and where you finish that counts!

Fast Fact

Did you know that 20% of the millionaires in the United States never attended college?

Money is not the only important measure of success, but you get the point. Do not victimize yourself by placing blame on an external event. The obstacles you face can usually be overcome with the proper strategy and dedication. You are blessed with amazing potential; you just need to access it. I could write an entire book on the importance of *critical reflection* but instead, I will validate this important recommendation with a simple example. If you want proof that this technique works, consider the following source and then maybe … just maybe … you will agree with me that critical reflection is effective.

> *One day, the mother of future Microsoft mogul Bill Gates (as of this writing the world's richest human being) walked in on her young son to find him sitting there doing nothing. She asked Bill what he was doing. "I'm thinking, Mom, I'm thinking."*
> —Walter Isaacson, "In Search of the Real Bill Gates"

If critical reflection is good enough for Bill Gates, who appears personally and professionally balanced and has given billions to tremendously valuable causes … it should be good enough for us!

Principle

To attain your career calling, you must agree to carve out time each and every day to assess your current situation and develop a strategic plan laid out in logical steps to achieve your destination.

START NOW! "Someday" Is Not a Day of the Week

> *"80% of your success will be a result of mastering your mind set and getting in touch with your authentic self, while the remaining 20% is a function of teaching you effective career search techniques."*
> —Chris Kuselias

The person who finds their calling in today's competitive job market does so by critical reflection, acquiring the best strategies on how to determine their passion, then marketing their skills through mastering the interview and evaluation process. Let today be the starting point for a new and exciting chapter in your life. Today begins your transformation from uncertainty and possibly frustration to clarity, exuberance and abundance!

> "Yesterday is history. Tomorrow is a mystery. And today? Today is a gift. That is why they call it the present."
> —Eleanor Roosevelt

Questions to Consider:

1. Isn't it time you seriously questioned yourself about what you want to do with the rest of your life?
2. Don't you deserve a career that provides challenge, reward, recognition and respect?
3. Is there a dream you want to pursue but keep putting off as the rush of life consumes your aspirations?
4. What do you daydream about? Starting your own flower shop, becoming a consultant, going back to school and being a teacher, writing a novel, becoming a 5-star chef? Are you living in the city or town that best matches your preferences for weather, schools, social activities and entertainment? What images or dreams dominate your thoughts?
5. Will the future be the best time of your life or have your career highlights and best times passed you by?
6. Are you living off old memories or creating new ones?

In order to get answers to these important questions, we need to immediately stop the "treadmill of life" and think about how you want to design the balance of your career. It does not matter if you are just starting your career or have been working for 40 years. Do you want a position that simply pays the bills and allows you to exist or do you want a career where you fulfill your passions and where you are making a difference?

Sadly, in my experience, most people spend more time researching a new dishwasher than they do in contemplating and planning for their career. They will purchase consumer reports, go online, study the warranty, compare and contrast models and makes, analyze the color and features, ask their friends and family for referrals, etc. But ask a person to ponder their career and conduct a similar analysis and they get stuck or procrastinate.

Why? The answer is that as a society we are not formally trained in the art of career selection or upward mobility, which is a fancy term for getting raises and promotions. Sure, we go to school, and most educational institutions offer career centers, internships, apprenticeships, alumni networks and on line job readiness courses. The problem is that few of these resources assist you in the process of determining what is truly unique and compelling about you as a professional; and once discovered, how to effectively market yourself in the 21st century workplace.

Fast Fact

10 years after graduation, over 50% of college graduates are working in a field totally unrelated to their chosen field of study!

Top 4 Reasons Unhappy People Used to Select Their Job

At this point, you might be beginning to understand how important it is to choose your career, instead of letting your career choose you! So how do most people make decisions concerning their career? Usually, their reasons are anything but rationale or logical.

Here are the top 4 reasons unfulfilled workers say were the basis for selecting their position:

1. *Fear:* Often, decisions are not based on potential benefit or the prospect of gain, but rather on the fear of loss
2. *Choosing The Path of Least Resistance:* People often select careers based on the least amount of effort or energy
3. *The Law of Averages:* People attempt to apply logic and select a career based on growth in a particular industry or job title as opposed to their passion or purpose
4. *Selection Through Familiarity:* People select or "inherit" a career (for example, the family dry cleaning business) vs. pursuing or investigating their true interests

To further illustrate how we often select a career without giving proper thought and consideration to our true motivations, I recently conducted an informal analysis of a group of college graduates to determine their motives for selecting a job. Here is a summation of my research. The answers to the question of what was the reason they chose their career path came back as follows:

- It paid the most money
- It was closest to my house
- I liked the interviewer (who they will most likely never see again …)
- The secretary of the person who interviewed me was hot!
- I was afraid it would be the only job offered
- To get my parents off my back
- So I wouldn't be the last unemployed graduate I know

These responses may sound ridiculous but when you consider that most of us have never been coached on the process of marrying our interest, skills and talents to an occupation that rewards these values, it begins to make sense why these seemingly preposterous factors often dictate career choice.

The Lottery Game

We all dream of becoming millionaires the easy way. But, have you sat down and actually thought about what would happen if you really did win the lottery? Other than a nicer house, car, etc.... (material possessions), the results may surprise you!

Questions

What would you do if you won 10 million dollars in the lottery (one lump sum and you don't have to share it with another winner)? Be specific.
How would you be different as a person?

Job Expectations: 10 Questions to Help You Develop a Clearer Picture

Working is indeed a rewarding pursuit for any of the reasons you listed in earlier exercises and for more reasons still. But you have to begin from the start. Even the most fun, glamorous, prestigious, high-paying, sought after jobs in the world have their downsides, and if you don't expect that reality, you will be disappointed.

Think about the occupation YOU really want and ask yourself these questions:

1. What exactly would you be doing?
2. Where would you work?
3. How much money would you make?
4. Is there travel involved?
5. What are the hours? Must you work weekends or holidays?
6. What clothes would you be wearing or how would you look at work?
7. In what ways would you be working with other people?
8. Why would your job be important to others?
9. What would you like and dislike about your job?
10. How closely would you be supervised?

Most career seekers do not contemplate such details. Let me ask you … How did you get to your current career position? What were your motivations? Did you incorporate a game plan? Who assisted you in the process?

I am confident that the process I am sharing here will become that essential coach, mentor, friend, and confidante needed to get you to take action!

I Know I Should Change … So Why Don't I?

> "*The world hates change, yet it is the only thing that has brought progress.*"
>
> —Charles F. Kettering

Like most career seekers, you most likely have never assessed your core motives or systematically planned your career. A job is a job, right? Wrong! My research tells me that only about 10–20% of all people truly love their careers and feel they have found their calling. The remaining 80–90% of the working population is stuck in apathy or a negative pattern of routine, fear, uncertainty and doubt about their future. Approximately 70% are unfulfilled in their jobs, 20% tolerate their work, and only 10% truly love what they do for a living. Many comfort themselves through comparison to others with less fancy job titles or by taking comfort in the fact that they at least have a job.

In order to transition from where you are today to a place where you are living your dream and are using your unique and compelling talents and making a contribution, *something* must change. Here is the reality … that *something* is you!

Most people know they should do something to change their life but simply do not know where to begin. They lack both a plan for determining their true motivations a user-friendly strategy for making it happen. Thus far in your career, you, like most, have probably been focused on making more money or getting ahead in your current occupation (often referred to as "climbing the corporate ladder.") Outside of work, you may have responsibilities: children, car payments, mortgage, credit card debt and perhaps school loans. If you require day care, there is yet another expense. Maybe you have had to carefully budget just to make ends meet and, for some, even take a 2nd job.

To meet these demands, you found yourself working for the money while trying to manufacture a small sense of satisfaction from your job or career. You justify your lack of passion for your work by convincing yourself you are making this sacrifice to meet the needs of your family. Promotions or pay raises may provide some temporary benefit, but deep down you know you are mismatched in what you really want to do for a living.

Since most everyone you know seems to be in the same position, with the same concerns, and responsibilities, you rationalize that "life s#@*% and then you die." Lost in this common existence is the fact that you are falling out of touch with your true talents, your true calling. *Something is lacking, and you can feel it at your core.*

It is time to be liberated from the inaccurate belief that work means spending time in a desperate pursuit of salary and benefits. Rewards like recognition and exuberance are not reserved for a few *lucky* souls and do not have to be sacrificed due to family obligations or financial responsibilities. It is time to follow your heart and not fall prey to a lifestyle less than you are capable of, or worse, exists to impress others. It is time to eliminate your limiting beliefs, leave behind constraining fears and obligations, and author a new life for yourself. With the exciting advances and opportunities of the 21st century workplace, it is the perfect time to rid yourself of limitations and become the person you truly aspire to be. It is time to reclaim your legacy!

"But, Chris," you might ask, "What you are saying sounds great, but is it *realistic*? I have *reality* staring me in the face. Sure I would like to attain all those exciting benefits and find my career calling, but who has time these days?"

You do! For starters, think about how much time you dedicate to watching TV or engaging in non-productive pursuits. I recently was astounded to learn that the average American watches over 6 hours of television per day. That is 25% of their lives devoted to watching actors and actresses get wealthy while you gradually erode your skills in this non-productive pursuit.

Success Tip

Stop watching actors on TV realize their career dreams and attain their calling and commit to starting right now to establish your own!

It is time to break free from the mentality of meeting your minimum basic needs and to adopt a more "me first" attitude. That's right, folks. I am recommending that you become more selfish! There is more to life than food and shelter and the ability to make the minimum payment on your mortgage, rent or credit card bills.

Consider the findings of Abraham Maslow, a famous behavioral psychologist who asserted that there are 5 fundamental human needs:

1. *Survival:* Meaning food and shelter.
2. *Security:* Meaning financial income to secure our lifestyle
3. *Belonging:* Meaning we feel part of a group and not isolated in our thoughts and actions
4. *Self-esteem:* Meaning the establishment of confidence, worthiness and the feeling that we are contributing to others. I often observe that people whose self–esteem was bolstered by their work experience a loss of self-esteem when they retire or lose their job
5. *Self-Actualization:* Meaning living a life where we are engaged in activities consistent with our self-image and which provide a deep sense of passion and purpose. Work moves from something you must do to something you truly enjoy doing.

Where are you on this continuum? Finding your career calling is the process of mastering each of these needs to the point where you are not just making ends meet, but building an accurate awareness of yourself that will help you systematically move to the self-actualization stage. It is here where most people who have found their career calling find themselves. My job is to assist you in getting to the *5th level of need,* the place and mindset where you enjoy a deep sense of purpose and passion. It is where the elite 10–20% of our workforce thrives!

What Does Finding Your Career Calling Feel Like?

Exuberance, exhilaration, accomplishment, relief, joy, energized, amazing... these are just a few of the words people use to describe what it feels like to have left behind an unfulfilling occupation and successfully entered into *the career calling zone.*

When you are on track to your calling you will:

- Be excited to go to work; there are no dreary Monday mornings and no "TGIF's"
- Experience a greater surge of passion, purpose and energy for the tasks at hand
- Take tremendous pride and enjoyment in both your work and in describing it to others
- Enjoy the people you work with and for and respect their contributions
- Realize your key values (recognition, respect, appreciation, compensation, belonging) on a consistent basis
- Know you are being rewarded commensurate with your value

What would you choose to do with your life if you did not have to work for the money? If you could literally begin any venture without limitation, what would be your choice of occupation? Here is a real life example to consider:

> Gerald Chertavian is a man I greatly admire, who is a husband, a father, a Harvard MBA and a former participant in the Big Brother program. After completing his studies, he began an incredibly successful career as a banker on Wall Street. Successful but not satisfied, he then formed a software company during the Internet boom and sold the business for several million dollars.
>
> Confronted with the unique opportunity to spend his time doing anything he wanted, Gerald decided to revisit the subject of his college thesis (closing the opportunity divide that exists in our country) and formed a non-profit company called *YearUP*. Leveraging his passion for working with young people, his belief in the power of the human spirit regardless of race, creed or color, and his substantial network of corporate contacts, he began a training school for disadvantaged youth. Today, *YearUp* has offices in several states with plans for national expansion.
>
> Gerald tells me he enjoyed both of his previous careers, banking and software, but has taken his passion to a whole new level with this latest endeavor.

How does it really feel? Finding your true career calling and experiencing passion, pleasure, challenge, profit, reward, power, and peace of mind is the difference between living and simply existing!

Please list 3 new feelings and emotions finding your career calling will provide for you ...

This should empower you and create an incredible surge of energy! You now have a written reason for action! I have personally observed people who have left behind an unhealthy career and achieved their calling realize incredible shifts in attitude and even health. People who were previously depressed experience a newfound zest and reason for living. Often, weight loss occurs as the person realizes more fun at work and feels less of a need to gain pleasure from the refrigerator. Individuals can eliminate acid reflux, spastic colon, and other ailments often caused or intensified by stress. Medications can be eliminated and headaches and body pains often disappear.

To experience these feelings, it is important to establish a plan, identify proven strategies that you are comfortable with, and implement them at a pace that meets your needs. Sometimes, however, external forces create a defining moment, where your pace of change is accelerated beyond what you expected or planned for. Whether change occurs for you because of a careful set of planned activities or it happens due to an unexpected event, I call the catalyst for this change a *defining moment*.

Habit Management

> *"For all our insight, obstinate habits do not disappear until replaced by other habits ... No amount of confession and no amount of explaining can make the crooked plant grow straight; it must be trained upon the trellis by the gardener's art ... "*
>
> —Carl Jung

THE FOLLOWING EXERCISES WERE designed to help you inventory your habits and serve as reinforcement to redefine or create new traits, beliefs and behaviors to propel you closer to your objective. The secret to re-inventing yourself and creating positive momentum is to build good habits and eliminate bad habits that are keeping you from truly living your authentic self and attaining the occupation that best meets your values, goals and aspirations. On the subject of habits, let us start with a simple question. *What is a habit?*

A habit is a behavior that you keep repeating. Any individual, who persists in establishing a new behavior, eventually realizes it has become a habit. Fortunately, you can reprogram yourself anytime you choose to do so. In my view, more people than ever are living for instant gratification. People purchase material possessions they really cannot afford, such as cars, furniture, appliances, entertainment systems, or the latest gadget. It is important that to obtain your calling and program your mind and body for this important change, you begin to focus on your positive and negative habits.

Key Question

What habits do I have that are roadblocks to attaining my career calling?

I live by the belief that 80% of our behavior is habitual. Think about a typical day in your life. Most likely, you rise at the same time, have the same routine for showering and getting ready, perhaps eat the same thing for breakfast, maybe watch the same morning news show, go online or read the newspaper, brush your teeth and begin your day.

Perhaps you kiss your loved one, wave to a neighbor, listen to the same morning radio station, take the same route to work, wave to your co-workers, plop down at your desk, grab a cup of coffee and start your work day.

Over time, perhaps you have developed similar patterns or routines when eating, working out, watching television, shopping, paying your bills or even having intimate relations with your significant other! You may be locked into a cruise control mode with unconscious negative patterns, which are inhibiting your growth and restricting your optimal level of achievement. Perhaps it's time to change things up a bit!

The key to "habit management," as I refer to this process, is to inventory both your good and bad habits. Simply put, make a list of the habits that will move you closer to your life goals (including those specific to obtaining your career calling) and those that are moving you further away from your goals and creating a comfort level that breeds mediocrity. Seek excellence and not conformity. I know people who go to the local coffee house and spend $5 per day ($25 per week, $1,250 per year!) out of sheer habit and routine. They follow the crowd and don't even really like coffee!

Habits ... Good and Bad

"The average American commutes 30 minutes to and from work, a total of one hour, every day. Over 5 years, this totals 1,250 hours, enough time to obtain the equivalent of a college education. The question is: How is this time being used? Making the radio talk show host rich ... or making you rich?"

—Chris Kuselias

Sample Good Habits	Sample Bad Habits
Early to rise/8 hours sleep per night	Excessive TV watching
No smoking; no excess drinking	Smoking/drinking
Regular exercise	Late night snacking
Read one hour per day	Trashy novels/tabloid newspapers
Return email/phone calls promptly	Procrastination
Save and invest 15% of your income	Over-spending/credit card debt

Your goal should be to *gradually* adopt more good habits and eliminate bad habits. Do not overwhelm yourself by trying to make wholesale changes overnight. You will only get discouraged and quit trying. Set a goal to add one good habit per quarter (every 13 weeks) and eliminate one bad habit every quarter. *Studies show that most behaviors that are repeated for a minimum of 13 weeks become permanent habits.* In one year's time you will have added 4 good habits and eliminated 4 bad habits. That is progress!

How to Change a Habit

Each of us has at least one bad habit that we would like to change. Bad habits might include smoking, overeating, or swearing. Good habits might include exercise, wearing a seat belt, and eating healthy. Success in life is a matter of establishing effective habits and eliminating the ineffective ones.

1. Be truthful
   Admit your bad habits and seek support from positive people for your efforts to change. Find role models or someone who practices the good habits you seek and avoid those habits you want to break.
2. Start with a simple change
   Don't try to do too much too soon or you will get frustrated. Make it a realistic change.
3. Make a commitment to your new behavior
   Write it down. Give yourself a reward for any step you may make in the right direction. Making a written plan has magical power. Tell a friend of your commitment to engage their support and benefit from the power of their high expectations of you.

Bad Habits vs. Good Habits

Objective

This activity is a step in the right direction to help you get started replacing bad habits with good ones. The most important point to remember when replacing bad habits with good ones is VISUALIZATION. You have to actually picture yourself in the old situation and how you will be when you adopt your new habit.

What to Do

Fill in your personal answers to the questions in the following table for a good habit you would like to add and a bad habit you would like to change. Use specifics. Try to think of where you will be, what your surroundings will look like, what you'll be wearing, who you will be with (or won't be with), and other details that will make the situation real:

Here are some great habits to add:

- Adopting the 5P's (passion, purpose, power, profit and peace of mind)
- I choose not to watch TV for 3 hours every night. Instead, I choose to invest one hour learning more about my career calling, business, financial independence, relationship, public speaking, writing a book or any number of other interesting activities that will further my calling
- I choose to start my day reading an inspiring autobiography or a spiritually uplifting message
- I choose not to become a workaholic
- I choose to schedule personal time off every week with my family and friends, as well as special time for myself, to be enjoyed guilt free
- Learning to take action and avoid procrastination
- Mastering your own mindset and avoiding your limiting beliefs
- Building your self-confidence and asking for what you want in life
- Meeting one great new contact per month who can educate or mentor you
- Putting your goals in writing and reviewing them every month
- Writing down your affirmations and reviewing them when you first wake up and just before bed
- Adopting one new good habit per quarter and eliminating one bad habit per quarter

Here is a list of habits that you should strive to eliminate:

- Not returning phone calls on time
- Being late for meetings and appointments

- Poor communication with spouse, family, colleagues and staff
- Not setting goals and a lack of clarity about expected outcomes
- Not attending to paperwork quickly and efficiently
- Allowing bills to go unpaid, resulting in interest penalties
- Talking too much instead of listening
- Working long days with no exercise or regular breaks
- Poor eating habits: Eating on the go, junk food or eating at irregular times of the day
- Leaving home in the morning without hugging your significant other or pets, neglecting family
- Taking work home with you or answering the telephone during family mealtimes
- Socializing too much on email or telephone
- Not taking enough time for fun and family—guilt free!
- Trying to control every decision, especially the small stuff
- Procrastinating on everything from filing taxes to cleaning out your garage

In closing, adding good habits and eliminating bad habits will have a profound effect on your career and life. It will open new doors and expand your possibilities. It will unburden you from limiting beliefs and negative patterns. It will create a new energy and zest for your daily activities. It will re-define you and make you feel brand new and improved!

The Power of ANTICIPATION

> *"I am not a has-been. I am a will-be."*
> —Lauren Bacall, actress

I am often asked if there is one single skill that is most essential to success. There are several factors that can dictate career success, but perhaps none more important than this skill. More than any other factor, the development of this single skill has had the most profound impact on my progress. My life completely changed when I adopted this philosophy in my personal and professional life. It can be argued that it is the single most critical skill to develop and is the basis for all progress. It clearly separates the exceptional from the mediocre. I am talking about *anticipation*.

I remember having the privilege to interview Wayne Gretzky, who is generally regarded as the greatest hockey player in the history of the sport.

My expectation was that he would be larger than life, the epitome of an athlete with muscles, size and power. Mr. Gretzky was my size and my build! I remember wondering how this average sized man with no distinguishing physical characteristics could so thoroughly dominate a sport like ice hockey where speed and physicality are so important to success. When he was asked how he was able to establish himself above all others he replied, "Most people skate to where the puck is; I skated to where the puck was going to be." The incredible power of anticipation was never more evident.

When I was asked by CNN how I was able to create an organization from scratch and build it into one of the country's fastest growing, privately held companies, I shared my strategy of developing a leadership team. "Most companies have managers; we have leaders. Managers are people who react to problems; leaders are the rare breed who anticipate challenges and fix them before they occur." This simple distinction permeates our core philosophy and is a primary reason for our incredible success.

So how can you learn to anticipate? Well, if you are currently working, be aware of what the future holds for you, your department, your company and your industry. Individuals who are downsized find themselves in this unfortunate and painful state because they were no longer competitive … they failed to anticipate!

Be in control! Find people who can assist you and who will promote your ability to anticipate. Mentors will not possess a magic pill, but rather a series of consistent steps based on an attitude of expecting to win. The common denominator is the ability to consistently anticipate changes and make plans to effectively deal with those changes before they become problematic. Anticipation leads to enhanced problem solving skills, the truest measure of success in life and business. How quickly you act and anticipate change will determine your success as a mom, saver, or business person. Most people wait until there is a problem and create tremendous anxiety and stress attempting to solve it.

You cannot live on yesterday's standards and expect to be competitive today! Think about a relationship. In a strong relationship, each partner learns to anticipate needs before their partner or children ask for or require something. When a family member and I disagree, it is usually about neglecting priorities and not anticipating each other's needs. Anticipation is a skill; whole industries evaporate when they ignore signs and don't anticipate market conditions in timely fashion.

For example, business guru Tom Peters, in his masterwork, *In Search of Excellence*, highlighted 43 successful companies, which comprised part of the *Fortune* 500. Of these, 14 were in financial trouble within 2 years. Why? They failed to embrace and anticipate change. These companies are a metaphor for your personal life

A key premise of this book is that you only have to focus on 5 areas to achieve balance. Forget all else and avoid distraction. A success in one area today may prove a major challenge in the future ($, relationship, diagnosis, etc.).

- Can you guarantee your relationship will be as exciting 5 years from now as it is today?
- Can you guarantee you will have the same occupation and that your company will be in business?
- Can you guarantee your savings account is safe?
- Can you guarantee you will be healthy and fit and won't develop a mental or physical disease due to poor dietary habits

The message: What was impossible yesterday is probable today!

The Power of Leverage

THE POWER OF LEVERAGE is another important concept used by successful performers. It is a technique to get you closer to your career calling whereby you accelerate your growth, knowledge and status by utilizing (leveraging) the power of your available resources, which includes your network, education, experience and skill set. In short, it is the process of itemizing and taking advantage of your best attributes and gifts to maximize your performance and eliminate obstacles that stand in your way.

Leverage allows you to:

Love your career and see it as a calling and not just a way to make money

Equip yourself with the proper resources to succeed in a highly competitive job market

Visualize yourself achieving your goals and successfully performing in your calling

Empower yourself to face the obstacles and make the necessary changes required to attain your career calling

Re-invent yourself as your values and desires change over time

Assess what methods are yielding results and which are wasting time and energy

Grow your reputation as an industry expert and contributor
Educate, enlighten and enjoy the ongoing process of finding your unique and compelling contributions

Benefits to Using Leverage

Have you surrounded yourself with trusted advisors with whom you've shared your vision and plans?

You cannot achieve your career calling and your highest level of success without leveraging your resources. You increase your chances of success when you leverage the power of sharing your goals with trusted advisors, who will serve as motivation to complete the tasks. Sharing your objectives with the right people is essential to success; choose coaches who will push you to excellence. You must surround yourself with mentors who will educate and empower you to make progress toward achieving your calling. It is this accountability that produces the leverage necessary to follow through with your aspirations.

Often, we all need that extra incentive to get us through those times where we lose confidence or focus. Leverage keeps us from losing site of our objective and the confidence needed to pursue our lofty expectations. Question: What is keeping you from making the changes necessary to climb to the next level? Could it be that you need a little leverage? Leverage adds tremendous value to your life and to the lives of your clients. Make a difference in people's lives by speaking. With leverage on your side, you have the opportunity to begin maximizing your unique gifts and abilities.

Standards and Their Amazing Effect

"Successful people have higher standards, period."
—Chris Kuselias

I WOULD NEXT LIKE TO share with you the importance of raising your standards. One of the keys to my personal success in life has been my ability to raise and maintain my personal standards, not by designer labels, status symbols, or by what others consider success, but rather by my own internal thermostat. I made a conscious decision to hold myself accountable to a guiding set of principles and conditions that absolutely required my concentrated focus, dedication and commitment to excellence. I am a student of *constant and never ending improvement.* I sincerely believe that you can never stay even; at the very moment you are reading these words, you are either progressing or regressing.

Once you accept and agree to this philosophy and adopt these principles, your life will undergo a sudden and dramatic shift from wasting time and partaking in non-productive activities to becoming acutely aware of your actions on a moment to moment basis. You will never again settle for that which does not meet with your personal and professional agenda; nor will you allow external forces to direct you into beliefs or actions inconsistent with your established standards. You assume control of the process and take responsibility for all of your actions. You are the pilot of your own life!

Success Tip

Create a list of things you are no longer willing to accept in your life. Do this now!

When I worked as a broadcaster at ESPN for a brief period, I had the good fortune to meet and share strategies with the world's most accomplished and celebrated athletes and entertainers. I interviewed and met personally with world renowned coaches, players, actors, directors, politicians and business tycoons. How? Simple. Everyone I talked with was involved with sports on some level: as a player, relative of a player, manager, or fan of sports. Today, the Super Bowl is like a who's who party of A-list celebrities and media personalities.

The one consistent theme that surfaced during interviews with every great achiever I ever studied or interviewed was their ability to set incredibly high standards for themselves; they refused to live their lives by the terms and conditions of their team, league or society. Great performers set their own mark and then go after it with unrelenting ambition and energy. Their practice habits, diet, research, and mind set are all carefully planned and executed. They are students of their craft and seek mentors for every aspect of improvement. What a wonderful example to the rest of us who seek greatness, not on the gridiron, field or court, but rather at the office, in the store, in the classroom or wherever we seek to establish our personal career calling.

I have always been a student of success. I am fascinated with what separates superstars from good or even great performers. How do you measure and quantify the difference? Michael Jordan is a person I admire and is generally regarded as the greatest basketball player of all time. It was a thrill and honor to watch him perform and exceed expectations time and again. He was truly dominant in his sport. While at ESPN, I asked numerous former NBA players to describe what set him apart from the world's other great players. While talent, drive, ambition, and work ethic were all part of the discussion, the single phrase that stood out was that "Air Jordan" had higher standards than the rest of the league. His peers were amazed that he never compared himself to others, but rather set his own standards when it came to points, wins or championships. He did not base his accomplishments on what others had done, but rather obliterated their records by setting his own bar … which was raised to the rafters. This lesson has stayed with me since and whenever I drift toward comparing my weight, earnings, relationship, parenting or any other area of my life to others or what society thinks, I remember 'Air Jordan" and it inspires me to be my best self. In fact, I keep a picture of him soaring to the basket in my home gym, and every day he serves as an inspiration to make my own mark and raise my standards!

The lesson is to raise your standards, become a true professional and act like one in all that you do, every day. There are no second acts or second chances at this game called life. We are here but for a short time and have a unique opportunity to capture our own glory and gold, not in the form of a medal, but in something much more profound and meaningful … in our legacy of contribution. You might not set the world record in 50-meter downhill skiing or inspire millions around the world in doing so, but you can alter and impact lives in your own way. You are here to contribute and by doing so will feel the same joy of accomplishment as an Olympic Gold medalist, NBA world champion point guard or Academy Award winning actor. The resume may read differently, but the emotional benefits are identical.

Another lesson I learned from this experience was to focus one's energy on your unique and compelling gifts. Superior performers spend their time engaged in thoughts and activities where they are brilliant and unique. They focus their time, effort and energy on these gifts like a laser beam. When you focus most of your time and energy doing the things you are truly brilliant at, you eventually reap big rewards.

Conversely, if you spend too much time working on your weaknesses, all you end up with is a lot of strong weaknesses! My question to you is this:

What percentage of your time do you spend on your brilliant activities? If you analyze your life and the activities that relate to obtaining your career calling, make sure you are spending a minimum of 80% of your precious time engaged in activities that lead to the outcome you seek and eliminate those that contribute little or nothing to where you desire and deserve to be!

The Quest to Outserve!

"The quality of a person's life is in direct proportion to their commitment to excellence, regardless of their chosen field of endeavor."

—Vince Lombardi

EARLIER, I STATED THAT passion is a privilege; it is a right and power that you possess. This being the case, it behooves you to pursue your passion and derive all of the benefits associated with that pursuit. Because you are stepping outside of the "norm," you must clarify your purpose and define your actions.

When you are faced with challenges along the way, your mind will provide you with a formidable defense against any threats to your passion. Your intellect can help you to define your purpose and develop a strategy for following your heart. Not only will you be able to integrate the pursuit of your passion into your life, but you will also be able to ensure that it remains a priority.

I ask you to consider your current circumstances, calmly, openly and honestly. You are reading this book for a reason and my guess is that you seek to change your current career path and aspire to a more fulfilling work life, one that unleashes your true talents and contributions in a powerful and meaningful way.

The message is: Do not focus on money, power, fame, job title or any other commonly accepted *external* measure of success. If you truly want success—the kind that brings inner peace and happiness—then adopt the internal belief system that contribution to your fellow man is the real secret to all success. *Outserve!* This above all else is the common denominator that makes all great achievers great!

Make a difference. *Outserving* as a philosophy works in both your personal and professional life. Any great marriage most likely practices the concept of outserving each other by putting the other person's thoughts and feelings ahead of one's own.

Make a Difference

One of the prevailing themes of this book is that to be truly happy and balanced, each of us must learn to make and *be able to acknowledge* our unique and compelling contribution to others. In my experience, it is the only thing that brings true peace of mind; the acquisition of material possessions or status will not. You must find what you were born to do! To illustrate, here is a story that I share in every group training activity I am associated with.

> A small boy lived by the ocean. He loved the creatures of the sea, especially the starfish, and spent much of his time exploring the seashore. One day he learned there would be a tide that would leave the starfish stranded on the sand. The day of the tide he went down to the beach and began picking up the stranded starfish and tossing them back into the sea. An elderly man who lived nearby came down to the beach to see what he was doing. "I'm saving the starfish, "the boy proudly declared. When the neighbor saw all of the stranded starfish, he shook his head and said, "I'm sorry to disappoint you, young man, but if you look down the beach one way, there are stranded starfish as far as the eye can see. And If you look down the beach the other way, it's the same. One little boy like you isn't going to make much of a difference." The boy thought about this for a moment. Then he reached his small hand down to the sand, picked up a starfish, tossed it out into the ocean and said, "I sure made a difference for that one."

While we live in a WIIFM (what's in it for me?) world, we can positively impact others, one person at a time. Through our work and belief system, we can influence a child, spouse, friend, customer, neighbor or total stranger. Make the choice to pursue your calling vigorously and leave no option other than attainment. Once experienced, you will find there is no other way! Let these words and exercises provide the blueprint for you to build the confidence, skills and mentors needed to make your dreams a daily reality. Stop the process of simply making a living and take the time now to design your life. Make a commitment to yourself and your inevitable success, which will occur if you follow this process.

Believe in yourself and your worthiness of acquiring your calling. Once you do, you will experience the incredible elation of contribution to others in tasks and activities that no longer feel like work, but pure joy. When you really think it through, that is what we are here for.

Success Is Built from the Inside Out, Not the Outside In

"I believe each of us is born with a life purpose. Identifying, acknowledging and honoring this purpose is perhaps the most important action successful people take. They take the time to understand what they are here to do, and then they pursue that with passion and enthusiasm."
— *The Success Principles*, by Jack Canfield,
coauthor of *Chicken Soup For The Soul*

Maybe you are like me and have suffered from what I called, *successful unfulfillment*. For years, I had individually attained high levels of achievement but often still felt empty. Adopting the concept of a calling and creating balance in my life hit me like a bolt of lightening! Focusing too intently on one area of life is a formula for disaster! Immediately, I could see why I previously felt pressure and anxiety and now had a plan to counter these negative feelings. What I was willing to do, and what many people won't do, was commit myself to the task of adopting a new approach.

My wife and I have made the conscious decision, on both an individual and collective basis, to lead a healthy, balanced life. We took a vow, both individually and as a couple. Initial goals like making millions, being in phenomenal shape and being in the social spotlight became secondary to finding our calling as a family and leading a balanced, healthy life. And amazingly, once we practiced the principles detailed in this book, our quality of life improved immediately!

As lifelong students, we had both read and studied successful leaders, authors and speakers, experts in their chosen field. In each case, the information that each expert shared was both enlightening and informative. However, we needed a system to put all of these individual strategies into a comprehensive plan. Adopting the strategies found in this book and making balance a priority was the answer. The process worked so effectively that I decided to share our good fortune with others.

Having spoken all over the world, the one factor I have found that prohibits people from succeeding more than any other single factor is *lack of purpose*. Most haven't answered the "Why?" question for their careers. *Often, the problem with people who are unfulfilled is that they're trying to build their life from the outside in, not the inside out.* They're looking for inner satisfaction from outward things. They are like billiard balls bouncing around the pool table of life. If you are reading this book, chances are you are a self-starter and highly ambitious. You must solidify your higher purpose in your life so that you are strong enough to weather the curve balls that life throws us and disciplined enough to leverage opportunity. With a clear purpose, you can establish a powerful foundation for achieving your calling and living in balance, the highest and truest measure of success.

We can all agree that making the decision to leave an incomplete professional existence, seek out and obtain your calling, and adopt a balanced lifestyle may sound simple, almost basic. The concept of "everything in moderation" is not a new revelation. The key is to not only integrate this belief system, but also to incorporate proven principles. Many people "talk the talk;" few however, follow through, take action and "walk the walk." I commend you for actually investing your precious time in learning a new strategy to benefit you and your loved ones. I am confident that if you practice the techniques enclosed in this book, you will yield similar results.

Success Tip

There is a huge difference between being interested in success and being committed to success. Everyone is interested in success; few are willing to dedicate themselves to attaining it.

Whose Job Is It to Ensure Your Career Happiness? ... Yours!

> *"How can I possibly require or educate my own kids to pursue their dreams if they don't see me pursuing mine?"*
> —Chris Kuselias

Who has the responsibility for your career happiness? At the risk of sounding harsh or overly direct ... *it is your responsibility to find your calling!* It isn't your current employer's problem or the Department of Labor's responsibility; it is your task and yours alone. If applicable, stop the blame game and take responsibility! Nobody cares about your happiness more than you do, so it stands to reason that you must be the one who does the work, sweats the details and basks in the glow of victory.

Often I hear people say that employers today have lost their sense of loyalty and compassion for employees. Here is a tip, folks: Employers are often as uninformed on the process of finding one's calling as the job seeker. The sad truth is that the people whose job it is to hire you often don't know how to find a good employee any more than you as a job seeker know how to find a decent employer.

As a member of the Society for Human Resources Management (SHRM), the largest human resources organization of its kind in the world, I attend strategy and training sessions and am extremely fortunate to be constantly exposed to the beliefs, thoughts and patterns of fellow members, who for the most part are key hiring authorities. My experience in countless meetings and strategy sessions with decision makers in personnel has shown that while these professionals are seeking to be the "employer of choice" in their industry, often these folks are as confused by the hiring process as the career seeker!

It is a fallacy that employers exist to work you to the bone and extract every ounce of your contributions with no consideration or caring for your feelings. The hiring authorities I interact with would prefer that you are content and like your work because they know a happy employee is a more productive employee; but often budget restrictions and the incredible pace of work these days preclude the individualized analysis or training needed to ensure this occurs.

It is your responsibility to ensure your career satisfaction! Your attitude will dictate if you master the process or succumb to excuses and resentment. Bottom line: While family, friends, co-workers and current and future employers most likely have your best interests in mind, the reality is there is only one person who will have the responsibility for living each day and night with either the happiness or disappointment of your chosen method of contribution and work ... and that person, my friend, is you!

Your Decisions Will Dictate Your Happiness

A husband and wife were enjoying a much needed vacation on a remote tropical island when suddenly a painful toothache threatened to derail their trip. Finding the only dentist on the island, the wife, who desperately wanted to enjoy the vacation, instructed the dentist to "pull the tooth without any Novocaine."

Confused the dentist said, "I applaud your braveness and appreciate your hurry, but pulling the tooth without any anesthesia will be very painful." Nevertheless, the wife insisted. "OK," said the dentist, "what tooth is it?' The wife turned to her husband and said, "Honey, show him which tooth is bothering you."

The lesson? Risk is easy, when it is not you taking the risk.

To conclude this chapter, I want to encourage you to take calculated risks and to present you with a list of decisions you will need to make. This will assist you in designing your own life vs. simply making a living. I want you to remain patient with what may at times seem like an overdose of questions, but trust me when I tell you that taking the time to ponder these is absolutely necessary and will be the most important element in defining who you REALLY are, what you REALLY want, and why you REALLY want it.

Finding your calling is not about creating a sharp resume and going on-line or through an employment agency to obtain an interview. It is about the process of peeling away your layers of societal conditioning and conformity to discover your inner aspirations, dreams and values.

The questions, activities and exercises throughout this book have been prepared in sequential order to create a "blooming effect" and provide you with a keener understanding of what will ultimately become your contribution … to yourself, your family and the world!

Take the time to find a quiet, uninterrupted place and contemplate each of the following life issues and your TRUE feelings about what you want … Reflect!

Careering   Whose career would you most want and admire? What have been the most pleasurable job functions you have had to this point in your career? What career would validate your existence?

Dreams   What do you dream about? What consumes your thoughts that, if acted upon, would produce amazing results? If a genie gave you 3 wishes, what would they be?

Education   Is there a course or subject matter you would like to learn more about? Is there a certain degree or accreditation you need to obtain to realize your goals? Is there a speaker or presenter you want to see?

Financial   It has been said that there are 2 kinds of people: people who choose to live to their means and build their lifestyle on the amount of their income AND people who first design their ideal lifestyle and then create a plan to earn enough to support this lifestyle. Which kind are you? What would you do if you won the lottery and money was not an issue? Do you have a retirement strategy?

Geography   Are you living in the country, state and city you would choose if there were no obstacles? Are you living in the climate you like? Are you visiting the places you dream about?

Hobbies   When can you honestly say that you are having the most fun? What activity or endeavor makes you smile, laugh or even giggle? Other than work and family, what are you doing for yourself? What is the hobby or activity you will someday take up?

Health and Fitness   Are you in peak shape? Are your vital indicators acceptable to you and your doctor? Are you committed to a healthy lifestyle vs. fad diets or inconsistent workout programs? Are your excuses for not being in the shape you desire real or imagined?

Relationships   Can you honestly say you are spending time with the people who are most important to you? Who inspires you? Who supports you? Is your partner or spouse a person you would pick again? (Remember this: the grass is not greener over here or over there … the grass is only green where you water it.) Are you nurturing your key relationships? Are you developing quality new contacts and mentors?

Finally   What is truly most important to you? What will you miss the most? What in your life would be most difficult to replace?

To conclude, there are 3 basic methods to obtain your career calling and improve the overall quality of your life.

1. The 1ˢᵗ is to analyze what you are doing well, that is, what is working for you in pursuit of your ideal career and internal happiness and SIMPLY DO MORE OF IT!
2. 2ⁿᵈ, analyze what is not working for you, that is, what is causing you frustration or moving you further away from your objectives AND STOP DOING IT!
3. And 3ʳᵈ, incorporate new ideas and routines, TRY NEW THINGS to find out which ones work for you and which do not and incorporate the good new habits into your daily behaviors.

Congratulations on finishing this 2ⁿᵈ chapter! Relax, take a deep breath and by all means do become overwhelmed with all of my requests to get in touch with your authentic (internal) self. Keep in mind that this is an ongoing process and not a finite task. Your goal is not to become perfect, but to simply get better. You have already learned a great deal about yourself and the process of finding your calling. You have been given much to ponder.
 Onward!

CHAPTER 3

Fame, Fortune, Meaning ...
The Choice Is Yours!

KEY QUESTION: WHAT DO I REALLY WANT?

In this chapter, you will learn:

KEY TOPICS

- Success versus *"Suck-cess"*
- Balance Is a Key to Your Success
- Defining Success on Your Own Terms
- Mastering Money Mindset

KEY MESSAGES

- Success is a personal choice; it is unique to you!
- Attaining balance is a key ingredient to true success and happiness.
- Consistent *progress* is the true measure of success.
- Highly successful people do not base success on the standards of others; they set their own mark and then pursue it!
- Commit to recognizing a steady progression toward your calling and you will soon live the life you previously thought was unattainable!
- Adopt a "Compensation Follows Contribution" mindset: *Learn then Earn!*
- The secret to increasing your income is to *increase your value*. If you want to earn more money, make a greater contribution!
- You must decide to be wealthy and reprogram your belief system to have positive associations to being wealthy.
- Improve your financial literacy: Seek out quality mentors who can educate you on cash, investing and retirement strategies.
- Determine your net worth: Value after all debt and expenses are paid.
- Analyze your spending habits: Keep an expense journal over a 3-month period (one quarter) and analyze areas you can reduce.
- Create a retirement plan: Start today!
- Pay yourself first: Commit to saving a minimum of 15% of your income.
- There are 2 kinds of people: those who adjust their lifestyle to their income level and those who adjust their income level to their lifestyle; be the latter!

> *"I'm not here just to make a living; I'm here to make a difference."*
>
> —Helen Bridges

Exercise: Getting to Know Me

"When it comes to careering, people are not born with a built in GPS mechanism."

—Chris Kuselias

Suppose you and I had an appointment for lunch. We have never met before. Write down 10 things that would help me get a good idea of who you really are. What would I need to know about your feelings, your personality, what you like, what you don't like, etc? Be sure to include your internal feelings as well as your outward actions.

Examples: Strong leadership skills, computer savvy, exceptional customer service, great little league baseball coach, compassionate friend, 12 handicap golfer, gourmet cook, amateur photographer, etc.

Who you are is a question that needs review before you discover what you really want. What most people want when asked is *success*. Let's review this concept.

Success versus *"Suck-cess"*

"Stop buying things you don't need, with money you don't have, to impress people you don't know."

—Chris Kuselias

I MEET COUNTLESS PEOPLE WHO confuse success with *suck-cess*. *Suck-cess* is a phenomenon whereby an individual feels they have achieved a degree of achievement based on others' standards or what societal conditioning has determined as the measure of success. People who are *suck-cessful* often try to gauge their happiness on material possessions or external measures, as opposed to what truly brings peace, joy and happiness in their heart. This process often *sucks* the life out of them.

Do you know anyone like this? I call this *suck*-cess because they may present the image of one who is content and proud, but deep down they remain restless, unfulfilled and are still searching for personal validation. Theses folks are not happy, healthy and in control, but rather strive to present the image to others that they have "made it." The problem is that individuals who fall into this category will often subconsciously sabotage their career in an effort to get to their inner, *authentic* self. Amazingly, some people can live their entire life trapped in this web of self-deceit and look back on their legacy with remorse and regret.

Still others immerse themselves in 1 or 2 areas of the 5 key life areas (career happiness, financial independence, health and fitness, relationship mastery and enlightened spirituality) at the expense of true balance, and neglect other essential areas. For example, we all know people who are deemed workaholics. While for some this sounds like a badge of honor, to me this always equals neglect in another essential area. Maybe the CEO spends so much time being *suck-cessful* at work that he or she is a failure as a husband, father, wife or mother. Perhaps, the focus on the almighty dollar has blurred the importance of family, contribution and personal satisfaction.

Take the time to determine what success truly means to you and yours and do not fall prey to family, friends, co-workers or societal definitions of what happiness means. The personal definition that allows you to sleep soundly and act confidently is the only measure that matters. The decision to pursue your calling and the establishment of sound reasoning for choosing to do so will make all the difference.

Erik's Story ... From the Courtroom to World Wide Leader!

"And now, ladies and gentlemen, here is your host, Erik Kuselias!"

How can a person modify their perception of work from a job to a calling? Let me share the story of my younger brother Erik, a member of the Mensa society who attended Brown University, Michigan Law School and obtained a Ph.D. from Columbia University. Upon graduation, he worked for 2 prestigious law firms before cofounding his own firm. He was highly successful, made a tremendous income and even ran for State Senator. He got married, had a beautiful baby, drove an expensive foreign car and built a gorgeous home in an exclusive neighborhood. The only problem was that being a lawyer was not his calling and these trappings of success only masked his growing disenchantment with the legal profession. By anyone's measure he had achieved external success but he had clearly not found his calling. For several years he was caught up in the cycle of building a solid career, albeit not his calling, and justifying his work life by comparing his success to others. He didn't dislike his occupation; he simply was not passionate about being a lawyer.

One day, he decided to volunteer with the local radio station to cohost a weekend sports radio show. He gave up his Friday nights for 18 months hosting a sports weekend radio show before having the courage to send a demo to ESPN, the worldwide leader in sports. After months of persistence, to his delight,

ESPN invited him to interview and subsequently offered to put him on the air for a trial period of one week. Having found his true passion and now in his element, Erik, although raw and inexperienced, displayed the fire and passion which resulted in an entry level offer to host his own show, even though it was the lowest paying and least listened to radio program on the ESPN airways. But it was with the "worldwide leader," and was a national show.

Erik was then confronted with the age old issue of ... be careful what you wish for ... The decision: Leave a partnership role in your own law firm after investing 7 years and over 200K on your undergraduate and legal education or begin at the very bottom in the radio broadcast business, making ⅓ of his current salary. There was the dilemma. Pursue his passion of sports or remain in the more practical career of law, which paid more but would never provide the passion and enthusiasm that a career in sports offered. This is what happens when you pursue your passion; you will often have to make a choice between passion and practicality. Erik received advice from everyone, including family, friends and trusted advisors, but ultimately he was the one who had to make and live with the choice. He had financial issues of mortgage, car payments and student loans to consider, (not to mention a wife and a new baby!) At an emotional dinner one night, I counseled and reminded Erik that living one's true passion has many more rewards than working for the money or prestige. If he loved the law and the future prospect of spending the next 40 years in that profession, great! If he was not passionate about it and didn't see "work as play," he should re-evaluate.

After careful deliberation weighing the pros and cons of a legal career vs. a start up career in media broadcasting, Erik made the decision to pursue his heart and took the ESPN job! As of this writing, he has his own radio show, has appeared on TV multiple times and is building a tremendous career in the media.

In summary, Erik used the Master Formula, the 5P's ... He found his passion (sports), then his purpose (entertaining others with his opinions and observations), built his power (he gained respect from the industry), increased his profit (he is now well into 6 figures) and sleeps well with the peace of mind that he has found his calling. Erik is the epitome of the career calling formula (the 5 P's) and has achieved *balance* in his personal and professional life.

Erik is no different from you or me. He simply had the courage and conviction to pursue his destiny and leave behind a life, which, while attractive to most, did not satisfy his personal measure of career success. Money, yes! Prestige, yes! Status, yes! Challenge, yes! ... Passion, no!

While I can empower you to consider alternatives to your current work situation and educate you on the value and benefits of finding your career calling, when presented with the decision of staying put or transitioning to this new endeavor of passion, the choice is yours and yours alone. Certainly you can get advice and counsel but the journey to your calling involves risk, and guts! People can remain stuck in the process of comparing and contrasting risk vs. reward, sometimes for years! The key is to start to create momentum towards an alternative lifestyle through research, finding quality mentors, volunteer work in a field of interest and following other specific strategies you will learn in this book.

Your Internal Struggle: How Your Mind Plays Tricks on You

"The sense of anxiety and guilt doesn't come from having too much to do; it is the automatic result of breaking agreements with yourself."
— David Allen, *Getting Things Done*

From years of experience, I can share with you that the decision to pursue your career calling is one that will challenge your heart and soul. It is a process that forces you to confront your personal belief system about the concept of *practicality vs. passion*. Not that the 2 are mutually exclusive, but people who actually get to the decision making mode often have second thoughts about what they have as opposed to the uncertainty of what pursuing their passion will yield. Get used to the idea of making and keeping promises to yourself or stress will become your constant companion.

Mike has been working in the printing industry for over 15 years. He is well established and respected, makes a better than average living, has a nice house with a mortgage, 2 teenage daughters and a late model American made sedan. Mike has a decent marriage but feels pressure to keep his wife happy; she also works part time to make ends meet. Everything seems pretty good except for one small problem ... Mike has no passion for his job and finds himself increasingly fantasizing about quitting and pursuing his passion for the outdoors. Every day slips further and further into being comfortably numb.

On many days he goes through the motions; has developed a predictable routine for lunch and work breaks that bore him to tears. His life isn't so terrible that he will simply quit, but enough is missing that he knows in his heart and soul he is missing his true calling. His friends express similar feelings and experiences but try to convince him that everyone is in the same boat and nobody likes their job. Mike is not willing to accept this. Mike feels alone and seeks a friend or other resource to share his growing disenchantment. He has even considered therapy. He wonders how he got to this place in his life and if others have escaped and found a solution to reclaiming their passion, without disrupting or potentially losing his family.

Maybe you can relate to Mike ... Upon making a decision to pursue your true destiny, the thought process usually goes something like this ...

The reality is: I don't get a lot of passion and purpose from my current job ... but

Then again, none of my circle of friends or family love their job either, work is work, right? ... but

What if I found a job I really loved where work and play felt the same ... but

Who am I kidding? I am destined to work at jobs I don't like ... but

Chris Kuselias' book suggests that anyone can find their career calling and that there is a formula ... but

Sounds like another scam to me. Finding a career calling is for suckers and dreamers ... but

What if it really works and I can save myself from a life of regret, boredom and unhappiness ... but

Everyone complains about or hates their job, right? I am no different, I am doing OK, it could be worse ... but

I am not everybody. I deserve better, I am smart, talented, I am just in the wrong place ... but

What if my friends and family laugh at me? After all, I have some status ... but

Who cares what they think? It's my life ... but

What if I try the process and I fail? I bet some people have lost their shirt in a new venture or job change ... but

What if I try the process and succeed and am genuinely happy! ... but

Why make any rash decisions? I will procrastinate today and start tomorrow ... but

No, I refuse to stay in a job I don't truly enjoy for even one more day. Life is in session ... but

The reality is: I can visualize, even picture a tremendously exciting career ... but

Chris, the reality is: I am scared!

This internal struggle is perfectly normal! Admit it; on some level you are anxious about the process of critical reflection and testing your worth. What if you fall short and do not attain your calling? Then you will really have failed! Some rationalize that it is better to not even try for fear of falling short of the destination. They pacify or suppress their inner voice by making statements like, "I am responsible or I have responsibilities; passion seeking is for others."

The primary reason why you have not pursued your calling is simply because you are scared of failing on some level and lack a specific plan for achieving your dream. You dream of something bigger and better but rationalize that being practical is more prudent. You may even blame your wife, children or loved ones for being the reason YOU haven't or cannot pursue your career calling. The process is a push pull activity that frankly, most people do not have the courage or patience to complete. We as human beings, do everything in our power to gain pleasure and avoid pain.

But here is my promise, the same one I made to my brother Erik. Putting yourself in position to realize your passion, purpose and demonstrate your unique and compelling talents is worth it! There are success stories everywhere! Consider these:

- The successful entrepreneur in Boston, Massachusetts, who, after a successful corporate banking career on Wall Street followed by the creation of a software business, which he sold for millions, started a training program for inner city youth in an attempt to narrow the opportunity divide in this country. His training program has expanded into multiple states and is growing!
- The banker who partnered with one of his former clients to open and co-manage a flower shop in San Diego, California!
- The former stay at home mom and her husband who leveraged their 401K to purchase and reinvent a revolutionary kids clothing store in Denver, Colorado! They enjoyed selecting fabrics, patterns and designing their 1st catalogue.
- The plumber who joined a non-profit organization, which accumulates clothing for underprivileged youth in the Bronx, New York. While he describes his duties as a plumber as respectable, his hobby of building a clothing closet may soon create a full time opportunity!
- The English major who followed her passion and is managing an upscale restaurant in Newport, Rhode Island. She loves every detail, including the menu design and choice of flowers to adorn every table.
- The former delivery driver in Nashville, Tennessee, who returned to school at night and became an elementary school teacher. He explains that teaching kids is his reason for being!

All of these examples have one thing in common ... while they sought counsel and opinion, the decision and effort was their own. You are the captain of your own career!

Success Tip

If you ever need a helping hand, look at the end of your own arm. The message: be self-sufficient.

To Educate or Not to Educate, That Is the Question

I am often asked about the importance of education as it relates to career happiness. Make no mistake, I am a huge proponent of education and urge you to feed your mind with quality schooling, seminars and useful success tools. However, there are countless stories of high school and college dropouts who poured their energies into a new concept, at the expense of completing a formal education.

As of this writing, 85% of CEO's and founders on the Inc. 500 list (the fastest growing privately held companies in the U.S.) have bachelor's degrees and 36% have postgraduate degrees.

Investors and venture capitalists (people willing to invest in an idea), tend to support ventures headed by college graduates. The perception is that the discipline required to obtain a degree bodes well for the issues needed to launch and maintain a new business. Given the choice, obtaining a degree is the way to go and many educational institutions are even funding student run businesses by providing both capital and office space to encourage entrepreneurship.

Education is one of the few things you can purchase that will last, in some form, your whole lifetime. It will not rust, corrode, or wear out. It cannot be stolen, repossessed, or destroyed. It becomes a permanent part of you, and once you have it, no one can take it away. Sure, your memory can fade with age or be interrupted by disease or accident, but you will always be further ahead with education and a lifelong habit of exercising your mind than you would have been without it.

Success Tip

Jobs requiring postsecondary education training are projected to grow more rapidly than those that do not!

While having a high school diploma or degree does not guarantee career success and happiness (there are numerous stories of people who achieve their career calling without the benefit of a formal education), it is clearly an asset. When you invest in yourself … you can't lose!

According to the U.S. Census Bureau, with the following degrees, here's how much you can expect to make in your lifetime:

High School Diploma: $1,100,000	Earns 35% more than high school dropouts
Bachelor's Degree: $2,100,000	Earns 116% more than high school dropouts
Master's Degree: $2,500,000	Earns 160% more than high school dropouts
Doctorate: $4,400,000	Earns 225% more than high school dropouts

Education really pays off. Continuous learning has been suggested as the source of everything better from health to happier marriages. The list of benefits continues:

- You can earn more money.
- You will be more likely to earn promotions at work.
- You will enjoy greater career satisfaction.
- You can build on your learning foundation, taking on more and more difficult subjects.
- You can continue to experience personal growth.
- You can enjoy improved social status.
- You can experience more self-confidence.
- You can grasp world events with more ease.
- You can have more economic and social opportunities.
- You can be better equipped as a parent.
- You can enjoy greater career flexibility.
- Your children are more likely to get farther in their education.

In short, EDUCATION IS A GOOD DEAL!

If you did not obtain a degree, fear not, my fellow career seeker; there are many ways to obtain your ideal calling. I myself was a mediocre student at best. To prove my point, here are a few individuals who took an alternative route to finding their career calling.

No Excuses   Here is a list of billionaires and multimillionaires who never graduated from college:

Bill Gates	Microsoft
Paul Allen	Microsoft
Michael Dell	Dell Computer
Larry Ellison	Oracle
Jay Van Andle	Amway
Richard DeVos	Amway
Steve Jobs	Apple Computers
Thomas Monaghan	Domino's Pizza
Jim Jannard	Oakley Sunglasses
Peter Jennings	ABC News
Walter Cronkite	CBS News
Harry S. Truman	U.S. President
Debra Field	Mrs. Fields Cookies
Steven Spielberg	Movie Director
Ralph Lauren	Clothing designer
Rosie O'Donnell	Actress/talk-show host
Ted Turner	Turner Networks
Wayne Huizenga	Blockbuster Video

A common denominator in all cases is clarity of purpose, mastering of mindset and limiting beliefs, a keen understanding of the *why*, and a focus on living a life of balance. While singleness of purpose is often a requirement to launching a new career, it is imperative that you do not do so at the risk of forgetting to relax, enjoy your family, exercise and open your eyes to the beauty that life affords us.

Balance Is a Key to Your Success

BALANCE IS NOT SOMETHING you can buy or sell. Balance is a feeling and you know in your heart and soul when it is right. You will experience joy, gratitude and enthusiasm when balanced, and stress, anger, restlessness and a sense of being unfulfilled when out of balance. People who tell me they love their work tend to love the people they are working with, while those who dislike their occupations often say they really dislike the people they are associating with.

Balance is often a function of the people with whom you choose to associate. Some experts suggest that you are a living, breathing result of the 5 people with whom you associate the most. Consider this carefully and answer truthfully if you are happy with the 5 people (and all of their tendencies, attitudes and idiosyncrasies) that dominate your time.

Consider this: If we are all living longer and better with more inventions to give us a better quality of life, why aren't we happier? I sincerely believe that while technology has it obvious benefits, it has also reduced the need for personal contact and the sense of belonging we all desperately crave. How many of us hide behind voice mail, email or other technological methods of communication, which replace personal contact?

All of my research, seminars, and analysis on the subject of what differentiates successful people from those who are still searching have resulted in one consistent theme: success in life is a function of balance. Although there may be numerous sub-categories, if you think about it, *success in life is really the continuous process of attempting to balance the following 5 critical areas of wellness:*

Health and Fitness Wellness   Diet, exercise, creating inner strength, belief system management

Financial Wellness   Money and banking, retirement planning, estate planning

Relationship Management Wellness   Marriage, parenting, family obligations, social activities

Spiritual Wellness   Prioritizing religious beliefs, getting closer to your god, serving others

Career Wellness   Determining your calling and your contribution to society

The key is to adopt these principals, commit to your calling and dissect each critical aspect of your life into these 5 manageable areas. See this book as a mentor, but not as your only mentor. Seek out and mirror actions of role models. I certainly have mine and credit a great deal of my success to their influence and guidance. This book was designed for anyone and everyone who desires balance and who seeks their own role model, in the mode of life they currently occupy. Examples include:

- The mom who wants to be shown just how another stay at home mother of 3 has effectively organized her life, taken her kids to programs, washed, dressed, and remained occupied with beneficial activities
- The business executive who wants to learn how others have managed to fit in time for family, exercise, health and spiritual pursuit, without sacrificing performance at work

- The teacher who is conscious of what they eat, but who just can't understand why they always feel tired and can never seem to lose weight and seeks a mentor to help them over the hump
- The parents who desperately seek a close family unit and who observe other families having fun and communicating but who feel distant from their own children and just cannot seem to reach a common ground of understanding
- The employee who toils day after day and wonders why they cannot ever be recognized for their efforts like other people they have observed who moved up the ladder of career success
- The everyman or woman who wonders how to re-capture their own lost energy and passion and who wants to learn how other people were able to tap into that inner spirit and re-invent themselves

Having spent the better part of my lifetime studying successful authors, speakers, coaches, business people, athletes and families, I have concluded that success is entirely predictable and can ultimately be defined by mastering this single word ... *balance.* Too much focus on a single area at the expense of another creates massive internal conflict!

Consider the following:

- Why do so many people hate their jobs and subscribe to mottos like, 'TGIF, Another day another dollar, same %#@* different day" or worse, become workaholics to mask their depression or to compensate for an unhappy or unhealthy personal life?
- Why do people continually begin diets knowing it won't yield the results they seek? Why do so many amazingly fit bodybuilders have such a high degree of emotional insecurity? Why is it that so many celebrities with wealth and fame become consumed with drugs and alcohol in an effort to alter their unhappy state of mind?
- Why do so many millionaires leave their fortunes to butlers or maids because they spent so much time accumulating wealth that they neglected their relationships and have no true family or friends? Why are most Americans 2 paychecks away from bankruptcy?
- Why do so many marriages fail? Why are most men hesitant to communicate their feelings? Why do so many mothers faced with

the challenging task of raising children neglect their physical appearance, lose their spontaneity and become unhappy?

- Why are people inconsistent with regard to their spirituality and seek assistance only when times are tough or a tragedy befalls them? At my church, you cannot get a parking space on Christmas and Easter Sunday, but the rest of the year, no problem!
- The answer is simple ... they all lack *balance.*

Do I have your attention? If so, the 1st step to attaining balance is to make a commitment to yourself and your loved ones that you will become a student of success. This commitment includes 3 aspects:

Desire—Faith—Action

Positively visualize yourself living a thriving, abundant life of balance and a work life that involves obtaining your career calling until your dreams become your daily reality. They say the hardest step in any journey is the 1st one. By reading these words, you have begun a journey, which will activate feelings, emotions, pride, and peace of mind that you may have thought was beyond your scope. Your potential is astounding and, through this process, you will begin to truly realize it. Life is now in session, so let's continue!

Achieving Balance Takes a Commitment

One great fantasy about success is that there is a magic pill or dust that makes it possible. The reality is that there are no shortcuts or magical secrets. Think about anything of value in your life, whether it is your career, your relationship with your spouse or children, the time when you were most fit, and they all have one thing in common ... effort. *There are no shortcuts to success, so don't bother trying!* From the earliest research into the study of success and human behavior, the same principles of success without effort have been marketed and sold under different phrases or clever gimmicks. They simply do not work! Ask yourself:

- How many people do you know who have achieved great wealth by purchasing real estate for no money down?
- How many marriages truly work without continuous effort to build trust or communication?

"It says here you were fired due to excessive illness and fatigue...
Was that a clever way to say they were sick and tired of you?"

- How many people who cut corners and seek the path of least resistance have great careers?
- How many diet pills or magical exercise machines actually achieve the promise of results and vitality?
- How many people, who at first glance appear to have it together, are in reality living a life of amassing material possessions or trophies, but lack peace of mind?

The simple truth is that you can achieve balance, success and peace of mind, but it takes a commitment to modify your current habits and lifestyle. As my grandmother used to say, "If you keep doing what you are doing, you will keep getting what you are getting." It is time to make changes ...

I typically begin by telling my audience that *success is entirely predict-able*. When they ask how, I tell them, "Success is based on many failures and high risk tolerance. Successful people possess great persistence and have tried and failed frequently, but they have learned from their mistakes. They made continuous but small improvements until one day they were living their dream and were the envy of their peers! Successful people also take more risks and know that they will never succeed every time, but win or lose they will gain valuable experience from trying. Truly successful, well-balanced people understand that life offers very few shortcuts.

But Chris, you may be thinking, it is easier to believe in a quick fix. And setting goals and achieving one's career calling seems like a difficult task. *Want some wine with that cheese?* Well, I am here to tell you that's its easier than you think! You have already achieved some remarkable things in your life; you just desire more! What you really seek is assistance in determining the measurable gap between where you are right now and where you desire to be. And here is a revealing fact, which you may have forgotten. *We all start at the same place!* It is our belief systems and personally imposed limitations that set us apart.

Regardless of what infomercials may claim, nobody has the perfect keys to success in life. It is a practiced art and we are all uniquely different beings with individual perspectives. From numerous examples, you know that being born into riches certainly does not guarantee success, nor does coming from a challenging upbringing ensure poverty. Remember this statement: *The essence of life lies in your development as a well-rounded person who sets a moral compass and lives by high standards.* Each time you study a subject matter expert, listen to a CD or read a book, you can save years of life lessons. Think of how much time, energy and money you will save and what strategies you will learn simply by reading this single book!

Quality of life is not achieved by taking shortcuts. And while there may be no shortcuts, there is a path, and it is that path that I would like to guide you to follow. You must be willing to examine your values and motives and become engrossed in the process. It is virtually impossible to read this book and not experience change. It is my *gift to you*. By reading it, I hope that you will formulate a better plan for your health, career, finances, relationships, and spiritual beliefs and achieve balance. You will begin the journey of continuous and constant improvement and never settle for an unfulfilling career again!

Learn to ask yourself 3 essential questions:

1. What are my unique and compelling gifts?
2. What are my optimal contributions?
3. What is keeping me from making them?

Through the enclosed exercises, you will formulate answers to these important questions.

Daily Balancing Act: Family and Work

Attaining balance is not a destination; it will always be a journey—designing and fulfilling our career calling, creating and maintaining quality relationships, accumulating wealth, discovering our unique and compelling contributions, understanding our beliefs and values.

Balance is an achievable destination. We must get there, because if we're always pursuing balance but never actually achieving it, we haven't solved any of the conflicts between work and family that can lead to painful outcomes.

So the big question is: *How does one design and follow a path that provides excellence in both family life and work without resulting in stressful conflicts between the 2?*

Being successful in our career calling—whether in business, the arts, health care, education, athletics, or any other occupation—requires a devotion and love for a career that makes balancing professional passion and commitment with family passion and commitment particularly challenging. Both beasts demand to be fed!

Success does complicate life by adding many demands in our career lives. Depending on our position, we may have employees, customers, and suppliers to consider, in addition to bosses. The demands of all these stakeholders add stress and conflict to our lives. In my personal experience, becoming more successful certainly had its benefits, but believe me there were more new stress contributors than I ever dreamed possible.

The greater our success, the more meetings, travel, negotiations, decisions and need for conflict resolution we are likely to encounter. There are requirements for public appearances, speaking engagements, and public relations. There are the additional temptations of power, wealth, position, and status if we are successful, and to be successful, we must devote more of our time. This push-pull leaves less time for our families and produces greater risk for becoming out of balance.

Being successful is an asset, not a liability, in trying to have both a family and career. The qualities and skills necessary to engage in a rewarding career are also needed in developing a stable family, and vice versa. Achieving a satisfying balance between your personal life and work will make you more effective and efficient at both. But how?

You don't achieve balance in life by accident but rather by establishing a consistent game plan that includes setting objectives, establishing priorities and creating boundaries and self-imposed measurement criteria. Bottom line: *You need to define your career calling and family success on your own terms and balance what is more important to you.* Balance cannot possibly happen on its own; you have to create it and commit to retaining it.

Unfortunately, many career seekers are misled into believing that their employers will dispense "life-balance" as a mandatory benefit of employment. This is a dis-empowering and dangerous way to think. We must be the captain of our own ship and chart our own course by setting our own priorities. There are 2 essential components in prioritizing:

1. Knowing how to establish priorities and what is most important to us.
2. Knowing what we have to give up. What has to go to the back of the line and wait?

In summary, it is important to select a calling that supports both your personal and professional balance. You need to be smart about your career choices because some careers are much more conducive to life balance than others. And once you are contributing within your chosen calling, you need to safeguard balance by making prudent decisions and developing a path that is uniquely yours.

Exercise: Balance Evaluation

Here is a helpful matrix to assess your current level of performance and establish a blueprint for success in the 5 key areas: Career, Financial, Health and Fitness, Relationships and Spirituality. Next to each category, I want you to honestly design your *ideal scenario*. From this, you will observe highs, lows and gaps that need to be addressed in order to feel balanced and healthy.

Career

Current calling _____

Future interests _____

Financial

Checking _____

Savings _____

Retirement _____

Health & Fitness

Weight _____

Body Fat % _____

Blood pressure _____

Cholesterol _____

Relationship Mastery

Marriage _____

Parenting _____

5 People you spend most time with _____

Spirituality

Meditation (15 minutes per day) _____

Defining Success on Your Own Terms

CHANGING YOUR PERSPECTIVE CAN influence your capacity to be happy with your priorities and your choices. I want your measure of success and happiness to be *internal*. When you fall into comparison mode, you are using external *benchmarks* for your success, and although this seems logical when competing with colleagues or neighbors, this can be a major obstacle in defining and creating your own balance.

Consider these common *external* benchmarks:

- Other people's career success
- Other people's salary or job title
- Other people's clothes, house, car, or vacation schedule
- Other people's wealth, assets, or acquisitions
- Other people's social calendar, parties or clubs

Consider these common *internal* benchmarks:

- Our feelings and associations about ourselves
- Our family and close friends' feelings about themselves
- Our contributions to others
- Our personal growth, improvement, and progress

The key to mastery is to learn to define balance on your own terms, using internal benchmarks to stop this comparison cycle and determine when enough is truly enough. There will always be people and families who have more than you and people and families with less than you. It is not about what they have ... it is only about what *you* seek and deem important for you and those closest to you. Forget keeping up with the Joneses; they probably aren't that internally happy!

Upon graduation from college, I competed for acceptance into a great business school. This was done to please my parents and increase my starting salary level, so I could say I was making more money than my classmates and friends. Upon being hired, I bought a fancy sports car to show my peers that I had made it, and I purchased clothes that had a fancy designer label on them, so others would know that I was successful. I read books that I thought made me look intelligent and current, saw movies so I could talk intelligently about trendy topics and even listened to music that seemed to show I was cultured and sophisticated.

One day I woke up in a cold sweat and realized that I was living someone else's life. What I had become was not who I truly was or where I came from. My values were screwed up! My internal identity did not match my external identity. Who was I? I was attempting to live up to an ideal that others perceived was successful, when in fact, alone in my thoughts, did not really equate to having made it. Who was deciding what was right for me and validated my actions? Not me ...

I was restless, anxious and no matter what I bought or acquired, it was never enough. There was always something better ... the next thing. Strangely, the wealthier I became and the more possessions I acquired, the less happy I became. There was no pride in ownership and I realized that I was consumed with impressing everyone else except the one who mattered most ... me!

My life changed when I made the decision to pursue my own passions and forget what the ads said I should wear and what lifestyle society deemed successful. Immediately, my stomach and mind relaxed, my health improved and my senses took hold. I lost the anxiety, began to feel a sense of self-worth and attained what I guess they call peace of mind. I am no longer the boss of many but more importantly, I supervise myself and my own life ... !

—*The Career Guarantee* seminar attendee, Charlotte, North Carolina

What You Can and Cannot Control

You and I must break free of others values and make some tough choices, because balance is achieved by letting go of those things that you don't want or need as much. Time to prioritize!

These lower-level matters may masquerade as first-tier priorities, but you can tell what matters most to you when you have to let go of something. Does it cause pain and, if so, how much? Is it a temporary ache or have you created a hole in your soul? Everything comes with a price—even achieving balance.

Try this simple exercise:

I will eliminate from my life:

- Negative habits like smoking, drinking, gambling and complaining
- People who pretend to understand my true feelings, be my friends and waste my time
- Hobbies or activities that would be nice to do but aren't really important to my mission
- Meaningless activities that don't create anything and that don't inspire me to achieve more important things
- Trivial gossip, mindless radio and TV shows, and other time wasters

To make room for:

- Uninterrupted, quality time with my family and loved ones
- Time to reflect on my true career calling and meet quality mentors who can educate me
- Exercise and diet to keep me healthy and vibrant
- Uninterrupted time to help my spouse or children or parents or siblings or significant other with their needs
- Time for de-stressing and refreshing myself

Be aware of what you can and cannot control. Consider these ...

Things you control	Things you can't control
Your career path	The economy, world events, interest rates, etc.
How you spend your time	Hours in a day
Choices of friends, contacts, risks	Layoffs, downsizing, etc.
What you eat and how you exercise	The aging process
Where you live and work	Weather, local economy, global competition

Some people attempt to separate their personal life from their professional life. It is an *illusion* that we can fulfill our career goals and our family goals at separate times during our lives. The reality is that balance and happiness are achieved by pursuing excellence for both career and family *simultaneously*. If you sacrifice your career objectives to satisfy your family objectives, you will not achieve balanced. If you focus on your career at the expense of your family, you will not achieve balance. The harsh reality is that you have to design a career plan carefully to be certain that it permits you to have enough time for your family responsibilities.

Involve Your Loved Ones in Decisions

Allow me to save you a great deal of frustration and wasted effort. You cannot create balance alone or in a vacuum. When you involve your significant others at home and at work in designing and refining your work-family balance plan, you will have greater success.

Here are 4 strategies to consider:

1. Involve all team or family members
2. Understand all team or family concerns
3. Be creative in the way you spend time with your spouse and kids
4. Make sure that both parents/partners have a chance to maintain balanced lives

In our household, we deal with these issues by frequently sitting down as a family and talking about the time we spend together and what each member needs. My kids are all in elementary school yet welcome the chance to be part of a team decision and actually take accountability for their actions. These processes sound so simple, yet most families do not engage in them.

I have had many surprises during these regular family conversations. Even my youngest daughter contributes! Schedule meetings with each other regularly to understand what all the different needs are. If you have a weekly meeting with your boss to make sure you're on the same page, why not with your own spouse, children or entire family unit? Without having some schedule and structure for family dialogue and activity, you may never get around to it.

When you are working ... work! When you decide to spend time with your family, enjoy it! Try not to combine the 2 where you are on an important business call while you are reading to your children or answering email during dinner. I don't know about you, but my kids are attuned to my presence and know when I am distracted and being disrespectful to our quality time together! Children are observant. Even if we are physically there, they can easily tell if we are not emotionally present. Don't cheat them out of their time with you!

Avoid Toxic Relationships

Another rule of mine is that 2 unbalanced parents or caretakers don't equal a balanced one. Nor can 1 balanced parent compensate for the imbalance of a spouse or partner. Some parents feel that because one of them can be at home and have dinner every night with the family while the other is at work full time, they have found the solution. There is no substitute for commitment to the family unit and uninterrupted, quality time with each member. Often, when one or both heads of the household are out of balance regarding happiness at work, problems can arise that can destroy the relationship or family.

This dissension can exist in any organization, even the company I founded. One of my very top associates, a person whom I trained and mentored and consider to be a confidante and friend, was truly passionate about her evolving career as a consultant and couldn't wait to share her good fortune and success stories with her spouse. She had adopted the 5P's (Passion-Purpose-Power-Profit-Peace of Mind) and was living her dream. Unfortunately for my associate and friend, her spouse was caught up in an unfulfilling career and was unwilling to do anything about it. It was easier for the spouse to complain and blame than to take positive action and alter this negative pattern.

Things got so bad that my associate and friend became increasingly reserved about sharing her excitement and began to almost feel guilty that she was so passionate about her career contribution, while her spouse was cynical and became resentful. It was tearing her apart emotionally before my very eyes. Finally, I had to counsel my friend that she had to confront the situation and make a choice as it was affecting her performance at work and overall attitude. She was becoming a different person!

Sadly, she was confronted with an "either/or" scenario as her spouse was unwilling to even consider a new strategy. Ultimately, she extricated herself from this unhealthy relationship and, while being single again was very painful and left her initially lonely, she has rebounded and found a new spouse who supports her and is genuinely happy for her success.

Sometimes beginning anew is the only option after all efforts have been expended. While I would never advocate divorce or ending a relationship over career matters, often a negative relationship where jealousy and resentment exist seemingly over career is symptomatic of a larger issue.

> *"Certain people are so negative ... if you put them in a dark room they would begin to develop!"*
> —Les Brown, *How To Remain Authentic*
> *(True to Ourselves)*

We can't possibly be superstars in everything. We are who we are. And we need to be satisfied with that. We must choose to balance those aspects that define who we are—to find and balance the unique combination of wants and needs that is authentically ourselves.

The greatest service we can do is to be true to ourselves by accepting that we can't be universally great and successful at everything. Don't try to be Rachel Ray in the kitchen, Tiger Woods on the golf course, Donald Trump in the boardroom, and Bill Gates in the wealth department. Be your best self. Here are 10 reasonable questions to ask at this stage:

1. Do you recognize what you are good at and what energizes you?
2. Do you fully utilize your most enjoyed skills?
3. Does your work further some interest or issue that you care deeply about?
4. Do you see yourself, through work, as making a difference in the world?
5. Do you view most days with a sense of enthusiasm?
6. Have you developed your own philosophy of life and success?
7. Are you taking the necessary risks to live your philosophy?
8. Do you feel a sense of meaning and purpose for your life?
9. Do you have active goals this year relating to that purpose?
10. Are you living your life to the fullest now instead of hoping that things will work out someday?

Understand that there are no shortcuts to building a life of substance. It is an ongoing process to become more than you already are. It is a worthy challenge. Now is the time to make a difference in your life and in the lives of others. Find your unique and compelling contribution! Don't simply read these words, place this book on a shelf and resume your old habits. That would be a waste, because nothing much in your life will change. And if you have taken the time to read this far, you obviously want to improve some things in your life. Many people have turned their lives into wonderful success stories simply because they decided to change.

Achieving balance is not easy to do, but when you seek a better quality of life, your life will be so much better … awkward at first, no doubt, but in the end it's worth it.

The evidence shows in the lives of people all around us. People get involved in infidelity, addictions, obsessions, compulsions, poor lifestyles or physical habits, poor communication and relationship skills, marital problems, money mismanagement, and fraud. Many people say that these things are causing imbalance in their lives. But many of the dysfunctional elements of people's lives are the symptoms, not the causes. The way to deal with disruption is through prevention; don't let your life get out of balance.

Success Is a Personal Concept

"I thought I was going to make crazy cartoons for the rest of my life. I didn't think I'd ever get paid for it, didn't think I drew well enough, but I knew it made me happy."
— Matt Groening, creator of *The Simpsons*

If we can agree that success is a function of balance, the next action we should take is to define success. Clearly, the concept of success will vary from person to person. As a starting point, Webster's dictionary defines success as *"favorable or desired outcome; also: the attainment of wealth, favor, or fame."*

In my seminars or personal coaching sessions, I often begin by asking the following 2 questions.

1. What is your personal definition of success?
2. What is your ultimate goal?

As examples, you may initially say:

- To make a difference ·
- Lose weight
- Raise great kids
- Finish my degree or go back to school
- Quit smoking
- Become a world traveler
- Buy a retirement home in a warm climate
- Win a beauty pageant
- Earn a billion dollars
- Retire at 50 years of age

All of these are reasonable, common responses. There is, however, one common element behind every goal or measure of personal or professional success, one driving force ... *the desire for happiness. You don't actually crave the accomplishment; you crave the feelings and emotions associated with the accomplishment!* Due to personal choice or societal conditioning, you may have chosen to link your perception of happiness to that particular accomplishment. Who told you Mercedes is the most prestigious car? Rolex is the watch to have? Armani is the suit to wear or a polo pony logo on your shirt means you have arrived? It is called "marketing" and advertisers spend billions to get you to associate success with their product or service. And guess what? It works! When you purchase or wear a trendy item, you feel like you have arrived, you are worthy.

I cannot say I do not pay attention to brands and labels, because I do, but I view them more for their practicality than for the prestige or status. Balance provides a consistent sense of pleasure in your life and you deserve it! *The principles in this book are about directing your mind to avoid or at least limit outside influences and societal conditioning to make you internally happy.*

As trite as it sounds, I want you to be "happy from the inside out and not from the outside in." Experiencing happiness on a more consistent basis based on your internal value system and not by an advertiser's created impression of success is the key. Stop buying into the false idea and misperception that some external influence will make you truly happy. Happiness cannot be bought; it's a feeling. Remember *The Grinch Who Stole Christmas*? At the end he attains a heightened sense of awareness and proclaims, "Maybe Christmas *doesn't* come from a store. Maybe Christmas … perhaps … means a little bit more." We all have a natural state of happiness that needs rekindling.

Why do millions abuse alcohol, drugs or food, gamble their hard earned money away or watch excessive television? Although the answers represent a complex set of individual circumstances, the practical reason is their desperate, conditioned attempt to seek happiness and they associate comfort to these activities or more likely, escape inner pain by numbing their senses with an external agent. Can you name the #1 retail-selling product in America with over $100 billion annual sales? Answer: cocaine. We now know that modifying your state of mind through drugs or alcohol is a short-term fix, and never lasts. Unfortunately, far too many people have not mastered their internal belief systems and constantly seek a quick, external escape to obtain happiness.

For example, people who are unhappy in their relationship often think, *let me divorce and find a new person who can make me happy.* They observe how in the beginning of a fresh, new relationship things are great (infatuation phase) until the reality of life pressures or having the confidence to show your vulnerability and shortcomings sets in. Careers are the same way. A new role seems great until you get bored with the tasks, commute, people or pay. The grass is not greener over there; the grass is only greener where you water it!

The answer lies in the message to stop trying to live up to the public's expectations and form one's own standards. By doing so, they would be less stressed, more content and less apt to turn to mood altering activities. To become truly unhappy, you actually have to distort your own reality. Happiness is a natural state of mind. If you don't believe me, go the hospital and observe the behavior of a newborn. I have been blessed with 3 beautiful children who, unless they were hungry or needed to be changed, would smile, giggle and laugh for hours for no apparent reason. Relatives and friends would come over just to observe the pure joy that a new human being has upon entering our world. It is only after societal conditioning that we learn hate, prejudice, jealousy, resentment and other unfounded fears and insecurities. These are learned behaviors.

I once conducted a seminar in inner city Miami where there was extreme tension between several groups required to work together. To reach my audience and effect significant change, I knew I needed a powerful message that every attendee could relate to equally. I walked on the stage that day with a cooing 6-month-old baby swaddled in a blanket and asked the audience by a show of hands how many thought that the baby was born with prejudice, hostility and resentment towards its fellow man. No hands were raised. We concluded as a team that each member had adopted these belief systems by choice or choice of habit and that it was not a natural instinct to harbor ill will towards others who had different opinions. Anger, resentment and hatred are conditioned traits; we are not born that way. We ended the coaching session with an understanding that each of us controls our emotions and to be careful as to how perceptions are formed.

The simplest way to change your attitude is as follows. Start with your own physiology. You have 80 muscles in your face; use them! Smile and you will feel better! Don't allow your mind to focus on negative thoughts; control your mind and do not let it control you! If your mind is undisciplined due to cultural influences like TV, school, or the media, you can fall prey to negative conditioning and become unhappy. Control your focus by asking effective and empowering questions.

Understand that your brain is wired to seek pleasure and avoid pain; it's a survival instinct we all possess. Don't rush to judgment. When I was younger and inexperienced, I used to believe happiness and success represented money. Then as I grew older, I began to focus on the value of my contribution. Now I realize it is a state that I can control. By choosing to consciously associate with happy people, I am creating pleasure and eliminating pain. Claim your ultimate power!

Top 5 Rewards Exercise

One of the exercises in my seminars or personal coaching sessions is to ask attendees to identify their 5 top rewards of achieving life balance and greater success. You may be surprised to hear that the following answers invariably make the list.

1. Respect of parents
2. Respect from spouse or children
3. Respect of peers or colleagues
4. Making a difference in others' lives
5. Never having to worry about money

Stop reading and consider your top 5 rewards?

3 Key Success Questions

Success is not a material possession, but the feelings and emotions that come from a consistent increase in the quality of your life. Anyone can have a single great game or day, but consistently achieving and increasing value is true success.

There are 3 key questions you should ask yourself every day:

1. Are you consistently increasing the quality of your life in the 5 critical areas?
2. Are you shaping your environment or is your environment shaping you?
3. Are you developing greater passion, material possessions, courage and wealth?

Consistent actions will improve the quality of your life; those actions are dictated by decisions, which are dictated by your standards and beliefs.

Why "Progress" Is the True Measure of Success

> *"If I am through learning ... I am through earning!"*
> —Chris Kuselias

Not only must you identify and document your progress toward achievement of your objectives, but you must also raise your standards with regard to your own expectations. When people in the media ask me to describe a defining moment in my life that helped shape my path to a successful, ful-filled lifestyle, I share the following answer: *When I made the firm decision to consistently raise my expectations and hold myself accountable to a higher standard than my circle of friends and acquaintances.* It was not a decision designed to obtain material possessions or social status, but rather one that was essential towards helping me obtain my calling and realize my true passion and purpose.

Every great performer (scientist, athlete, actor, doctor, researcher, con-sultant, teacher, entrepreneur, social worker, insurance salesperson, cus-tomer service rep, banker, lawyer, maintenance worker, etc.) consciously or unconsciously adopts the philosophy of out-working, out-thinking, and out-innovating their peers. Their standards are simply higher, and medioc-rity is not tolerated. Here are 5 steps to ensuring constant and never ending improvement:

1. Identify what you truly want and don't want
2. Set high standards regardless of your position, title or field
3. Document your sincere desires in writing
4. Adopt a belief system with a strong enough why behind each desire
5. If you do, one day you will look up and notice you are exactly where you wanted to be, but by that time you will have estab-lished new objectives as progressive people always do.

> ... Remember, if you set a goal to travel to the place as far as your eye can see, when you get there, you can always see farther!

Genius is in the details; little things count. Progress needs to be in small incremental shifts, not huge advancements. Consider these examples:

- Finances: Consider the power of compounding.
- Relationship: One big dinner and night on the town doesn't fix a damaged or neglected relationship, rather everyday sacrifices and contributions build a consistent foundation. Set a goal to out serve your spouse, record on paper how you are achieving this goal, understand how and why this will benefit your family, and watch it happen!
- Fitness: One mega exercise per day won't work; it will only serve to reinforce how much it hurts and your fitness level will remain stagnant. Set your goal, determine why you want to be in shape (longevity, endurance, vanity), start with a walk around the block

THE CAREER GUARANTEE

and build until it leads to running a marathon, if you have that desire. Establish a consistent rise in your cardiovascular fitness and muscle tone and you will achieve your fitness goals!

I want you to take inventory of where you are in each of the 5 areas (career, financial, health & fitness, key relationships, spiritual enlightenment) and then take decisive action toward your destination. Commit to constant improvement in all 5 areas. Create affirmations like this one ... *I will be balanced, accumulate wealth, have a passionate relationship, find a challenging, contributing career.* When you are growing in each area you will be happy; if you are not growing and learning you become complacent, bored and unhappy. Achieve to be happy!

The better you feel about yourself, the more inspiring you will be to others and the greater the contribution you will make. That's when life explodes! When you become a positive role model to kids, friends, and employees, because you have balance, you are like a magnet to those around you.

Success Tip

Great coaches and business managers don't talk about outcomes or winning, they focus on improvement and know by doing so, winning is certain to follow!

How Do You Know If You Are Progressing?: 3 Key Questions

Every day, I ask myself 3 important questions:

1. What did I learn today?
2. What have I improved or contributed?
3. What have I enjoyed?

Each day, constantly improve the overall quality of your life in all 5 critical areas (Career, financial, health and fitness, relationships and spirituality) and you will leave a legacy and enjoy a meaningful existence.

- Your life is not a function of world events, but of your reality, which is what you choose to focus on
- If you wish to change your reality, change your focus (avoid negative news, gossip, excessive TV)
- If you want to change focus, ask yourself new questions, adopt positive self-talk to condition your mind to seek positives.

Thinking is a summary of the questions you ask yourself every day.

Success Tip

Commit to recognizing a steady progression toward your calling and you will soon realize you are living the life that you previously thought was unattainable!

How Will You Know When You Are Successful?

The other reflection you need to focus on is how you know you are moving closer to your calling. In other words, how do you know when you are successful? It continually amazes me how in my seminars I can ask 20 different people to "define career success" and get 20 totally unique answers. Try these:

- Become a millionaire
- Attain a specific title
- Flexibility in my work
- Security
- Creativity
- Recognition
- Early retirement

As you can see, some people judge career success by a dollar amount, some by values and others by title or responsibility. What is important is how YOU define success, so let's find out!

What Is Your Definition of Success?

The secret of success is getting ahead ... but not a big one!

As stated earlier, success is defined by Webster's dictionary as "A favorable result or the gaining of wealth, fame, etc." I define career success as "The ability to choose a job that you like to do, and to be finally, emotionally and spiritually rewarded for doing a good job at it!"

What Is Your Definition of Career Success?

"Life is never stagnant. If you are not moving forward you are falling behind."

—Chris Kuselias

SHOW ME THE MONEY ... Mastering Money Mindset

Did you hear about the umbrella salesman who saved his money for a sunny day?

Let's talk now about raising your financial standards. Have you ever really stopped to consider how much you are really worth? I do not mean what they could sell your physical body parts for (that's kind of gross ...) but rather what your *intellectual property* is worth.

The chart below will assist you to quantify this question, but my point is to be conscious of engaging in any activity that reduces your hourly value. Stop wasting time browsing through pointless email, engaging in non-sensible telephone conversations or working in a job that limits your growth and the full utilization of your talents.

How Much Are You Worth?

Your Income	Income Per Hour	Your Income	Income Per Hour
$30,000	$15	$120,000	$60
$40,000	$20	$130,000	$65
$50,000	$25	$140,000	$70
$60,000	$30	$150,000	$75
$70,000	$35	$160,000	$80
$80,000	$40	$170,000	$85
$90,000	$45	$180,000	$90
$100,000	$50	$190,000	$95
$110,000	$55	$200,000	$100

Like all the other concepts covered in this book, creating and maintaining a strong financial position begins and ends with your mindset. Money is a natural by-product of career success. Individuals who pursue their passion find their purpose and realize the true power of working in a career that they absolutely love; such individuals work smarter, harder and more efficiently because it is a labor of love. As a result, these select few put in the extra hours, conduct the extra research and are rewarded more handsomely than a person who shows up, punches a time clock and leaves.

Following the principles contained in this book and subscribing to the master formula introduced earlier (passion, purpose, power, profit and peace of mind) inevitably leads to this sequential order of accomplishment. This means that each step is important and leads to the next step. I want to spend some time on the 4th P, *Profit*, as it has a profound effect on your happiness and often derails great intentions for reasons that may seem incredible.

Let us begin with the premise that if you aggressively pursue your calling, build your knowledge and obtain the reputation as an industry expert, *you will inevitably earn more compensation*. I want to teach you to anticipate and expect this reward and to make certain you do not sabotage your own success because you never had money before or have been conditioned to think that making lots of money is a bad thing.

> The late Coco Chanel, a pioneer in the fashion industry, once said, "Some people think luxury is the opposite of poverty. It is not. It is the opposite of vulgarity."

How is it possible that people establish a negative belief system about money? Consider these common phrases:

- Money is the root of all evil
- You can't buy happiness
- You have to have money to make money
- Money does not grow on trees

We all know of a person who seems to have acquired a lot of money by fooling others or providing questionable service, but these people are the exceptions. More likely, people who attain a high degree of wealth and prosperity do so through hard work, sacrifice and by discovering their unique and compelling skills and then providing a substantial contribution to others. You will ultimately get rewarded for your level of service and expertise.

Certainly, we have all experienced a phase in our life when we were under appreciated or underpaid, but trust me, this is a temporary scenario. Your talents will ultimately be recognized and rewarded if you exceed expectations and become a recognized expert in your field or industry. (This is what I mean by the power in the 5P's). The problem is that many folks feel they deserve more compensation simply because of tenure. In the 21st century workplace, reward is not about tenure, but rather about a commitment to constantly improving one's value and contribution. Being able to document this value with specific examples is a must!

Success Tip

If you want to earn more money, figure out a way to make a greater contribution!

It seems like a lot of people have spent a lot of time creating negative publicity and fancy sayings to discourage those who have a desire for success and who then reap the rewards of contributing to such a large extent that their compensation rewards them handsomely. Nonsense! If used ethically and productively, money and compensation is a wonderful result and measure of recognition of a life dedicated to service and contribution. Money funds education, starts non-profit organizations, builds schools and roads, provides medical care when insurance will not and many other worthwhile causes.

The Scary Truth about Spending and Saving

With so much emphasis on the almighty dollar and so many Americans apparently working for the money, it would seem that U.S. families must be basking in the glow of financial independence and prosperity, right? WRONG! Here are the latest troubling statistics concerning the average household:

- 107 million households are overly indebted
- 52% of employees live paycheck to paycheck
- 20% of 401(k) participants have loans outstanding (they are borrowing on their retirement monies!)
- 10 million households are financially distressed
- 8 million consumers declared personal bankruptcy in the past 6 years

Not only are the majority of Americans working for the pursuit of money and missing the incredible joy and happiness associated with having a job with passion and purpose, but they are spending more than they have and jeopardizing their future way of life by tapping into the funds that will support their golden years! If this is you, my advice is to immediately take charge of your career and earning power and desist from using your 401(k) or retirement money to keep up with the Joneses. You will regret it if you exhaust your retirement funds. Ask any of the elderly folks you see waiting on tables in a fast food restaurant, not because they choose to, but rather because they have to! Don't be forced to spend your golden years at the golden arches because of poor planning!

Limiting Beliefs About Your Money

Thomas J. Stanley, Ph.D. who wrote the #1 New York Times Best-Seller *The Millionaire Next Door* states, "Extraordinary levels of economic productivity can be accomplished by searching for and finding the vocation that evokes and conjures up emotional energy."

The message is this: If you truly want to make more money, you need to spend your time in a career that stimulates your passion and energy. Every great performer interviewed on the secret to abundance consistently shares a passion and emotional investment in the day to day activities leading to expansion.

My question for you: *What person or persons in your life have had the greatest impact on your view of money and wealth attainment?* One of my clients was restricting his own progress because he had adopted the limiting belief that if he became wealthy it would be at the expense of someone else. He had adopted his parents "old school" belief system that one could only become affluent and well off by exploiting poor people or those less fortunate. He possessed an inner voice that cautioned him to do well, but only to the extent that it would not cause his parents to become critical of his wealth. He was, in essence, sabotaging his own career calling by only progressing so far before pulling back on his career accelerator. This may sound ridiculous, but we all possess these internal "associations" which often come from our parents, teachers, friends, or former bosses.

Consider my personal circumstances. For me, this concept of making money and having limiting beliefs about wealth accumulation tested my own values. My father worked for over 40 years in corporate America with the same employer as an Advertising Manager. He was highly successful and provided a better than average lifestyle for his wife and 5 children. As a kid growing up, I aspired to equal his achievements; he was my hero in many ways.

Can you imagine my own shock when I realized that I was holding myself back? Why? Because subconsciously I did not want to make my wonderful father feel inferior if I achieved greater prosperity. Foolishly, I felt it would hurt his feelings. My dad always wanted his children to learn from him and go on to achieve great things. He put us through school and pushed us to take risks. For some reason, I felt incredibly guilty driving a nicer car, having a larger house or traveling to more exotic locations on vacation. I also found myself not wanting to "out do" my siblings and needed to rid myself of the limiting belief that I would somehow become less close to them if I did exceedingly well. The problem was mine. So how did I cure myself of this internal conflict?

I began by writing down my limiting beliefs. Simply seeing the words on the page made me feel stupid and opened my eyes. Of course my family was rooting for me. As it turns out, I was the one who had the problem! I began to formulate an internal defense to this limiting belief that somehow my success would alienate me from my family and in some weird way, make my father feel less significant. I worked hard to change my association regarding the acquisition of money and the effect it would have on my family relationships. Instead of needlessly worrying about criticism or envy, I envisioned their appreciation for my hard work and took pride in discussing the people I was helping. I also was cautious of preaching my concepts to family members and had to remind myself that they were the people I should help the most, as they were the people I loved the most!

I began to recite affirmations that my values and success were a function and result of my upbringing and that my family was genuinely proud of my accomplishments. My curiosity regarding what made people happy and content came from a positive family environment and desire for others to share in this wonderful experience. My father remains one of my biggest fans and support systems. I am so proud to have confronted and mastered this limiting belief about money and my family, as opposed to letting it control or limit my progress and happiness. Do you possess a limiting belief about money?

Strategies for Earning and Deserving Wealth

> *"In order to become financially well off, you must 1*st *decide to be wealthy and 2*nd *condition your internal belief system to have positive associations to being wealthy."*
> —Chris Kuselias

I take money very seriously and advise you to do the same. It was money that provided my education, funded my research, and now enables me to share my knowledge with millions of people by starting one of the most successful wellness businesses in America, which, among other accomplishments, has successfully employed over 10,000 former welfare recipients. The money also allows my family to make a significant contribution to our church and has made it possible for, my father to experience a radical cancer treatment in another country (not funded by his insurance) which ultimately saved his life.

It is also money that will fund my retirement and allow my family to pursue their individual callings and hopefully leave their positive mark on society. The list is endless. Money provides opportunity. While this is not a book about financial planning or achieving financial independence, I would like to share a few of my beliefs about wealth.

To begin, from this day forward, I want you to commit to understanding how much you have, how much you owe and how much you need to save in the event of a crisis. Briefly, there are 5 important money areas to consider:

Improve Your Financial Literacy   Seek out quality mentors who can educate you on cash, investing and retirement strategies. Today, easy to use software programs make the process easier than ever.

Determine Your Net Worth   Net worth is what you have after all debt and expenses are paid. Strive to build a positive value and never return to debt status.

Analyze Your Spending Habits   I suggest keeping a journal of everything you spend over a 3-month period (one quarter) and analyzing areas you can reduce spending.

Create a Retirement Plan   As one of my good friends says, "Don't spend your golden years working for the golden arches (McDonald's)" unless, of course, you want to! Learn the value of compound interest. As Einstein said, "Compound interest is the 8th natural wonder of the world and the most powerful thing I have ever encountered."

Pay Yourself First   Commit to saving a minimum of 15% of your income

Compensation Follows Contribution

Success Tip

Determine the measurable gap between where you are right now and where you desire to be.

Successful individuals are constantly taking actions to improve the chances that they will attain their designated objectives. They know that their outcomes and results will determine their rewards in life. You get recognized and paid by your contribution. If you wish to improve your rewards, simply formulate a plan to improve your contribution to your customers, coworkers or supervisors in a manner that they can clearly see the value you bring.

If you remain stagnant and do not continually improve your skills (language, computer, managerial, organizational) and subsequent contributions (revenue, customer satisfaction, service) your value will decline.

Remember, if you are not moving forward, you are falling behind! We never remain stagnant. If you are suffering from job insecurity, it is most likely because your employer cannot quantify your value or contribution to the mission. Study your contribution, each and every day!

Make More or Spend Less?

If you really think about it, there are only 2 definitive ways to accumulate more money. The 1st is to analyze your spending habits, find areas where you can reduce and spend less money. The 2nd is to figure out a way to make more of it.

> *"There are 2 kinds of people ... those who adjust their lifestyle to their income level and those who adjust their income level to their lifestyle."*
>
> —Chris Kuselias

Personally, I subscribe to the "make more" philosophy. To make more money, all you need to do is follow the formula described in this book. The 5P's identified earlier are the key to earning more money and loving what you do for a living. To review these:

Explore Your *Passion* I am a believer in pursuing your passion and linking these emotions and rewards to an occupation where you can experience these positive energizers as often as possible.

Find Your *Purpose* Passion at work leads to an understanding of why you are here. Your contributions are the basis of your purpose.

Develop Your *Power* Because of the energy and enthusiasm expended in a pursuit that you love, you no doubt will become a recognized leader in your chosen field or endeavor. That is where you accumulate your power; others will seek you out for inspiration and knowledge. The fact is that it is hard not to be great at something that you love to do and commit significant time to.

Profit Inevitably Follows   Because only about 10%–20% of people are truly passionate about what they do for a living, it is easy to identify them. As my grandma used to say, "They stick out like a sore thumb." If you are engaged in a career pursuit built on passion and purpose, your income will rise in accordance with your increase in value. If you want to make more money, simply decide how to increase your value. Most people never understand or apply this basic formula.

Peace of Mind Is the Ultimate Result   The gift of knowing you mattered and made a difference to others through your unique and compelling gifts and skills is what truly validates your being.

Pay raises or promotions are not an entitlement in the 21st century workplace. More income and the benefits associated with the acquisition of more money are reserved for those who create a game plan for increasing their value in the marketplace. To sustain a positive flow of healthy income, you must agree to and abide by the philosophy to continually increase your skills, value and contribution.

While going back to school or obtaining the appropriate certifications are valuable and sometimes essential, do not make the common mistake of trying to be absolutely perfect (or obtain the ultimate certificate) before deciding to pursue your passion and earn what you are entitled to. There is no perfect scenario! Sometimes the best plan is to simply start moving and gain momentum.

For a time, I procrastinated on writing this book. I wanted to find the right publisher, the best agent, the free time needed to create the text, and other associates to whom I could allocate some of my responsibilities so I could conduct the proper research. Finally, I decided that all of those issues were masked excuses. I just had to sit at my computer and start typing. From there the project took shape. The message: Get started now!

3 Steps to Making More Money!

Success Tip

To increase your income ... simply increase your value.

If you are truly committed to making more money, begin the process by determining exactly how much you want to earn. You will learn to apply the awesome power of *affirmations* (projecting in your mind what you seek to have, become or do before you actually attain it) and how your *reticular activating system* (the part of your brain that helps you focus on priority commands) can highlight opportunities for massive income.

To initiate the process of making more money, let me share 3 steps you need to take.

Step 1 How much do you want or need to make?

For starters, here is a simple but unbelievably complex question: How much money do you want and how much do you need to be wealthy? Said in simpler terms: How much is enough? I would be willing to bet that those of you who have an indefinite response to this question or answer with a generic statement like, "enough to be comfortable," have not attained wealth to this point in your life. I will also make the bold prediction that if you do not change this philosophy, you *will never achieve financial independence!*

This may sound harsh, but the truth is that unless you have a definitive goal for how much you want to earn and how you will go about acquiring this wealth, you are merely describing a prayer that lacks any foundation to even remotely become true. Wealthy people don't hope for money, pray for money, wait for a winning lottery ticket or count on their rich Aunt to die and leave them a substantial inheritance. Instead, wealthy people begin with a plan for how they can make a significant contribution that will be generously rewarded.

By now, it should not surprise you that I am forcing you to speak in terms of specifics as opposed to generalities. Specifics create plans and plans foster action. Actions produce results. If it is financial reward you seek, you must be clear on *exactly* how much you intend to make it.

To this point in your career, you have produced a certain financial return on your contributions. I suspect this result is not acceptable. It is my objective to teach you how to increase this amount by providing you with the inspiration and techniques required to make positive changes in how you derive compensation from contribution.

Your challenge will be to create a career path that takes you from where you are today to where you feel you will have realized your passion and purpose. By doing so, you will acquire power and, by extension, profit. Ultimately, this will produce peace of mind and a sense of contentment associated with knowing you have validated your existence.

To illustrate the degree and detail of clarity you need, I want you to answer the following;

My current net worth is _____

My current level of debt is _____

To become debt free, I must _____

My current income is _____

My target date to achieve my career calling is _____

My desired income is _____

I will save 15% of this annually, which equals _____

Step 2   Ask yourself: How can I increase my current value or level of service?

Said another way: What product, service or contribution can I make that my current employer, industry or customers want and need?

While the purpose of this book is not to detail every available strategy for increasing your level of service, I do have a few helpful hints. First, always be on the look-out for new and better ways to solve problems, especially those faced by customers in the industry you are most passionate about. If you aspire to earn more, identify what I call "vacant needs," meaning areas where a need is not being fully met. You must then use your passion to formulate a solution to this vacancy. Doing so will often make you wealthy beyond your wildest dreams.

> *"I never perfected an invention that I did not think about in terms of the service it might give others ... I find out what the world needs, and then I proceed to invent."*
> —Thomas Edison

Have you ever had a great idea for a new product or service? I think we all have at one time or another. Most times, this brainstorming occurs because we perceived a need or were frustrated because this new idea, product or solution would improve the quality of our own lives if it existed. Did you ever walk into a store and see "your great idea" on the shelf? I have! The fact is that every great invention you can name was created because some enterprising person identified an opportunity and invested the mental and emotional energy to create a solution. That is how inventions like

Tivo, Google, automatic car starters, Hooked on Phonics, polio vaccines, the idea of a mutual fund and any other innovation you can name or benefit from got started. Somebody stopped daydreaming about an idea and took action!

eBay, currently the world's largest online auction service, was invented by a man named Pierre Omidyar, who originally sought an easier way for his then fiancée to distribute and trade Pez candy dispensers! Talk about identifying a need, seizing an opportunity and taking action! I am certain that Mr. Omidyar incorporated the suggestions of several mentors to help his vision become a reality, and you can do the same. You must learn to look for opportunities; they are everywhere!

To increase your momentum with regard to seeing opportunities, begin by becoming a student of your industry. The more you know about how the processes work in your area of interest, the faster you will be able to identify missing links or opportunities for enhancement. It is the ability to identify and provide these enhancements that makes people rich! Mentors are essential because most of us are not trained inventors and are unsure as to how to bring a great idea to practical application. That is where a good coach or advisor can assist you in the process.

What issues ignite your inner flame? Where is a need in your current industry or field that you can adopt as a project? If your plan is to leave your current field because you lack passion for it anymore, where is a need in your next career that requires your time, effort and energy to solve? Train your mind to be solutions oriented and you will see results!

Step 3   Determine: What is the best *distribution channel* for my value?

By distribution channel, I mean best industry, best employer, best department, or position that will afford you the chance to demonstrate your unique value in an acceptable time frame. Ask yourself this critical question: Can I provide this newfound contribution (product, service or ideas) in my current capacity or do I need to change companies, industries or start my own venture? One of the most challenging aspects of the process is to find an outlet for your vision or solution.

Many people start by presenting their ideas to their current employer or by volunteering or even originating an internal task force to study a problem area. Most companies encourage this practice as they seek people who look to protect the company's interests. Do not be so paranoid about someone else stealing your great idea; document your concepts and you will be fine. If you enjoy your current field but are a little burned out or bored, create a buzz by seeking a new solution to better the company. At the very least, you alert your employer to the fact that you are an *intrapreneur* and someone who takes their role and the company seriously.

Other suggestions include volunteering in a new field or industry or joining one of the many entrepreneurial groups, non profits, charitable foundations (of which there are currently over 18,000) to brainstorm on your next big idea or solution. One thing is certain: You simply cannot be stagnant, or you will most assuredly realize the same or less progress.

If you feel the need to start your own venture, I caution you that owning and managing a business takes more than just a great idea. Take it from someone who has started several ventures, including *Career* T.E.A.M., LLC, which was recognized by *Inc. Magazine* in 2001 as one of the fastest growing, privately held business' in America.

While I encourage you to pursue an outlet for your passion and purpose, I strongly advise you to act prudently and cautiously before deciding to leave a promising career or investing your hard earned money in a start-up enterprise.

Who Are the Millionaires?

"Anyone who thinks $5 million is enough is not the kind of person to earn $5 million in the 1st place."

—Warren Avis

Millionaires rarely work for the money; more likely they have found something that sparks their interest. Bill Gates, Donald Trump and Oprah could quit tomorrow and not have to worry about money. They continue working because they love it! It feeds their minds and fulfills their passions. Most of all, they are contributing to others. Sure they have egos, some larger than others, but make no mistake, these people are dedicated to their craft and committed to excellence.

If you seek to be rich and enjoy the many benefits of an abundant lifestyle, be advised, that the greatest number of millionaires can be found under the category of entrepreneurs. Most millionaires are people like you and I who invest the time and energy to understand their passion and purpose and figure out where they can make the greatest contribution to others. While celebrities and their rich and famous lifestyles dominate the news, the real secret is that less publicized passion seekers dominate the list of wealthy families. Millionaires are plumbers, real estate investors, franchise owners, dry cleaners, carpet cleaners, trainers, driveway sealers, computer repair experts, pet store owners and small manufacturing players.

For your consideration, here is a chart of how millionaires earned this distinction.

Who Are the Millionaires?

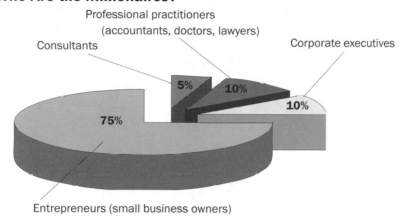

Professional practitioners (accountants, doctors, lawyers)

Consultants

Corporate executives

5%

10%

10%

75%

Entrepreneurs (small business owners)

Choosing a Financial Expert

Given a choice between having their gums scraped at the dentist with a dull knife or mastering financial planning, many career seekers would opt for the dentist chair. Effective financial planning is a complex challenge that involves expense control, cash management, investments, retirement planning, estate planning and knowledge of taxation issues. The key is to find a professional (certified financial planner) who understands your needs, wants and values. Like any occupation, there are professionals and then there are hackers. When it comes to your hard earned money, you cannot afford to put your trust in anything but a qualified, reputable professional. Here are my suggestions:

- Try to obtain a referral from a person whom you know and trust, someone who has significant experience with finances and shares your asset level and risk tolerance for money.
- If you do not know a good contact, contact the Financial Planning Association (www.fpanet.org) and obtain a minimum of 3 referrals in your local area.

- After you obtain a referral, conduct a thorough background check to include: certifications and credentials, references, products and services offered and how they charge for their services. Also, conduct your own personal interview to make sure the investment advisor shares your ethics, values and vision. Avoid any financial planner who tries to gain your business by promising unrealistic returns. If it sounds too good to be true, it usually is!
- Remember, while a good certified financial planner can be extremely helpful, it is still your money and responsibility to ensure it is managed, protected and growing at a rate you are comfortable with. Do not relinquish your power; it is your money, and a CFP is only there to help coach you along the way.

Next up, let's set our goals!

CHAPTER 4

People *without* Goals
Work for People *with* Goals!

KEY QUESTION: WHERE AM I GOING?

In this chapter, you will learn:

KEY TOPICS

- Goal Setting Is Essential to Living the Dream
- Effectively Forecasting Your Future
- 10 Keys To Effective Goal Setting
- Establishing a Clear and Definite Focus

KEY MESSAGES

- A definite, well thought out career plan will stimulate and motivate your internal potential to succeed.
- 3 types of goals: short-term (up to one year); medium-term (1–5 years); long-term (5+ years).
- Professionals do not leave career success to chance; plan your life and makes things happen!
- Goal setting will ensure you are experiencing constant and never ending improvement.
- Quantify the benefits (for example, more money, recognition, creativity) you will gain by obtaining your career calling compared to the downside to remaining in your current function (is it powerful enough to make you take action now?).
- The more specific your career goal the greater the chance you have to achieve it;
- Hope without a plan is not a strategy!
- Every morning, recite your personal and career goals out loud. By doing so, you will succeed in embedding your career objectives into your subconscious mind.
- The decision to pursue, the strategy, the actions taken, the dedication to achieve, and the acceptance of a new career offer all reside in your personal control!

A wise man once said that those who do not have goals wind up working for someone who does.

Goal Setting Is Essential to Living the Dream

> *One day Alice came to a fork in the road and saw a Cheshire*
> *cat in a tree. "Which road do I take?" she asked. His response*
> *was a question: "Where do you want to go?" "I don't know,"*
> *Alice answered. "Then," said the cat, "it doesn't matter."*
> —Lewis Carroll, *Alice in Wonderland*

All Goals Must Revolve Around Your *Purpose*

THE ABOVE IS ONE of my favorite quotations because the message is so profound. How can any of us possibly expect to find genuine career happiness fueled by passion, purpose, power, profit and peace of mind (the 5P's) if we are clueless with regard to our ultimate objectives?

If you do not have a plan to help you determine what you really want from your profession and cannot find or are unwilling to devote the necessary time to the process of uncovering what you truly value, you will most likely be destined to a life of regret and wasted talents.

© 2009 Learned

"This next little exercise I like to call goal-setting!"

Without a plan, you are relying on hope, and hope is not a strategy. When planning your career, it is important to look at the process in 3 stages: past, present and future. How did you get to this point, where are you now in the process and where do you want to be?

Most likely, you will not transition from your current occupation directly into your ideal career calling. There will inevitably be a progression of well planned roles leading up to the culmination of your experience and education. Some call this a *career ladder* because with each rung of the climb you are ascending closer to the top. While there may be a series of job changes, internships, volunteer work, part time jobs, or continued education in some form, your ultimate destination needs to be defined.

The process of attaining your ideal career calling begins with the establishment of your passion and purpose. Passion and purpose are how we serve others. Once defined, you then will create your required steps to success, called *interim goals*. All of your goals should be established around your purpose, which requires critical reflection. Your purpose will not magically invade your body or fall from the sky. It must come from an exploration of what makes you unique and compelling as a human being and how you can best serve others through your talents.

Be certain to create your career plans from critical reflection (self-awareness) and not from guilt, boredom or panic. For example, many people after a holiday season of indulgence and overeating look in the mirror at an unflattering image of themselves and set a New Year's resolution to lose weight. After 2 or 3 days of punishing themselves during an internal struggle to consume fewer calories, they regress to established habits of snacking, 2nd or 3rd helpings, or desserts every night.

There are several potential reasons for this behavior (belief systems, identity, comfort level, habit, positive or negative associations to food) but all point to one missing ingredient: if there is not a clearly defined purpose or strong enough *why*, people revert to their established comfort zone. Find a compelling reason to achieve your goal and you have a chance; without a strong enough *why*, you will fail.

Measure your career and life like a one-time opportunity and act as if there are no 2nd chances because, in reality, there are not. There are no dress rehearsals or do-overs. Enjoy each successful experience and sensation in your development, no matter how small or insignificant.

Often, life presents us with unexpected and wonderful possibilities, which are not initially apparent. Seek the hidden treasures in a chance encounter, a follow up email to an author who moved you, a unique opportunity to voice a new idea in your next staff meeting, or a conference where you could be inspired or meet your next new partner.

Effectively Forecasting Your Future

"Give me a stock clerk with a goal and I will give you a man who will make history. Give me a man with no goals, and I will give you a stock clerk."

—J.C. Penney, founder

S CIENCE HAS TAUGHT US that the human mind is a performance based organ. This means that whatever command you send to your subconscious mind, it will focus 24 hours per day to attain. The more specific the request, the better results you will achieve. *How much* and *by when* are 2 essential aspects to any command you send to your subconscious mind. "I think I would like a career in health care" is not as powerful or effective as, "I will be a licensed practical nurse at Yale New Haven Hospital working the 2nd shift earning $45,000 annually by January 1, of next year."

One client of mine purchased a graduation ring from the law school he wanted to graduate from the day he was admitted to their evening program. Because he was working a full time day job and going to law school at night, he needed every incentive possible to ensure he completed his studies. He wore the ring every day and kept the ring on his night stand as a visual reminder of his dream and looked at the ring every night before bed; just so he would not quit school and would stay focused on his desired outcome.

When I decided to author this book, the first thing I did was design the book cover and locate it in front of my desk so I would imbed the goal into my subconscious mind to help create this work. Whether you seek to create a revolutionary exercise program, design an innovative website, become president of your class, start a new non- profit organization, host a television show or climb Mt. Everest, I suggest you adopt the same practice.

Success Tip

I require my clients and leadership group (the highest ranking staff members of *Career* T.E.A.M.) to carry their key objectives with them at all times. You should too!

One of my favorite examples of forecasting your future achievement comes courtesy of the actor and comedian Jim Carrey, who as a struggling young comic in Los Angeles, wrote himself a check for $10 million, dated it 5 years ahead and wrote on the check, "for services rendered." He carried the check in his wallet from that day forward until movies like *Ace Ventura: Pet Detective*, *The Mask* and *Dumb and Dumber* escalated his per movie fee to over $20 million! When Jim's beloved father died in 1994, he honored his dad and biggest fan by placing the fake check into the coffin. The lesson: Conceive it, believe it and you will achieve it!

A Look Into Your Future

To create a compelling perspective, here is a great exercise to help you visualize your future, understand how you are progressing and how quickly the days, months and years actually pass us by.

	Age Today	Age in 5 Years	Age in 10 Years
You			
Your Spouse (if applicable)			
Each Child By Name (If applicable)			
1.			
2.			
3.			

The 1st time I personally completed this exercise, I thought, *Wow! I am getting up there in age!* My 2nd thought was to realize that time does not wait for anyone; it simply progresses. The question is: Are you progressing at the same pace as time and will you be happy with your career and life choices as you reach each benchmark? When you see this on paper, it illuminates how important it is to create a game plan and assign action items to ensure you are happy with your accomplishments.

10 Keys to Setting Effective Goals

WHAT I FIND MOST helpful is to start by describing goals in general terms before you become specific with regard to your plan for establishing and obtaining your career calling. To be effective, your goals must be:

1. Balanced (Career, Financial, Health and Fitness, Relationships, Spirituality)

2. Beneficial to Others (Contribution goals are the best kind!)

3. Challenging (If they are too easy, what is the point?)

4. Flexible (Goals must be fluid and you must remain versatile)

5. Measurable (How many pounds, by which date, what job title, etc.)

6. Mirror Your Values (And make sure they are in sync with your identity)

7. Purposeful (They must have a reason that you can articulate)

8. Realistic (Regarding time frame to achieve and credentials required)

9. Supported (By family, friends and mentors)

10. Make Them Your Own (Not mine or someone else's but yours alone!)

The Yale University Study

To illustrate the importance of goal setting, a study was conducted of Yale University's class of 1953, which asked the following questions:

1. Have you set goals?

2. Are your goals in writing?

3. Do you have a plan to achieve your goals?

In response, only 3% of the class had written goals accompanied by a definite plan of action. 20 years later, in 1973, the same class was re-surveyed and the results were predictable. The 3% of the class who set goals and wrote them down were earning, on average, *10 times as much money* as the 97% of Yale graduates who did not. Although monetary reward isn't the only true measure of success, it certainly validates that setting and writing down objectives has a profound effect on income.

5 Proven Success Strategies

The process of goal setting is certainly not a new concept and most likely you are currently in the practice of formulating objectives in at least one area of your life. Maybe you have set a fitness goal to lose weight after the holidays. Perhaps you aspire to save a certain amount of money each month. Setting specific career related goals is challenging because most individuals are short-term thinkers, and long term career planning is often overlooked. This is a huge mistake! Not setting goals at all is well … self-sabotage!

Here are some of my favorite strategies:

1. *Study high achievers in your chosen field*
   Setting goals is powerful stuff and will elevate you to the top of your field. For example, I am often asked to speak at conferences attended by industry professionals, who seek a competitive edge. To illustrate my point, I will inevitably ask the participants to raise their hands if they can identify the most efficient and effective people in their chosen field. How many of you know who the people are who have set the standard for success in your field, industry or occupation? Almost every hand in the room is typically raised, because most people are aware of those individuals achieving excellence in their field (a.k.a. the top dogs!).

   My next step is to request again by a show of hands, how many of them have ever made the effort to meet these top performers. Often, not a single hand is raised!

   Why are people so hesitant to learn from others who may become a mentor to us and who have obviously figured out how to achieve excellence? It seems so obvious that we could benefit from their wisdom, experience, information or techniques. Most assuredly, you can bet that these top performers are in the regular habit of setting goals. The message: *Make it one of your priorities and set a goal right now to identify and meet the top 2 or 3 performers in your chosen field!*

   My suspicion is that you will find that these high achievers are in the practice of not only setting goals, but also have a definite plan for where they want to be 1–5–10 years ahead. From this day forward, I want you to employ the concept of beginning any endeavor with the end in mind; that is, decide what you ultimately want and then fill in the steps needed to get there.

   Do not enter into a career or start in a new industry without a plan for exactly where you aspire to end up. Not to oversimplify, but you would not just get in your car and start driving aimlessly, hoping you find a great view or restaurant. No, you hopefully begin your journey with a destination in mind and a set of directions.

2. *Purchase a mini recorder or notebook*

Goals often originate from our vision or ideas. Purchase a recorder and create an Ideas Book—this is simply a device or notebook where you record or write down your day-to-day observations and insights. It is a powerful tool to expand your awareness.

Did you ever have a big idea in the middle of the night? You sit straight up in bed and your mind is racing. Usually, you only have a few seconds to capture that idea before you lose it, or your body says, "Go back to sleep, it is 3 o'clock in the morning!" In fact, you may drift back to sleep, wake up hours later and have completely forgotten what your great idea was. Never lose a great thought again! An old saying I like is, *"When you think it, ink it!"*

3. *Establish family goals (at an early age)*

Personally, what my family and I do is create goals around the following categories:

Career
Financial
Hobbies/Entertainment/Vacations
Health and Fitness/Relaxation
Relationships
Spiritual/Contribution/Reflection

What we have determined as a family (and what my wife and I instill in our children) is that when you let other people determine your success, you are sabotaging your future. Personalizing your goals is one of the most important aspects of the goal setting process. Although we have family goals, we encourage each of our children to formulate objectives in key individual areas, even at their young ages (keep room clean, clear the table, school attendance goal, save their pennies, etc.).

Goal setting requires discipline and consistency, which is why most people set goals but do not follow through. If you do not adopt the practice of consistently setting and modifying your goals, you will live to regret it. It is said that there are 2 major pains in life. One is the pain of discipline; the other is the pain of regret. We want our kids to live without regret and teaching them the discipline to formulate goals is an important lesson in this process.

Even though my kids are very young, we already have a *mandatory* family conference every Wednesday night from 7 PM to 8 PM. We create a positive, fun environment, make popcorn and sit in our assigned seats. We keep the meeting notes in a binder and as a family we discuss and address "important issues," like room cleaning, television shows we are allowed to watch, snacks, allowance, trash removal duties, setting the dinner table and vacation plans. The important thing is that my children and family know that there is structure, accountability and a plan for our future. We are setting an example of the importance of goal setting and monitoring progress for *each* member of the Kuselias family. I suggest you do the same with yours. Make it fun, educational and allow ALL members to share their opinions and objectives. The results will astound you!

In each of our children's rooms, we have created a wall of fame (we also have one in every *Career* T.E.A.M. classroom around the nation) where their highlights are visually depicted. Each and every day, these accomplishments (including graded papers, drawings, and photographs with their friends, awards, certificates, etc.) are embedded into their minds and I am convinced have a positive effect on their attitude, mood and behavior. The building of self-esteem is another important benefit of this process. The last thing my kids see and observe before going to sleep each night are the positive aspects of their young lives, visually reinforced. *Research shows that what you see, hear and read 30 minutes before you turn in for the night influences both your sleeping pattern and energy for the next day.*

The lesson? Be careful what you fill your mind with right before going to bed. High achievers fill their mind with positive reinforcement, affirmations of their goals and critical reflection of a great day spent contributing to others. Avoid watching mindless TV, depressing news of war, rape, murder, gangs, scandals, or unproductive reading material. If you decide to have these things in your life, don't do them right before bed. I end each day by brushing my teeth and reflecting on how I assisted others and made the world a better place. I ask myself a single question, which is: "How could I have been more effective today?" I do not dwell on my mistakes or question my decisions, because doing so will only negatively affect my rest and abilities the next day to inspire my wife, kids, family, associates, customers and new people I meet.

4. *Purchase a photo album to create a visual reinforcement of your key goals*

   Next, I want to introduce you to the importance of creating visual reinforcement for all of your goals and objectives. Here is a fun strategy to set and visualize your goals:

   Buy a large photo album and create chapters for each area you wish to set goals. Within these chapters, I want you to start collecting pictures, which visually emphasize where or how you want to end up. Again, start with the end in mind but reinforce and create a visual reminder of the outcome you seek. Examples include:

   A photo of the body you want

   A picture of the house or car you desire

   A mock certificate of your targeted educational degree

   A mock business card of the title you want to hold

   A phantom copy of a charitable donation you aspire to make one day

   My son has a photo of Derek Jeter (who he wants to someday play catch with … I have the same photo of Jeter in my book; just don't tell my son!)

Author's Note

My personal success journal has pictures of:

- The current list of best selling books designed to help others. One of them, by Jack Canfield, motivated me to spend the long days and nights it took to author this book!

- Photos of my favorite seminar leaders, like John Maxwell and Steven Covey shown in front of large audiences

- Photos of helpful television hosts like Suze Orman, who have their own television or radio program created to assist the general public improve their quality of life

- A picture of my personal fitness trainer to remind me to seek fitness every day

- An article based on interviews with Warren Buffet, a man I respect and admire for his financial savvy on investment strategies

These are just a few of my personal inclusions; what are yours? I think you will find this exercise enlightening and invigorating!

5. *Create a goal setting journal*

Every successful person I know, have counseled or study, practices the art of setting and monitoring their goals and objectives. The best seem to make a practice of writing down their most important aspirations in a user-friendly format that they can reflect on and feel positive about their progress in life.

To demonstrate that I practice what I preach, here is sample from my current personal goal setting journal. I have recorded my goals in this format for the past 20 years and now have it computerized in a file entitled Annual Goals. Please see www .thecareerguarantee.com for more information on goal setting. It is inspiring to go back in time and observe what I once thought was a stretch or goal that would be a challenge. Today, some of my goals seem so elementary or simple it is almost a joke. But guess what? That shows the amazing progress I have made over 20 years by using the same techniques and strategies you are learning. Imagine the fun I will have in 20 years when I look back on what I think is a challenging goal today!

Each year on December 31, I sit at my computer and record my goals for the upcoming year. I begin with a paragraph affirmation and follow up with 5 categories, which contain my major life goals. These include:

1. Career
2. Financial
3. Health and fitness
4. Relationships
5. Spirituality

Each month, I review my goals and modify them as needed. I may increase or add new goals based on opportunities that arise throughout the course of the year. Regardless, I have a blueprint to follow, which provides the course for that given year. Please remember to be as specific as possible and include dates, names, numbers, percentages, locations, and amounts. Here is my latest submission (excluding certain confidential information), which begins with an affirmation:

Affirmation

I am a healthy, spiritual, loving husband and actively involved father of 3 children with incredibly strong family values who focuses his professional energies on creating and distributing life enhancing products and services through *Career* T.E.A.M., TV, radio, speaking and authorship.

Career

- Celebrate another anniversary of *Career* T.E.A.M. as a national leader in human performance coaching
- Establish www.thecareerguarantee.com as the premier careering website for those in pursuit of their career calling
- Expand CTL government contracting division to serve all 50 states
- Media
  - Have *The Career Guarantee* appear on *New York Times* bestseller list
  - Create a draft for a new Career TV Show that provides quality advice and inspiration
  - Pursue syndicated Career Radio concept to assist millions of career seekers in need of practical, empowering career advice

Financial

- Maintain and expand a diversified portfolio of quality investments
  - Generate minimum income of …
  - Expand personal net worth to … (excludes business valuation)
    Real estate/house/net worth: …
    Life insurance of $ …
    Investment portfolio $ …
  - Expand investment portfolio to …
    Cash: $X
    Investments: $X
    Retirement: $X
  - Monitor will/estate plan (completed DATE, revised DATE)
- Maintain professional advisory team
  - Accounting:
  - Investment advisors:
  - Legal:
  - Public relations:
  - Image consultant:

Health & Fitness

- Conduct a complete annual physical to include all vital indicators
  - Maintain a body weight at 175 pounds max
  - Keep cholesterol under 180, blood pressure at 120/80, body fat at max of 12%

- Workout minimum of 5x per week in personal home gym or when on the road
- Maintain daily vitamin program as prescribed by nutrition mentor
- Dental makeover to whiten my teeth
- Purchase roller blades for my family/ride on new bike path near our house
- Begin martial arts training 3 times per week to increase flexibility

Relationships

- Spend 15 minutes uninterrupted conversation with my wife/celebrate annual wedding anniversary (with 2 day retreat to renew our commitment, passion, hopes and dreams)
- Spend minimum of 15 quality minutes every day with each of my children (reading, story, listening)
- Take a minimum of 3 quality family vacations per year (for example, Disney, Italy, Newport, Aruba)
- Explore potential to purchase a beach house on the water in Madison, Connecticut
- Treat myself to a weekly massage (Friday at 12:45)

Spiritual

- Attend church regularly on Sundays with my entire family, practice tithing
- Positively contribute to my community/volunteer my time
- Empower one million new people to achieve life balance through my research and guidance
- Spend 10 minutes per day meditating and reflecting on my good fortune

Hard Work and Persistence Are Usually Rewarded!

"If people knew how hard I worked to get my mastery, it wouldn't seem so wonderful after all."

—Michelangelo

Every individual I know who has amassed incredible success has taken risks and worked hard. One of my favorite movies is the inspirational story of Rocky Balboa, written by a then unknown actor named Sylvester Stallone. While those of us who have seen his movies enjoy the experience, the behind the scenes work to get to the screen is amazing in itself.

The Real Rocky Story

As a child he grew up a loner and was often beaten by his father. An academic advisor once told him that based on aptitude testing, he should consider a career as an elevator repairman. In 1974, Sylvester Stallone was a broke, discouraged actor and screenwriter. While attending a boxing match he became inspired by a "nobody" boxer, Chuck Wepner, who "went the distance" with the great Muhammed Ali. He rushed home and in a 3-day burst of creative output produced the 1st draft of the screenplay entitled Rocky. Down to his last $106, Stallone submitted his screenplay to his agent.

A studio offered $20,000 with either Ryan O'Neal or Burt Reynolds playing the lead character. Stallone was excited by the offer but wanted to play the lead himself. He offered to act for free. He was told, "That's not the way it works in Hollywood." Stallone turned down the offer even though he desperately needed the money. Then they offered him $80,000 on the condition that he wouldn't play the lead. He turned them down again. They told him that Robert Redford was interested, in which case they'd pay him $200,000. He turned them down once again. The upped their offer to $300,000. He told them that he'd rather not see the move made if he couldn't play the lead. They finally agreed to his terms. He was paid $20,000 for the script, plus $340 per week, which was the minimum actor's wage. After expenses, agent free, and taxes he netted about $6,000 instead of $330,000.

In 1976 Stallone was nominated for an Academy Award as Best Actor. The movie Rocky won 3 Oscars: Best Picture, Best Director, and Best Film Editing. The Rocky series has since grossed over $1 billion, making Sylvester Stallone an international movie star!

The lesson: Pursue a higher calling, never compromise what you know in your heart is right and you will achieve your goals! Stallone's quote: "Success is usually the culmination of controlling failure."

Goal Attainment Requires Abundant Energy

> *"Having all the money in the world isn't much if you can hardly get out of bed in the morning to enjoy it."*
> —Author Unknown

When I decided to author this book, I knew I would spend considerable time on health and fitness and the link between high levels of career success and vitality.

You will never achieve or maintain your ideal career calling without a commitment to health and nutrition. Many people today are so tired and out of shape that they can barely make it through the day, much less have the stamina and energy required to pursue and attain professional greatness and life balance. One essential ingredient for career success continues to be a requirement for an abundance of mental, emotional and physical energy.

To demonstrate my commitment to fitness and my strong belief in the incredible benefits of living a fit lifestyle, when we purchased our dream house, *the very 1ˢᵗ room we finished was our home gym.* In fact, we built an entire wing for our fitness center. Before we had furniture or even a bed to sleep in we had a sanctuary for building our minds and bodies to be in shape to accomplish our life goals.

Why is fitness so important to obtaining your career calling? Without your health nothing else matters. I once visited a very wealthy friend dying in a hospital bed who commented he would spend his entire fortune if he could have 10 more pain free minutes to run through a field. Wow! What good is money, fame or fortune if you cannot sing a tune, attend the ceremony, play the game, or be there when the horn sounds?

My family, while not what I would term fanatical (we enjoy pizza and desserts as much as anyone else), make a conscious commitment to educating ourselves on food, nutrition, supplements and, of course, exercise. I want to still play full court basketball when I am 60, ride the waves in Maui all day long with my kids if I choose to, or play 3 sets of tennis without an oxygen machine.

I want to have the energy I need to live the life I have designed and be there for my children. The technology and research on improving health has never been better; we are truly lucky to live in a country and an era where the average life span is nearly 80 years!

Because of our knowledge and belief in adopting a fitness lifestyle, we outfitted our 1,000 square foot home gym with our favorite fitness equipment, inspirational photos and quotes on the walls, a water machine and fridge for protein bars, healthy sports drinks, juice and supplements. We installed a big screen television and audio system so we could play our favorite "pump up" music. You don't need to go to this extreme or invest that kind of money if you don't have it (*yet don't worry, you will ... if you can conceive it and believe it, you will achieve it!*), but make a decision to purse a fit lifestyle without excuses.

If you can only afford a used pair of sneakers to run outside, fine. It doesn't cost anything to walk or run outside. But do something to increase your stamina and, as you build your wealth, invest in your fitness and study the advancing technology, which can add years to your life and zest to your pursuit of your career calling.

I tell you these things not to impress you, but to impress upon you that you can have all the best objectives and plans in the world, but without the ability to maintain the peak energy needed to think, strategize, act, move, study, plan, execute and maintain, you will fall short and become another person with unfulfilled potential. For my family, this sizeable investment forced us to justify its usage; it was an incentive!

The top performers in every field of study know a secret … that to get and stay on top requires an abundance of physical, mental and emotional energy. You now know it as well, so do something about it!

3 Essential Areas of Fitness

Here are my other beliefs about fitness, mostly gleaned from my health and fitness mentors:

1. *Physical exercise:*
   - Success requires an abundance of physical energy! Strength training is essential for muscle tone, posture and appearance.
   - Morning cardio burns the greatest amount of fat, so get it done before you shower or eat. (Personally, I rise at 6 AM, put on my shorts and T-shirt, grab a 16 ounce bottle of water, stretch, jump on the treadmill, recumbent bike or elliptical rider, turn on ESPN and burn those calories for at least 30 minutes!)
   - Conduct strength training (circuit) a minimum of 3 times per week.
   - Chart your strength progress and number of monthly sessions.
   - Vary your workout routines to avoid boredom (change your reps, exercises, music, time of day).
   - Post visual pictures of your ideal physique to stimulate your mindset.
   - Seek spouse support (ideally, work out together!).
2. *Diet and nutrition*
   - Eat right: Proper diet means fruits, vegetables and whole grain foods; the body is 70% water, so eat foods that are 70% water, including fruits and vegetables.
   - Eat lean protein
   - Drink lots of water. When you are dehydrated, your digestion slows and you become tired more easily.

- Avoid white flour, sugar and salt. Canned foods are often 50% salt. White flour, introduced in the 1800s, initially caught on because of its appearance. In order to create white flour from whole grain wheat, wheat must be ground, and the kernels, which contain the nutrients, must be removed. The flour is then bleached for whiteness. Enriched white flour means nutrients have been added back in, but, when they bake the bread at 350 degrees, the heat kills the added vitamins.
- Supplement your diet with vitamins and minerals: Antioxidants, found in proflavenols, green vegetables and certain vitamins remove free radicals, which are responsible for disease.
- Try to avoid combining proteins and starch, which stimulate acid production (acid reflux is a growing epidemic!).
- If you are overweight, write down everything you eat for a full week, then analyze your diet for modifications.
- Create a list of 10 healthy food choices by meal (breakfast, lunch, dinner) that you enjoy, post on your refrigerator and when shopping, purchase those!
- Create a simple list of 10 *to-dos* and *not-to-dos* (for example, replace white with wheat) and post on your fridge.
- Remember, the better your diet, the less you need to exercise
- Limit caffeine, sugar and salt; eat small meals 5X per day and do not eat after 7 PM.

3. *Mental nutrition*
   - Change your association to food from pure pleasure to food as a fuel required to keep your body's sophisticated system in tune (your body is a temple, make sure it is not the temple of doom!).
   - As harsh as this sounds, visually picture your own arteries hardening before you decide to ingest transfats or foods that contribute to high cholesterol.
   - Choose vitality as a lifestyle and post photos of a fit lifestyle in your kitchen.
   - Associate feelings of good health as more powerful than desires fulfilled by a few pleasurable minutes of ingesting food.
   - Over 50 million Americans are obese. Invest in a scale and weigh yourself every day, record your weight and monitor trends (holiday gains).

- Monitor your vitals with an annual physical to alleviate health worries or concerns (remember, when the mind hurts, the body suffers!).
- Remember, ulcers are not the result of what we eat, but rather what is eating us.
- Avoid thoughts and emotions that negatively affect health: negative thoughts depress the body and mind. They sap your precious energy and weaken your immune system. Focus on self-talk and feed your mind, like your body, with positive nourishment.
- Exercise to your favorite music and television shows to avoid boredom or painful joints (TV or music can take your mind off aches and pains).
- Get your rest and sleep (8 hours per night plus regular mini vacations).

Using Goal Setting to Find Your Calling

Goal setting is a critical component to obtaining your career calling. They provide direction and serve as the basis for helping you get what you want from life. Formulating goals is a detailed and time-consuming process, but a critical process.

Everybody has goals. Individuals have goals. Families have goals. Businesses have goals. Governments have goals. And even nations have goals.

Goals can be divided into 3 basic components: short-term goals (1 year); medium-term goals (5 years); and long-term goals (until the end of your work life).

It is not a lack of time that most unsuccessful career seekers suffer from, but a lack of direction. Direction creates more time and motivation creates energy. When setting your career goals, don't be discouraged if you share your goals with other people and they laugh. Only your close friends will really be rooting for you.

One of my favorite sayings is: *If you don't have a destination, you'll never get there.* So it's important that if you are looking to change careers, or re-enter you have a specific agenda. Through seminars, workshops or email, job seekers will regularly ask me to tell them what they want from a career. That's not possible. It's like having a favorite flavor of ice cream; it's an individual preference. You as an individual have to find your ultimate calling because only you know what work-related activities inspire you.

Aren't you a lot happier at things that you like to do? Didn't you perform better in roles or former courses that you were passionate about? Of course you did. There are the winners who go out and make things happen, participate and achieve. When winners encounter failure (as anyone who has stretched their limits is bound to do), they view it solely as a temporary setback and something to gain experience from. Others, conversely, procrastinate, blame their failures on other people and make excuses. Often these folks are spectators in the game of life, individuals who watch things happen or choose not to do anything at all. Recognize that "some day" is not a day of the week. Which category are you in? This is your life plan! Every monumentally successful career seeker that I have ever coached understands their motivations. They can enthusiastically articulate the *why*! Was it the feelings from doing a great job? Was it a specific monetary reward if they fulfilled an objective? What is the why behind your want?

Success Tip

It's the "why" that is the power and strength behind setting your goals and committing yourself to achieve them.

The other important aspect of goal-setting is that it forces you to analyze where you are right now in the career planning cycle. And once you assess that where you are right now, today, is not really where you want to be, you can quantify a difference in your mind. And once you determine that there is a difference, you can measure that difference. Once you measure that difference, you can determine a plan of action on how to close the gap. So here is an essential exercise. *Quantify the measurable difference between where you are today and where you want to be.* Ask yourself: What must change today? Part of achieving satisfaction through setting goals is to realize that right now, today, you are unfulfilled with your current professional status. Utilize your disenchantment to your advantage. That's right. Feel unhappy. Stop reading and do this now! What you will realize is that there is real energy in realizing that "Hey, I'm not happy in what I'm doing today. And I'm spending a large portion of my time, approximately ⅓ of my life, doing it."

Once you admit you are misusing your talents, let yourself experience the pain and frustration of this unhappiness. That may sound like strange advice, but if you don't you'll never have the drive or the motivation to change. For some, the decision is like a lightning bolt; for others it is a more gradual awakening. Change happens in an instant!

Think of some of your most important decisions. Most likely, they involved only a few words but those words were powerful indeed and resulted in significant change. How do these sound ... *I do* ... *I will* ... *I quit* ... *I love you* ... *I'm pregnant* ... *I want a divorce* ... *It's cancer* ... *You're fired.* These words represent defining moments that will motivate you to change. Analyze the things that you really dislike about your current career path.

Don't confuse activity with accomplishment. Don't just go through the motions. Experience dictates that many job seekers don't like to make career commitments because it creates pressure on them. Nobody likes to feel pressure. But once you set a goal, then you're committed to fulfilling that goal. And if you confide in trusted advisors or a coach, and you don't follow up, these individuals will provide the peer pressure or positive reinforcement needed to succeed.

Quantify the many benefits you will realize if you attain your objectives. And then think about what will you lose or what you will be sacrificing if you don't achieve your goal. Compare and contrast the benefits vs. the consequences of not taking action.

I personally review my short-term goals on a daily basis, my larger career goals on a weekly basis and my lifelong career goals on a monthly basis. I'm constantly re-evaluating myself. Letting other people know what my goals are serves as motivation for me to fulfill those objectives, as does continually asking myself the "why" behind each one of my goals.

Don't make your career goals just an exercise of writing the words on a page and wondering if they're going to happen and randomly attacking it. Have a systematic approach. Only you can determine if your career goals are realistic. If your goal is to become the CEO of a *Fortune* 500 company, that may be a realistic goal or it may not be.

You see, I can't tell you, because I can't get inside your head and see what kind of commitment or dedication you're going to make to the goal. Quite frankly, I've been pleasantly surprised by people who I thought had set a career goal far beyond their own expectations or qualifications and, yet, they were so committed and so dedicated internally that they went on to achieve the goal.

> Never underestimate yourself. Create in your own mind a strong enough justification for achieving the goal. Develop an internal pressure by telling other people what career goals you have set for yourself. And then be committed to them.

Getting Started

S O, HOW DOES ONE get started? One thought-provoking exercise is the brainstorming exercise. The overall mission is to attain your ideal career. As a secondary goal, let's say you want to earn $100,000.00 a year. Ask yourself, "What can I do to earn $100,000.00 a year?" Begin by eliminating distractions and then write down 20 answers as fast as they come into your mind. Then generate action plans related to the answers on your list. This process of defining specific tasks will ultimately help you achieve your career goal.

Where Are You Now?

1. List the 3 best aspects.
2. List 3 missing aspects.
3. Where do you ultimately want to be?

How have the duties, responsibilities and experiences of your prior jobs prepared you for your newly defined career calling?

5 Career Choices

A common theme of my coaching is to continually require you to articulate exactly what it is you truly want. The 1st question regarding your career involves the capacity in which you want to demonstrate and contribute your unique and compelling skills. Depending on life circumstances (children, divorce, age, energy level, care of an elderly parent, education status, etc.) you will want to identify a plan that fits your obligations and life style. To guide you in this decision, let me ask you to define your current objective. Do you aspire to be a . . .

Full-time employee
Part-time employee
Consultant (freelance or work at home job)
Entrepreneur (start your own business)
Volunteer (often an effective strategy for entry into a field where you have no prior experience)

The Brainstorming Exercise

Ask yourself: "What steps can I take to attain my ideal career"?
Take some time and write your 20 answers on paper.

- Hint! Remember the 80/20 principal, which states that 20% of the things that you write will be the most important things you will have to do.
- The more specific your career goal, the better chance you'll have to achieve it.
- Formulate short-term, medium-term and long-term goals.
- Review your goals each morning by reading them aloud to yourself. By doing so, you will succeed in embedding your objectives into your subconscious mind.
- Understand that there is no one person or thing to blame for not achieving or attaining your ideal career. You are the captain of your own ship!

Establishing a Clear and Definite Focus

THE MOST IMPORTANT ASPECT to successfully attaining your career calling is a clear and definite focus on exactly what you want. Most career seekers who do not reach their career potential fail because they have not identified a specific target.

The follow exercises will help you narrow your interests and create a specific career direction. As you get closer to your actual goal, you will feel yourself gaining momentum, gaining confidence, and improving as a person.

You and I were all put here for a special reason, a unique purpose. Each of us has a unique talent that must be realized in order for us to feel complete. Your mission is to find out exactly what your contribution will be and in what career you will be best able to demonstrate your special talents.

A few hints and suggestions:

Focus on the feelings that you will have if you attain your ideal career.

Compare these feelings to your current emotional state.

Observe the differences.

Use this discrepancy as the motivation to achieve.

Make your goals realistic and attainable.

Model successful people in the fields that interest you.

Determine the exact steps and actions required to be successful in your quest.

Monitor your progress daily and alter your approach if necessary.

Assign specific times and dates for the completion of your goals.

Specify your career goal. The more specific your goal, the better your chances to achieve it.

Formulate short-term (1 year), medium-term (2–5 year), and long-term (6 years plus) career goals.

Avoid procrastination. Reduce the job search into small, workable steps.

Review your goals each morning by reading them aloud to yourself. This transfers your objective into your subconscious mind.

Recognize that there is no other person or thing to blame if you do not attain your ideal career. The decision to pursue, the strategy chose, the actions taken, the dedication to achieve, and the acceptance of the offer all reside in your personal control.

Good luck! (Hint: These steps apply to any goal you want to achieve!)

The Worthwhile Goal Exercise

1. Describe 3 experiences in your career or in another area of your life in which you have achieved a worthwhile goal or felt excited about an accomplishment (for example, high school graduation, diet, etc.).
2. Then go back and describe why you were excited or pleased.

Next, I want you to describe a typical day in your ideal career. Let your thoughts run wild. How do you start your day? When do you go to lunch? Who are you with? How does the day end?

Your Ideal Career: A Typical Day

Describe a typical day in your ideal career (adjust the hours for 2nd and 3rd shift jobs accordingly). This should help you to formulate realistic expectations!

AM

8–9 _____

9–10 _____

10–11 _____

11–12 _____

12–1 _____

1–2 _____

2–3 _____

PM

3–4 _____

4–5 _____

5–6 _____

6–midnight _____

Make this a fun exercise and don't include sleep, eat, or nap every other hour! Have you included time for physical exercise?

Exercise: Setting Immediate, Short Term and Long Term Goals

(Hint: Use the steps and next steps from your brainstorming exercise.)

1. My short-term goal (1 year) is to be a _____

   A. To obtain this position, I must begin by _____

   B. The date that I have set to obtain this goal is _____

2. My medium-term career goal (2–5 years) is to be a _____

   A. To attain this position, I foresee myself having to _____

   B. The date that I have set to obtain this goal is _____

3. My ultimate (long-term) career goal is to be a: _____

_____

   A.In this position I will perform the following tasks: _____

      _____

      _____

   B.The date that I have set to obtain this career goal is _____

Think long term! Your career is a marathon … not a sprint!
  Now that you have identified a career path:

1. What kind of professional will you need to become?
2. What qualities will you need to develop in order to be a success in your quest? For example, do you need to be more organized?
3. Will you need to become more knowledgeable on a particular subject?
4. Do you need to develop special skills?
5. Should you become a better dresser?

Hint: Consider your attitude, skills and outlook.

Exercise: 5 Reasons You Truly Want to Attain Your Calling

How would you feel if you became this type of person? Again, identify the "why" behind the "what." Why is it important to achieve your ideal career? *Remember, if you can't list the reasons why you want to achieve your calling, then you're really not totally committed to attaining the goal.*

1. _____

2. _____

3. _____

4. _____

5. _____

Exercise: 5 Obstacles You Must Overcome to Attain Your Calling

List 5 obstacles you will have to overcome to obtain your career calling. First and foremost may be to overcome procrastination. That's a big one for everyone.

1. _____

2. _____

3. _____

4. _____

5. _____

Key People Exercise

List 3 important people who can help you attain your career goals. These should be individuals whom you must contact or get to know in order to help you. Can you identify them? How will you benefit from meeting these people? Can they hire you? Can they introduce you to someone of importance? Can they coach or teach you? Can they serve as motivation for you?

1. Name: _____

   Benefit: _____

2. Name: _____

   Benefit: _____

3. Name: _____

   Benefit: _____

Keep track of your progress and monitor your success. Research studies show that without goals you will waste half of your time in extraneous activities that contribute little or nothing towards attaining your objectives. Theroux tells us, "If one advances confidently in the direction of his dreams and endeavors to live the life he has imagined, he will then meet with a success unexpected in common hours."

Establish the confidence that you can do anything you set out to do. *Setting goals is an exercise in keeping a formal record of your accomplishments in a specified time.* Begin by setting the actual goal and developing a plan of action to attain your career calling. Then monitor these achievements to make sure that your plan is being executed properly.

5-Step Process for Achieving Your Goals

1. Set the goal! (What do you want?)
2. Define why you want to achieve this goal. (What are your reasons?)
3. Identify what obstacles stand between you and your goal. (What will prevent you from achieving your goal?)
4. Identify people and resources that can help you. (Who can help?)
5. Assign specific dates to achieve each step in the process. (When will this happen?)

If the career calling objective that you set depends entirely on luck or fate, then it's not really a goal but just a hope.

I referred earlier to formulating a specific goal and targeting your ideal career. Let me share with you a story you may find beneficial.

The Story of Jody

I was assisting a young woman recently who had an interest in the sports marketing industry. Jody had been interested in sports since she was a youngster and had played sports her whole life. She loved the nature of competition. She knew all the players on the teams and kept track of their performance statistics. She could even tell you the seating capacities for all the fields. That's how passionate and knowledgeable she was. She came to me and said, "Chris, I've tried selling insurance. I've worked in a bank. I was a waitress. And I just find the only activity that fills me with a sense of passion is when I'm involved in sports.

So I told her, "Hey, why don't you try to get into the sports marketing industry?" Her answer was one of a typical nature. "I don't know how." The 1st thing I instructed her to do was to write on a blank side of a business card the name of the company she would like to work for, the name of the title she'd like to hold and exactly what she'd like to do in the sports marketing industry. In other words, I was narrowing her focus. I was asking her to be specific. And her answer came back, "I can't complete that exercise, Chris. All I know is that I have an interest in sports." So I encouraged her to assess why she was interested in sports, that is, to identify the "why" behind the "what,"

After initially moving her out of her comfort zone and forcing her to analyze the basis for her passion about sports, we determined that the reason she liked sports was because of the camaraderie, the teamwork, the togetherness, the competition, the discipline that sports offers, the excitement and the notoriety of being a good athlete. Also she loved the enthusiasm and excitement that being around sports gave her. Some people like computers, others like to write, some to manage, her passion was sports.

So her 1st step was to target a position outside of actually playing because, quite frankly, she wasn't of professional caliber as an athlete. She needed an education as to the specific occupations within the sports marketing industry that she might be interested in. She began by researching specific occupations in sports marketing. She visited websites, learned a few buzz words, read a few articles on the largest sports marketing companies and read up on some of her favorite athletes. She read articles on agents, the business of sports, event planning and those who were negotiating contracts. She learned that in her regional area there were actually 2 headquarters of large sports marketing companies. Taking the traditional methodology, this individual would probably have sent a resume to these companies, received a rejection letter and wound up discouraged and continued on in her unhappy and dissatisfied lifestyle.

Together, we formulated a plan of attack. We reviewed her research. After preparing a script, rehearsing and building her confidence, she then contacted the secretary of a large sports marketing company, dialing directly into the switchboard, introducing herself as an individual who was very much interested in the sports marketing industry. Jody recognized that the people in the building were probably very busy, but that she had a goal to learn more about it and nothing was going to stand in her way. She asked if she could have some company information. The secretary was pleased and delighted to assist her and immediately sent her out a company overview, not already on the website., which talked about some of the more influential people in the organization and their accomplishments. Everybody likes to brag, including large, medium and small employers.

She waited anxiously until she received the information and immediately read through it. I then quizzed her on some of the more pertinent points of what the documents she received revealed in regards to number of employees, areas within the sports marketing area this company was noted for, and future targets. This line of questioning helped her identify potential growth. Jody then said to me, "Chris, I've acquired knowledgeable about the industry. I learned about 1 or 2 of the particular companies in my state. I could even tell you the name of the presidents of the companies. But I'm still an outsider. How do I get on the inside?"

Does this sound familiar to anybody? Her next step was to target a specific individual within one of the organizations with whom she could meet. Jody had targeted her ideal industry, learned about specific functions and components of the company by asking for information, and built a working knowledge. Her next step was finding a mentor or somebody she could talk to on the inside. Through using the information interview and contact strategies, which I will showcase for you in a future section, Jody cultivated her contact network and made some friends within the organization.

Thus far, Jody had achieved 4 of her goals and set up an information interview. She identified her targeted industry. She learned about specific companies within the industry. She learned specifics about those employers as far as growth and long-term potential. She had targeted an individual within that company who she could rely on for information, guidance, resource, knowledge, as well as how to get her foot in the door.

Whether you are a job search veteran or just beginning your career, when setting your goals, I recommend highly doing what Jody did. Jody had absolutely no idea what she wanted to do when she 1st started. But as she started building momentum and learning more about her area of interest, her passion, she asked herself the "why" behind the "what." Why did she want to get into sports? And she learned about the fact that she liked competition, teamwork, togetherness, and the unbridled excitement of sports. She gained confidence and momentum. Most importantly, she asked herself *why*. She then went out and researched the occupation.

Remember the 5P's? I'm happy to report that Jody started in an entry-level position and was so enthusiastic (passion) about being in the industry, her efforts were noticed by her superiors in the organization (purpose). Because of her effort, she is respected for her knowledge (power). She's moving up the ladder and earning more money (profit) and is just thrilled to be in the sports marketing industry (peace of mind). Jody is a total success story. Quite a change from an individual who had earlier said, "I have no idea how to get my foot in the door and penetrate that hidden job market in my chosen field."

You have the potential to do the same thing that Jody did in your own quest for a particular career. You just need to identify your goals and realize that goals are to be set in stages, short-term, medium-term and long-term. Jody now has long-term aspirations of getting into a higher-level management position and making important decisions and policies. Jody has found what I am preaching to you ... When you pursue your passion, purpose, build your base of power, increase your profit and achieve the rare feeling of peace of mind ... good things happen!

Take a tip from the story of Jody and do the same thing in your own career. Obtain information to become more knowledgeable about your specific industry and target the exact goals that you want in that career. Brainstorm and write down a list of things that you can do to get involved in the industry you'd like to be a part of. Penetrate that hidden job market by being a person who sets goals for themselves and assigns dates to achieve those goals.

Jody tracked her progress and gets a kick out of looking back when she was just learning about sports marketing business. Maybe someday in the future she'll be shaping the direction of that industry.

Reviewing the 5 Step Process for Goal Setting

In closing, the simple 5-step formula for setting and achieving your career goal is as follows:

1. Set the goal. Choose the target and look to people who make their living in your ideal occupation. Find role models.
2. Write down *why* you want to achieve it. The "why" behind the "what." Justify your choice. Ask yourself if it is realistic. Does it match your values?
3. Identify any obstacles that stand in your way of achieving your goal, and list them. Identify what's preventing you from attaining your ideal career.
4. Identify people, groups or organizations that can help you achieve your goal. Write them down. Whom do you have to meet? What groups do you have to join? How do you have to elevate your current status in order to achieve your goal?
5. Assign specific dates to achieve each short-term, medium-term and long-term goal.

Final Thoughts

Learn to put your goals in writing and constantly re-evaluate your current position. If your career goals are not working for you or are too ambitious, they can always be adjusted. Don't be afraid to aim high. The funny thing about goals is that if you look as far as the eye can see and set a goal to get there, when you do get there you can always see farther. The message is that goal setting should be a continuous process. Never stop setting goals. Constantly re-evaluate and set new goals.

By now, you are on track to deciding on your specific goals. You have a career industry and maybe a specific position in mind. You've learned about the specific opportunities that exist within your chosen field or fields. You've learned to program your mind to think long-term and not just on a day-to-day basis. You look to the future. Where are you going to be 5 years from now? Think long-term.

You've become aware that procrastination can be a silent killer as far as destroying your career aspirations. You need to dedicate time each day to review your goals. I can honestly say that every day for the last 25 years I have set aside time each day, usually 1st thing in the morning for 3 to 5 minutes, to review and record my progress towards my own goals. I consider health, financial, spiritual, emotional, social aspects of my life as all-important areas requiring specific objectives.

I'm a firm believer that a goal properly set is already half-accomplished. It's the little things that make a difference between success and failure. Successful people just do things a little differently, and are more persistent than those who fail. There's no consolation in almost getting hired, almost winning the game. As Knute Rockne said, "Show me a good loser and I'll show you a loser."

Learn to enjoy victory and associate positive feelings towards winning and achieving your goals. If you fail, bounce back quickly with a modified goal. Learn to crave success. All great performers, regardless of their industry, have an overwhelming desire to succeed. *Do you?* Understand that rejection is a reality and you're going to have certain hardships in your life. Remember, it's the people who can learn to accept failure as a temporary setback and get back on the track to their goals who are the true achievers, who view failure as a detour, a valuable learning experience and not a dead-end.

Finally, work hard. There's no substitute for continuous effort. There's an old saying among business owners that, *you can prevent losing your shirt by keeping your sleeves rolled up.* Abigail Van Buren said, "If you want a place in the sun, you have to put up with a few blisters." Learn from the mistakes of other people because you can never live long enough to make them all yourself. When an obstacle arises, change your direction towards the goal and not your decision to achieve the goal. Also, be aware of self-imposed limitations. And don't sabotage your own success. Learn to feel success as a comfortable and natural part of your character. You deserve it!

Remember that finding your ideal career begins with a look inside yourself. The objective is to consider all the career opportunities prior to narrowing your interest. And once you narrow your interest set objectives that will create momentum.

Have you identified the obstacles that stand between you and your career goal? Remember, if there were no obstacles, you would already have achieved your goal. Successful people can identify the specific obstacles, list them and then comprise a plan of action to overcome and eliminate these obstacles. To overcome obstacles, you need a strategy, which is an organized set of actions and a systematic arrangement of your resources. Start with the total universe of jobs, review your interests and then narrow these down until you target a workable number that you really feel you have an interest in. Just like Jody did in the sports marketing example cited earlier.

I want you to know that I have not asked you to complete one single exercise or example that I personally have not done or do on a regular basis. Career seekers all over our great nation have completed them and found their career calling. You will too! Successful achievement takes work. And everything in life really has a price. Do not at any cost sacrifice your health, your morals or your integrity to attain your career goals. There is no job or profession on earth that is worth that price.

Above all, be true to yourself. Good things—in your career or in some other area—may come to those who wait, but those who wait only get the rewards left behind by those who hustle. Go get your ideal career. The sky's the limit!

CHAPTER 5

Master and Commander ...
of Your Mind and Career!

KEY QUESTION: WHY DO I WANT IT?

In this chapter, you will learn:

KEY TOPICS

- Mastering Your Thought Process
- The Power of Attitude
- Conquering Your Limiting Beliefs
- The Power of Affirmations
- How To Live in the Now
- The Power of Visualization

KEY MESSAGES

- Decisions will dictate your career success.
- Commitment starts and ends with managing your thoughts and beliefs.
- Finding your calling is not just your right; it is your obligation!
- Your attitude determines your altitude.
- Beware of limiting patterns of behavior.
- Progress not perfection ... that is the goal!
- Guard your mind from negative thoughts!
- Transform your inner cynic into your inner coach.
- The secret: Start with the end in mind.

"The greatest revolution of our generation is the discovery that human beings, by changing the inner attitudes of their minds, can change the outer aspects of their lives."
—William James, Harvard psychologist

Mastering Your Thought Process

IT IS TIME TO learn how to harness the power of your most valuable asset ... your mind! Your mind is the absolute key to your life and yet most people have no clue as to how to harness this incredible power! Experts tell us we are only using about 10% of our brain capacity, I know some people who use even less! The question is ... How much of your brain capacity are *you* using?

> *"If a 100-foot oak tree had the mind of a human, it would only grow to be 10 feet tall!"*
>
> —T. Harv Eker

Your mind is like a giant super computer. Information that enters your mind is labeled and stored in files for easy retrieval. What make us unique is *where* we file, *how* we access and *when* we access stored information. You make choices as to what your "customized" mental database looks like, what is retained and in what situations you choose to access it. When fear occurs, what file is accessed? When conflict arises, where do you go looking? When ambition is needed, what file dictates your programmed response? Be aware of what books, magazines, articles, television and other stimuli you install into your supercomputer mind. Like a computer, the saying, "garbage in, garbage out" applies.

I want to help you edit and "install" some new files, which may open up a world of possibility for you. These include examples, stories, quotes and guidance. Chapter by chapter, we are re-programming your "career files" with successful strategies. By adding these new files we are creating new options for you, new choices to accelerate your career. From this, you will develop new habits, beliefs and attitudes, which are the genesis of greatness. Going forward you will observe greater success simply by having better files.

Fast Fact

If your subconscious thermostat is not "set" for career success, there is no technique or strategy you can learn that will make a difference.

Your *career identity* is simply the mental and emotional picture you have of yourself. This includes what you believe you are worthy of, capable of, comfortable with and how talented you are. Why is your career identity important? Because we as human beings always "self-regulate" to the person or level we are comfortable with. Being in sync with our identity is one of the strongest desires human beings have. We will always act in accordance with our identity. The secret to progress is not to try and fool yourself into being someone else, but rather, to take steps to alter your identity to be the person you are capable of being.

Resistance to this change will come in the form of habits, prior momentum and conditioning from family, teachers, friends and media. This is why I am so cognizant of what my children are exposed to (television, violence, negative thinkers, cynics, etc.) because early exposure shapes identity and will create their *foundation* for life. It takes courage to make a change and explore why you are like you are and do what you do. It is almost like career therapy. But trust me. Making these changes will give you what you ultimately seek, greater happiness and peace of mind!

Consider lottery winners. Studies have shown that people who win the lottery eventually return to their original level of income, the amount they are comfortable with. *The amount they identify with!* We all think we need excessive amounts of money, but unless we modify our belief system (our comfort level) to feel deserving with this financial windfall, we will feel incongruous and sabotage ourselves until we return to our natural state. Sounds crazy, but its true!

Whether it is a golfer who double bogies the last hole to sub-consciously maintain their handicap thermostat, a salesperson "programmed" to make $50,000 annually who suddenly hits a slump in the 4th quarter to maintain this figure or a student who gets C on the final exam to maintain their B average, there are countless examples of *self-regulating behaviors* that occur unbeknownst to us. Where are you self-regulating or as some say sabotaging your own success? Can you see now why you are acting this way? It is because your identity and goals are not in sync. You want to weigh 110 pounds, but your identity says you weigh 130 pounds. Until you *identify* with 110 pounds, you will be engaged in a constant struggle with your own identity and most likely remain at 130 pounds. This is why diets result in frustration.

The secret? The minute you reprogram your mind and truly see yourself as a 110-pound person (a 110-pound identity), it will begin to happen. The mind is indeed a powerful force!

Letter From Steven in St. Louis ...

After years of frustration caused by bouncing from job to job, I finally decided to get some professional guidance and attend your *The Career Guarantee* seminar.

I was initially skeptical but after learning about the importance of my identity, I immediately adopted this plan to change my internal view of myself rather than hoping that some external factor or achievement was the answer. The answer was inside of my own head, and I was my own worst enemy! Once I felt entitled to success and saw myself as a high earner, my career passion and purpose exploded. My career thermostat is now set for excellence!

P.S.: My favorite song is ... "Ain't No Stopping Us Now" by Luther Vandross

The Million Dollar Question:
What Is Your Career Thermostat Set For?

Like the thermostat on your wall, you are currently set at a specific temperature. Unlike the thermostat on your wall, you are conditioned for a certain level of success. Your character and belief systems are essential parts of your ultimate career success. Certainly having superior careering strategies is important, but without taking the time to learn how your own mind and emotions work, you, like millions of others, can get a job, but not your ideal career.

So who are you? What are your habits? What do you believe in? Can you manage your fears? Are you deserving of a great career? Will you take risks? Are you programmed for career success? Observe yourself and your thoughts, fears, habits, actions and lack of action. Study yourself ... that is the 1st step towards changing your career identity.

Success Tip

Your career will grow only to the extent your mind does

Let me begin by reminding you that you have a conscious mind and a subconscious mind. You should be aware that whatever your conscious mind wants, your subconscious mind will accept. It is not capable of an argument. If your conscious mind commands your subconscious mind that you are not deserving of a raise or promotion, your subconscious mind will work tirelessly to make it true. Conversely, if you instill a positive thought that you truly deserve, your subconscious mind will work to make that a reality. All of your internal dialogue and self-talk should be aimed at moving you closer to the attainment of your life goals, including your career calling.

Although we have not personally met, I will make the bold prediction that what you are capable of is much more than what you have demonstrated to date. Will today be the day that you decide to make your life consistent with the quality of your spirit? Remember these words: *I will not be denied.* You cannot be denied in your quest to find your passion, purpose, power, profit and your peace of mind.

Establishing Your Priorities

The 21ˢᵗ century workforce requires constant change and adaptation. It becomes critical to invest the mental and emotional energy in pursuing your calling. By simply making slight changes, you can yield dramatic results! And you need not be especially intelligent or gifted to realize your aspirations. You just need to be clear on your desired outcome. The most important question you can ask yourself is: *"What do you really want?"*

You control your direction … not the economy, not the president, not the political landscape, housing market or oil prices, etc. You are not a victim, but rather the captain of your own ship, master and commander! You will no longer focus on external forces because you have an internal plan that makes such considerations—while relevant—not deciding factors in your personal course of action.

Remember these 3 keys:

1. The objective of careering is a contribution that makes you truly happy, referred to as your *calling*
2. Feelings and emotions are more important than material possessions or external rewards
3. You possess the power to find your calling; it is not a random event or based on luck

As the great motivator, Zig Ziglar, points out, "Most people are wandering generalities" vs. "meaningful specifics." I have found that most people spend more time analyzing what automobile to purchase (model, make, consumer reports, gas mileage, safety tests, etc.) than they spend on improving themselves! As a result, they drift through life without purpose or direction.

What do you stand for? I have a close friend who is fond of saying, "If you don't stand for something, you will fall for anything." Have you recently stopped and considered the reality you are building for yourself? The combination of your thoughts, both positive and negative, comprises your reality. What is your reality?

Here is a dose of reality. *Every role model you identify as a success did not get there without adversity, obstacles and challenge.* They simply focused on their outcome and did not allow themselves to become sidetracked with guilt or excuses. "Ask and you shall receive, seek and you will find." They focused on exactly what they wanted and formulated the internal belief and attitude that it was attainable. The common denominator to success and life balance is attitude.

Did you know that it takes the same amount of energy to formulate a positive thought as it does a negative one? Positive thinking is ultimately about structuring your belief system; that is, substituting positive images for negative ones. It is the process of consciously filtering out unhealthy thoughts and cleansing the mind.

The *Why* Behind the Want

> *"You do not want to get to the top of the ladder and find out you were climbing the wrong wall."*
>
>   —Anonymous

It was the great philosopher Aristotle (340 B.C.) who originally adopted the belief that the most powerful and compelling objective of every human being is *the desire for happiness.* I believe, as Aristotle did, that every action you take or decision you make is predicated on this desire to attain a greater sense of happiness. For each action you take to achieve success, your ultimate reason will be because you crave the need to feel happy. Why do you seek a career calling? Why do you want a better relationship? Why lose weight? Why attain a certain level of savings? Why start your own business? Why become more spiritual? The reason: So you can feel happy!

Attaining true happiness requires continuous growth and the establishment of a solid identity. One of the strongest human desires is to live in accordance with our own identity. When people try to be something they are not and lose touch with their authentic self, we call this an *identity crisis.* That is why a person who subconsciously "sees" themselves as overweight will never be thin until they change their identity and "see" themselves as thin.

A person addicted to drugs or alcohol who "believes" they are an addict will remain one until they create a new image (and believe it at their core) of being drug or alcohol free. A person in jail often is planning their next crime when it comes time to being released. Why? Because this individual has developed a belief in their own identity as not a free person, deserving of freedoms that you and I enjoy, but rather that of a prisoner, an inmate. They do not internally feel worthy of being free, so they sabotage their own freedom so that reality is consistent with identity.

We all have a tremendous desire to be congruent with whom we perceive ourselves to be, regardless of whether it is logical. Regarding your career, unless you feel worthy and deserving of a raise, promotion or the establishment of a new venture, you will struggle and sabotage your chances. Why? Because we all have a tremendous desire to live in accordance with our self-perception.

Finding your ultimate destination is simply a function of expanding and enhancing your internal identity and formulating a belief system that makes the attainment of this vision truly attainable. You must believe you can do it! Belief without passion *and* conviction is simply a lie. In fact, if you look carefully at the word belief, you will see something interesting. The word B – E – L – I – E – F actually contains the word lie! One of the root causes of behavioral dysfunction is an inability to connect our belief systems with our actions. We may want something, but if we do not believe it with conviction, we will create an internal struggle that leads to massive stress. People can spend years in therapy trying to break through when often it is a matter of choosing goals in sync with our character and true selves vs. trying to live up to others' expectations.

The key is not to try to change your behavior, but rather, to help you to create a new identity. My goal is to assist you to re-shape yourself to become the person needed to obtain your unique calling. Together, we will visualize you already engaged in your career calling and then provide steps to make it a reality. Research tells us that there is almost no difference in brain function when visualizing something and actually doing it! That is the incredible power of your mind!

I also know that the clearer your images and objectives, the more successful you will be in attaining them. There is a direct correlation between low self-esteem and a lack of clarity. People who are successful are clear in their wants, needs and desires. Those less accomplished tend to be less focused. Avoid being vague!

The exciting news is that you and I can systematically alter our current identity to help us make the changes we need to make in order to realize our true potential. Understand that there is a direct link between what you think about yourself and your career success. If you seek a particular career calling, you must develop the proper *self-concept* needed to live into this occupation.

The fact is that you will attract into your life, the people and opportunities in sync with your most dominant thoughts. The person you decide to become is a direct correlation to how you decide to structure your values and belief systems. Character comes from what you focus on and allow into your mind, what you choose to expose your emotions to and how you react to circumstances.

The key to obtaining your calling is to create massive momentum or what I call *leverage* behind your purpose or desire. In other words, you need to build a strong emotional tie between the outcome you seek and the effort required to achieve the objective.

Said another way, you must clearly establish, *"the why behind the want."* What was the real reason you decided to invest time and energy in finding your unique calling and learning the importance of life balance? Are you broke? Are you tired or dissatisfied with being mediocre? Are you restless for more? Do you seek peace of mind? Whatever your motivations, you need to understand your desired outcome and *why* you seek that outcome.

80% of achievement in life is in developing a strong enough *why,* the psychology behind your ambition. The other 20% is in the mechanics, the actual carrying out of your plan. If you have momentum toward a prior behavior or bad habit, your mind will resist your initial efforts to change this conditioned response.

For example, if you took 20 years to put on weight through poor eating habits, it will take a strong effort to avoid the body's conditioned response to seek a certain quantity or chemical composition of food. If the conditioned habit has been to be non-communicative (silence) during an argument with your spouse, and you want to become a good communicator (instead of using silence to express your feelings), your momentum will try to keep you from communicating by pulling you toward the familiar pattern of silence.

You must adopt a new philosophy and through positive self-talk and leverage (a strong enough justification for fighting through your natural conditioned response, for example, it will enhance the quality of your relationship), you can adopt a new conditioned response to conflict, in this case, not silence but communication!

Before you decide where you want to be, you must first determine where you are today. Recently we purchased a new car that had one of those fancy navigation systems, which supposedly helps men like me (who hate to ask for directions!) find their destination. The 1st step to using this new technology is to program your origination point, where you are now. Finding your career calling works the same way. Before you determine your ultimate destination, you must first take careful inventory of where you are today.

Again, we only use about 10% of our brain power. You no doubt have hidden potential that has never been identified or put into practice. Without realizing your potential and continually growing as a person, you will remain unemployed, unhappy or undervalued in the workplace. We all have a unique gift or contribution to make, let us discover it together and put it to good use!

Where Is Your Ultimate Destination?

"The indispensable 1ˢᵗ step to getting the things you want out of life is this: decide what you want."
—Ben Stein, actor and author

Another bit of obvious but important advice: Do not keep your credentials a secret! Learn to identify and demonstrate your most significant strengths. If you are currently employed, don't wait for the employer to find a role that maximizes your talents; make it your responsibility. Take control!

The game plan is to itemize your collective skills and talents and then empower you to describe them to a potential employer in a language you are comfortable with. That is what self-marketing is all about!

You will not only recognize your unique talents and skills but will apply them to your newfound calling. Develop the confidence to demonstrate

© 2009 Learned

"Human Resources informed me they will hire your replacement as soon as they figure out what you actually did!"

you are uniquely valuable and your attitude and skills are transferable into the position sought. Your success path won't be a direct line. Think of a ship traveling across the ocean at night. The commander won't always be able to see if he's on the right track and he may veer off course by a couple of degrees. But he has a compass, which helps him monitor his goal. Ultimately, even if slightly off-course, he winds up at his destination.

Success Tip

Where is my ultimate destination? That's an essential question you have to ask yourself.

7 Questions To Help You Set Your Direction

If your responses total more than 2 no's, it is time to take control of your decisions and chart your own course. To take control, begin by focusing on your decisions ...

1. Am I living in balance?
2. Am I enjoying myself and fulfilled at work?
3. Am I making a measurable contribution that makes me feel good?
4. Am I challenged in my current role?
5. Am I improving and learning?
6. Am I surrounding myself with good role models and supportive colleagues?
7. Am I fairly compensated for my efforts?

Decisions Will Dictate Your Success

It is time to strengthen your *decision-making muscles*. To improve, start making more of them and become conscious of them. Any skill you possess gets better the more you use it. If you want to play better golf, get to the driving range. If you want to build your vocabulary, commit to reading more or invest in a vocabulary building program. If you want to perform better when it comes to making love ... practice, practice, practice! (Sorry, that last one got away from me.)

Design your life instead of just being subject to the whims of everyday occurrences. The most important decision you can make is to take accountability for and control of your professional life. *Who you are is not a function of what has happened to you in the past, but rather what you choose to focus on.* For many, life is like being thrown into the river rapids; and the current pulls you wherever it wants to. Be aware of these current events—when you come to forks in the river, if you don't make a decision, you are subject to whatever direction the river pushes you.

Are you controlling your life, or is life controlling you? The critical impact of my message is this: Your life will not change by itself; it changes through your actions. If there is a key person you wish to meet, seminar you want to attend, or occupation you crave, act on it! Concentrate on those forces that can accelerate you towards your objective and act!

This process will set in motion your conscious and subconscious mind to achieve your goal. I would suggest that any 2 people reading this book have had very similar opportunities in life. Some readers have simply acted more decisively than others. And it is these decisions—*the ability to take action*—that separate the successful person from the person who is still searching. Decisions shape your life. Do you have the insight, the guts, to make a decision when a unique opportunity presents itself? Or, do you procrastinate, and delay taking action?

Preference Versus Decisions

> *"Everything begins as a thought. Everyone manifests. Some people manifest abundance. Others manifest lack. If you want a better harvest, you must plant better thoughts. Poor thoughts will not produce prosperity."*
> — Mark Victor Hansen & Robert G. Allen,
> *The One Minute Millionaire*

Most people don't realize the difference between making a decision and what our preferences are. Anybody can tell you what their preferences are, what they hope for. Very few people can tell you what they have decided to do. The difference between a preference and a decision is that when you make a decision, you leave no other option.

Henry Ford once said, "If you believe you can do a thing, or believe you cannot, in either case, you're probably right." Helplessness, worry and apathy are adopted behaviors. If you have these behaviors, you have made a decision to adopt them and allow them in your life. This second, you can decide to eliminate them.

When I founded my company, *Career* T.E.A.M, we set out to assist 10,000 welfare recipients become economically and emotionally independent and transition off welfare. To do so, we adopted this same philosophy regarding decisions. Our strategy was to make getting off welfare, not a "should" but a "must"! Our key was to change our clients' *core belief systems*. Our staff fostered an environment of a fresh start. This was our unique and compelling strategy and how we became nationally recognized. Other programs focused on mechanics (the resume or interview process); we focused heavily on client mindset and changing poorly shaped identities.

Students didn't have a *preference* to become self-sufficient; they made a *decision* to become independent. We did not offer welfare recipients a *preference* of a new lifestyle; we asked rather that they make a *decision* to commit their heart and soul to no other alternative than to be self-sufficient, to no longer rely on a government check to feed their family, clothe their babies, send their children to school, buy a car or go on a vacation. This single mandate made all the difference in the world and branded *Career* T.E.A.M. as a national workforce provider. We were even invited to the White House to share our success formula!

Your success in obtaining your unique and compelling career calling will be a function of the *decisions* you make in your life: who you network with, what risks you take, what positions you accept or reject, and where you choose to live. These are all important decisions that will dictate your success or failure. Your decision to go back to school, to get married, to have children, to drink, to smoke, your decision about your health and fitness, lifestyle and religious beliefs, those decisions ultimately shape who you are. The 5P's (passion, purpose, power, profit and peace of mind) require you to make decisions about how you want to live and thrive.

If you make excuses about where you came from, how your family failed you or how you weren't afforded the right opportunities, stop right now! These excuses are useless! We all know people who have had advantages, whether they are genetic, environmental, family advantages, educational advantages and still fail. We also know people who overcome barriers and lead exceptionally abundant lives.

Success isn't an entitlement for the rich or the wealthy or those born into fortunate circumstances. It's yours if you want it and can *identify* with it. You just have to develop the courage to claim it and incorporate a strategy to find your career calling. And that's my calling, to help you manifest and develop that courage and realize the true potential that you have within you so you can go out and claim what is rightfully yours—your calling.

Napoleon Hill, author of the classic book, *Think & Grow Rich*, said it is a self-fulfilling prophecy that "you will become what you think about." The sum total of what you deposit into your mind is what you will become. Garbage in, garbage out! If you want to find a problem with your career or why you will never obtain your unique calling, guess what, you will find it. The bible taught us: "Seek and you shall find."

If you're looking for an excuse to fall short or be negative, your mind will absolutely find it. Conversely, if you seek out the positive, you will find that instead. Is the new message in America today: "Expect very little, this way you won't be disappointed?" I cringe when I hear people say, "Be realistic." That's a fancy word for saying, "Be negative and don't expect anything." Imagine if Barack Obama told himself he could not become President or that his chances as an African American were unrealistic?

You can never achieve your career calling if you adopt a defeatist attitude. A little negativity can go a long way towards destroying your career dreams. Negativity is like poison. You don't need a quart of poison to kill you; all you need is the tip of a poisonous arrow. It doesn't take a lot of negative thinking to destroy everything you've worked for. Be careful who you associate with and take advice from!

Others choose not to make any decisions and simply wait for fate to direct them. If you adopt the philosophy that success is based on fate and choose to be directed and manipulated by the ebb and flows of life, that is also a decision, albeit a poor one. You are disempowering yourself because you are victimizing yourself and relinquishing control of the process. Remember, *you* control the game and the intensity and pace at which you play it!

Good things may come to those who wait, but only those things left behind by those who hustled!

Coming from a dysfunctional family, having limited opportunities, being born to a certain race or gender are not excuses that are tolerable for why you aren't where you want to be in your career. These are merely *conditions* of your life. Most important are the decisions that you make to overcome conditions and your ability to commit to seeing them through.

Let today be the day that you decide what makes you *unique and compelling* and apply these attributes to a career that allows you to contribute and enrich the lives of others. Your true career potential is greater than what you have been demonstrating to this point. Making a decision is one that eliminates any other possibility than the calling that you seek. Working simply for the money or prestige is simply not an option!

Avoid the "victim" mentality and instead emerge the victor! Do not become one of the many working individuals who dislike their job, blame the boss, or are directed by their external environment. Choose to carve out your unique place in the world, a place where you are afforded the opportunity to contribute your reason for being along with your unique and compelling values and standards.

Anticipate the future! The problems we encounter 5 minutes before we go over the side of Niagara Falls, could probably be avoided if we made better decisions upstream. People often unconsciously sabotage their professional life. They envision the worst-case scenario and struggle to overcome those limiting beliefs. Some link such pain and anguish to being disappointed that they stop trying. They sabotage real progress in their life because they associate negativity and pain to potential rejection. They are defeated before they even begin! And they remain stuck in a dead end career. The final result is that we have extraordinary people who settle for mediocre lives.

Only about 20% have found their career calling, take pride and experience passion on a daily basis. The other 80% are mired in fear, uncertainty and doubt. You don't want to fall into that trap. Peel away the conditioning, fear and apprehension and together, let us show the world what you have to offer, the real and amazing you!

Are You *Interested* In Finding Your Calling ...
Or *Committed* to It?

> *"Do or do not, there is no try."*
>
> —Yoda from *Star Wars*

If you are familiar with my career, you know I am often interviewed by various magazines, television and radio stations about how I became "so successful."

I didn't come from an affluent family, went to a state university, wasn't a great student, but here's my secret. I began to achieve success when I decided I was absolutely *committed* to being successful for myself and my family, and I was absolutely certain that I had passion, purpose and power to help individuals. I realized I had a contribution to make and that I was absolutely committed to becoming an Ambassador for the subject of career success. That decision, more than anything else, shaped my destiny. In your life, when you make a decision and commit to whatever it is that you decide you want, only then can you achieve a life of abundance.

If you met me in an elevator and had 45 seconds to describe your specific career calling and dedication to achieving it, what words would come out of your mouth? Remember, 45 seconds ...

Because "the road to success is always under construction," it is very important that you create a foundation and standards for things that you can control in your personal and professional life. What I am professing is orchestrating a career blueprint.

Commitment Starts and Ends with Managing Your Thoughts and Beliefs

> *"When you are inspired by some great purpose, some extraordinary project, all your thoughts break their bounds. Your mind transcends limitations, your consciousness expands in every direction, and you find yourself a new, great and wonderful world."*
>
> —*The Yoga Sutras of Patanjali*,
> quoted in *The 8th Habit*, by Steven Covey

Focus on the twin towers of pain and pleasure. Human beings have a desire to move towards pleasure and move away from pain. Everything we do is geared towards that activity. The challenge is: We all associate different things to obtaining pleasure or avoiding pain. Do you want a secret to life? Here it is: *The ability to change and alter what you link pain and pleasure to on a proactive basis will be the entire difference for you.*

For example, if you link pleasure to smoking, you are always going to smoke. But people who have quit smoking have figured out a way to link pain to smoking. If you link pleasure to victimizing yourself and having others feel sorry for you, guess what? It will become a habit. What you associate pain and pleasure to will dictate the course of your life and your ability to make positive change in your personal and professional endeavors.

Do you associate enough pleasure to finding your career calling that you will endure some pain (critical reflection, making new contacts, finishing this book, etc.) to achieve it?

There is even a name for this science called neuro-associative conditioning or NAC, which is the process of programming your inner self and linking positive beliefs to the things that you want. Although it is not my desire to provide a historical lesson on the study of managing your conscious and subconscious mind, for the purposes of this book, let's agree that NAC is a powerful science, a conditioning process that deserves mention.

Once you understand and master this technique, you operate on automatic pilot. It is like driving a car. You don't have to think about every single action when you are driving from home to the office. You may be daydreaming about what you did yesterday, what you're going to have for dinner that night, a conversation you had … you are on automatic pilot. It's the same process with neuro-associative conditioning. You condition your mind to look for success and it simply comes to you more often.

Mastering your mindset correlates to your level of self-esteem.

As a nation, we are suffering from an epidemic of low self-esteem. Only 1 in 3 people based upon national studies have positive self-esteem. 2 out of 3 people have low self-esteem. Self-esteem is your life energy. Protect your life energy! So many people have great dreams and aspirations but daily activities, incongruent lifestyle and poor personal life drain your life energy. Being in sync with your identity is an important process to invest your time and energy. Make sure that your life choices are not incongruent between who you are and what you do; that's what causes friction and massive stress. Are your actions and choices meeting the expectations of others, or are they meeting your own expectations? Have you found yourself in a mode of predictability and comfort in life, but not one that gives you passion? When you look back on your life when you are old and grey, you do not want to say, "It was OK, but I could have," and worse, "I should have done more." Create a *defining moment* where it is no longer acceptable to ignore the passions you have within you.

My 5th grade son came home from school and asked me if I wanted to participate in his school's "career day" where parents would present a 15 minute overview of their current job and responsibilities to his class. The idea was to begin to educate the kids about working and certain options available to them when they reached working age. As I thought about what to say, it dawned on me that I wasn't a big fan of my own job functions and when I really thought about it, was afraid I would have to fake enthusiasm to make my job sound more glamorous than it truly was. It was like an out of body experience as I realized I was in the wrong field; I was living someone else's life! Talk about your breakthrough or defining moment! Feeling like a fraud, I decided to explore my passion and purpose as suggested in *The Career Guarantee* and have since made a transition into a marketing role. I cannot wait to present to the kids during the next career day when I can share my genuine enthusiasm for my occupation!

—Troy from Philadelphia

Talk about a defining moment! Many people need a layoff, illness or, in the case above, embarrassment to obtain the clarity needed to make a significant change. For others, a defining moment may be a movie or the messages in a book or simply the desire to do more and better.

I'm not suggesting you immediately quit your job and move to a different place in the world; what I am saying, however, is that making changes doesn't necessarily mean a change of occupation, relationship, or ever geography. It is a process of managing your internal circuitry; the greatest computer ever invented—your mind!

The Importance of Self-Concept

> *"During one-on-one coaching, seminars or workshops, I have often heard people use the phrase, "they have yet to find themselves." Be aware that the "self" is not something a person finds, but rather something one creates and develops."*
> —Chris Kuselias

You, an organism that offers contribution, value and solutions, are in constant development. You are in production. You are unique. There has never been another individual exactly like you, ever. You are continually evolving and you are never stagnant. You are moving toward an ultimate destination, based on your current talents and potential.

I have a question for you: Is it possible that you are a uniquely exciting individual who has not realized your career calling yet? Is there a universe of potential within you? Is who you really are and what you have to contribute to others being utilized or wasted? If your self-concept isn't in line with your identity, you are simply cheating yourself, your loved ones, your children and everybody else that you hold dear. The plan is to save you any more wasted days, weeks, months or years and ignite that passion in you. The process of *self-concept* is about reconnecting to yourself, living in balance and achieving your full career potential.

Try this exercise … I want you to think back to the last time you felt overcome with joy, a time you were truly happy and in a passionate state. Maybe it was at work, had something to do with your family or when you were engaged in a hobby. I want you to rekindle those flames and remind your emotional self what that felt like. I want to restore and have you remember a connection. That is the feeling that ultimately creates a peace of mind and has a calming effect on your soul. You probably felt you were doing what you were born to do with the people that you were meant to do it with, feeling the way you were meant to feel.

How can you develop that passion in your career? To begin, are you doing what you truly enjoy doing? Are you passionate? My guess is no or you might not be reading these words. So, assuming you are not, if you could do anything your heart desired, what would it be? Pretend money was not an issue. Would you keep your current career and do it differently or change to something completely different?

> Study the common trends of your own *happiness states* and you will see that success leaves clues to how and where you should be spending your time, that is, a calling.

The happiest people I know are those who have found a way to earn a living doing something they are passionate about. My advice is to keep your antenna up and notice the times when you experience the most zest, joy and happiness and record those times in a journal or some organized system.

> The key to happiness is so simple it sounds elementary. Spend more time doing what you love to do.

You can obtain the control that I am talking about, but effort is required. Being *too busy* is not an excuse I will allow. Are you so *busy being busy* that you let the passion and joy erode from your life? You have immense potential that is not being utilized: spiritual, physical, mental, emotional, career, relationships and financially. Time to open the faucet!

"Life #@&*+# and then you die," is not a mantra I subscribe to, nor should you. Seek substance over appearance. An early mentor taught me the importance of spending more time on my internal self than my external self. While we all seek to make a good appearance, I advise you not to spend too much of your precious time working on your *appearance* instead of your *substance.*

Many people spend 1–2 hours in the morning getting ready so they can look good, and they don't spend 5 minutes on the essence of who they are, their substance. How much of your life energy is absorbed by the superficial vs. what you know in your mind and body and heart really, truly matters? I am not really interested in your *social mask.* When did you stop living and start simply existing? When did it become wake up, go to work, grab a latte, worry about money, come home, worry about work, worry about the future. When did that pattern take hold? Develop your passion and build that into your unique purpose.

I know that each one of us has passion and purpose that when ignited, makes life immeasurably more meaningful. I also know how easy it is to succumb to daily pressures and conformity. Can you imagine if Michael Jordan didn't pursue his dream of becoming a basketball player? Can you imagine if Elvis went into the moving business instead of pursuing his passion of being a singer? Can you imagine if I had stayed on my path to become a lawyer and I didn't fulfill my dream? How about you?

Success Tip

If you don't stand for or believe in anything, then you can be suckered into anything.

Without passion, superficiality and material possessions become the alternative and the measure. It's called keeping up with the Joneses. False goals, like money, the accumulation of material possessions and approval from others, take the place of real inner peace and purpose. You can be suckered into what to purchase, what to wear, how to feel, how to look, how to dress, how to behave!

Make a commitment right now to view life from the inside out and to pursue your rightful place in the world. Focus on who you really are and what you really want and then contribute your gifts by developing your skills and expertise in whatever field or endeavor ignites your inner flame of passion.

You Were Born with Passion ... How Did You Lose It?

> *"The biggest mistake people make in life is not trying to make a living at doing what they most enjoy."*
> —Malcolm S. Forbes

Enthusiasm is derived from the Greek word *entheos,* which translates "to be filled with God." I believe there is a direct correlation between your spirit, which exists in your mind, body and soul, and your passion for contribution to others. Your career is an ideal opportunity to express this contribution. The challenge is that this passion is often tarnished by societal conditioning, life events our own apathy.

You had this passion. You were born with it. Don't believe me? Take a look at any new baby. Every time each of my children was born (I have 3)

I was amazed by the excitement, the passion, the pure joy that they were born with. They would laugh and giggle over the smallest details: a smile from a stranger, a music box and even the discovery of their own belly button! When did this unabashed joy fade away and be replaced by fear, uncertainty and doubt? When did you lose this childlike playfulness? Are you saying maturity and the loss of fun and enjoyment go hand and hand? When did cynicism replace love of life? You didn't lose it at one fell swoop; it wasn't surgically removed.

Most likely, this zest faded a little at a time, like an ocean gradually erodes a shoreline. Here is the good news! You can rekindle that. It is not extinct but simply dormant. Don't become one of those people who talk about how crazy and fun you used to be. Create new memories. Be aware of where your joy is.

Are you accepting that the most fun and fulfillment you'll ever have is in your past? *But Chris,* you might be thinking; *now I have responsibilities and bills and kids and jobs, etc.* That is a rationalization for the choice you've made to neglect yourself and what matters to you. Yes, you have more responsibility. But, that is why even more than ever it is so important to carve out time to spend on you and not just watch mindless television or get lost in a novel reading about somebody else's exciting life. It is not enough to live vicariously through actors or actresses who are getting paid and living their dream; we must live our own dreams.

I possess the belief that the older we become, the easier our career should be. We are supposed to understand things better. You should have seen some of my prior outfits or hairstyles, yikes! While we no doubt benefit from modern conveniences, life is in many ways more complicated. It certainly goes by at a faster pace than ever before. We are now so programmed and over-stimulated that we often neglect to conduct an internal check of our thoughts and emotions.

Success Tip

At the age of 40, over half your work life is still ahead of you.

When was the last time you just sat around and day dreamed? We are over-stimulated (24 hour cell phone access, hand held computers, internet, 600 television channels) to the point we have lost our career goals and can no longer hear our self-talk because of outside stimulus. We have lost ourselves in the speed and complexities of the modern world. We have an appointment with stress overload and it is often only a matter of time.

If you are stressing your system mentally, physically and emotionally, you are going to get old before your time. Medical experts tell us we can lose as much as a decade off our life by enduring the kind of stress I am describing to you. I coach people every day who are in so deep a rut I need a team to pull them out! Life, apathy and poor career choices have eroded their passion and zest for life and it takes a great deal of courage and momentum to fix what ails them. Fear not, you can change and improve if you are willing to put the brakes on and ignite that lost flame.

Breaking Destructive Patterns

You can break destructive patterns in your life by creating a new reality. As an example, I wanted to have an office in my home and listen to Frank Sinatra music while I create. I also wanted to be around my kids more, especially when they were young before they went to school a full day. I often take my eldest daughter Alana to meetings, introducing her as my publicist or the "heir apparent." Surely, it is unconventional. People might ask, "What kind of unprofessional guy brings his kids to meetings?" I didn't care, because it's what I wanted to do. It didn't impact them negatively, and it didn't derail the meeting. Maybe they thought it was unprofessional because somebody told them it was.

Recently, I had a 2-day meeting in Boston. I took my young son C.J. with me. His bedtime is normally 7:30 PM. After my meeting that day, which he spent coloring Spiderman books, we went to see real live sharks at the Boston Aquarium and to Fenway Park to watch a Red Sox game. When we got back to our hotel, we jumped around in our underwear, raided the mini-bar of the candy, and watched cool movies until 10:00 PM. We had a great time, and he will probably never forget it. I certainly will not!

I could have gone on a business trip myself, sat there, maybe done some work at night and eaten dinner alone. Instead I had a wonderful bonding opportunity with my son. Unconventional ... yes! I broke a pattern by making a change and it was great!

This is your one shot at life. This is not a dress rehearsal. Children learn what they live, and you want to teach them by example. If your kids see you miserable and not living a life that is your true self, they will probably be drawn into a similar pattern. Is that what you want for your children? Do you want them complaining about the lousy hand they were dealt in life or blaming the economy?

I promise you, it's not what I want for mine. I want them to find their authentic self, their true self, to hear their inner voice, and not get bogged down with outside distractions or information overload, but to spend the time to figure out who they are, and what gives them purpose and passion. I want them to stake their claim and make a contribution. I want them to live life with passion and zest and have no regrets. This takes planning as a family to make sure that happens. I suggest that you incorporate these exercises and philosophies and do the same for yours.

Finding Your Career Calling Is Your Obligation!

I want you to be able to say, "I'm proud of my career." I want you to have a level of enjoyment and peace as you pursue your purpose and passion. I want you to put what's important to you on your to do list. If you don't pursue your passions, you are cheating the world out of your unique contributions. When you neglect your calling, you are not only cheating yourself, but everybody else around you, including your family, friends and professional associates.

Most people answer the question *who are you?* with what they do, because they can't answer the question with who they are. Perhaps they don't know or haven't spent the time to think about it so they can articulate it properly. "I'm a mom. I'm a doctor. I'm a parent. I'm a husband. I'm a wife. I'm an electrician." The true essence of who you are is not what you do; it is so much more.

Be True to Yourself

> *"Jacob was left alone. And a man wrestled with him until the break of dawn."*
>
> —Genesis 32:23–32

Is there restlessness, a yearning, or, as my mother likes to say, "A hole in your soul?" If there is, be careful what you fill it with. Make sure it's not an affair, overeating, smoking, or worse. The energy it takes to suppress your true inner self is amazing and will drain your life to the point where you won't have the energy to succeed. Are you using most of your energy to suppress your inner self?

I always relate to the analogy of the swan, so perfect and graceful above the water, but underneath the water line, the swan's legs are kicking and clawing against the tide or current to keep it afloat and appearing graceful. Are you showing the world a graceful exterior, but internally there exists a frenetic, restless soul? It consumes your strength and ultimately exhausts you.

People often describe me as contagiously happy. I have found my purpose and passion and it can't help but radiate in the way I speak, act, and think. That is my wish for you. When a person attains their calling and exhibits pride in their profession, others will be drawn towards you and look to you for guidance. That is how you will develop power.

To attain this distinction, it is important to set aside time to focus on *you*. Many people are caretakers, who take care of everybody else first and leave little or no time for their own development. Is this you? Do you always put others in your life first—family, kids, spouse, partner, boss, co-workers, church members—and take care of yourself last? To truly love your profession, you must absolutely commit to exploring your inner genius; that is your unique and compelling self. Set aside the kids, the diapers, the lawn, the chores, the PTA meetings, the family obligations, and carve out time for you!

A challenge you face is that all of your momentum is probably focused on limiting beliefs, societal conditioning and the fear of failure. You may have developed this mentality over weeks, months or even years. You must change this pattern of beliefs and "shock your system" with a breakthrough or defining moment and the complete acceptance of the positive feelings associated with the benefits of finding your true career calling.

I am of the belief that our maker is truly wise. Each of us, including you, has everything within you—everything—that you will ever need to be, do and achieve your career purpose and passion. You are in possession of all the ingredients and the tools you need. There is greatness within you!

Employers today are spending millions to try to find people who can match their interests with their products or services. They know a happy employee works harder, has fewer sick days and performs better. The field of industrial psychology is based on the pairing of tasks and duties with an individual's core self and their base skills. Companies that do that the most effectively, win. You will have a competitive edge!

More good news: This process of self-discovery will empower and energize you. I have come to believe that at the core of every human being is uniqueness, a compelling person with a different set of passions and contributions. Make no mistake; the visual analogy is that of putting yourself under a microscope.

Once, while being interviewed on the process of uncovering and achieving one's true career calling, I surprised the skeptical host by equating the process of finding your career calling to finding your soul mate. I asked the interviewer, who shared with me that they were divorced, if they would go on a date without first assessing if the person had similar values and belief systems. In other words, if you are looking to find a soul mate, isn't the 1ˢᵗ step to determine what *you* seek in a soul mate? You do not compromise on important values or considerations. You don't just randomly date without considering what is important to you or you are simply wasting time and *hoping* to find Mr. or Mrs. Right.

My point is to spend more time in analyzing what you'll do for a career since you're going to spend so much time on it, much like you would do when evaluating a car or appliance. People continue to just grab jobs as if it didn't matter to them. They will fail. Some very intelligent people are stuck in occupations that are destroying their vitality and zest. A friend says this: "He has more degrees than a thermometer but he can't find his calling because he doesn't know what he values in his work life."

Learn to focus on your values and work smarter, not harder. You are the captain of your decisions and behaviors. When you choose the behavior, you choose the consequences. When you attain your calling, you will have a new responsibility because as the saying goes, "Of him to whom much is given, much is expected."

The Power of Attitude

Building a Positive Career Attitude

"We do not sing because we are happy, we are happy because we sing."

—William James, philosopher

It is estimated you have approximately 50,000 thoughts per day . . . and over 90% of them are negative. Think about it. Is your self-talk positive (*I was great, I am so proud of myself, What a great job of anticipating the problem I did . . .*) or negative (*How could I be so stupid? Why did I say that? Why am I so fat? . . .*). If you are like most people, chances are you are beating yourself up internally with your own negative thoughts. Each time you send a negative message to yourself you erode your confidence and self-esteem.

Here is a phenomenal exercise. Place a rubber band around your wrist and every time you think a negative thought, snap the rubber band on your wrist as a penalty. Have your spouse, significant other or a friend join in the process and participate. The plan is to go as long as you can without thinking a single negative thought. See how long you can go. My experience is that you will be snapping away within seconds. Gradually, as you get better at mastering or filtering your negative energies, you can go longer without hurting your wrist with the snap of the rubber band. When you make progress, an hour may go by before you have to snap it. You will continually get better. Condition yourself for success!

You are building your positive-focused energies. You are eliminating a negative-focused mentality. This simple exercise gets you in the habit of noticing what you do have instead of what you don't have; what's great about your life vs. what's not. Become a person who focuses on solutions and not problems, that is a key to changing your life.

Focus on positives and minimize your attention to negatives. Develop the habit of giving compliments because it will help you to focus on the positive activities of others and not their faults or shortcomings. To give a compliment, you have to be focused on something positive about another individual. When you start to program your mind to do that, you start to look for the wonderful things in life. This will begin to build a more positive career attitude. Go out and give 3 compliments today!

Attitude Determines Altitude

> "There exists a hidden psychology to career success, which the majority of individuals are unaware of. It is why most people never achieve career happiness and life balance. Career unhappiness is not your challenge; it is merely a symptom of the lack of clarity inside of you."
>
> —Chris Kuselias

There are more incredible career opportunities than there are people seeking them. Skill level or a better resume isn't the problem, but rather attitude and confidence. Have you ever heard the saying, "It is your attitude, not your aptitude that will determine your altitude." When a person walks into a room, before they even open their mouth, you notice their attitude and formulate an opinion. Studies show that the majority of our communication is non-verbal and only a small percentage is through the spoken word. You see it in tone, posture, pace, body language, and hear it in voice and inflection. We often see before we hear.

When I was asked by CNN to describe our success in transforming thousands of unemployed individuals with low self-esteem, I illustrated the importance of starting with posture and body language. I would select the most bored, inattentive member of the audience and ask them to join me in front of the room as a volunteer. I would ask them to mimic a person they have met who was bored, depressed, angry, possibly out of work and lacking purpose and passion. I would then request that they walk the length of the room in the posture that this unhappy person exhibited. They would be overly dramatic with slow pace, slouched shoulders, head down, etc. and we would record a list of attributes which confirmed this person was down on their luck.

After itemizing all the non-verbal attributes of an unfulfilled person, we would then ask the same volunteer to suddenly change their demeanor and act and walk like a person who had: a great career that filled them with passion, a plan for their life, a person who was confident they were a positive role model for their children, a person who had attained some money and was experiencing success. Suddenly, my volunteer would transform from the shrinking violet to a bold, confident individual who strolled across the room at a faster pace, head high and with a confident wave to his fellow audience members! The crowd would be hysterical and hoot and holler at this newfound transformation.

I would then reinforce the importance of focusing on how you conduct yourself and what your body language communicates to the world. The bored, tired, disinterested audience was now at rapt attention, anxious to see what we would do next! Awareness of their body led to a change in momentum and belief.

When you meet a person for the 1st time, whether it is a new customer, potential new business partner or an interviewer, *people formulate a powerful first impression of you within the first 12–30 seconds.* This is typically before you have even spoken your first word! We judge people on their appearance and general demeanor. You can tell a great deal about attitude (especially professional interviews that literally see hundreds of candidates) from a first impression. Attitude ultimately determines success.

Success Tip

Were you aware that how much you respect and like yourself defines your self-esteem?

Who are you really and how much do you like yourself? Your exterior demeanor is a mirror of your interior thoughts, emotions and beliefs. I call this your "mental fitness" and like physical fitness, it requires regular and sometimes intense training to improve. Learn to nourish your spirit and feed your mind with optimism, much like you nourish the body with healthy foods and vitamins.

If you eat junk food, you might eventually develop high blood pressure, clog your arteries, experience low stamina, have increased body fat and generally feel lousy. If you eat healthy and exercise, you become vibrant and alive! If you dwell on problems, debt, marital issues, world tension, you will soon become an unhappy person and push people away. When you focus on goals, outcomes, solutions and formulate a visualize picture of your optimal self, it is as if you injected happiness into your veins! Next time you are in a crowded place, observe which individuals are passionate and which are moping from task to task. Which person are you? Is there bounce in your step or does your body language suggest lethargy?

You can improve your body language and overall demeanor by training your mind to focus on the positive aspects of your life. Discipline yourself to focus on the outcomes you seek and the positive steps required to achieve each new success. Make a commitment to reject negative thoughts, make excuses or assign blame to anyone but yourself. Be accountable! Replace fear, worry, procrastination and doubt with optimism, upbeat, happy thoughts and emotions and, like the impact of eliminating fat, sugar and salt from your physical diet, you will observe a change.

Success Tip

This powerful combination of taking personal responsibility for your performance coupled with a clear vision and purpose provides a solid foundation to achieve excellence and balance.

What's Wrong with a Neutral Attitude?

We often hear of someone having a "good" attitude or a "bad" attitude, and as you would expect, "good" or "bad" things usually result. What about a neutral attitude? Someone with a neutral attitude goes with the flow, is not particularly motivated or extremely happy with their life, but is not miserable either. What is wrong with that?

Let's take a closer look at what happens to those with neutral attitudes. Answer: Not much of anything.

- They tend to stay in the same job, even if it makes them unhappy or no longer meets their needs.
- They have difficulty making new friends or starting new relationships.

- They don't learn and grow.
- They don't grab opportunities and run with them.

Is that how you want to describe your life?

How Attitude Shows in Your Language

Whether you are aware of it or not, your attitude shows—*in everything you say and do.* Make it reflect well on you! Attitude is evident in:

- Word choice
- Tone of voice
- Gestures, expression, and body language

Let's take these one by one and look at how exactly our attitudes are reflected in them.

Word Choice

Positive:	Yes I will	I can Of course	You bet I'm certain
Negative:	No It wasn't my fault	I can't I don't have time	I'm afraid No way
Neutral:	Maybe I doubt it	I'm not sure If ...	Wait and see

Progress, Not Perfection, Is the Goal

> *Asked which of his works he would select as his masterpiece, architect Frank Lloyd Wright at age 83 replied, "My next one."*

Attitude is clearly a key to attaining your career calling and enjoying every Monday morning. News flash! You are never going to be perfect. You are going to say things you shouldn't say, do things you shouldn't do, make mistakes, fall into negative patterns. That makes you human. The goal is just to get better every day. The only way you truly fail is if you quit. And if you learn something in the process and you contribute at the same time, you're ahead of the game.

Your reality is controlled by the information available to you, what you do with this data and ultimately what you *focus* on. This thought process forms your own personal reality. Think about some of the great people in history, like Walt Disney, who was told that his theme park idea was ridiculous and turned down by practically everybody.

> Steve Jobs was only 21 years old when he cofounded Apple Inc. in his garage. This first personal computer, named Apple, sold for $666. As of this writing, Jobs serves as chairman and CEO and was listed by *Fortune* magazine as the most powerful businessmen of 2007. In the beginning, there were doubters.

In 1996, Congress introduced the Welfare Reform Act, which put a term limit on welfare and created a sense of urgency to transition people to successful employment. The Welfare Reform Act said that people had to get off welfare after 60+ years of conditioning. This was a huge shift in culture and belief conditioning. Many people felt entitled to a check because they had grown up that way.

As a company, our vision was to mandate empowerment and motivation training into helping us solve the welfare problem in this country. We as an organization thought that you must be dedicated to changing mindset, building identity and empowerment. I remember distinctly that many of our inexperienced funding sources said, "No, no, just give the participants an overview of the mechanics of job search like resume and interview." They literally laughed in our faces and told us they would never fund a training program with a focus on changing mindsets. Their limiting belief was that welfare recipients would not absorb nor appreciate the content. Today, (10,000+ placements and counting), changing mindset is essential for this type of training.

Developing a Chief Executive Officer (CEO) Attitude

During the course of my professional career, I have been both an employee and a Chief Executive Officer (CEO), the ultimate authority and final decision maker. One thing I have learned is that the most successful people in life, regardless of position or title, learn to think like a CEO, even if they are in an entry-level position. This is a key ingredient to finding and keeping your career calling. Below is a chart of the differences between those who think like employees vs. those who adopt a CEO mentality.

Employee Mentality	CEO Mentality
Pays only for what can be reimbursed	Invests money in their professional development
Associates with anyone who will listen	Associates with positive influences
Reacts to interruptions	Minimizes unproductive interruptions
Keeps safe client	Terminates unprofitable relationships

Employee Mentality	CEO Mentality
Confuses activity with accomplishment	Is results focused and reduces unproductive tasks
Thinks quantity is more important than quality	Knows quality creates more quantity
Puts process before people	Puts people before profits
Puts revenue before reputation	Puts reputation before revenue
Builds business ahead of capacity	Builds capacity ahead of business
Prioritizes schedules occasionally	Schedules priorities daily
Is short-term oriented	Is long-term oriented
Relies on quick turnaround	Relies on client trust
Succeeds by accident	Succeeds by design

How you *think* as a professional will determine how you *act* as a professional. Until you begin to think like an owner, you won't consistently take actions that maximize your professional talents.

At *Career* T.E.A.M., all Project Directors (appointed leaders in each city where we have a location, see www.thecareerguarantee.com) are groomed to adopt an owner mentality and treat their assigned project as if it were their own money invested, even though it is not. They manage revenue brought in and watch every penny spent as if it were their own checkbook. Our culture provides incentives on how they run "their business site" and an ownership mentality prevails as a result.

When these associates talk about *Career* T.E.A.M., they use phrases like "my organization" or "our company." I often get email on weekends or evenings because there is tremendous pride and they feel invested in the process and outcomes. Each person knows they matter and contribute to our success or failure. They have an ownership (CEO) mentality and build their skills on their own time, without having to be told to do so. I believe developing staff with a CEO Mentality is the #1 reason we were named one of *Inc. Magazine's* 500 fastest growing, privately held companies.

Other keys:

- How you work matters more than where you work
- How you present yourself matters more than what you have to present
- How many hours you produce matters more that how many hours you work
- Getting loyal business matters more than how much business you get

- Having trusted associates matters more than how many associates you have

While you must first *think* your way to the top, mere thinking is not enough. You must actively invest in your development as a professional to grow. To be a leader in your field, you have to become and remain more competent, innovative, and attractive than your competition.

Conquering Your Limiting Beliefs

I remember reading the amazing story told by Dr. Bernie Siegel, who was studying patients who were diagnosed as schizophrenics, people who were challenged with multiple personalities. In his work, he recounted how when some of his patients were deliberately prompted to shift personalities (by hearing a certain phrase or forced to remember a certain trigger event) that not only did their personality change right before his eyes but that physical characteristics like rashes, posture and even eye color would change. This points out how powerful our mindset is when our mind can actually initiate physical changes due to strong belief with conviction!

A LIMITING BELIEF IS A self-imposed limitation regarding your ability to accomplish a certain task or activity. It can also be a limitation regarding your mindset or ability to change. The good news is that belief systems can be changed or altered, but to do so requires a commitment to that change.

For years, I held the limiting belief that it was impossible for me to be both a great businessman and a great father. I had it in my mind that to be a great businessman and effect change to millions through my research, one had to spend so much time at work or on the road that family life would suffer. To be a great father, one had to restrict or even sacrifice one's career and ambition in order to satisfy family obligations. I was not of the belief that one could be proficient at both. It was not until I made a conscious effort to study role models who had attained excellence in both, that I began to eliminate this limiting belief. When I saw it was possible in others, I knew it could be possible in my life as well.

Today, I have achieved my objectives as both a professional and as a father and continue to build confidence and proficiency in both areas. Unlike before, I now believe it is possible to be an excellent business professional and an excellent husband and father.

To illustrate the power of limiting beliefs and how they can inhibit your development, let me share with you the facts concerning one of the largest species on the planet, the elephant. Due to space limitations associated with captivity, a baby elephant is conditioned at birth to be restricted to an extremely limited space. This is accomplished by having the baby elephant's trainer attach an extremely short rope to both a metal post planted in the ground and the baby elephant's leg. The baby elephant establishes a comfort zone determined by the length of the rope. The baby elephant quickly learns that he can only move in accordance with the length of the short rope, and soon establishes a limiting belief (its reality) that it can only move a short distance. Being a baby elephant, it does not yet possess the physical strength to yank the post out of the ground. It is trained to remain in this designated area; an artificial ceiling has been established.

Incredibly, when the elephant matures and reaches its full 4- or 5-ton weight (with the capacity to now easily break the rope or pull the post out of the ground with a decent tug), it doesn't even bother trying because it has been conditioned that it cannot be done. The end result is that the mature elephant requires the same small space as the baby elephant, even though the mature elephant weighs 5 tons! Talk about a limiting belief!

Perhaps you feel like the elephant when it comes to attaining your career calling. The key is to establish a new set of beliefs based upon role models who accomplish similar goals. If we are not internally convinced that

© mblain / stockxpert

completing the necessary steps to achieve our calling (starting with completing this book!) will result in enhanced pleasure and benefits, we will procrastinate and remain where we are—incomplete and unfulfilled.

> *"All the resources we need are in the mind."*
> —Theodore Roosevelt

Every resource that you need to accomplish your calling is within you. We are all special, uniquely conceived beings who have a purpose and a destiny that is our duty to fulfill. Unfortunately, we often develop a pattern of behavior for addressing emotional or labor intensive changes if we are confused regarding the actual pain vs. pleasure it may bring.

You will act aggressively when the benefits are crystal clear, or the pain of remaining in your current situation becomes too great to bear any longer. The moment you make this change is called a *defining moment*.

You can only experience new results (that is, achieving your calling) if you are able to get leverage on yourself and define what it is you truly want. The catalyst for action is your new emotional state.

Have you ever seen a common housefly trapped in the window of a room? It is there because it first seeks light and thus finds itself banging up against the glass, sometimes for hours. The fly in this case is extremely motivated to make a change (get outside) and even has leverage to do so. The problem is the fly refuses or is incapable of changing its approach to the challenge of getting outside, so it continues a pursuit of the same tactic, without success, until it tires and dies. Despite its desire, the fly is stuck in a non-productive pattern of behavior. The only way that the fly can achieve freedom is to step back and seek another exit (alternative).

> *Consider the words of genius Albert Einstein: "The significant problems we face cannot be solved by the same level of thinking that created them."*

Have you ever felt like the fly in the window? You are trying to further your career, but not getting anywhere. The lesson is to change your pattern or you will experience the same results. Changing your pattern is often as simple as modifying your current approach.

For example, have you ever wanted to arrange a meeting with someone you knew could help you further your career but for some reason (fear of rejection, shyness, laziness) you missed the opportunity? Next time you find yourself in this situation, avoid the pattern that suggests you will feel the pain of rejection, but rather zero in on the pleasure gained by having the courage to ask the contact for their time and consider the benefits to their guidance and wisdom. Replace your old limiting belief with a new alternative.

How to Avoid Limiting Beliefs

> *"If you realized how powerful your thoughts are, you would never think a negative thought."*
>
> —Peace Pilgrim

By now, you may have heard the story of Roger Bannister, the 1st runner in history to break the 4-minute mile. His contribution was so powerful that ESPN made a movie about the event. Even more amazing than his record setting pace, is that within a short time of breaking the record, several other runners suddenly also ran a mile under 4 minutes. This was after centuries of no human being ever accomplishing this feat. What happened? Simply put, Bannister eliminated the limiting belief that no human could run the mile under 4 minutes and opened the door (and mindset) that others could do the same. My question: What limiting beliefs do you have in your life, holding you back from greatness?

You have the ability at this very moment to exceed all previous measures of success. There is no skill you cannot improve, no relationship you cannot develop, no goal you cannot attain if you eliminate limiting beliefs and foster the power of your potential.

Ray Kroc was a 52-year-old milkshake salesman when he bought out a restaurant owned by Mac and Richard McDonald. Many people are thinking of retirement at that age, but not Ray. His dream was to create a franchise for their delicious burgers, so he bought out the brothers in 1961 and created McDonald's, the most successful fast food company in the world.

There is resentment to success. Why? Many are not willing to sacrifice and find it easier to bring others down, to make excuses and formulate blame for their shortcomings. They have fear and lack courage to tackle success. Avoid the "something for nothing disease," which is thinking you will get back more than you put in. They rationalize that successful people are lucky. You and I know different! The truth is that life mimics effort: superior performance rewards superior effort. Many people don't strive for major success because they fear what may result if they don't succeed. Learn this: Failure is inevitable if we attempt bigger things. Failure can be very beneficial—enlightening us at times.

The only way to combat failure is to decide to see it as an opportunity to improve your direction. Attaining your calling in life is a life-long process of continuous and never-ending improvement. Reaching the pinnacle of success in the 5 critical areas (career, health, financial, social, spiritual) is not so much what you receive from achievement as it is what you *become* by achieving.

You are responsible for upgrading your talents as well as being aware of your true worth. Think of yourself as a Stock Exchange symbol. Are you a stock that everybody wants to buy or a stock that no one wants? Remember, winners always focus on solutions, while losers focus on the problem. Winners always look to what they can do and how they can improve, while losers always look at who is to blame for their shortcomings.

The Power of Affirmations

"All battles are won or lost first, in the mind."

—Joan of Arc

AN AFFIRMATION IS A statement that determines what it is you want with the assumption you have already attained it.

> Here is how self-talk works: Replace the beliefs or thoughts that are keeping you from achieving your career calling with a revised statement that empowers you and will actually move you closer to your calling.

Napoleon Hill said it best when he said, "The only thing you have complete control over is your own mental attitude." That is the ticket to career success and balance! One hour of planning truly saves 3 hours of execution. Most people don't plan; when you fail to plan, you plan to fail!

Consider the story of the woodcutter who is attempting to chop down a huge tree. He begins by swinging his axe over and over in the same spot. Over time, his axe begins to dull due to usage, but he is afraid to stop swinging because he feels it will waste time and delay the falling of the tree. What he fails to realize is that the down time spent stopping to sharpen his axe blade will actually reduce the time it takes to fell the tree. The blade, once sharpened, cuts through the tree easier, saving the man from reaching complete exhaustion.

Have you been approaching the process with a dull blade? Have you taken the time to replenish your energy by formulating a clear and distinct vision of your desired outcome? Often, people are grinding away at a task without stopping to sharpen their dull blade, instead of recharging, planning and executing the task more expeditiously. Affirmations will help keep you sharp!

Using Affirmations

To use affirmations, decide exactly what you want and describe yourself as if you already achieved the goal. I, Jane Doe, am financially successful. Or, I, Jane Doe, have a great job. Actors, athletes, and executives successfully use this technique to improve their lives.

Visualize Your Goal   Picture in your mind exactly what it is you want. Remember: There are no limits to your imagination. Try these:

I, _____, am healthy.

I, _____, am energetic.

I, _____, exercise regularly.

I, _____, get along with many different kinds of people.

I, _____, eat wisely.

I, _____, use time wisely.

I, _____, am a good test taker.

I, _____, am a good speller.

I, _____, sleep soundly.

I, _____, am smart.

I, _____, learn quickly.

I, _____, am sensitive to people's moods.

I, _____, have good relationships.

I, _____, work hard.

I, _____, know how to play and have fun.

I, _____, am physically fit.

I, _____, like myself.

I, _____, am liked by others.

I, _____, budget my money wisely.

I, _____, earn income that exceeds my expectation.

Writing Your Affirmations

Affirmations work in every area of life. The important thing is to define them carefully, so that you know exactly when your affirmation statement becomes true. For example, "I exercise regularly" may mean "going to the gym 4 times per week" for some people. For others, it may mean walking to the corner or sweeping the floor every day. The definition depends on the person. Measurable outcomes matter!

Consider the power of small changes to make a big difference in your life. If you smoke 3 packs of cigarettes daily, an affirmation like "I, Ron Lung, am a non-smoker," might be more discouraging than empowering at this point in your life. So, work up to it. "I, Mr. Needa Patch, smoke only 2 packs per day."

Write an affirmation related to your personal life. (Define your affirmation carefully with details.)

Write a work-related affirmation. (Also include details.)

10 Words to Exclude from Your Affirmations

Can ... Will ... Try ... Would ... Could ... Should ... Might ... More ... Maybe ... Hope to ...

How to Live in the Now

Success Tip

Don't live in the past unless you like guilt and don't live in the future unless you like fear.

I AM BLESSED TO HAVE great mentors who have coached me to live in the now! I live my life with the belief that in the final analysis, life is a series of moments, some positive and some challenging, but moments nonetheless. I recall the most vivid memories as almost a mental scrapbook (my wedding day, my children being born, my 1st contract, my best speech, meeting the President of the United States in the White House, my 1st television appearance, my 1st million dollar bank statement, the new cross we donated to our church, the look and smell of the study in my home where I created this book, etc.).

Here are success tips to help you become a *live in the now* person:

Success Tip

Question: Are you living off old memories or creating new ones?

Do not be one of those people who talk about how fun life used to be; live in the present. While I am a believer in living in the now, I am an advocate of focusing on the future because each of us will be spending the rest of our lives there.

Success Tip

Right now you are either living your dream or someone else's.

Most people live their lives based on others' expectations or to please someone else's desires (parents, spouses, kids, co-workers, friends, bosses).

Success Tip

It is virtually impossible when in a passionate, purposeful state to feel depressed!

Affirmations keep your momentum going during rough spots. By supplying your subconscious mind with exciting thoughts, visual pictures and images (your new business card, signed purchase of a new franchise, 6 figure bank account, exotic vacations, etc.) you can begin to stretch your capabilities and develop a larger comfort zone. Affirmations allow you to expand your comfort zone and pursue greater possibilities.

The 1st step in actually achieving your career calling is visualizing precisely what it is (what it looks, feels and tastes like) and the 2nd step is by expanding your confidence (comfort zone), which will instill a new belief system that it can be obtained. Once your passion is ignited by these visuals and your confidence is built, your feelings of hopelessness, anxiousness or futility diminish. And *you* control the entire process. Emerson said, "Why should the way I feel depend on the thoughts in someone else's head."

Success Tip

Every weakness has potential to be converted into an enormous strength!

Debate your own pessimism. See yourself as the problem because only then can you take ownership of the solution. Both the problem and solution are within you! When you perceive yourself as the victim, you lose the power to solve it! Recite this statement every morning: "I own the problem, and I am the solution."

Maximizing the Power
of Your Reticular Activating System (RAS)

"If you think sand trap during your backswing, you will usually get sand."

—Mike Kuselias, golfer, 10 handicap

Why is it important to be specific when it comes to visualizing your objectives? At the risk of sounding technical, there is a part of your brain called the reticular activating system (RAS), which is basically a filter of your thoughts.

In May of 1957, the publication *Scientific American* introduced an article on the discovery of the reticular formation at the base of the human brain. This formation was described as the gateway to conscious awareness. Acting as a search function, your RAS is programmed to focus sensations consistent with your internal belief system. The bottom line: Whatever you focus on in a clear and distinct way, your brain seeks out and looks for.

For example, when you drive a car, you may observe, smell and hear numerous sounds en route to your destination, but only remember the essential details that prevent you from crashing and successfully finding your destination. Your brain (RAS) serves to focus on the critical needs in any situation you face. It constantly amazes me that my wife can sleep through normal houses noises, traffic, pounding rain storms and probably a hurricane, but even in her deepest, most peaceful sleep, if my youngest daughter should so much as make a peep from the other end of the house, she jolts upright and is immediately in action.

How is this possible? Simple, her RAS has prioritized the sounds of my daughter and filters out all the other distractions, even if they are louder and more pronounced. Her subconscious mind has been trained to "hear" her child, and block out all else, even while sound asleep. I find this incredible. The implications for your career success based upon what you are choosing to block out or not block out and allow into your most valuable asset, your mind, are profound. How effective is your filter?

How have you programmed your RAS? What have you consciously or subconsciously deemed important that your brain focuses on? Does it contribute to your desires or take you further away? Have you conditioned yourself to fail? Do you subconsciously EXPECT to fail so your mind seeks out conditions or activities where you will fulfill your internal commands? These are very powerful questions that must be mastered if you have a true desire to achieve your calling. The key is to program your RAS to look for and recognize actions that bring you closer to your objectives, including the attainment of your career calling.

My career changed dramatically when I learned to change my RAS to focus on *specific* achievements. Yours will too! Everything I want and identify with I spend time "programming into my RAS" so I am on a search and find mission. It is how I met my wife, started my business, and acquired the material possessions I value, found key mentors in my life, achieved financial independence and sustained every other conceivable item or value I possess.

You will learn that in order to acquire, you must first identify and project an image into your RAS, which will then serve as a radar detector. Does this sound like hocus pocus? Hardly! The bestselling book, *The Secret*, which gained internally acclaim, is based on the "Law of Attraction," another way to describe this concept.

Once you understand how powerful your mind is and how you can dictate the controls, you will begin to move toward your objectives at warp speed and never allow negative thoughts or beliefs to invade your most trusted resource, your mind! Never again will you allow trashy television, negative media or societal pressures form the basis for your RAS; you are in control!

Your RAS filters out anything that does not bring you closer to your goal (again, when you are driving if the house on the left does not aid you in getting to your destination while your eyes may see it, your brain ignores it) and focuses intensely on actions that will help you achieve your goals. Your RAS will target, focus on and process anything that coincides with your belief system and identity.

The key is to uncover your unique and compelling skills, attach these to an occupation or career path where you can utilize these skills, find key mentors and role models and create a mental picture of yourself *already* doing that job.

Commit 15 minutes per day without distraction to close your eyes and visualize your most important desires. Some call it meditation, I prefer "critical reflection." Whatever you call it, I strongly suggest you create an area and start the process! Use this time to monitor your filters, now that you know how powerful they are and the effect they can have on your life.

Guard Your Mind!

"Each thought you have will either be an investment or a cost. It will either move you toward happiness and success or away from it. It will either empower you or disempower you. That is why it is imperative you choose your thoughts and beliefs wisely."
— T. Harv Eker, *Secrets of the Millionaire Mind*

Successful people filter out useless information and focus on productive, nourishing data. Think of your mind as a filter; is it clogged with soot and dirt in the form of negative images and pessimism? If you have not yet conditioned yourself to guard your mind, and you are consumed with tabloids, negative stories and defeating mindsets, it is time to make the firm decision to pursue healthy input. To achieve your career calling you must be prepared to make certain changes in your behavior. If no changes were required, you most likely would already be in your desired occupation and on the path to contribution and abundance.

I was astonished to learn that the typical American watches television an average of 6 hours per day. My guess is that it is not spent entirely on educational or spiritually enriching programs.

At an average of 6 hours per day, by the time a person is 60 years of age, they will have used up 15 years of their life plopped down in front of the boob tube.

Do you really want to waste a quarter of your life watching actors and actresses (some who are not that talented) get rich entertaining you, even as you sit unfulfilled in your own professional pursuits and are reduced to desperately seeking enjoyment from a glass tube?

If the average American could simply eliminate 2 hours per day of watching television (a 33% decline) they would free up an additional 700 hours per year, which equates to over 4 months of work related time! What could you do with 4 months if instead of watching re-runs, you put your energies into a new business or new relationships or training?

"I find television very educational; every time someone turns it on, I go in the other room and read a book."
— Groucho Marx

If you do, your personal and professional life will accelerate to levels you never thought possible. You will train your mind to avoid distraction. For years, I thought of myself as an average reader. Today, I am so clear on my thinking that when I read a reference book, the important or relevant points that apply to me seem to jump off the page like they were illuminated! I know what I am looking for and what sections are not relevant. My RAS kicks in and I now average about a book per week! This stuff is like gold!

Pursue quality information that nourishes your life. Negative thinking is about who is to blame, who is at fault, excuses, rationalizations. A negative thinker operates from fear rather than faith. It is easy to think negatively with news, media and talk show television full of crisis, terror, fires and murder. That is like mainlining a negative serum directly into your veins! Do not fall prey to the destructive power of negative thinking. Dare to be great!

One question I always ask in my seminars is: "How many of you live a life filled with passion, have found your career calling, achieved balance and are consistently improving and growing as a person?"

Invariably, only a few hands go up! I will submit to you that only a precious few people are living the life they deserve. They are not contributing or making a difference to the level they should or could. In fact, I almost named this book, *If Every One Else Is Doing It, Don't,* because my research provided me with sobering thoughts as to how few people truly are happy and living the life they desire. Very few people look at life in a different way or commit to investing in their own success. Focus on your vision, contribution and value and not the struggle.

Why do we struggle? In simple terms, there is a struggle going on between your internal belief system and societal conditioning. It is a normal instinct for all of us to *fit in.*

Trust yourself! There is a price for following the crowd, meeting the norm, and going with the flow. Advertisers know this. Social acceptance is one of the most compelling methods to influence human behavior. When we are unsure of how to act or feel, we look to others for guidance and how to behave. Many people feel that if enough people are doing something, it must be right. Think of all the horror stories of apparently safe and tested drugs, which turned out to have devastating side effects.

Stop looking for advertisers to help you formulate an effective, healthy diet. With the advent of fast food and the like, today, one of every 3 people die of cancer and one of 2 die of heart disease, which is related to lifestyle.

Consider advertisers who for years, promoted that smoking was not a health risk and, in fact, had socially redeeming qualities. How ridiculous! Guard your mind from the crowd mentality. Be careful of your decisions. We all follow styles, fashion trends, hairstyles and hot designers. There is strength in numbers, so we seek acceptance from our fellow human beings. We are conditioned to seek validation and comfort, but by whom?

I propose a different alternative. Be unique. Of all the profound advice that I have had the privilege to receive in my lifetime, *guarding my mind from negative thoughts* is one of the best. If you maintain your individuality, set your standards and properly research your decisions, I will welcome you to a select group of achievers!

Why Self-Talk Is Critical to Finding Your Calling

> *"We have to learn to be our own best friends because we fall too easily into the trap of being our own worst enemies."*
> —Roderick Thorp

Did you know that of the 50,000 thoughts the average person has per day, the vast majority are negative? In fact, research indicates that up to 96% of human thought is negative. People have either remorse about the past or are worrying about their future. Look at any newspaper headline or network or cable news story; each story is more horrific than the next. Most of us are very good at mentally beating ourselves up over our decisions, weight or stupidity. How many times have you told yourself how dumb you were for acting a certain way? This seems to come naturally.

What is the only plant that grows naturally in your garden? Weeds!

The words you have programmed your mind to use will in turn dictate your emotional state. Here is a simple exercise: Try smiling when you are really unhappy, or frowning when you are excited or thrilled. It is nearly impossible!

There is a great deal of research currently being conducted on "self-talk." First off, I am a huge fan of programming your mind with positive messages. Your subconscious mind, like a computer, does not have the capability to think or make decisions. It only takes instructions and reacts. It does, however, control your attitude, emotions and personality. Because your subconscious mind takes orders, you can literally talk yourself into evolving into the person you desire to be.

> When you first begin the new process of incorporating words like, "I love myself, I am balanced, I am wealthy, I am in control of my destiny," it may feel awkward or strange. When a new set of instructions is affirmed and clashes with old beliefs stored in your subconscious mind, psychologists refer to this as *cognitive dissonance.*

Simply put, you have an internal conflict over old bad habits as new habits try to take over. This is as normal as your body feeling sluggish when you make the decision to eliminate sugar or caffeine from your diet. There is internal conflict as your new habits are fighting to replace prior beliefs. It is almost like sore muscles after you first begin working out, after having neglected exercise for a time. When you first begin, you will experience pain and soreness but very quickly you adapt until you feel exhilaration and strength pouring through your veins when you improve your physical fitness.

> If you call yourself stupid, your self does not argue, it accepts!

You can literally change your entire life and send it into a wonderful new direction, simply by adopting the technique of asking better questions! Delete non-productive or obsolete files or your mind will become cluttered. If you want to be a great person, ask yourself great questions.

Think about it. Our most fascinating contributions and innovations came about because a single individual asked himself or herself the question: *What if?* What if we could travel to the moon? What if we could vaccinate polio? What if we treated all people as equals? What if we create www.thecareerguarantee.com and help millions of Americans find passion at work?

> There is the story of a father and young son who were hiking up a mountain. The boy slipped and fell down the mountain into some bushes. Scared but unhurt, the young boy cried out, "Somebody help me!" A voice called back, "Somebody help me!" The boy looked confused and surprised and shouted, "Who are you?" The voice shouted back, "Who are you?" The boy, now upset, yelled, "You are a Coward!" The voice shouted back, "You are a Coward!" The agitated boy screamed back, "You are a fool!" The voice screamed back, "You are a fool!"

By now, the boy's father had climbed down the mountain to where the boy was and helped his son to his feet. "Dad," the boy asked, "who is that?" The father laughed and said, "Son, that is called an echo but it is also a great lesson about life." The father proceeded to shout at the top of his lungs, "You are awesome!" The voice shouted back, "You are awesome!" The father shouted, "You can do it!" The voice shouted back, "You can do it!"

The father turned to his young son and said, "You see, that is exactly how life is. Whatever you send out always comes back to you."

Whatever you ask yourself, you will get an answer to. If you ask, what is *wrong* with me, your brain will answer and formulate a list of issues. For example, if you ask yourself, how come I can never find a nice guy? Your brain will tell you all the reasons ... because you are too desperate, too needy, controlling, or overweight!

Conversely, if you pose the question, what is *right* in my life, what is great about me, you will hear positives. You need to ask yourself better questions if you seek better answers. JFK asked a nation, "Ask not what your country can do for you, but what you can do for your country." His genius was getting an entire nation to ask a better question while simultaneously challenging the country to find a contribution. What can you give, and not what can you take. What Power! *Negative talk hurts!*

To conclude this section on self-talk, I want you to complete this important exercise:

What are the 3 most common questions you ask yourself? For many:

1. Why can't I find a good job?
2. Why do others seem to be happier in their career?
3. What can I do to improve my position and earnings?

Instead, create positive questions such as:

1. How did I improve today?
2. Who did I assist today?
3. What will I do with my newfound wealth?

The differences are subtle but powerful! Be extremely careful about how you talk to yourself. Constantly ask yourself if your current thought is helping you or hurting you? Is it getting you closer to your objective or taking you further away? Is it empowering you or diminishing your energy, self-esteem and personal power? Ladies and gentlemen, if you learn nothing else from me, learn this ... Monitor your self-talk!

Transform Your Inner Cynic into Your Inner Coach

It is estimated that 90% of physical ailments are emotionally induced!

Wow! That statement jumps off the page and should cause you to truly assess your inner cynic. The old proverb says, "When the mind hurts, the body suffers." When your thoughts are negative, studies show that you actually weaken your immune system. Many "sickly" workers are really folks who are hurting from the inside out. They may be displaced, underutilized and are manifesting their grief through physical troubles.

> The challenge is that while we are all born happy (children laugh an average of 450 times per day while adults only laugh 24 times per day) due to cynicism the majority of us lose this happiness.

Did you know that most heart attacks take place on Monday morning at 9:00 AM? Care to guess where most people are at that time? They are working and the stress of facing another week of working without passion or purpose is literally enough to kill a person! Also important is to eliminate negative phrases from your vocabulary. Here is a list of negative phrases: *Same S——, different day, Life is a b—— and then you die, Another day, another dollar, TGIF, The old ball and chain (when talking about your boss), I will never get a raise or promotion, Nobody likes their job, right? You are lucky to have a job ...*

During a seminar with a corporate client, I observed the following sign on one of the top manager's cubicle walls: *"The only difference between this place and the Titanic is that the Titanic had a band."* What is the corporate culture like in your organization? What message is being communicated to others? What is your mantra?

Many people I consult with actually develop a mood to fit the day of the week. For example, some people have the Monday morning blues to start their uninspiring work week, Wednesday is hump day, which signals their misery is at the halfway point and, of course, we have instituted TGIF to signal the end of another unfulfilling work week. Can you imagine conditioning your mind and behavior to fit the day of the week? How would you feel if you were stranded on a desert island without a calendar and did not know what day it was? You would probably have an identity crisis!

When you are truly inspired, the day doesn't matter. Your mindset is focused on a clear mission and you are building for an exciting future through an important and measurable contribution. Stimulate your thought process with empowering questions, which will serve to motivate you to achieve balance. There are 2 types of questions you should be aware of:

1. *Possibility Questions* (What if I lost 20 pounds and increased my energy level? What if I borrowed 50K and opened my own business? How would I be different if I became a millionaire?)
2. *Necessity Questions* (What must I do to fight off my cancer diagnosis? What is my game plan now that I have been laid off? Where will I find a partner with complementary skills so I can expand?)

Life is a healthy balance between possibility and necessity!

Countering Mindset Woes

Common Fear	How to counteract fear
Poor Health	Learn more about good health habits, nutrition, exercise and your genetics.
Losing your job	Become so valuable that you can't be fired. And if you are, your special skills will open up new opportunities. Keep refining your strengths. Focus on your brilliance; develop excellent connections.
Loneliness	Surround yourself with positive, supportive people. Be a giver. To attract friends, become a friend.
Uncertainty	Most of the jobs in the future haven't even been invented yet. Focus on developing your greatest talents. Design exciting goals.
Dying	It happens to all of us. Have Faith. Live every day to the fullest. Explore spiritual truths.
Failure	The spiritual side of you proves there is a bigger plan. God gave you talent. Seek it out. Surround yourself with winners. "Failure" is an opportunity to learn. Making mistakes is essential for long-term success.
Making major decisions	Think on paper—plan ahead—seek good advice.
Rejection	Don't take it personally, especially if you're in sales. We all experience some form of rejection every week. Become thick skinned.

Common Fear	How to counteract fear
Ignorance/Lack of knowledge	Practice the habit of learning something every day. Read. Study, and become more conscious. Remember: The use of knowledge is your greatest power. Become an *expert* in what you do best.
Losing your family	Continually nourish your most important relationships. Build a lifetime of positive memories you can cherish forever.
Public speaking	Join Toastmasters, take a Dale Carnegie course, join the National Speakers Association, choose a great mentor, author a ten-minute speech on your favorite subject. Practice. Accept opportunities to speak when asked. Hire a speech coach.
Poverty	Learn about money and how it works. Check your belief system. Find an excellent financial coach. Set specific goals to save and invest a portion of everything you earn.
Success	Embrace the fact that success comes from study, hard work, good planning and taking risks. You deserve all of this.

Build Your Vocabulary

If you want a key ingredient that will immediately create confidence, build your self-esteem, establish newfound respect and admiration and accelerate your personal and professional happiness, while moving you at warp speed towards your career calling ... (drum roll, please) ... *build your vocabulary!* If you do, euphoria, exuberance, abundance and pleasure are words you will become familiar with.

The simple example I am known for is when a man compliments his wife (which I do on a regular basis and suggest you do as well with your loved ones), which sounds better to you? Consider these options:

Option 1: "Honey you look "good" or ...
Option 2: "Honey, you look "radiant, spectacular, gorgeous, intoxicating, and delicious!"

The benefits to building a better vocabulary are profound ... and in this case your chances of getting lucky went up significantly! To further emphasize this important point, try this simple exercise:
- List 3 words that empower you.
- Now, list 3 words that disempower you.

Your assignment: For the next week, try to use the empowering words as often as possible and try to avoid using the dis-empowering words like the plague.

Remember, you decide what words you use, how you act and feel. And the best news is that you can at any moment decide to replace a negative thought with a positive thought. If you are depressed or unhappy, you chose to feel that way. Conversely, if you are vibrant, excited and energized, it is because you decided to be.

One of my most important discoveries was that I could literally act a certain way until I began to feel consistent with my actions. I could program my subconscious mind by behaving as if I was already in great shape or had achieved a level of wealth. Any characteristic I sought, I could begin to act as if I had already achieved it. And guess what? My subconscious mind followed right along with my self-talk and actions and generated emotions consistent with my new behavior.

For example, before I go on TV or do an interview (when I am always a bit anxious), I already have conducted a world class presentation in my mind. As a result, my confidence level and positive attitude shows.

Right now, you probably have a list of challenges, fears or problems that consume some portion of your thoughts. For some people, they dominate their thoughts; for others they appear more happy or carefree. My advice is simple, yet effective: Discipline yourself to focus on solutions to your problems and not the consequences of the problem.

> When Walt Disney formulated a vision of reality to build a worldwide brand and needed money, he was turned down by over 300 bankers. Were it not for his persistence, we would never have experienced the splendor of his vision to unite children and families at his theme parks.

My success is based on persistence and my trained ability to take action to resolve my challenges and not occupy my mind with non-productive worry. Think about where you want to go and not where you have been. Spend your time on what your future will look like and not the disappointments of the past.

Do this! Buy a scrapbook today! Establish a visual picture for the person you seek to become and adopt a plan to feed your mind with positive ideas or images consistent with your desired outcome. I call this my "vision board."

- Post pictures of the physique you seek
- Create a fictitious spreadsheet of the bank account you desire
- Cut out a picture of the car you will be driving
- Create a scrapbook of your ideal wardrobe
- Include your ideal vacation spot
- Take a favorite photo depicting your most valued relationships and absorb the emotions

Every year, I purchase the same scrapbook from a small store near my house. It is a ritual that I look forward to at the beginning of every New Year. I replace the insets that have yet to be accomplished into my new book. This year promises to be my best yet! My scrapbook has photos of the physique I want, beach house I desire, motorcycle I cherish, headshots and bios of the mentors I want to meet, donations I want to make, vacation destinations, places I want to explore with my family and other relevant desires.

These are specific images. If you want a beach house, do not simply cut out any photo from a magazine but find the EXACT location and address of the beach house you want! If you desire a new designer watch, determine the make and model you want. The more detailed your imagery, the more likely you are to obtain or achieve it.

Visualize your outcome and through positive and consistent self-talk, convince your subconscious mind that you are worthy and deserving of these attainable outcomes. I now have a scrapbook of previous material possessions (houses, cars) I wanted and non-material items (poems, letters), which were attained because I conceived it, then believed it and then achieved it.

Once you establish a clear picture of what you want, you will begin to notice people, things and circumstances that will draw you closer to each outcome. Remember, we become what we think about!

Question ... what is currently on your "Vision Board?"

The Power of Visualization

IN 1989, MY BELOVED father was diagnosed with esophageal cancer and told he had less than 6 months to live. We posted photos of all the things he loved and valued. In essence, we were creating a visual framework for why he should endure the pain and anguish of fighting the disease. Every time he began to lose faith, he had photos of his grandchildren whom he wanted to see grow, his favorite vacations spots, golf courses he wanted to play, healthy strong bodies, etc.

As a family, we were developing a mental image of health and vitality and a justification for not giving up when all looked lost. Each day, he would sit quietly in his favorite chair and visualize the cancer in his throat evaporating and a healthy throat passage instead. As of this writing, he is alive and well with a 10 (golf) handicap! I know for a fact that this process significantly aided in his recovery.

With regard to your desire to achieve your career goals, the lesson is to create a mental image of who you truly want to be as a professional and then live into that image as if it were already true. People who have achieved their calling utilize this technique every day. They create the vision before it is their reality and live into the photos or videos.

Keep in mind that there is no training on this subject, at least not in any school I have attended, visited or consulted with. I used to think everyone was issued an instruction manual for how to find the ideal career and lead a balanced life, and I must have missed that day. Not the case. Thought by thought, I want you to replace the old cynical you with the new visionary you. We are re-inventing your professional persona and making you better than ever!

Why does visualization get so much attention in the study of the human mind? For starters, scientists have determined that our brains cannot truly distinguish between visualizing an occurrence or belief and it actually happening. The internal processes (neuron activity) are identical. If you program yourself to continually visualize your wants and desires, and "pretend" that they have already occurred, your subconscious mind will frantically attempt to create consistency between what you visualize and what is real. The gap will be bridged through your thoughts. Subconsciously, your mind will attempt to create synergy between what is real and what is imagined.

Visualization is one of the most powerful techniques to help you achieve your ideal career. Top performers from every field employ the use of visualization to preview a successful ski run, foul shot, important speech, acting performance, brain surgery, negotiation to purchase a new property, etc.

I have advised some of my education clients (schools) to show the students their diplomas on the 1st day of class; and have them create their guest list for graduation. The goal is to help these students internalize the end result and visualize their success. This kept many in class who would have otherwise quit.

Tiger Woods, arguably the world's greatest golfer, consistently practices a swing and visualizes each and every shot before actually hitting the ball. When you watch him at a tournament, you can see him follow a pre-determined routine. He imagines solid contact, appropriate backspin, elevation of the fairway or green in advance of addressing the ball and making the shot. Many top NBA free throw shooters mimic the shooting form before actually taking the shot.

Before going on stage to make an important speech, I always visualize a positive response from my audience and forecast an empowering delivery in advance of my actual performance. For your interviews, it is critical that you visualize the first impression, the questions asked and a confidence level that will get you the position.

I am a firm believer that we not only visualize a positive outcome to our endeavors, whether it be an interview, meeting with a new mentor or creation of a new business venture, but that we actually create a wish book of everything we want in our lives.

I want you to picture yourself waking up in the morning, say next Monday morning, and imagine the feeling that you are going to work in your ideal career, the job that fills you with a sense of passion and pride, the job that allows you to exercise your creative juices, the job that provides you with incredible reward, recognition, the most happiness and which provides you with the type of compensation you deserve. Picture what it feels like to be truly passionate about your role and actually look forward to utilizing your unique gifts.

How would you conduct yourself getting ready to go to work that morning? And what attitude would you have as you were commuting to work? What would you be wearing, driving? Covet these feelings and ingrain them into your subconscious. That's the 1st step to really wanting and desiring something, to experience the feelings and establish an emotional attachment.

Now picture yourself unemployed or going to your current job. How do you feel about that? Maybe you're complacent ... another day, another dollar, as the saying goes. You're into the same routine with no pride, no energy and no enthusiasm. People are most depressed when they are not making a contribution and growing as a person!

Now revert and picture yourself going to that ideal career . What makes it your dream job? Is it the people that are there? Is it location? Is it creativity? Is it because you know there's going to be a bigger and better paycheck? Is it part of your identity?

Itemize those differences and review them daily. And take positive actions until you have achieved all of those listed items.

The Secret? Start with the End in Mind

When it comes to attaining your career calling, I want you to start, not at the beginning, but at the end. To reach your goal, you must begin this very moment, to become the person you want to be and *then,* take the actions necessary to actually be that person.

One secret to success is that great performers behave and act to their objectives before they actually attain the goal. This may include believing like, thinking like, dressing like, walking like, talking like, researching like and *feeling* like the mentor you seek to emulate and ultimately become. By acting the part, you are not creating an unhealthy fantasy, but rather sending powerful messages to your subconscious mind to *lock on* to those elements.

You are programming your RAS for success by teaching it to focus on signals that will bring you closer to your goal. The more leverage you create, the more momentum you foster towards living, being and doing your career calling, the faster you will achieve it.

How would you dress if you were the CEO? How would you train if you had only 10% body fat? What would you be reading if you were a successful millionaire? Whom would you entrust to manage your finances if you had an abundance of cash? How would you conduct yourself if you achieved celebrity status? Begin to look, feel and behave like the person you need to be, in order to live your dream. Start today with the end in mind!

Here are 3 simple steps for creating a vision with the *end in mind*:

1. Visualize your desired outcome (that is, you working in your dream career)
2. Visualize yourself achieving greatness and experiencing tremendous emotional satisfaction
3. Visualize the exact tasks, duties, meetings, qualities, roles, people and location of your desired outcome

Think of a career change as a chance to meet new friends, to wipe the slate clean and improve upon your previous challenges.

Having a great career will have a positive effect on your attitude, sleeping habits, physical appearance, the way you feel about yourself, how you get up in the morning, the money you earn and a great many other factors. There are many benefits to having a terrific career where you are making a difference and not just punching a clock. And it's the only way, in my opinion, to go through life. Make your career dreams become your daily reality.

Change is inevitable; progress is not. Your body, metabolism, hairstyles, fashion, career, financial position, relationships and view of the world are all guaranteed to change. Achieving progress in each of these areas is not a guarantee. It requires dedication and commitment.

CHAPTER 6

How to Overcome Fears and Avoid Procrastination

KEY QUESTION: WHAT IS *HOLDING ME BACK*?

In this chapter, you will learn:

KEY TOPICS

- Change Is Great … You Go First!
- Defeating Fears
- Mastering Rejection
- Avoiding Procrastination … The Silent Killer

KEY MESSAGES

- Career change is inevitable; career progress is not.
- Be absolutely clear on the numerous rewards of obtaining your calling.
- All of your fears are *learned* behaviors and thus can be changed or eliminated.
- Start the process today, someday is not a day of the week.
- Take the words "I'll do it later" out of your vocabulary.
- There are 2 primary causes of career procrastination: 1) you are overwhelmed by the process or 2) you perceive the process to be unpleasant.
- To avoid procrastination, condense the entire, often overwhelming task of finding a great job into a series of attainable, workable actions and make it fun!
- View career hurdles as temporary setbacks and a learning experience and not as permanent failures.
- Not making mistakes means you are playing life too safe; stretch your potential!
- Minimize what others think; life is your one shot to work and live as you choose.
- Avoid making excuses; accept responsibility for your actions.
- Stay clear of negative thinkers and associate with positive people.
- Use the loss of a job as a new starting point and replace the words "I have to" with "I choose to."
- Consider WIIFM (*what's in it for me?*), make the benefits of achieving your ideal career outweigh the frustration of not taking action or remaining stagnant in your current occupation.
- Itemize what you will gain or lose by achieving or not your ideal career? (Your answers should serve as the motivation to pursue it!)

> *"You do not have to see the whole staircase. Just take the first step."*
>
> —Dr. Martin Luther King

Change Is Great ... You Go First!

According to a survey conducted by careerbuilder.com, almost 75% of people interviewed said they aren't working in their dream job because of financial responsibilities, lack of education or fear of the unknown.

When you have one of those "I hate my job" days, try this: On your way home from work, stop at your local pharmacy, go to the thermometer section, and purchase a rectal thermometer made by one of the pharmaceutical giants. Be very sure you get this brand. When you get home, lock your doors, draw the curtains and disconnect the phone so you will not be disturbed. Change into comfortable clothing and sit in your favorite chair.

Open the package and remove the thermometer. Carefully place it on a table or a surface so that it will not become chipped or broken. Now the fun part begins. Take out the literature from the box and read it carefully. You will notice that in small print there is a statement: "Every rectal thermometer made by our company is personally tested and then sanitized."

Now, close your eyes and repeat out loud 5 times, "I am so glad I do not work in thermometer quality control at that company." HAVE A NICE DAY AND REMEMBER, THERE IS ALWAYS SOMEONE ELSE WITH A JOB THAT IS MORE OF A PAIN THAN YOURS!

OK, SO MY HUMOR is a bit lacking ... Seriously, let me ask you this: Are you really living or just existing? Whether you realize it or not, you have been changing every day of your life. Don't you believe me? Take a look at your high school yearbook photo, old clothing styles, trends you followed, relationships, jobs, friends who have come and gone, etc. Change is a mandate in the game of life. It is also a fact when it comes to the subject of your career. Your skills, needs, wants, values and beliefs about work, projects, tasks and responsibilities will change over time. I don't know about you, but I don't want the same things now that I did 10, 20 or 30 years ago. I want a new level of expression and responsibility! I want to live with passion and have fun!

Some career seekers attempt to prevent change and resist it with every fiber of their being. They resent having to learn new technology, hate the convenience and productivity of hand held computer devices and may even resist a change in their daily tasks or evaluation criteria. Here is a fact: *Career change is inevitable; career progress is not!* Just because things are changing does not automatically mean you are progressing. In fact, if you are not making a conscious effort to embrace change or enhance your skills, you are probably losing your value in the marketplace.

Defining Change

Change is modifying specific tasks or behaviors to be able to take on new or different responsibilities. The degree of difficulty involved in modifying ourselves professionally is evident when we consider all the adjustments we make in our knowledge, attitude, individual or group behavior.

Question: What specific changes, both personally and professionally, do you want to make, and why?

What does change feel like? Try this experiment ...

- Fold your arms across your chest normally as you would when you are relaxed. Wait one minute.
- Now try to fold the opposite way, with the opposite arm in the top position.
- How does it feel? Odd, right?

Even simple changes often feel uncomfortable ...

When it comes to careering, there are 2 types of change, both of which are impossible to control but important with respect to how you respond. One is called *cyclical change* and the other is called *structural change*.

Cyclical Change   Refers to variable changes that are normal and natural. Examples include the weather, the seasons or stock market fluctuations. We expect certain cycles where we can anticipate the change. For example, if you live in a 4 season climate, you have a feel for when to put on your skis or uncover the swimming pool.

Structural Change   Refers to changes that advance society and often make the prior way of doing things obsolete. For example, in my company we often assist clients whose industry, employer or job responsibilities have been replaced by technology. Examples: assembly line workers have been replaced with mechanical robots, in-store retail shopping has decreased due to on-line purchasing.

Changes will continue to occur and often will impact your occupation. Tracking the developments in your industry will prevent you from being blind-sided or eliminated.

Any change you make will be based on one single common reason: *the desire to gain pleasure and avoid pain*! The challenge is that each of us has adopted a different pattern to achieve these states. Some people drink alcohol, do drugs, watch TV or read to escape boredom or pain, etc. For those who do, these activities somehow yield pleasure. The key is to associate intense pleasure with finding work that feels like play.

Accepting change and obtaining your career calling will create a sense of internal happiness because you are making a positive contribution. In the modern, global economy, change and uncertainty are the norm and not the exception. The average job tenure is now less than 4 years and there is no guarantee that your career or current employer will even exist tomorrow. Change management is no longer a "should" … it is a must!

So here is the question: Is the process of seeking your career calling and the changes you will be required to make a positive for you or a negative? Change can sometimes be uncomfortable. As human beings, you and I would typically prefer to be comfortable than uncomfortable. By choosing to remain comfortable, you are in essence, making a decision to forego your full potential, inner passion and are settling for less than you could or should become.

Career progress requires some level of discomfort; there is no way around it or shortcut. You must learn to develop and accept the skill of being *comfortable while being uncomfortable.* Say what, Chris?

What I am suggesting is that to accomplish a major event like a career change, you are going to have to accept the prospect of living in an uncomfortable state, where new habits, contacts and behaviors will inevitably occur. There is simply no other way to transition from your current state of affairs to a life of abundance and happiness. Changes in behavior, routine and belief are essential ingredients.

Here is the good news: You have been successful at making major changes your entire life; a career change is simply another level of progress. I remember how incredibly nervous I was before: the birth of my 1st child, my 1st bank loan, 1st mortgage, 1st kiss, 1st move and 1st new business venture. All required me to manage my anxiety until this new behavior became part of my routine and personality.

You must ultimately become the change you seek. Simply put, being out of your element is a natural and normal part of progress. Embrace this as part of the process of making change in your life. People do this every day; you can too! You must commit to persevere through the challenges and break the bad habits that have resulted in a career and lifestyle that do not meet your current standards.

Are You Open to Change?

Change is inevitable … except from a vending machine!

This quiz measures how open you are to change. It is a perfectly normal and natural human response to resist change, so answer truthfully. Seeing your answers on paper will help you overcome some of your aversion to change.

True or False?

1. In these days of rapid progress all around us, I am quick to learn new ways of doing things.
2. I must be certain that doing something differently is worthwhile before I try it.
3. As soon as I hear about something new, I like to try it.
4. Too much time and energy is wasted, I believe, on experimenting with new ideas before enough is known about them.
5. I always try to keep myself up to date on current events.
6. When it comes to using new methods of doing things, I prefer to be a follower rather than a leader.
7. I am always eager to learn about new opportunities.
8. If I like things the way they are, I see no reason for making changes.
9. If I hear about something new, I feel restless until I try it.
10. Making changes creates too many problems and pressures. I'd rather relax and enjoy what I have.
11. I'm always looking for new ways of doing things faster and better.
12. Years of experience have made things the way they are—dependable. There's no reason to change things now.

4 Barriers to Change

> *"As soon as you trust yourself, you will know how to live."*
> —Goethe

I suggest that in order to change, we must trust our decisions. You cannot fight yourself over the changes you need to make; you must truly believe they are necessary and in your best interests. So if we know we should change and it is necessary to do so to remain competitive in the 21st century workplace, why do we still resist? The answer is simple ... it is *because we possess barriers to making change.*

We seek to maintain a comfort level, which often has been artificially created by our families, schooling, advertising, peer pressure or other conformities. Some people live by the philosophy they should not attempt to pursue their career calling because trying and failing may cause them emotional pain, so why bother? "Do nothing and worry" is the mantra of many 21st century job seekers.

Barriers are not the enemy; they are our friends! They provide a clear road map for change and help us to understand specifically what is holding us back. What are the barriers to making change and adopting a long-term career plan? In my experience, the 4 key barriers are as follows:

4 Key Barriers to Change

1. *Laziness:* People find the process of exploring inner passions, finding purpose, making change and re-inventing themselves too difficult ... so why bother?
2. *Anxiety:* Fear often prevents action while a lack of direction encourages complacency.
3. *Ignorance:* I have a job ... for now ... so leave me alone! I don't have to worry about finding my career calling, right? Wrong!
4. *Confusion:* Change is happening so fast, I am overwhelmed, confused and don't know where to start. So I do nothing.

Get Better ... Or Else!

> *"You cannot live on yesterday's standards and expect to be competitive today!"*
>
> —Chris Kuselias

If you have attended one of my speaking engagements or seminars, you know firsthand why I have the reputation as one of the most passionate and enthusiastic presenters ever to hold a microphone. Quite frankly, I get downright loud and excited! I am *that* passionate about helping others understand and achieve their career calling.

But believe it or not, at one time I was extremely nervous about speaking in public! Before I would get ready to speak I would adopt the same pattern. First, I would start sweating, my heart would beat, I would envision a loss of confidence, picture ridicule, etc. I processed every negative emotion possible and thought about all the terrible things that could happen and psyched myself out. I would start slurring my words, lose my concentration and become consumed with fear to the point of total loss of confidence! To obtain this emotional state, I had to repeat this pattern each time!

How did I conquer the fear? Only by consciously linking a new set of emotions to my nervous system that provided not negative emotions and linkages, but positive thoughts. I focused on how my words would help people. I focused on my research and knowledge of my subject matter. I envisioned the audience clapping in appreciation for my appearance.

What I learned is that *the decision to change happens in a moment.* When you heat water to 212 degrees Fahrenheit, it will boil; at 211 degrees it will not. A major change happens at the instant the temp hits 212. Prior to that, there is a build up and momentum is created. People in therapy can review the same incident or topic for years, until, in a moment, some analogy, word or action results in a new set of emotions, and the adoption of a new belief system unbinds them and allows them to progress! The quicker you change your link to past negative associations the faster the change and new belief will occur!

People marvel at my ability to get people to not only find their career calling, but to also effectively lose weight or quit smoking. They often mistakenly call me a guru and wonder if I have magic dust in my pocket. I promise you, I have no secret formula or magic. The truth is, I have a more powerful formula, which is the ability to help people change their *neuro-associations.* My gift is the ability to get them to do it quickly and not take months or years!

For example, if you associate dieting and weight loss with pain and deprivation, you will never achieve your goal to lose weight. The only way to lose weight is to associate negative feelings to the foods that you are *polluting your system* with, the foods that may lead to the development of cancer or heart disease, the foods that may destroy you, even kill you. It may prevent you from seeing your kids grow, graduate and marry, or living to see your grandkids. Do you see what I mean? You need to associate a passionate and compelling reason for change and adopt a negative belief about the foods or substances that cause the obesity. *Change is about establishing a new set of beliefs!*

For a change to be effective, it must not be solely at the intellectual level. At an intellectual level, you *know* that being overweight is unhealthy, that it destroys your immune system, puts stress on your joints and ligaments, causing long term health risks like diabetes, etc. You know these things!

"But Chris," you may say, "that pasta and meatballs and white bread dipped in olive oil and creamy salad dressing and chocolate cake and ice cream for dessert are just soooooo good!" And you would be right, if you associate extreme pleasure to eating and excess consumption, you will never achieve a fit, trim and attractive figure. Your neuro-associations link pleasure to the process. The pleasure gained by consuming the meal out-weighs the pain associated with looking in the mirror at a stomach that hangs over your belt or having hips that won't allow you to button your pants or not being able to purchase the latest fashions because you cannot fit into them. When you hit your pain threshold or find a compelling rea-son to look and feel better, only then will it happen.

In sum, in order to make a change, you must implement the pain versus pleasure litmus test and create both intellectual and emotional justifica-tions for adopting any new behavior. This is true whether you are trying to quit smoking, lose weight, stop screaming at your kids, save more money and, of course, if you are interested in transitioning to your unique and compelling career calling.

5 Master Steps to Creating Change

> *"The definition of insanity is doing the same thing over and over and expecting a different result."*

So how does one master the art of change management? *By simply com-mitting to becoming a change agent.* This is a skill that you need to improve if you hope to live a life of abundance and enthusiasm. Here are 5 simple steps to changing, which can help you find your calling:

Step 1: Decide exactly what career you want, not what you *don't* want, but what you *do* want and why! What is stopping you? Are you linking negativity to the change? At some level you fear the change. Why? As creatures of habit we are programmed to fear change. Make a decision compelling enough and you will do it! For example, I created and manu-factured 5,000 of my 1st program, *The Career Coach* CD kit, before a single order was placed. I had to market them! Get your decision-making mus-cles in shape; often people can't make a menu decision much less a major change!

Step 2: Make the attainment of your career calling an absolute *must* and not a *should*. Make it compelling! You can do this in all key ar-eas of your life. Saying, "I *should* save more, be nicer to my spouse, go to church or start my own business," doesn't cut it. Make it a *must*! If you are angry because you are overweight, it means you have chosen to consume more than your body needs. Since you made the decision to start, you can decide to stop. You now know you must change your associations of pain and pleasure. Eliminate any other possibility or outcome. When I sought to leave my 1st corporate job and become an entrepreneur, I used my entire life savings to start my company and left no option but success! Find role models who have found their calling and crave that same feeling they describe. And then ask yourself: What am I missing out on by not attaining my true calling?

Step 3: Change your belief system, actions and interrupt patterns of a boring, dull professional lifestyle. If unhappy, many blame the boss or the economy. But ask them if they have time to reinvent their personal brand, inventory their credentials and begin a networking campaign to meet new and exciting contacts and suddenly they feel tired or too busy. When I interview people for positions in my company, I begin by asking basic questions such as: "Tell me about yourself. What is your greatest strength? Before they can answer, I then purposely interrupt and break their pattern with a question such as, "Why are manhole covers round"? The person invariably looks puzzled, then smiles and can relax. The real interview begins, facades are gone and the true person presents themselves with spontaneous rather than canned or rehearsed answers. How can you use this technique in your personal relationships? Next time you are arguing with someone, switch sides. When I argue I often switch roles, adopt the other's side and presto!, the conflict is usually resolved as we enjoy representing each other's interests. Adopt the other's perspective! In our welfare to work classes, we observed untrained students who often slouched with poor posture and had low self-esteem. We broke their pattern of negativity and low self-esteem immediately by a physiology change ... we forced them to sit up straight, walk tall and smile. Be as outrageous as possible with the power of visualization.

Step 4: Find a new alternative to your existing or established career behavioral patterns. Did you ever notice that you often react the same way to the same challenges? For example, I can tell how certain associates of mine are going to react to certain news before I even tell them. I know who will get angry, who will take the time to process the information before reacting and who will need a hug! We all have established patterns, but most of us have not analyzed why we respond the way we do. Some people hold the belief that they can never be promoted or become a team leader in their organization. In the workplace, they consistently behave and act in accordance with how a subordinate would act, even though deep down they possess leadership qualities. They are stuck in a negative pattern of behavior.

We once hired a new associate in my company who was a smoker and as she became familiar with our messages, indicated a desire to quit. Intellectually she knew she should and had tried on several occasions. I explained to her that emotionally she had not yet adopted a strong enough why or pleasure association to quit. I began by asking her why she smoked and why she would consider quitting. I had her go to the white board in a classroom and draw a line down the center.

I had her create a list of pros and cons. Here was her response:

Why Quit Smoking	Why Keep Smoking
Not classy, bad smell	Excuse to get out of the office
Unhealthy, expensive habit	The breathing pattern eased stress
Secondhand smoke	Mental break and something to do

In analyzing her pain vs. pleasure, we quickly decided that quitting would mean linking more pain and potential danger to smoking than the pleasure smoking provided. What she really valued was not the taste or style but rather that smoking, in her mind, equated to relaxation. Knowing this, all we needed to do was replace smoking with a relaxation alternative. The solution: We merely replaced her pleasure associations with another, less expensive habit without depriving her of the relaxation she valued. That was the key to her decision to eliminate her smoking habit.

Step 5: Condition the new desire and pattern of attaining your career calling until it becomes part of your regular belief system and part of your identity. You cannot fool yourself; it must be a reflection of who you truly are. Remember the old saying, "A person convinced against their will is of the same opinion still." Reinforce a new belief or connection in your mind until it becomes part of your dominant thought process. For a change to stick, it must become part of who you are and what you believe. Conditioning yourself to accept and embrace change takes practice, but the more you do it, the easier it becomes.

Like you, I also struggle with conditioning new patterns. I will share with you that one of my personal challenges is that I have a voracious sweet tooth! Pies, cake, cookies, ice cream … delicious! I rationalize eating sweets by pointing to the fact that as a child I had dessert after very meal. My dear sweet mother is a great baker and also kept a plentiful supply of ice cream, cake and pie on hand to conclude every meal. I was addicted! Like Pavlov's dog, even breakfast was not complete without a dessert! It is a challenge for me to create a negative association to sweets ... but I am trying! I now link cholesterol level, blood sugar and weight to sugar and as I want to maintain a peak state of physical endurance to keep my busy work schedule and to keep up with my 3 active children, I cannot afford the extra weight or potential doctor visits. Thus, my sweet tooth is now under control.

How Change Will Accelerate Your Progress

Some changes can be anticipated, but all changes cannot. Events like terrorism, industries disappearing overnight, the Berlin Wall coming down in Germany and the Soviet Union being dismantled are good examples of unanticipated change. Today, many products are designed with only a 6–9 month life cycle, jobs are fleeting, more subcontractors are being used and company loyalty is disappearing. You must commit to reinventing yourself! Often, when you do, change occurs slowly but then accelerates rapidly.

> There is a certain species of the Chinese bamboo tree that, when you plant it, you see nothing for 4 years. Just a tiny sprout peeks out of the ground and that's it. You weed, water, cultivate, nurture and do everything you can to make it grow, but you still see nothing. In the 5th year, this particular species of the Chinese bamboo tree grows up to 8 feet tall!

If you are considering a change of career, keep in mind that you are ultimately seeking 2 types of rewards:

1. Internal: Emotions, feelings
2. External: people notice, compliments

Those in search of their career calling, while aware of external rewards, understand that true success and happiness are found through internal rewards. My goal is to provide you with a compelling future by helping you adopt a "must" attitude regarding finding your career calling and developing a compelling enough set of "internal" rewards to make it happen!

Who you are and what you are truly capable of is far beyond what you have accomplished to date. Tap into your dormant resources. Turn resources into significant assets to dramatically improve your overall quality of life. 2 important questions:

1. What do you want to change about your career?
2. What *needs* to change in order to attain your current career calling?

Typically, people I work with are trying to change either:

1. Their feelings or perception about their career
2. Or their behavior, that is how they act or react to situations in their professional life

Redefining yourself and your capabilities is essential. Maybe you feel imprisoned by your past. I mastered this once limiting belief that I could never be successful because I was afraid to speak in public. For a person like me who aspired to deliver seminars and workshops or who sought to appear on TV or radio, this was a big problem!

Through effective mentors and associating pleasure and not pain to speaking, I began to alleviate my fears. I trained my mind not to follow the pattern of sweaty palms and worst-case scenarios, but rather to focus on the value I was providing to others. Speaking was an obligation and a privilege, not something to be feared. The loss was not only mine if I did not master my limiting beliefs, but also the people who needed my strategies and techniques. I believed it was a selfish act if I could not master my own emotions.

I now associate pleasure to: the contribution I make, helping others break through barriers, and compensation I receive for my diligent hard work and research to produce exciting strategies. By thinking this way, I have eliminated prior embarrassment and negative feelings. You can do the same, whatever your fear or limiting belief! But start today ...

Success Tip

Someday is not a day of the week!

You need to find your highest and best use in this life and then pursue it! Most people aren't bothered by change itself, but rather that they didn't anticipate the change and its effects. This is what causes stress and abuses. Think daily about the future. Learn to ask good questions. Try these ...

1. Is your mate or spouse growing in the same direction and sharing feelings?
2. Are your children getting the resources they need to compete in an increasingly complicated world?
3. Are you saving the right amount to retire? Is your profession or business being fed the resources it needs to remain competitive in the future?
4. Are you increasing or modifying exercise and supplementation programs to resist the aging process and maintain the energy needed to obtain or retain your ideal career?

5. Are you investing the proper time in meditation and spiritual pursuit?

Success Tip

Create a path where a path never existed before.

Stop the Blame Game

"A lousy career is merely a symptom of what is going on inside your head."

—Chris Kuselias

One of the biggest myths in America is that we are entitled to a fantastic life, or that the government or employers carry the responsibility to ensure our happiness, fulfillment and prosperity. The truth is each of us is responsible for every aspect of our lives including our fitness, career future, financial obligations, relationship quality and spiritual peace. It is disturbing to notice an increasing number of people that take comfort in assigning blame to others for their shortcomings or challenges or failures: parents, spouses, bosses, terrorists, economy, etc.

Stop looking outside yourself for the things you don't have and start looking internally. It is you and you alone who produces, or doesn't produce, your quality of life. Stop making excuses or rationalizing why you haven't achieved your goals and realize that it doesn't matter where you have been, but only where you are going.

To stop the blame game and take a more active role in your own self-growth, follow these 5 valuable tips:

Stopping The Blame Game ...

1. Take 100% accountability for everything that happens to you.
2. If you keep doing what you're doing, you will keep getting what you are getting, and if you don't like it—make a change!
3. Blaming others is a complete waste of your time. No matter how often you do it, it won't change your outcome.
4. If you seek a different result, simply change your response or approach to the situation.
5. It is your attitude, not your aptitude, which determines your altitude in life.

Defeating Your Fears

Your Fears Are Self-Imposed

> *"F-E-A-R = False Events Appearing Real"*
> —Sign on *Career* T.E.A.M. office

Fear is natural; every human being experiences it. The challenge is that most people allow fear to control them to the point where it prevents them from attaining their goals and potential. Success stories also have fear but rather than letting it control them, they control *it*. These individuals know that fear should be recognized, experienced and can be used as a benefit. Fear is my mind's way of telling me to be alert. It is my thermostat for when I should proceed with caution. Acknowledge that your fears exist but do not let them prohibit you from completing your agenda.

All fears are *self-imposed*. Fears are created in the mind by making a decision to imagine some terrible or problematic outcome occurring if a certain event takes place. For example, if you are afraid of rejection in an interview, your command to your own mind may work like this ...

"I want to get a better job, one that moves me closer to realizing my true calling, but I create fear within myself by imagining that the interviewer will think I am underqualified and reject me, which will crush my self-esteem and diminish my spirits. This will make me experience sadness and frustration, which I want to avoid at all costs, so I think I will stay where I am. At least I am not being rejected and won't have to feel bad about myself."

In order to experience fear, you have to imagine the worst case scenario or some negative outcome.

How about these common career related fears? I am fearful to ...

- Explore my passions
- Look inside myself for the truth
- Quit my current position for a new one
- Tell my spouse I am not fulfilled in my career
- Ask for a raise
- Join a networking group where I know nobody
- Start my own venture
- Take a loan to pursue my dream career business

You have to decide right now if the fear of failure, rejection or the potential to feel bad on a temporary basis is worth not pursuing your career calling, a place and mindset where you will experience joy, happiness and the incredible feeling of contribution on a daily basis. Stop focusing on the worst case scenario and concentrate on the fact that it is your obligation, your right to aggressively pursue your unique niche in the world. To get there, you will have to experience some level of discomfort, but it will be well worth the temporary discomfort.

Conquering Your Fears

> *"I will not learn about fire by thinking about fire but by burning."*
> —Carla Needleman, *The World of Craft*

So what is preventing you from finding your career calling? The primary obstacle is not talent or intelligence. There are countless stories of individuals who have overcome incredible obstacles to become significant contributors. No, the primary reason most people do not attempt to improve is *fear* ... fear of failure, ridicule or rejection. Everyone is afraid of something.

I recall a humorous anecdote by the great comedian, Jerry Seinfeld, who pointed out in one of his now famous monologues that the 2 most common fears in life were death and public speaking. He jokingly asked the audience to ponder the dilemma that if you were at a funeral and possessed both of these fears, "Would you rather have to deliver the eulogy (a public speech) or be the person in the casket?" Some choice ...

Are you destroying your god-given imagination by worrying about events that never happen or focusing on the worst-case scenario? General George Patton said, "Fear kills more people than death, death kills us once. Fear kills us over and over again, subtly at times and brutally at others." I believe that people often fear death because they have not lived a full life. If this is the case, then isn't it time to get started? This thing called life is not a dress rehearsal!

> *"Do not anticipate trouble or worry about what may never happen. Keep in the sunlight."*
> —Benjamin Franklin

To avoid or reduce fear, focus on your physical body and sensations you experience in order to place yourself in a state of fear. Maybe you begin to sit a certain way, fold your arms in a defensive posture, breath differently, or become quiet. Perhaps you have a conditioned pattern of behavior that

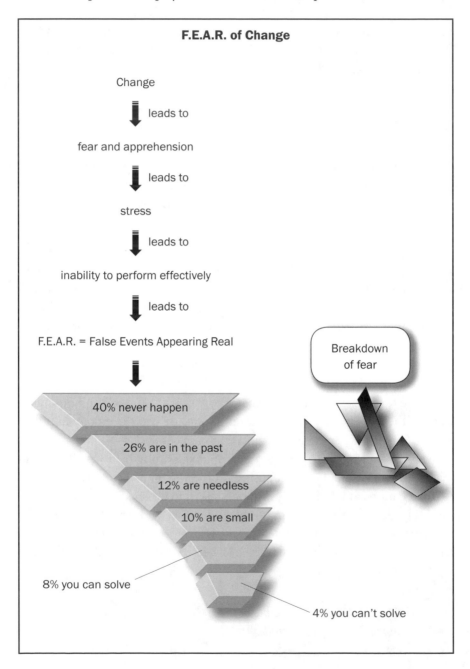

F.E.A.R. of Change

Change

leads to

fear and apprehension

leads to

stress

leads to

inability to perform effectively

leads to

F.E.A.R. = False Events Appearing Real

40% never happen

26% are in the past

12% are needless

10% are small

8% you can solve

4% you can't solve

Breakdown of fear

even feels comfortable to you that you adopt to become comfortable within the fear. Next time you are on an airplane, watch the behavior of passengers who become quiet, agitated, engrossed in a book or magazine, or even become chatty in an attempt to control their fears. Each of us has a different conditioned pattern of response to fearful or uncomfortable situations.

The solution to overcoming your fears is to condition your mind and belief system not to focus on negatives or worst case scenarios, but rather to concentrate on positive outcomes and expectations. When I fly, I always have a certain degree of trepidation but I always focus on the benefits to traveling to my desired destination. If I am going on vacation, I concentrate on the warm weather I will be experiencing, visualize myself on the beach or playing in the surf with my kids, the friends or family I will be seeing, the relaxation I will experience, etc. By doing so, I can literally feel the tension leaving my hands, feet and entire body. I encourage you to utilize this technique to conquer your own fears. Become a fearless flyer!

To manage your fears, build confidence by focusing on prior accomplishments. You have achieved so much already, all we are seeking is an upgrade to a career and lifestyle that is even a better fit. Do not diminish the effort and risk it took for you to get where you are today. While it might not seem like much, it no doubt involved stretching your capabilities and expanding your comfort zone.

Progress requires this. Often times people become so engrossed in the anxiety of the moment (for example, obtaining a bank loan, meeting an influential contact, asking for a raise, an important interview, speaking up in a group session), that they literally forget their prior successes and lose their confidence. Concentrate on your confidence. Your next interview may certainly produce stress, but unless it is your very first job, you have already been through the process and were successful.

Consider this, you weren't born with your existing group of friends or contacts, at some point you networked. You are a work in progress, you have done some great things, you merely seek to do even more ... and accelerate your pace!

3 Strategies for Confronting Your Fears ...

How Walt Disney, founder of Walt Disney, Inc., conceived Mickey Mouse ... Mickey Mouse popped out of his mind onto a drawing pad on a train ride from Manhattan to Hollywood at a time when his business fortunes and those of

his brother Roy were at the lowest point and failure seemed
almost inevitable.

Though it may sound strange, sometimes stress can actually empower your creative center. Here are 3 strategies to confront fear and establish courage:

1. Reduce the worst-case scenario. Try this simple exercise. Take out a sheet of paper and draw a line down the center. On the left side write your desired career calling. On the right side, write the worst possible occurrence that could happen if you took action toward achieving that goal. In most cases, you will be surprised to learn that the direct consequence is not so bad!

2. Instead of consequences, focus on the benefits and happiness you will derive if you take action toward your desired outcome. Create a list of the benefits associated with changing your current routine and the incredible joy of living your calling on a daily basis. What stresses will be removed? What moments of happiness will become lasting in your memory? Remember, all decisions are based on our desire to obtain happiness.

3. Be willing to take risks and be persistent. I often to speak to several thousand people at a time and have hosted my own national radio show. There was a time that I had a tremendous fear of public speaking. Whenever it was my turn to introduce myself to a group, I would work myself up into a negative frenzy and nearly get physically sick. I would do anything to avoid having to address a group of people and felt my skin crawl as it came closer to my turn … I overcame this fear by following these 3 steps and realizing that the worst-case scenario was not that bad and the benefits of mastering my fear were incredible! Thomas Edison, generally considered our greatest inventor, was also a tremendous failure as several of his inventions never amounted to anything. Babe Ruth, the sultan of swat, had an incredible number of strike-outs. Oprah had significant obstacles, but pushed forward and became an icon. The biggest risk to your calling is your inability to master your own fears and self-imposed limitations.

Don't Wait for an External Event to Create Internal Change!

"Is this all there is?"

—Anonymous

Let us begin with a review of the reasons why people seek to make a career change and pursue meaning and purpose. The top reasons are:

1. A Desire for More   Most people are always thinking about the possibility of more responsibility, money, creativity, reward or recognition. Sometimes the sheer frustration of repeating this internal pattern finally results in action: a trip to the bookstore or visit to a career counselor.

2. Getting Fired or Laid Off   Most people, guilty of procrastination up to this point, use the loss of a job to confront their true ambitions and desires. They are "off the treadmill" of life and have time to think and contemplate. This time often sparks an interest and allows for critical reflection.

3. A Change in Current Job Responsibilities   Often a person will get serious and confront real alternatives when they find their duties modified or reduced. They can see the writing on the wall and demand change as their current role has lost some of the passion due to a reduction or change in duties.

4. A Change in Marital Status (for Example, Divorce)   In my experience, often making a change in one's relationship is followed by a change in career. This occurs as the newly single person has time to look at his or her career from a new perspective, without the restrictions or limitations of their former spouse who may have been unsupportive or envious regarding a career change.

5. Celebrating a Landmark Birthday   This often signals a change in outlook and intensifies the desire to leave a positive legacy. I find many people when turning 40 or 50 feel often make a change hoping to realize or validate their dreams.

6. Retirement   Many people take advantage of an early retirement offering, are forced into retirement or simply retire as expected and still feel the need to contribute. This typically includes starting one's own business, consulting or part time work. In my own experience, I find about 75% of retirees maintain a desire to keep working as opposed to the traditional view of retirement.

7. A Brush with Death   Have you ever known a person who has had a near death experience? I have met and advised countless individuals who have experienced an event or scenario such as a terminal cancer diagnosis, surviving a plane crash or being saved from drowning; events which brought them face to face with their own mortality. In my case, it was a tumor on my spine in my early thirties and the very real threat of becoming a quadriplegic for the balance of my existence. I will never forget the day I received this news while sitting in the doctor's office. Talk about a wake-up call and a life-altering event! Individuals who experience these instances rarely return to their prior state of mind; the occurrence serves as a catalyst for permanent change. These people adopt a different perspective about life. Little things are less bothersome; stress is no longer a main ingredient in their personality and their priorities shift from material concerns to a greater sense of community and service. They have a unique perspective, and are less inclined to complain about insignificant concerns and worry about mundane issues.

I am not suggesting that you go out and seek a life-changing event or near death experience; that would be ludicrous. My point is to not wait for a crisis or life-altering event to serve as the catalyst for getting you to claim your rightful destiny. Be proactive and *crave* the incredible feelings and emotions associated with knowing you have found your calling. Too often, I meet people who describe their lives as *"OK."* Why settle for mediocrity when you have within you every single thing you need to be a monster success? You have been blessed with enormous potential! As a human being, you already have the mental, emotional, and attitudinal gifts required to be a great contributor. It is there for the taking; you need not wait to be laid off, destitute or receive an unfavorable diagnosis to get your butt in gear! So what is stopping you? Easy ... *what is hindering you is your inability to master your internal belief system regarding failure and its potential consequences?* You are scared!

Master your fears. Remember, you were not born with your current collection of fears; they were absorbed into your personality and became a fixture in your emotional make up over time. Societal conditioning has contributed to your own self-imposed limitations (for example: I did not graduate college so my earnings will be limited ... My parents were hourly workers, so I must be one as well, ... Having a decent job is better than risking it all for a pursuit of my calling).

Fears are not a virus, they are an adopted belief that was not there previously. Guard your mind from negative thoughts and screen out associates who drain your life energy. When confronted with a challenge (such as the decision to pursue your career calling) there are really only 2 options, bravery and cowardice.

1. Bravery: The ability to act in spite of your fears
2. Cowardice: An inability to act because one is consumed or controlled by fears

At the risk of oversimplifying, acts of bravery lead to the trait of courage. The opposite of fear is courage. Fear is your deadliest enemy. It retards your growth and restricts you from achieving your calling. So the real challenge is: How can you become more courageous?

The Risk of Not Taking Risks

> "It is not a coincidence that the top home run hitters in Major League Baseball historically are among the league leaders in strikeouts. The message: If you swing for the fences, you will also have plenty of misses, but in the end, it is worth it!"
>
> —Chris Kuselias

I am going to make a statement here that will no doubt be controversial to those of you who tend to be conservative when it comes to risk taking: if you are risk-averse in today's competitive workplace, you are endangering yourself and your family. Those candidates who are unwilling to take risks are extremely vulnerable to obsolescence; meaning their skills and attitudes may no longer be in demand. I see a huge correlation between people who are drifting aimlessly in the job market and an unwillingness to try new methods or strategies. Over time, any individual who does not re-invent with fresh new skills, knowledge or stimulating solutions to problems in their industry will fail.

The most powerful, wealthy and congruent people I know are those who went left when everyone else went right; for them, conformity was almost a dirty word. Said another way, the price of entry for obtaining your calling is a willingness to *zig* while others *zag*. Like it or not, we now live in a world that not only craves innovation, but demands it! *The ability to demonstrate a unique and compelling skill set, creativity or solution is the secret to career success in the 21st century workplace.*

Need an example? Consider the medium of television. For decades, television programming, generally regarded as the most powerful and influential medium ever created, provided news, talk show formats, sitcoms or dramas. Then a risk taker, someone who was thinking outside the proverbial box, unveiled a new concept called *Reality TV.* Regardless of your opinion of reality television (I am personally not a huge fan), immediately it seemed as if every new show was a spin-off of one reality show or another.

Next, someone conceived the idea that viewers were tired of their existence and wanted to change their lives; thus was born the creation of the makeover television show, which immediately began to generate a huge following. Currently, there seems to be a makeover show for your house, relationship, physical features and, who knows, maybe we will see a successful version of a career makeover show! The point is, for years, television followed the same basic format; then suddenly, due to risk taking and a new vision, it changed its complexion.

I would rather have you attempt a uniquely compelling approach and fail than adopt a conformist mentality and be frustrated by your inability to differentiate your skills and credentials to a potential hiring authority.

> Hiring authorities are begging for innovation ... they want Baskin-Robbins 32nd flavor of ice cream, the 58th variety of Heinz steak sauce, the new formula for Kentucky Fried Chicken or the job search candidate who can solve their challenges in a non-traditional way.

There is not a single employer on the planet looking for a mediocre candidate. Hiring authorities have preferences. You will never appeal to everyone, not intellectually, emotionally, physically or creatively. Who says universal acceptance is the solution to anything? You need to focus your efforts on creating a personal brand and establishing a niche group in your desired field.

Never Stop Competing

One of your nation's greatest leaders knew defeat throughout his life. His resume was a mess. The following is his less than smooth rise to success. Can you name him?

1831	Failed in business
1832	Defeated for legislature
1833	Failed in business—AGAIN
1836	Suffered a nervous breakdown
1838	Defeated for speaker
1840	Defeated for elector
1843	Defeated for Congress
1848	Defeated for Congress—AGAIN
1855	Defeated for Senate
1856	Defeated for Vice President
1858	Defeated for Senate—AGAIN
1860	*Elected President of the United States of America*

Abe Lincoln was a champion who never stopped competing even with failures that would have left most devastated. He just kept competing until he finally won!

Your Fears Are Learned Behaviors

> *"There are 2 types of speakers; those that are nervous and those that are liars."*
>
> —Mark Twain

An important breakthrough for you will be to learn that *all fears are learned behaviors*. The good news is that if fears are learned, they can also be unlearned. Understand that we all start at the same place. You may be thinking, "But, Chris, I am a worrier, it is part of my personality. I was born that way." Nonsense! Remember that worry, like fear, is a learned behavior, one that you have chosen to adopt. Fear's first cousin, worry, is the habit of focusing on the negative or dwelling on what you don't want to occur.

In my *The Career Guarantee* seminar, I present a recently born baby (fake doll), swaddled in a warm blanket. I show the audience the baby's face and make it a point to reinforce how innocent and vulnerable the newborn is. The audience and I then list learned behaviors such as racism, prejudice, anger, alcoholism, drug dependency, stereotypes, jealousy, stress, envy, insecurity, fear of flying, fear of public speaking, fear of rejection, etc. We list over 100 learned fears and behaviors, none of which this precious baby had developed.

The question is then posed: What events, relationships and experiences will shape this child and create these learned behaviors? It is truly a compelling exercise and one that reinforces the fact that we all start at basically the same place. It is our experiences that create our associations of pain and pleasure and then dictate our legacy. The child in this example will learn to adopt fears, but can also learn to eradicate them.

Here are 3 thought provoking questions:

1. What one great thing would you attempt if you knew you would not fail?
2. What person or persons has or have experienced the same disappointments, setbacks or limitations that you have, yet has or have attained the career objective you seek ... despite these obstacles?
3. What is *really* keeping you from your goal—Laziness Apathy? Fear?

If you focus on the negative, you will hear more ambulances, be attracted to more negative newspaper articles and most likely continue to target destructive relationships. You will program your mind to become a magnet for negative occurrences. Conversely, if you focus on the positive, you will see more beauty, observe kind acts and be drawn to contribution.

Mastering Rejection

IF YOU TRULY ASPIRE to attain your career calling, you must learn the skill of mastering rejection. You might be asking who would want to be good at a task that most likely involves a certain degree of anger, failure and a loss of self-esteem. Where do I sign up for that? The reality is that rejection is a normal part of life; we all face it. Usually the more successful the individual, the more rejection he or she has confronted.

When I first founded *Career* T.E.A.M., we spent months formulating a solution to our 1st major assignment, the challenge of moving welfare recipients (many of whom had never worked, never attended high school, could not read or write, had suffered physical or mental abuse and had

"I got three responses today ... 'Get out,' 'Stay out,' and 'Don't come back!'"

multiple children without day care or supervision) into meaningful careers where they could begin the process of becoming self-sufficient.

As a team, we wrote and created an empowering course, which included our best strategies and techniques on limiting beliefs, goal setting, affirmations, taking responsibility, values, conquering fears, skill identification, habits and job readiness. We poured our heart and souls into a curriculum we believed would revolutionize welfare to work programs. We engaged direct feedback from American corporations that shared their internal processes for hiring and rejecting entry level candidates. The course offering was empowering, educational and informative and we were confident that any participant would be motivated to make the transition to self-sufficiency.

Our 1st presentation was to an established government funded workforce development board that had posted a Request for Proposals on the Internet to serve the welfare recipients in their region. For over a week, we created an elaborate presentation complete with video, audio, student guides and a power point presentation with sophisticated graphics. We were ready! We dressed in our best professional attire, got to our appointment early and were ready to rock and roll!

I began by thanking the attendees (a group of 5 high level and credentialed workforce managers/decision makers), introduced our team and began our presentation. I began in my usual motivational tone to explain that our philosophy was that the challenge of transitioning a welfare recipient to gainful employment was more about addressing their internal belief systems and self-imposed limitations (understanding of self) than about work readiness training (resume, interviewing techniques).

Our program would begin with a focus on the individuals' mindset before addressing the mechanics of the job search process. The lead manager immediately folded her arms, stood up and stopped me in mid sentence. Her next comment nearly floored me as she stated, "I certainly hope you are not here to waste our time discussing the psychology of careering or *voodoo* training when what *these people* really need is a new resume and a kick in the butt."

As calmly as I could, I attempted to address her observation and provide a reasonable explanation as to why we felt that any person with significant barriers needed to be trained and developed from the *inside out*. Before I could finish my 1st sentence to rebut her assertions, the funding source manager stood up, held up her hand and rudely stated that the meeting was over and that we had wasted their time. She concluded by stating that there was no place in welfare reform coaching or career training for topics like mindset, affirmations, limiting beliefs, etc. With that she left the room, leaving our team to feel confused and rejected. We had worked so hard only to be crushed by the opinion of a misguided decision maker.

We were left with 3 options: quit the business and forget we ever considered the challenge of welfare to work, compromise our program offering to comply with providing only the work readiness training (what we knew was a surefire formula for failure) or re-group, find an alternative customer and stick to our guns. We chose the latter and went on to become one of the most respected welfare to work programs in the nation. As a side note, one year later we were delighted to learn that the funding source, which had rejected our plan, now made empowerment and self-discovery mandated components of their welfare to work training. I am pleased to tell you that *Career* T.E.A.M. was subsequently awarded several million dollars in workforce funding.

The lesson is to never stop competing and to not let rejection derail your vision, especially if you believe in your heart that you are right and your intentions are honorable. Every celebrity, athlete, politician or person of influence you can name has experienced rejection in their climb to the top of their profession. If you are not experiencing rejection on a fairly regular basis, I suggest you are either complacent or playing it safe and not taking enough risks. As your coach, I view it as my responsibility through my words, to get you to see that rejection is merely an opportunity to refine or re-shape your vision. Never take it personally. It may be that the timing was wrong, you were ahead of your time, or some other justifiable reason. Somebody out there is interested. There are over 6 billion people on earth; someone will see things your way, agree with your vision or appreciate your perspective. The key is to find the outlet, organization or individual who can make your vision a reality. Don't quit!

> Sergey Brin and Larry Page were schoolmates and friends who had a vision for a new Internet business. They packaged their concept and approached several potential partners, one of whom was Yahoo!, who could have acquired the friends company for a handful of stock. Yahoo! passed on the project and the 2 friends, although rejected but not discouraged, went back to work. As of this writing, Sergey and Larry's company is now worth billions. You may have heard of it ... their company is called Google.

Rejection is simply an opportunity to learn and build from. Try to find out why the other party does not see things your way; the experience is invaluable. Assess if it was a good fit after all; many times it is not. I cannot tell you how many job interviews I was rejected for that would have potentially sent me to on the wrong career path. You control your reaction to rejection; it is up to you to condition yourself to see rejection not as a personal attack or criticism but rather as a chance to learn.

I remember reading about 2 men whose work I greatly admire, Jack Canfield and Mark Victor Hansen, who had a vision to create a series of empowering short stories and were rejected by over 30 publishers who said the concept would not work. Undeterred, the 2 authors attended the American Booksellers Association conference and received another 130 rejections on their concept. Finally, persistence paid off when a struggling publisher of addiction-recovery books took a chance on them. The 1st book went on to sell 8 million copies and turned into a series of 80 best-selling books that have been translated into 39 languages. Perhaps you have heard of *Chicken Soup for the Soul.*

Be Persistent!

> *Did you know that according to scientists and people who study aerodynamics, the bumble bee is technically incapable of flight? Its body weight should not be able to be propelled through the air based upon its wing capabilities. Yet, we all have seen a bumble bee in flight! The bee simply decided it needed and wanted to fly, despite these scientifically confirmed limitations.*

If you were to ask people who know me what my most compelling character trait is, they would say without hesitation, *persistence.* I simply do not give up ... ever. Perhaps it was because most things never came easy to me or that I have had to work extremely hard for everything of value that I have.

Whatever the reason, my research has confirmed that top achievers (to include people who get to live out their career dreams on a daily basis) have all worked extremely hard to develop themselves and share the common trait of *incredible persistence.* These folks lock on to a goal and invest their entire being into achieving their objective. Certainly obstacles confront them in their quest, but they never lose sight of their dream and press on through detours. They do this because, unlike most, they have created such a strong *why* and have developed such an internal emotional benefit to the attainment of this objective that nothing will stand in their way. Simply put, persistent people have a clear understanding of exactly what they want and are willing to do more than most to obtain it.

> Growing up, I was infatuated by professional athletes and had a dream to become a major league baseball player. When I got to college, I found myself competing with 16 other shortstops for 2 spots on the roster. My arm strength and range were simply not good enough and if I did not find another position, my baseball career would be over. Instead of being cut from the team, I decided to convert to the outfield, where I had a chance to succeed. I spent countless hours before and after practice improving my outfield skills. Despite skeptics and never having played the outfield position until college, I mastered the position and was selected as an outfielder to play in the New England All Star game held in my dream field, Fenway Park in Boston, Massachusetts, home of my beloved Red Sox! The reason? Persistence and a commitment to constantly improve my skills, knowledge and expertise.

Commit To Constant and Never Ending Improvement

> *"If you are willing to do more than you are paid to do, eventually you will be paid to do more than you do."*
> —Sign on the wall of a Career T.E.A.M. office

I experienced a breakthrough when one of my mentors pointed out what now seems like simple advice. I had, by any measure, achieved tremendous success in my career, yet on some level I was not enjoying each accomplishment as it occurred. I had the mentality of *achieving to be happy* instead of one where I was focused on *happily achieving.*

My mentor pointed out to me that the Japanese have a word for constant and never ending improvement, which is *kaizen.* The concept of constant and never ending improvement serves as a philosophy for the modern Japanese economy and was originally conceived as the age-old philosophy for Japan's warriors. When I heard this, a realization hit me like a hammer. Stop focusing on the end result in order to obtain a sense of accomplishment, but enjoy each step of the journey and be happy along the way to greatness. What I was doing was checking off each task of the process but not relishing or enjoying each of these accomplishments. I was like a robot that was only focused on the mission's objective, without taking credit for the skills and key decisions each step required to keep my momentum.

Today, I *happily achieve* in all of my undertakings and enjoy the ride! Ask yourself:

1. Am I injecting passion into this experience?
2. How can I improve my results?
3. How can I be more efficient?

Exercise: The 4 Quarters of Life

If you ever find yourself losing confidence or need a morale boost, try this exercise. What I often do when I begin to doubt myself or feel like I am getting off track, is return to my accomplishments and refresh my spirit. In short, I itemize my success stories into 4 quarters (can you tell I am a huge sports fan!). Ideally, select one accomplishment from each of the following 3 categories: personal, educational and professional accomplishments in your quest to map out your credentials.

1st Quarter: From Birth to Age 25

Personal: Named National High School Scholar Athlete and inducted into the Hall of Fame

Educational: Graduated 15th in my high school class and admitted to UCONN School of Business, accepted to law school

Professional: Authored initial business plan for future career coaching enterprise

2nd Quarter: From Age 25 to Age 50

Personal: Married my soul mate and beautiful wife Susan and had 3 beautiful children

Educational: Attended over 50 seminars from world renowned educators and innovators

Professional: Founded *Career* T.E.A.M., LLC, a company dedicated to coaching individuals, government and organizations to make positive changes to improve performance

3rd Quarter: From Age 50 to Age 75

Personal: Continue to build a world class family based on trust, honesty and communication

Educational: Develop an international seminar/workshop series to bridge growing opportunity divide

Professional: Assist 1 million people find their career calling

4ᵗʰ Quarter: From Age 75 to Age 100 (Can You Tell I Am an Optimist?)

Personal: ?
Educational: ?
Professional: ?

Avoiding Procrastination ... the Silent Killer

TO PROCRASTINATE IS THE art of putting off doing something today until tomorrow or to continually delay action towards achievement. Procrastination is what I call the silent killer. In my opinion, it is the number one reason that keeps people from achieving what they really want in their careers. Procrastination is something that starts small and kind of creeps up on you. That's why I call it the silent killer, until it becomes a bad habit and part of your personality.

The best strategy to combat occupational procrastination is to take consistent steps and positive actions towards the attainment of your ideal career. Resist the temptation to let the "procrastination virus" become part of your daily routine or part of your personality because, if it does, it will severely limit your progress, growth and attainment of your career objectives.

Career procrastinators create a lot of excuses or alibis for why they have not begun their career search campaign or why they aren't in their ideal career and blame others for their shortcomings or problems. They refuse to accept responsibility for their own actions and view difficulties and temporary obstacles as permanent problem areas, which will prevent them from reaching their career goals, rather than viewing their failures as temporary setbacks and something to learn from.

So how do you overcome this dilemma? Stop worrying about what other people think. Don't give in to a fear of criticism.

"Honey, how's the resume coming along?"

Ignore other people's comments because they're probably procrastinators themselves who obviously haven't read *The Career Guarantee* and are envious of the fact that you have taken decisive action to improve yourself. Many people don't like others to succeed because it reinforces their own inability to take action, their apathetic attitude or pure laziness. So, they root against everyone and criticize those who pursue greatness. Surround yourself with positive thinkers and progressive personalities. You may even need to change your circle of acquaintances to a more positive group of people who don't succumb to fear.

Be the kind of person that says the glass is half-full and not half-empty. In fact, I heard a cute analogy about how an optimist goes to the window every morning and says, "Good morning, God," while a pessimist goes to the same window and says, "Good God, morning."

It is human nature to want to stay in a comfort zone, and not to feel insecure by moving out of that zone. Ask yourself if you have become complacent or unhappy. Ask yourself if you're in a rut.

You are a human being, not a human becoming ...

Good Morning Exercise

Your status or title does not always equate to true career satisfaction. In fact, the majority of workers are unfulfilled. Please answer the following question. Do I get out of bed happy or am I miserable when the alarm clock rings?

Signs that you are not happy with your current situation:

- Repetition
- You welcome every weekend
- Tired
- Insomnia
- Poor appetite
- Illness
- Hostility
- Lack of concentration
- Cynical attitude
- Excessive television watching

If you have any of the above signs, *please concentrate on finishing this book* so that you can achieve career happiness, regain your confidence and self-esteem, and obtain a more productive and health lifestyle.

Do you have any of these symptoms? Be honest with yourself. Try to get out of these bad habits. Bad habits are easy to form and hard to live with, while good habits are hard to form but easy to live with. Once you've had a taste of security, it becomes difficult to get yourself out of that state.

5 Reasons to Quit Your Job ... Now!

It is perfectly normal to experience a certain level of frustration no matter what job you hold, company you work for or country you live in. There is no perfect job, just like there are no perfect human beings. Understanding the difference between an acceptable level of unhappiness and a dangerous level of dissatisfaction is an important distinction. Although every situation is unique, extenuating factors often can alter the decision. Here are 5 circumstances that should typically result in an immediate change in employment or, at the very least, result in a heart to heart talk with your trusted advisors.

1. Loss of Pride   Do you observe a decline in the quality of your work? Do you no longer take pride in your work to the point you avoid talking about your career? If you find yourself sheepishly avoiding the question, "What do you do for a living?" because you have lost the spark and pride in your job, company or industry, consider a change. If you find yourself cutting corners, sleeping late, taking longer lunches, gossiping about the negative, or hanging out with company malcontents, these are clear signs you are not being challenged, have outgrown the tasks, and become complacent. If you are in this situation, do not act irrationally and quit today. Rather, assess your situation and consider what needs to change to reclaim your passion. Volunteer for a new assignment, take more risks, take a part time job in a new field, but make sure you take action before you fall into a difficult funk. If you have, move on!

2. Loss of Passion or Self-Esteem   Do you feel like you have lost some of your passion or self-esteem? Are you bored, indifferent or apathetic? Do you get overly excited about the weekends or snow days? Is TGIF your favorite restaurant not because of the food, but because of the title? Do Monday mornings bring a sense of dread? Keep in mind that most of us work 8 hours a day, but if you add in commute time, overtime, time thinking about work or time getting ready to go to work, we actually spend more time working than any other aspect of our lives! If work is a downer, your personality and vitality will suffer. This can negatively affect your attitude, love life, interest in friends and family, hobbies, etc. If this has occurred, move on!

3. Loss of Health   Is your job negatively affecting your health or even jeopardizing your life? Has your stress level increased to the point of being a health risk? Every job involves a certain degree of stress. In fact, I believe certain kinds of stress are actually healthy as they can empower you to greater achievement. But if you have headaches, feel stomach sick, or worse, experience heart palpitations, it is time to change gears, my friend! Chronic career stress can lead to serious health issues including depression, insomnia, heart disease or gastrointestinal conditions. Make sure you are taking adequate vacation time to recharge your battery and find stress relieving outlets like exercise or meditation. All work and no play not only make Jack a dull boy, it can put him in the hospital! Before this occurs, move on!

4. Loss of Balance   Does your current position require you to be a workaholic? Has your work life negatively affected your life balance? Is your travel schedule out of control? Do you see the hotel concierge more than your loved ones? Do you find yourself missing important life events, like your children's plays, parent teacher conferences, workouts, favorite shows, vacations, social events, etc.? Remember, there are 5 key life balance areas: career, health and fitness, financial stability, relationship mastery, and spiritual enlightenment. Emphasis on any one area at the expense of the others is a recipe for disaster! If you simply cannot attain balance due to your current career duties, move on!

5. Loss of Faith   Is the culture of your organization so negative that you simply have lost faith in the mission and cannot stand the environment? Is your supervisor inhibiting your career progression? Is the company you work for unprofessional or unethical? Have you maxed out your progression so that you are destined to stay put forever? Clearly, you have a responsibility if not an obligation to do everything in your power to be a positive force in whatever organization pays your salary. However, if you have exhausted all of your options regarding reducing negativity amongst your peers, improving unethical behaviors within the organization or your supervisor makes it clear you are going no further towards your career calling, move on!

Excuses Are Useless ... If Only ...

Be cognizant of your feelings and surroundings. Constantly have your human antenna in working order to gauge if you are on track to your calling. We all have good days and bad days but monitor if you are off course with no hope of success. If you are not happy, make certain it is not an excuse or that your blame is not improperly directed. Consider if these excuses are familiar ...

- If only I'd gone to a better school
- If only I weren't a woman, a man, white, black, Hispanic, Puerto Rican or a Martian
- If only I were younger
- If only I could meet the right spouse
- If only I were more of a risk-taker
- If only I didn't have a wife and kids to take care of
- If only I didn't have a husband and kids to take care of

- If only my boss knew how well I was really doing
- If only I didn't worry so much
- If only my health weren't so bad
- If only I had been born into riches instead of poverty

I have met people who have come from some of the most discouraging and disheartening backgrounds who have gone on to achieve tremendous wealth, peace of mind and career success because of the fact that they took action and didn't let their excuses dominate them. They didn't allow themselves to fall prey to an unfulfilling comfort zone or secure position, which didn't provide passion and purpose. They took specific career action and they forged ahead.

- Oprah was born an African American female in an industry dominated by white males. Her story is well documented and she now spends her days empowering millions with her TV and media empire.
- Steven Spielberg was a college dropout who never lost faith in his dream to be a premier filmmaker. Some his most famous movies are: *ET, Indiana Jones, Jurassic Park,* and *Schindler's List.*
- Ray Charles was born blind but never let that be an excuse to stop him from becoming one of the world's most beloved performers.

The list of individuals who achieved their calling despite having every conceivable excuse to fail is endless. If they can do it, so can you!

PROCRASTINATION EXERCISE

Did you know that a city block of fog can be condensed into a single cup of water?

Finding your calling is simply a series of well orchestrated and choreographed steps. It is a process and not an outcome or destination. Procrastination is the enemy and needs to be managed and eliminated. Procrastination can fall into any area of your life, career included. 2 things cause procrastination. Number 1, the activity at hand is unpleasant or, number 2, the activity or job is overwhelming.

Name a previous situation when you were guilty of procrastination
Looking back, why did you delay action?
What problems will you encounter if you "put off" the career search
    process and delay action?

Finding a job or changing careers can easily be deemed unpleasant by people who don't like to inventory or list their accomplishments. They avoid
critical reflection. Taking inventory is a mandate, you will most likely be
pleasantly surprised!

You may have better credentials than you think; once you assemble
them, list your accomplishments, and strategize on methods of improving
your credentials, it can be an exhilarating exciting process!. The challenge
is that many of us don't realize the talent and credentials we already have.
Let me give you an example.

Jason the Gym Rat

In one of my recent seminars, I had a young man approach me and indicate
he was passionate about working in the health and fitness industry. We sat
down and discussed his specific accomplishments, in essence, inventorying his
achievements.

Jason cited job-related activities that he had been involved with. At one point
he said to me, "Oh, and by the way, Chris, I worked in a gymnasium. I was a gym
worker. In fact, I was a certified trainer." I said, "But wait a minute. Wait a minute. Tell me more." And he said, "Well, basically I would run people through the
exercise equipment, showing people how to use the machines. You know how it
works." And I said, "No, I don't know how it works." And he said, "Well, you know,
I would guide them as to how many seconds to bring the machine forward and
how to go back and the techniques and everything about health and how long
it took them to exercise and what a good basic program they should be on and
how regularly they should be on that program and what they should eat and so
forth and so on. You know, Chris."

And I said, "Well, wait a minute. Basically, you were a coach or mentor to
them. Would that be right?" And the young man said, "Well, yeah." And I said,
"Well, basically then you could say that you were a consultant to them. Would
that be a fair assessment?" And he said, "Well, yeah, I guess you could probably
say that." And then I said, "Well, in the overall objectives of these people in the
gym, why were they there?" And he said, "Oh, of course, they were there to get
healthier, to get fit, to improve the quality of their lives, to improve the way they
looked, I guess to be more fit."

So I said, "In other words, fitness is the key here." And he said, "Yes." So I
said, "Would it be accurate to say that you were a fitness consultant? I mean
you are certified." And he said, "Gee, I never thought of it in those terms." I said,
"Well, it sounds much better than 'I work in a gym,' doesn't it? I'd rather be

called an exercise fitness consultant than a gym worker." He got the point immediately and I think you do, too. We both smiled and went on from there. *Not
so unpleasant ...*

The gym story is an overly simplistic example. But you can do the same
thing with your own activities. And remember, word choice is very important on your resume or when you're promoting your achievements. The
phrase, "I worked in a gym" may not sound so glamorous. But if you can
get yourself thinking "Hey, I was an exercise fitness consultant" and use
proper voice inflexion, your outcome may improve. You will feel excited
about what your credentials rather than embarrassed about your previous
occupations.

We've all heard the cute example of how, "I'm a typical housewife," translates into, "I'm a domestic engineer." That's a little cliché, but start thinking
positively of your prior positions.

Procrastination is also caused because a career search is *overwhelming*.
Whenever I encounter an overwhelming situation, I do the following. First,
I ask myself, "Chris, what is the overall objective that you seek from this
endeavor?" Secondly, I assign a list of realistic short-term and long-term
goals that I can easily fulfill, and that helps me complete this larger task.
In essence, I break down the larger task into smaller manageable activities.
In concluding this segment on procrastination, don't tell yourself, "I have
to do something." Instead, when you're involved in a potentially unpleasant or overwhelming situation, try, "Hey, I choose to do this. I'm making
a choice." Take the words "I have to do this" out of your vocabulary and
substitute it with the words "I choose to" or "I want to." And that will help
you avoid procrastination. Don't internalize "I have to find the job of my
dreams." Repeat ... "I want to find the job of my dreams." Say it loud and
proud ... "I choose to find my ideal career because there are many benefits
to me and my family in doing so." And reflect on those benefits. Write them
down in a place where you see them every day, mine are in my wallet.

What happens to me if I do procrastinate? Is it the money that I'll lose
because I'm not happy in my current job? Is it the fact that I only go through
life once and I'm not passionate? Is it the fact that when I look back at my
life when I'm older, I'll have a lot of regrets for not taking risks and finding out what was my special, unique contribution to society? What are the
consequences of not taking action? What's the down-side risk?

And then actualize the feelings if you achieve your ideal career. Picture
yourself getting up every morning, getting dressed and going to work.

What are the positive emotions of that dream job? Is it the creativity? Is it the incredible relationships you'll make? Is it the money you'll earn? How will your life be better? What improvements will you see?

Focusing on the positive will help you avoid procrastination. Again, develop the habit of reciting out loud, "I want and deserve the job of my dreams," not "I have to go through the motions" or "I have to write my resume" or "I have to make some phone calls" or "I'm afraid to network because people are going to hang up on me." Tell yourself, "I want to. I choose to." Start today!

> *"The secret of getting ahead is getting started. The secret of getting started is breaking down your complex, overwhelming tasks into small manageable tasks, and then starting on the first one."*
>
> —Mark Twain

Being concise will also help you eliminate the tendency to procrastinate.

No Matter What!

> *"Knowing is not enough; we must apply. Willing is not enough; we must do."*
>
> —Goethe

I am asking you to provide no less than 100% of your attention and dedication to the process of attaining your career calling. Nothing less is acceptable! Together, we will get there, no matter what! Sometimes in life a good effort or quasi commitment yields acceptable results, but not in this case! When it comes to finding that magic formula for your career calling, 99.9% is not good enough. There is too much competition and life moves too fast to not provide your complete and undivided attention. To illustrate what 99.9% yields versus 100%, here are some dramatic examples. If 99.9% was good enough:

- Your heart would fail to beat 32,000 times each year!
- Doctors would accidentally drop 50 newborn babies every day.
- 16,000 important pieces of mail would be lost every day.
- 2 unsafe airplane landings at O'Hare International airport every day.

- 20,000 incorrectly filled important drug prescriptions every year.
- 500 surgical operations performed incorrectly each year.
- 1 hour of unsanitary drinking water every month.

The difference between living your career dreams or not is often that close! Why take the chance or settle for anything less than you desire and deserve to be? The answers lie ahead ...

CHAPTER 7

How to Identify Your Unique and Compelling Career Calling

KEY QUESTION: *HOW* DO I GET THERE?

In this chapter, you will learn:

KEY TOPICS

- How to *Reinvent* Yourself
- Time to Take Action
- Narrowing Your Focus

KEY MESSAGES

- Determining your unique career calling requires a look inside your heart and soul.
- Make sure you truly understand what motivates your actions.
- Successful career seekers get in touch with their authentic self.
- An understanding of your authentic self and your most important emotional needs are paramount to achieving career success.
- Design your ideal business card; review it every day!
- 4 key steps to career success: *Formulate* an Idea, *Envision* the outcome, *Plan* for your success and *Do* it!
- A successful career is measured by *your* internal happiness and not by material possessions, societal conditioning, prestige, title or validation by co-workers, neighbors or family members.
- Your career is an extension of your personality, but not a measure of your worth.
- Strive to be considered an expert resource by understanding and articulating the incredible value of your unique and compelling contributions.
- Career searching requires you to effectively market your abilities. Know your product (yourself) and continuously update your credentials. Never allow yourself to become obsolete!
- Update your qualifications and add 1 new career enhancement per month.
- Mistakes mean you are taking enough risks; zero mistakes equals complacency!
- With fundamentals comes confidence, with confidence comes success, with success comes pride, and with pride comes career happiness.
- Understand what truly makes you unique and compelling in the eyes of the employer.

> *"Where talent and the needs of the world cross, therein lies your vocation."*
>
> —Aristotle

How to *Reinvent* Yourself

"Given the right circumstances, from no more than dreams to determination, and the liberty to try, quite ordinary people consistently do extraordinary things."
—Dee Hock, *Birth of the Chaordic Age*

The Story of Maria

The Challenge

Maria is a 40-year old woman of Mexican Hispanic decent who made the difficult emotional decision to leave her family in Mexico in search of a better life for herself, her teenage son and her young daughter. Recently divorced, she came to the United States with very little except the strong desire to provide for her family. As the sole breadwinner, Maria successfully worked her way up from entry-level hospitality jobs to a job with the state as a case manager, which meant she processed claims for people on public assistance. Being bilingual was a benefit to Maria as many of her clients were relatively new to the country and not proficient in English. Maria built a decent career for herself and her 2 kids but never made enough to enjoy any extras. She has a small condo in a questionable neighborhood and drove a compact care that always seemed to need minor work. Playing the role of single parent and the sole breadwinner left little or no time for herself and the pursuit of her own dreams. She also sent money home to her family back in Mexico, which occasionally strained her ability to pay her bills on time. Maria had little or no money saved for retirement and was one bad break away from bankruptcy. Maria yearned for a chance to pursue her true passion, which was to leave the paper-pushing job she had and transition to a position that allowed her to teach others in a fun and exciting way. On a daily basis, she watched clients move from one station to the next with little or no progress.

The Turning Point

One day, after her daughter came home from school detailing a disturbing event between a student and a teacher, Maria decided she had enough of her job and troubled neighborhood. She did not want her children exposed to poverty and negative influences, which seemed to permeate her neighborhood. With this as her motivation to find a more rewarding job function, earn more money and ultimately relocate, Maria made the decision to approach the Director of her entire department, a person who was 3 levels above her own supervisor and whom she was extremely nervous to be around due to their elevated status. Word from her fellow employees was that when the "big boss" walked through the office and near your cubicle, it would be a good idea to look the other way. Maria ignored the office rumors and summoned up all of her courage to ask the Director's assistant for an appointment with the Department head. The request for an appointment was granted and took 2 weeks to occur, but that gave Maria time to prepare. Maria outlined her thoughts around a revised plan for teaching clients in need of bilingual services, using her own previous experience as a client as an example. The Director was impressed and was not the unapproachable dictator her co-workers suggested she was. Instead, she welcomed Maria's proposed ideas and applauded her initiative!

The New Calling

As a result of the meeting, one month later Maria was asked to sit on a new internal task force designed to create a plan for assisting those with limited English skills. Maria was the lowest ranking person on the committee and the only member who was a former client. Suddenly, going to work was no longer a chore and an obligation, but rather a chance to fulfill her passion! Maria felt invigorated by the very thought of empowering Hispanic clients to make it in this country and was appointed to conduct one on one appointments with eligible clients. Her days of shuffling paperwork and another day another dollar attitude were gone.

The P.S.

Maria has recently developed what is now considered the recognized guide for transition by Hispanic clients (with help from an editor) and is asked to speak on the subject to other departments engaged in similar activities. There are plans to even make it a web-based tool! As a result of her initiative, she received a raise and promotion and even has her own assistant to help her stay organized. With her raise, Maria rented an apartment in a more desirable part of town and her children adore their new school system. Maria employed the 5P's: Passion-Purpose-Power-Profit-Peace of Mind to transition into her calling!

"I Don't Know What I Want to Do" ...
3 Questions to Help Narrow Your Focus

"Everyone has a genius inside them waiting to find their niche."

—Chris Kuselias

I N MY *THE CAREER GUARANTEE* seminars or personal counseling sessions, people often ask me, "Chris, what is the ideal formula for finding career happiness?" My answer is always the same: "Forget what industries are growing or even what jobs are available out there. The simple secret is to obtain a clear understanding of who you are, what unique skills you possess, link these to an occupation where you can contribute, and the money and happiness will surely follow."

The challenge is that in today's fast paced, competitive world, most do not spend 5 minutes to contemplate personal aspirations or consider what would truly make us feel happy and fulfilled. "Keep quiet and do your job" seems to be a common mantra, but will not move us closer to our inner desire for greater passion and purpose.

To help you begin to understand this new way of thinking, I want you to carefully consider these 3 questions:

1. When you daydream about your ideal job, what do you see yourself doing?
2. What career path and daily activities will feed your inner passion?
3. Whose career do you want or admire most? In other words, if you could change places with somebody you know personally or have met, ask yourself who would that person be and why would you want their occupation? Why their occupation?

If you cannot answer these questions, don't panic! The following will help you build a solid foundation as to who you truly are and what you value; in other words, what will make you happy. And happiness is a rarity in today's often superficial, win at all costs world. Despite having more "stuff," Americans are more disillusioned and disenchanted than ever before. A bigger house (bigger mortgage, larger SUV, 100″ TV screen, etc.) is not the answer. Don't believe me? Look around. Today there are millions of people who are unemployed and the majority of those who are employed are disenchanted with their careers. Most workers today can be classified as underemployed. That is, they are not fulfilling their true career potential or earning the compensation they deserve. Don't be spend your life making excuses and blaming the system. Strive to achieve and don't fear success.

It's not lonely at the top; it's crowded at the bottom.

I believe that an individual, business, educational institution and even a complex government system *must determine their unique and compelling qualities* if they are to thrive and sustain.

As you can imagine, I spend a great deal of my time speaking to groups and associations on the topic of career and organizational success. Whenever I am asked to speak to a group of entrepreneurs, individuals looking to start their own business or purchase an existing venture, I am inevitably asked to share my opinion regarding the secret to creating and maintaining a new business in the modern global economy. I typically begin by sharing with the audience that over 75% of all new ventures fail within the first 3 years, which immediately silences the room.

I then provide my recommendation, which is, that for any new concept to initially succeed and maintain market share, it must absolutely be able to *identify its most unique and compelling features, benefits and competitive advantages.* In sales, we call it the unique selling proposition (USP). If you cannot provide a quick, succinct description on how your service benefits other consumers, how it can be cost justified, who it will benefit or why it is needed, you will not be successful, period. The same formula applies to interviewing. In our work lives, it has become absolutely essential to be able to identify our unique interests and contributions, if we have any hope of obtaining our career calling. Keep in mind that these interests can change over time. The 1st step begins with the identification of your passions and focusing on finding what work activities don't feel like *work.* When you cannot differentiate between work and fun and are lost in the joy of creating, problem solving, contributing, you are on your way. You are careering.

The transition from your current situation to the attainment of your career calling often starts with the process of *reinventing yourself.*

In my personal experience, Nordstrom's department store has to be considered one of the premier customer service organizations. I always have a pleasant experience there and am impressed with their knowledge of my buying habits and personal style. Their staff is 2nd to none. While shopping one day, I noticed a new slogan for their ad campaign: *REINVENT YOURSELF!* What a great way to look at your life. You remain the same person, but reinvent certain aspects of your character, outlook, and beliefs. Create your own career brand. *If Evian can brand water, you can brand anything!*

Think about it. We live in a time of information overload: 600 television stations, unlimited, high speed Internet access and multi-media advertisers bombarding us with slogans, jingles, threats and promises. *Today, more than ever in history, it is essential to get clear on what you want and filter out all the nonsense that threatens to poison your mind or confuse your goals.* When it comes to how you spend your time, learn to focus on knowledge that furthers your agenda (that is, your career calling) and steer clear of information that does not contribute to your desires.

Here are some exercises to help you narrow your focus, get in touch with your unique and compelling strengths, successes and accomplishments, and understand who you truly are and what you sincerely desire. These will effectively serve to get you in touch with your hidden motivations and begin to direct you towards your career calling.

5 Key Considerations When Defining Your Career Calling

You *must* understand your passions and interests, unique skills and talents all factor in your values to attain true career success. Consider:

1. Location of the position
2. Desired compensation
3. Any additional education or training required
4. The organizational culture
5. Authority and type of people you work with or for

Let's further define your unique requirements:

Exercise

What Motivates Your Achievements

What motivates you? Take this quick assessment to find out. Be sure to check all that apply.

20 Self-Awareness Questions

There is an ancient legend that speaks to the challenge of finding your inner wisdom. Back when people had access to the knowledge of the gods, many chose to ignore this incredible source of knowledge and wisdom. The gods apparently tired of the people's apathy so they decided they would hide this valuable information in a place where only the most dedicated seekers could find it. Their thought process was: If people have to work harder to obtain this knowledge, they will appreciate it more and cherish it more carefully. As a result, the gods convened a meeting to discuss the optimal place to hide this information. One god suggested that it be buried in the deepest ocean while another recommended it be hidden on the highest mountain top. After much debate, one of the wisest gods suggested that

The Success Tree

© tawng / stockxpert

Success is not achieved by accident or twists of fate. It sprouts from the seeds you have planted. Fill in your tree of success. On each root write one of your strengths, skills, aptitudes, or good qualities. On each fruit write one of your successes, accomplishments, or special achievements.

they hide this wisdom deep inside the people themselves. "They will never think to look in there." ... and so it came to pass and continues today.

Career seekers have been guided to focus on external factors and the mechanics of job search (resume, cover letter, interview, etc.) as opposed to looking inside for the answers. If you learn anything from this book, learn

Self-Test: What Motivates Your Achievements?

List your accomplishments here	Feeling of Accomplishment	Pleasure	Challenge	Recognition	Obligation	Pressure	Winning	Acceptance	Friendship	Helping Others	Security	Freedom	Money
	What Motivated You? (Check all that apply												
EXAMPLE: Organizing bake sale	✓	✓	✓	✓	✓	✓				✓			
1													
2													
3													
4													
5													
6													
7													
8													
9													
10													
11													
12													
13													
14													
15													
16													
17													
18													
19													
20													
Total the number of check marks in each column. Write the numbers here.													

that your destiny and greatness is found by conducting an internal evaluation of your wants, needs and desires. Most of the advice contained in this book is designed to get you thinking, dust off the cobwebs and force you to contemplate your authentic self.

There is no growth without examination …

Here are thought provoking questions to further clarify your objectives. Providing honest answers will narrow your focus, eliminate areas of non-interest and create momentum towards your ideal career calling. Please be sure you are uninterrupted and give EACH question serious thought.

1. What are your general interests? Are they related to people, information, other?
2. Do you express yourself well in oral and written form?
3. What daily activities provide the most satisfaction?
4. Do you like responsibility?
5. Do you have an aversion to following directions?
6. What kind of work environment is important to you?
7. Would you rather work indoors or outdoors?
8. Are you more comfortable with regular routines?
9. Do you enjoy new concepts and situations?
10. Would you prefer a regular salary, commission, or a combination of both?
11. Would you like to work a regular schedule (for example, 9 AM to 5 PM)?
12. Would you prefer flexible hours?
13. Are you willing to travel?
14. Do you see yourself as a leader?
15. Do you prefer to work on your own or with other people?
16. Do you work well under pressure?
17. Would you like to work in a big city or in a more rural environment?
18. Do you prefer to work for a large, medium or small employer?
19. Would you be willing to relocate?
20. Would you prefer to work days or evenings?

Once you review each question, see if you can identify any trend or theme as to what is the ideal career scenario for you. Most people have never been challenged with this level of career planning detail; and for many, this exercise creates an "Aha moment" as to how to best direct their career search energies. You are now "careering," as I like to say. How does it feel?

Time to Take Action

Walk the Walk, Talk the Talk

> *"The beginning is half of every action."*
>
> —Greek proverb

I AM OFTEN ASKED TO define what separates high achievers (those who find their calling and are living their dream) from those that do not attain their objectives. While there are many circumstances that dictate success and failure, one concept rises above the rest on the question of what makes up the difference between success and failure ... *the ability to take action!* Successful people, those who have found their calling are highly action oriented individuals who not only create a plan, but implement the plan in a swift and decisive manner.

Do not confuse activity with accomplishment.

It continually amazes me how many people confuse activity with accomplishment. People will research, plan, strategize, analyze and talk until they are blue in the face. All are important steps but without action, they are meaningless. I am not suggesting that these actions do not constitute momentum; they do. Just be sure you are not consumed with *process as opposed to progress.*

When I decided to write this book, the 1st thing I did was set up the files on my computer for the table of contents and outline. Up until that point, I had thought about the book, talked to others about it and even studied similar works to familiarize myself with the process. I researched publishers and marketing options and conferred with my staff as to how this book would benefit our organization and further our brand development. I even designed a writing schedule as to when I could create without interruption. All of these were quasi-actions; the real book did not take shape until I typed the very 1st word. That is when the real *action* began.

As another example, I have a contact in the television advertising business who indicated that, incredibly, 18% of American consumers who purchase a new product or service via an infomercial never actually use the product or even open the box! They have satisfied, at some baseline psychological level, their need to fulfill an internal void. Perhaps they feel they have taken action by simply ordering an exercise machine. But unless they actually assemble and then use the product, they have not truly taken action. What a waste of time and money! Are you simply satisfying yourself in some area of your life and not taking the appropriate *action*?

Often, making a decision to adopt a new plan serves as enough leverage to see it through. As Woody Allen said, "Success is simply a matter of showing up." If you show up, you are ahead of 85% of people. If you show up on time, you are ahead of 90%. If you show up on time and have a plan, you are ahead of 95%. And if you show up, on time, with a plan and you put that plan into action, you are ahead of 100%!" Make sure you fulfill all steps when it comes to targeting a new career calling.

When conducting a seminar for career seekers, I often hold up a copy of this book and inform my audience that I have a solution to the challenge of finding one's career calling. I then ask them, "Who would like this free copy?"

Inevitably hands will be raised and many will shout their name. After a while, one of the audience members will leap from their seat, come up on stage with me and grab the book. After the person goes back to their seat (with a free copy of the book for their effort), I ask the audience to describe what the individual did that made them unique?

The answer: THEY TOOK ACTION! They simply took action while everyone else pondered, considered, analyzed, and evaluated the situation. As a group, we then itemize the reasons why everyone else in the room did not take action. Typically, the answers look something like this ...

1. I wasn't exactly sure what to do
2. I was afraid I would look foolish or stupid in front of others
3. I did not want to appear greedy or desperate for a free book
4. I thought you were kidding or setting us up
5. I was seated too far back

What would you do in this scenario? Maybe you could guess that your reactions in this instance are a microcosm for how you react to other opportunities in life. Many of these excuses permeate your life and are preventing you from becoming all you could and should be. Stop waiting for permission, further instruction, the right job to fall in your lap, your boss to recognize your unique talents, the economy to improve, enough money, your past to disappear, etc. Action makes the difference! There is always a voice that tells us what could go wrong; ignore it! Focus on the reasons why you will be successful and suppress those conditioned fears that someone else may make a judgment or laugh at you. P.S.: The next time you are in one of my seminars and I offer a free book … grab it!

5 Questions to Stimulate Action

Success Tip

When you begin to develop greater clarity about your future, you will immediately become more efficient in your present!

A word of caution: Many people start self-help projects or play "the New Year's game," where their plans are vague, too general and don't possess the intense commitment to follow through. Without enough leverage and a commitment to adopt a new belief system, changes are intellectualized, but never emotionalized and thus, are rarely effective.

Here is a list of questions to help consolidate your thinking and promote you to take action:

1. What are your highest value activities?
2. What are your personal results areas?
3. Do you like where you are?
4. How can you make a difference?
5. At this exact moment, what is the most valuable use of your time?

4 Steps to Success

> "If you were to ask me to explain the secret to my success, I would tell you it is because I understand that there is a power greater than myself that rules my life and in life if you can be still long enough in all of your endeavors, the good times, the hard times, to connect yourself to the source I call God—call it whatever you want to—the force, nature, Allah, the power. If you can connect yourself to the source and allow the energy that is your personality, your life force, to be connected to the greater force, anything is possible for you. I am proof of that. I think that my life, the fact that I was born where I was born, and the time that I was and have been able to do what I have done, speaks to the possibility. Not that I am special, but that it could be done. Hold the highest, grandest vision for yourself."

—Oprah Winfrey

Oprah gets it! She clearly understands that getting in touch with your authentic self and nurturing your highest and best vision yields incredible results! Here is a 4-step strategy for converting your career dreams to reality.

1. *Idea:* Every great career story begins with a thought. Ignite that spark!
2. *Envision:* Create a mental picture of yourself already engaged in your career calling
3. *Plan:* Create a series of carefully planned steps to make your vision a reality
4. *Do:* Take action and monitor your progress

I remember hearing how J.K. Rowling envisioned and created the Harry Potter character while riding on a train from Manchester to London to look at a new apartment. She did not even have a pen when the vision hit her. She created a plan and then authored the 1st book. Take initiative, go above and beyond the call, take risks, *stretch.* The choices and outcomes you experienced in your past do not dictate your future growth or potential. You are constantly moving forward, progressing. You are evolving! We have all made bad, often painful decisions. That person was simply an early version of the person you are now. You are new and improved!

Taking Control: *If it's to be, it's up to me!* You are accountable for your success or failure in any given situation. There is no substitute for hard work and dedication. Many people are lazy and seek the path of least resistance. According to Robert Half International, the typical employee actually works less than 50% of the time they are paid! Your objective should be simple: Be in the top 10% of performers in your chosen field. Use your time wisely; the quality of your life will be determined by how you spend each precious day, hour and minute. Equally important is to recognize that how you spend your time will indicate your true values. You cannot save time; you can only spend time. High achievers spend a greater percentage of their time in activities of higher value. Discipline yourself to focus on tasks in order of priority.

Develop a long-term view, which will improve your short-term decision-making. Less than 3% of people have a long-term perspective. Most live day to day. Short-term sacrifice for long term gain and security is paramount to success and happiness. Every action you take should ultimately lead to this mission: to provide the practical strategies and techniques needed to achieve life balance and, in turn, leave this world a better place!

Identifying Your Most Marketable Skills

> *"Those who love their work would continue to do it even if they didn't get paid (if they could afford to), who become absorbed in their work, who integrate their work with their values, their lives, their very being-these people have a calling. In addition, those with a calling see their work as meaningful, with a wider purpose, and ideally even contribute to the greater good of society or the world."*
>
> —His Holiness the Dalai Lama
> and Howard C. Cutler, M.D.,
> *The Art of Happiness at Work*

You may be wondering how and why I chose *careering*. A number of years ago, I was a college graduate, out of a job and totally frustrated. I had little

© 2009 Learned

"Does being a toll collector in an exact change lane qualify as a skill?"

self-esteem, and I needed guidance and support. I looked around and I didn't find any, and I soon learned I was not alone. I did not have a plan of action. I was an enthusiastic incompetent! I was stagnant because I was unaware of what I had to offer and had not developed the proper vocabulary or mindset to inform potential hiring authorities what I could do to help their company. (Some people never move off this square in the chessboard of life and remain stagnant and frustrated.) Lucky for me, my frustration resulted in action!

Regardless of your age, education level or job status, you absolutely need to identify *your most marketable traits*. Ideally, your interests and hobbies should correspond with your aptitude, meaning we usually pursue endeavors we receive praise for and are good at. This is a secret to career happiness. Ask yourself what's unique or compelling about me? What is my professional contribution based upon my education, work history and personal experiences? To help you determine your worth, please complete the following.

If I asked you to identify your 3 most marketable or problem-solving capabilities, what would they be and how would they differentiate you from your competition? Is it your organizational skills, your ability to inspire others, technical knowledge, customer service, physical strength or something else?

In order, what do you consider your 3 most marketable or problem solving capabilities (for example, leadership skills, creativity)? Once you decide, please provide specific examples (word stories) of each choice.

This is an excellent strategy for identifying your competitive edge. If you cannot identify your 3 most marketable or problem-solving capabilities, spend the time reflecting on your life and what makes you unique, because employers and lending sources today are looking for problem solvers who know their own unique value.

Thought-Provoking Questions

Passion

What Do I Love to Do?

What activities give me happiness?
What excites me about life?
What is my secret ambition?
What are my hobbies?

Talent

What Am I Good At?

> What do I get complimented on?
> Where have I excelled in the past?
> Where have I been successful?
> What are some of my strengths?

Values

What Is Most Important To Me?

> What would I do if I were wealthy?
> What do I stand for?
> What won't I stand for?
> What would I risk my life for?

Destiny

What Was I Born To Do?

> What is my unique mission in life?
> What does my maker want me to do?
> What are my unique opportunities?
> Where can I make a difference?

If you are a student, focus on schooling or training programs you recently completed. You don't want to be one of those people who is out of work for 6 months after graduation and then settles for a job that doesn't provide you with your personal or monetary objectives. More experienced career seekers should put more attention into accomplishments and recognition by previous employers. Identify something unique regarding your education, work history or personal achievements and you will immediately begin to separate yourself from your competition.

The Business Card Exercise

Here's a great exercise for those of you who don't know exactly what you want to do with your career. Turn over any business card and on the blank side write your full name, the professional title of the position you passionately seek, and the specific company or organization that you would ideally like to make this contribution for. I suggest you also research and author your IDEAL JOB DESCRIPTION. These 2 simple tasks will force you to narrow your interests and be SPECIFIC about your future. Once completed, review the card every day, visualize yourself in this role and take action until it becomes your daily reality!

Focusing on a specific career involves targeting 2 critical factors:

1. Your ability to identify a specific organization or company that will be your ultimate work location. Hint: Target companies, not job titles.
    Design your ideal business card!
2. Your ability to identify the specific title you desire. Also, you should be able to write a paragraph of your ideal job description.
    Author your ideal job description!

Once you have an ultimate objective, the other elements to the careering process will fall in place. If you don't have a specific focus, the view will remain cloudy. You can't hit a target that you can't see.

The Swap Technique

If you could exchange careers with any individual (whom you know personally) for the next 3 years, who would that person be, and briefly explain 3 reasons you chose this person (for example, earnings, title, salary, challenge, attitude, etc.).

Think about why it was that you chose that individual. Is it the nature of their work? Is it the money they're earning? Is it the travel they're involved with? Is it the creativity? Is it their independence? When you consider the reasons for your selection, it should immediately provide insight into what career values are important to you.

Many people follow in their parents', uncles' or relatives' footsteps because of the fact that they've been exposed to that occupation. It makes sense that the more familiar you are with an occupation, the more apt you are to pursue it. If you narrow down your opportunities or your familiarity count to one or 2 people or occupations, there is a good chance you may wind up in that occupation and regret it later. Stretch your list of professional contacts or you will limit your outcome!

... my great grandfather was in waste disposal, my grandfather was in waste disposal, my father was in waste disposal, I am in waste disposal and, doggone it, my baby girl will be in waste disposal!

Required Career Benefits

My strong suggestion is to get involved in as many diverse fields as possible before narrowing it down to a few that peak your interest. I can't tell you how many unhappy career seekers I have counseled who had selected their occupation because their father's father made a decision to work in a particular field many years ago and the job was handed down to them. *Choose your career ... don't let it choose you.* Otherwise, you may find yourself unhappy and unfulfilled.

Let's turn our attention to developing your niche. Why work? What is paramount to you in a career ? Is it a sense of belonging? Is it the money? Is it the recognition? Is it obligation, the need to feed your family, send a child to school or pay the mortgage? Is it the status? Does your ego need to be fulfilled? Is it important to you to feel that you have to make a contribution to society? What exactly is important to you as an individual? Carefully consider these questions and see how your answers fit into your quest to obtain your career calling.

5-Step Strategy for Finding Your Calling

Step 1   Determine your (unique) most marketable skills and find people currently in positions you seek.

Step 2   Narrow your focus to a specific field or industry.

Identify a strategy to market your capabilities to potential employers in your field of choice. Do not limit your strategy to a mass-mailed resume or posting a resume on the Internet and waiting for the phone a reply email Be more proactive and take control of the process.

Step 3   Become a master in the art of researching specific employers where you have interest.

To illustrate the process, consider the following scenario where a career in sales is the objective. For the purposes of this example, the product or service is irrelevant. If I were interested in marketing or sales, I would create my ideal business card and target a specific job title and employer who offered both a position and the product or service (a.k.a. my contribution). I would conduct research on the targeted employer or industry. For starters, target company website, Annual Report, trade journals, articles, etc. You can research scope of services, mission statement, board of directors, locations, etc. To be successful, you need to master the art of employer research.

I would write to the employer and request an information package . Many Public Relations Departments of large companies have information packages, which can familiarize you with their mission, both today and in the future. Even small companies today have informative websites or on line brochures.

For this sales and marketing exercise, you do not have to know the assets, the return on debt and detailed financial data. You should be familiar with their product line, their performance and distribution sources. Are there any new developments in the industry? Who are their major competitors? By doing this, you will differentiate yourself from most people who, amazingly, conduct little or no research. Through a little data gathering, you can obtain the key information you need to know to nail the interview!

Step 4   Narrow your focus to a particular state, city and employer.

After I decided where I wanted to work, and what city and state, I would find out if they had any offices in my desired location. Researching the Internet, telephone directory or company publications, you would find out where the main office in your ideal state or city was.

Step 5   Make contact with your targeted employer.

You would then call the main number of the employer and ask to speak to the Marketing assistant or secretary, who is an *influencer* but not usually a *decision maker.* Remember, in this example, we desire a marketing or sales position. You would ask the assistant, "Who is the number one marketing manager or salesperson with your employer?" They will probably ask who is calling and you would respond with confidence. "I'm going to be an outstanding marketing manager or salesperson some day and I have an interest in your organization. I would like to contact this person and learn more about it." Do not under any circumstances let them pass you off to human resources or the website! You are only calling to gather information.

When you engage the *influencer,* find out, "Who is the best person you have there? Who is number one?" And they might tell you, "Well, it's Joe Smith" or "Jane Smith" or whoever it might be. And then ask her what they thought of the company. Establish a rapport. How do they like the employer? How are the people there? Are they nice? Establish that connection that's so important for serious candidates.

Then ask, "What is the best time to reach Joe or Jane Smith? Is it in the morning before work? Do they like to stay late? I certainly don't want to bother them when they're busy." She may say, "Well, they come in early. They leave late." Be sure to get a specific time to call that individual and acquire the specific number then and there.

Note: I wouldn't send an email, write them a letter or send them my resume. I would get on the telephone the very next day with all the information laid out before me and I'd introduce myself as an individual who is really interested in getting involved in marketing or sales who has really done his homework on that employer. State that you understand that they are the hardest worker or best that their company has. "That's what the people that I've asked tell me about you." Appeal to their ego. And the person might say, "Well, you know, fine. Maybe I am the best. Some people think I'm OK. I do my job and I work hard."

Follow by stating, "I'm interested in getting involved in marketing or sales. And, of course, I'm not asking you for a job. But would you mind if I took a half-hour of your time? I'll take you out to breakfast or lunch, at your convenience, of course. I'd just like to get your opinions on your organization and the industry as a whole. Also, I'd like to know what differentiates your company from your competitors. Why did you choose your current employer? Why are you the best here?" And they may say, "Well, I don't make the hiring decisions, but if you put it that way, maybe I can find some time next week. How about next Tuesday? Come in at 8:00 before I start working or come in at lunchtime or meet me at a certain restaurant." Nobody's going to turn you away if you tactfully feed their ego and applaud their efforts. *Keep in mind that most people enjoy the process of mentoring others and sharing their hard earned knowledge.* Top performers take pride in their work and like to talk about what they do. Take my word for it.

Now, if you have the chance to sit down with a contact and talk about specific information towards the hiring process, it's important that you don't lead with your resume. You don't just say, "Well, here's my resume. Can you get me in the door?" Your next goal is to impress that individual, by talking about what you've done. Ease into the conversation. Find out their background. Try to establish a common bond. You might reinforce how eager they were when they first started looking for a job or lost a job and needed to change careers. They'll appreciate the fact that you took the risk that you did to get their attention.

And once you have their attention, then you can tactfully find out, "Well, when you came to this employer, what was the interview process like? Why did you select the employer? Was there a referral involved or did you just walk in off the street? Did you answer an ad? Did you use the Internet, attend a job fair, learn about the position through the alumni network or through a friend of a friend? How did you get in the door?"

There is nothing more impressive when seeking employment than to have somebody, especially the number one marketing or salesperson in the organization, provide a referral. Wouldn't you like to have a letter to the Sales Manager or the person who can hire you from Joe or Jane Smith stipulating, "Hey, I came across a candidate, (insert your name), who is very sharp. He got my attention. He took me out to lunch. And I've got to tell you something; we could use more people like him." Clearly, if they take the time to sit with you, they'll take the time to advocate for you. And people take pride in their organization. Believe it or not, they want talented people in the organization.

That is how I would go about pursuing my career calling. I wouldn't wait for it to find me. I'd be proactive and not reactive. Once I contacted 2 or 3 employers and did some informational interviewing or informal data gathering, I'd be on my way. And I'd start doing that ASAP. For now, recognize that there is a very specialized job market out there. And you need to become proactive and unique; go beyond the methods that everybody else is using.

Narrowing Your Focus

THE PURPOSE OF THESE exercises is to guide you towards a general career direction or field from which to explore specific occupations. My objective is get you to narrow your options, inspire you to explore your interests and share specific exercises, which will gradually enlighten you and ignite the spark to help you achieve your career goals.

After completion, you will realize, "Now I have a better understanding. I don't know when it happened. But after completing the exercises, at some point I suddenly had a better feel for what I wanted to do with my career."

I would like to change our focus and begin by listing for you a number of career values that I have found most people consider when analyzing their employment options. For many people, advancement, benefits and creativity are important. For others, spare time is desired. Assisting or helping people may be another's most important value. How about independence, work location, money or problem-solving? Stability is important to some people as is status associated with a career or position. Does your ideal occupation involve travel? Do you want variety? Do you need change?

Or do you like consistency and order? Is there another area that I didn't mention?

Once you have rated your values, identify how each value will be of importance to you in your next job.

Those are just a few examples of job values that you need to begin thinking about when assessing a new career or deciding if you should remain in your current occupation. Some people don't want to change their career; they just aspire to do it better!

Next, sit down and list your strengths. Here are some examples …

25 Examples of Personal Strengths

Check which strengths you have or which traits describe you. Check as many as apply, or add your own.

□ Artistic	□ Perfectionism
□ Communicative	□ Personable
□ Compassionate	□ Physical Fitness
□ Confident	□ Responsibility
□ Creative	□ Self-Assurance
□ Dependable	□ Self-Control
□ Energetic	□ Sensitivity
□ Enthusiastic	□ Stability
□ Expressive	□ Time Management Skills
□ Hard Working	□ Trustworthiness
□ Imaginative	□ Versatility
□ Independent	□ _____
□ Leadership Ability	□ _____
□ Motivation	□ _____

1. Identify what types of careers require these strengths.
2. Give examples of how you have demonstrated these strengths.
3. Pick your top 5 strengths. Tell exactly when you displayed these strengths. Be specific!

Top 5 Strengths Others See in You

List the 5 strengths that your parents/family/significant other/friends see in you:

Hint: Now is not the time to be modest. Brag away! (The next exercise will bring you back down to earth).

Now list the 5 strengths that your employer (or former employer) sees in you, or, if you have never been employed, list the 5 strengths you have, which you believe make you attractive to an employer.

My Weaknesses

Did you hear about the elevator operator who lost his job because he couldn't learn the route?

Everyone has weaknesses; sometimes, unfortunately, they are even easier for us to list than our own strengths. In this exercise, we will zero in on how we are going to improve. So, go ahead and list those weaknesses, but don't dwell on them. Put all your energy instead into finding solutions, improving what needs improving, and turning those weaknesses into strengths. (In fact, the act of working to overcome a weakness is a strength!)

List 3 weaknesses that your parents/family/friends see in you.

List 1 thing you can do right away to improve each of the weaknesses:

Now, list 3 weaknesses an employer might see in you:

List 1 thing you can do right away to improve each of the weaknesses:

3 Reasons to Celebrate Your Mistakes

Rather than denying your mistakes or blaming others for your errors, look at them as the opportunities they are—real life chances to learn, grow, and get smarter at whatever you are doing. Why celebrate your mistakes?

Reason #1 Mistakes create valuable feedback that moves you closer to your goals.

Reason #2 Mistakes are made by the world's smartest and most successful people (you are in excellent company).

Reason #3 Making a mistake means that you are taking risks (playing it safe limits your ability to learn and grow).

Rate Your Character Traits

How well do your know yourself? Read the following list of character traits commonly found in successful people. Rate how strong you believe you are in each category. Make sure you mention these traits when you are in your self- promotion mode.

Successful People Have	Your Own Rating (1 = Weakest / 5 = Strongest)
1. The ability to communicate	1 2 3 4 5
2. Intelligence	1 2 3 4 5
3. Self-confidence	1 2 3 4 5
4. Accepted responsibility	1 2 3 4 5
5. Motivation	1 2 3 4 5
6. Leadership	1 2 3 4 5
7. High energy	1 2 3 4 5
8. Imagination	1 2 3 4 5
9. Flexibility	1 2 3 4 5
10. Interpersonal skills	1 2 3 4 5
11. Self-knowledge	1 2 3 4 5
12. The ability to handle conflict	1 2 3 4 5
13. Useful job skills	1 2 3 4 5
14. Specific goals	1 2 3 4 5
15. Reliability	1 2 3 4 5

Rating Behaviors and Attitudes

Use the following table to rate your own characteristics on a scale of 1–5. Then use the "Friends Rating" column to indicate how you think one of your friends would rate you in that same category.

Behavior or attitude	Self-rating	Friend's rating
Ambitious	1 2 3 4 5	1 2 3 4 5
Cheerful	1 2 3 4 5	1 2 3 4 5
Confident	1 2 3 4 5	1 2 3 4 5
Cooperative	1 2 3 4 5	1 2 3 4 5
Dependable	1 2 3 4 5	1 2 3 4 5
Enthusiastic	1 2 3 4 5	1 2 3 4 5
Hard Working	1 2 3 4 5	1 2 3 4 5
Helpful	1 2 3 4 5	1 2 3 4 5
Neat	1 2 3 4 5	1 2 3 4 5
Outgoing	1 2 3 4 5	1 2 3 4 5
Patient	1 2 3 4 5	1 2 3 4 5
Respectful	1 2 3 4 5	1 2 3 4 5
Persistent	1 2 3 4 5	1 2 3 4 5
Self-Centered	1 2 3 4 5	1 2 3 4 5

Behavior or attitude	Self-rating	Friend's rating
Serious	1 2 3 4 5	1 2 3 4 5
Shy	1 2 3 4 5	1 2 3 4 5
Tactful	1 2 3 4 5	1 2 3 4 5

1. What can you learn about yourself by thinking about how others see you?
2. Why are some of the ratings different?
3. Do you wish some of the ratings were different? How can you change the way others see you?

Note: Please pay close attention to any behavior or attitude that is 2 or more points different between your own self-rating and your friends. Analyze why you feel differently, are you giving off the wrong vibe?

Skill Building

There is the story of a man and woman who one day noticed the great artist Picasso sitting nearby. Hesitantly, they approached the incredible legend and asked him if he was in fact, Picasso. Picasso acknowledged his identity and went back to what he was doing. The couple then took out an old piece of scrap paper and asked Picasso if he would be gracious enough to draw a quick sketch for them. Picasso obliged with a quick drawing and handed back the scrap paper. The couple, delirious with excitement, asked if they could offer Picasso something for the privilege of his drawing. Picasso replied that it would cost $100,000.00. The couple, taken aback, asked him how the drawing could be so costly when it seemingly took such little effort and only a few seconds for him to complete the drawing on the scrap paper. Picasso smiled and said, "You are mistaken, it took me a lifetime to develop my skills." The message: Never underestimate your skills and what it took for you to acquire your unique and compelling talents.

Solutions are created by skills. Your skills comprise the essence of your personal *brand*. I would like to help you further narrow your focus with respect to the identification of your unique and compelling skills.

What Is a Skill?

A skill is something that you can DO. Most people have literally hundreds of skills, but can't identify what they are. Some activities or tasks involve mastering a group of smaller skills. Think about driving a car. Driving a car is just one example of using many skills together in order to perform an activity.

Here is a partial list of the skills involved in driving:

- Reading road signs
- Judging distances and speed
- Interpreting speedometer reading
- Pumping gas
- Planning and charting maintenance schedules
- Calculating mileage per gallon
- Anticipating other's actions based on their various signals
- Hand-eye coordination to steer the wheel
- Hand-foot coordination to hit the gas and apply the breaks
- Memorizing routines: get in, close the door, fasten seatbelt, turn the ignition key
- Ability to interpret and convert information in a rearview or convex mirror
- Maintaining concentration and avoiding unnecessary distractions (*to drive long distances with kids in the back seat*).

Could you have come up with a list like that on your own? If not, you can probably add to it now. Now that you understand, identify your own skills as you might present them to an employer. You have a much better chance of getting hired if you can effectively demonstrate your skills to an employer by having concrete examples.

My top skills are:

	Personal Skills	Educational Skills	Employment Skills
1			
2			
3			

The Skills Triangle

1..Self-management skills  2..Transferable skills

3..Job content skills

Self-Management Skills	
Skills that you use in everyday life. These skills describe a person and give the employer an idea of how you might fit into their work environment. These are part of your personality. (Examples: well-organized, enthusiastic, good leader)	1. 2. 3.
Transferable Skills	
Skills that you use in many life situations. These skills include those which you can transfer from job to job. They are not unique to any one position but instead can be used in many job functions. (Examples: good math skills, pleasant telephone manner, speak Spanish)	1. 2. 3.
Job Content Skills	
Skills that are required to do a specific job. These are specific skills, which would be listed in job descriptions. (Example: operate a cash register; know how to change oil in domestic and foreign cars, any kind of certification—teaching, nurse's aide, CPA, CPR	1. 2. 3.

The *Prove It* Model: How to effectively present your skills

To an employer, it's not a skill until you *prove* it's a skill. So prove it!

Name one of your skills (for example, leadership and problem-solving).

Use it in a real story ("Last year, I was elected to serve on my apartment association because of my reputation as a leader and problem-solver"):

Give numbers (To prove the skill—"I can type,"—give numbers:"40 words per minute with only 1 error in a 5-minute test").

State positive results   ("My safe driving earned me a $200 discount on my annual insurance promotion):

Relate the skill to the job   ("I built up my upper-body strength after 6 months in a wheel-chair from a car accident. Now I can lift any box in your warehouse!").

How You Will Be Evaluated During the Interview

Every interviewer has their own style and asks different questions depending on the position. Each hiring authority also formulates an impression of you as a candidate. That over-all impression is based on how you present yourself in these 5 key areas.

Have pointed statements prepared for each of these areas. Be able to present them with conviction. You are well on your way to getting a yes!

5 Areas Employers Will Evaluate You

Personnel departments and their respective decision-makers hire on the basis of *potential*. Potential heads up the list of what I term the 5 specific areas that you will be evaluated on when you're seeking employment.

Those 5 specific areas include, and not necessarily are in this order:

1. Your past performance or your track record
2. Your willingness to compete and take risks in previous circumstances
3. Your skill development
4. Your understanding of self, which makes the process of self-awareness that much more important
5. What benefits do you provide to the company or, in essence, what is your current/future value?

With these 5 areas in mind, it is important to gain a clear understanding of your most marketable skills and strengths. It is important to understand your true value and what you bring to an organization.

5 Career Skills Sought by Employers

These 5 career skills involve areas of strength or ability and thus define your potential worth as a candidate.

These 5 areas are:

1. Analytical or problem-solving; for example, finding solutions
2. Management or leadership activities

3. Research or the ability to assemble information
4. Writing or speaking in terms of your presentation skills, promoting a product, communicating abilities
5. Your technical skills, such as computer knowledge or servicing customers via product knowledge

Consider your strongest areas. These 5 career skills provide the foundation for what a sampling of employers have targeted as the 15 most marketable employment aptitudes that a candidate can possess. These aptitudes should be expressed to interviewers, people that you talk to in information interviews and in your daily networking conversations.

Identifying Your Most Marketable Employment Aptitudes

Aptitude	Example
Administrative	
Compiling Data	
Computer Skills	
Imagination/Creativity	
Managing	
Organization Skills	
Persuasive Skills	
Presentation Skills	
Public Relations	
Public Speaking	
Quantitative Skills	
Research and Analysis	
Supervisory Skills	
Teaching/Training Skills	
Writing Skills	

Identify the marketable employment aptitudes you possess. Give examples!

You have just concluded an amazing process—identifying 5 areas that you will be evaluated on, your 5 basic career skills as your primary categories and the 15 most marketable employment aptitudes employers seek.

I believe your answers provide incredible insight into your authentic self.

What were the strongest *shoulds* proposed on you? In other words, when you were growing up, "You should go to college. You should be a doctor. You should make a lot of money." What you need to do is break those strings because you are an adult now and can determine your own *should*.

10 Clarifying Questions

1. My childhood fantasy job was to be ... (professional athlete, princess, fireman)
2. This was my dream job because ... (cite emotional, spiritual, social, financial reasons)
3. What one person has been most influential in your life? Why?
4. What were the strongest *shoulds* when you were growing up? (that is, "you should")
5. Before I retire, I want to ...
6. I like and admire people who ...
7. Describe the type of people you would like to work with.
8. Describe the type of people you feel uncomfortable with.
9. What career would you choose if you won a lottery worth 10 million dollars?
10. What individuals have been most influential in your life?

Another question: "Before I retire (I recognize that some of you may not have even started a career yet), I want to what?" What do you want to do? Do you want to leave a positive contribution to your society? Do you want to earn a lot of money? Do you want to achieve all your goals? What do you want to do? Only you can decide. The next question: "I like and admire people who"—who what? Then describe the type of people you'd like to work with. And, lastly, describe the type of employer you feel uncomfortable working with.

Finally, what career would you choose to do if you won the lottery and could work because you like to and not because you have to? If tomorrow you bought a lottery ticket and you won several million dollars, what would you do? What would you do with your time each day? Is there a job or contribution you want to make because you enjoy the work and not because you did it for the money?

The Self-Introduction Exercise

Imagine that you have been scheduled to appear live on the most popular talk show in the country. In a couple of paragraphs, please provide an introduction of yourself to an audience who knows nothing about your personal background, education and professional accomplishments. Hint: Why would anyone want to listen to you and not change the channel? Are you interesting? Are you a person of significance?

This process will prepare you to answer the 1st interview question, which more often than not is "Tell me about yourself."

This exercise should provide you with the impetus to start thinking about what you've done with your life and what's unique and compelling about you as a candidate. Ask yourself again: What is your unique contribution? Have you figured it out yet?

The Narrow Down Technique

The strategy for obtaining your calling is to begin by the process of elimination. This means that we want to exclude certain fields, which hold absolutely no appeal to you and have no redeeming qualities. Below is a comprehensive list of various industries (clearly there are new ones being created daily) from which I would like you to select a workable number.

For example, if you've chosen the field of marketing, you may list a sales representative or a field representative, an account executive, a sales consultant or a marketing sales assistant or a sales assistant or a product manager, a real estate sales person or a person who does market research or people who develop market programs or a market specialist.

You could specialize that even more to say retail marketing where, for example, you may want to be a management training person. That may be your goal. Or to be a buyer of merchandise, an individual who purchases the merchandise displayed on the floor of the retail store. Or there's a buying training program for that. And you may want to have your goal to get into that buying training program. Or you may want to be a person who puts up and sets up the displays or decorates the retail office or is responsible for the advertising and layout or doing some of the promotions. Or you may want to become an assistant store manager or be a sales manager of the store. The possibilities are endless!

Brainstorm on the specific industries that you have chosen and it will get you thinking about what it is that you really want to do. And having done this, your next step will be to target specific companies or employers for whom you can work. Visit www.thecareerguarantee.com for more information on career selection.

Accounting	Gardening	Physical fitness
Advertising	Government services	Physics
Aeronautics	Health care	Police work
Agriculture	History	Politics
Animals	Hotel and motel	Public speaking
Architecture	Industrial design	Publishing
Automotive	Insurance	Real estate
Banking	Interior design	Recording
Biology	Investments	Recreation
Bookkeeping	Journalism	Recreation
Botany	Law	Repair services
Broadcasting	Machine work	Retailing
Children's services	Management services/staffing	Sales
Commercial art	Manual labor	Secretarial
Communications	Marketing/public relations	Service
Computer/MIS	Mathematics	Social work
Construction	Medicine	Sports
Cosmetology	Mental health	Synthetics
Counseling	Metal work	Telecommunications
Ecology	Nutrition	Television
Economics	Oceanography	Textiles
Education	Office services	Transportation
Electronics	Performing arts	Travel
Entertainment	Personal services	Weather
Fashion	Personnel	Woodworking
Finance	Pharmacology	Zoology
Fine arts	Photography	Other

Exercise

1. Circle your top 10 choices.
2. List your top 3 choices out of the top 10.
3. Choose 1 of the top 3 choices.
4. List specific job titles within that field.

Note: Although you may have chosen to study a specific skill or trade, you should be able to write down specific occupations (job titles) within this chosen career field. Then start researching and conduct at least one information interview for each specific position in which you have interest.

Next up, building a world class network of mentors!

CHAPTER 8

It Is Who You Know ...
Building a World Class Network
of Career Mentors

KEY QUESTION:
WHO CAN HELP ME OBTAIN MY DREAM?

In this chapter, you will learn:

KEY TOPICS
- Why Mentors Are Essential to Achieving Your Calling
- A Guide to Meeting Mentors
- Best Strategies for Making Connections

KEY MESSAGES
- Building a career contact network will ensure the attainment of your desired career calling.
- The secret to networking is to give 1st to get back 2nd!
- You can get whatever *you* want by helping others attain what *they* want.
- It's not what you know; it is who you know and how you can help *each other.*
- The people who find their career calling know how to cultivate helpful contacts who can educate, inspire and inform.
- You know approximately 500 people; learn to benefit from all your contacts.
- Set a goal to increase your contacts by one per month, which translates into 12 valuable new contacts per year!
- Keep an active, organized file of your contacts.
- Where do the best opportunities exist? 75–80% are hidden jobs (not advertised), only 20% are found in published ads for jobs (advertised), 5% of people are self-employed.
- Challenge: 90% of all job seekers target the 20% published job market, while only 10% of all job seekers target the 80% hidden job market where the best careers are found!
- Preparation determines performance; overcome your anxiety of contacting a new mentor or employer by creating a script and by being prepared to effectively respond to objections.
- Information interviewing is an important and necessary strategy to meet new contacts and learn about valuable career opportunities in your chosen field.

Connecting to mentors and building your network is like a muscle; the more you work it, the larger it gets.

Why Mentors Are Essential to Achieving Your Calling

ONE OF THE KEYS to my success is that I have had many quality mentors, some of whom have influenced my life with a single look, gesture, word, phrase or sentence. Every high achiever regularly employs the practice of finding and interacting with people of influence. Now it is your turn to build your all-star team!

One of the most important aspects of career happiness is establishing your contacts, people who can help you transition from where you are today to where you want to be. The old axiom applies: *It's not what you know but who you know.* People who attain their career calling are not necessarily those who are the best qualified candidates, but are those who are the best qualified as to *how* to obtain it. Building a career contact network will ensure the attainment of your desired career calling.

Thus far, you have learned to identify your unique contributions and had an opportunity to define success on your own terms. You have learned new strategies for confronting your fears and been educated to avoid the silent killer, which stifles all action, procrastination. You know the importance of critical reflection (self-analysis) and have identified your professional strengths, wants, weaknesses and desires. You learned that the "why" is more important than the "what" and that success comes from identifying your passion and pursuing a vocation that satisfies those desires. You addressed the importance of formulating short and long-term goals and narrowed your focus to career paths and titles in specific industries in which you will demonstrate passion and purpose.

> *"A single conversation across the table with a wise man is worth a month's study of books."*
>
> —Chinese proverb

We will now develop your own *personal advisory board* of influential contacts and penetrate the *hidden job market,* which accounts for 80% of all the opportunities. That's right! 80% of all the opportunities out there are never published. You never hear about them through Internet, want ads or other media sources; they are a secret.

While the hidden job market accounts for 4 out of 5 open positions, the published job market (want ads, internet boards, help wanted signs, etc.) accounts for only 20% of all vacancies. You will learn to master both sources using combined strategies ranging from the telephone, letter, Internet and via the most important technique in the whole program, *the information interview.*

This chapter will focus on building contacts that can empower you, educate you and provide you with insight into vacancies that may not yet be advertised.

The Secret to Networking: Give to Get!

> *"There are 2 types of people: anchors and motors. You want to lose the anchors and get with the motors because the motors are going somewhere and they are having more fun. The anchors will just drag you down."*
> —Wyland, world renowned marine artist

A fact of life is that no matter what your targeted calling, whether it be to start your own consulting firm, teach kindergarten, operate a non-profit to assist the homeless, design websites, discover a new cure for cancer or become a flight attendant, there are a great many people whose assistance and guidance you will need. The secret to productive networking is to understand that in order to receive, you must first give. Some equate networking with "connecting," that is, sharing *your* collective wisdom, ideas and contacts with others as a core philosophy before seeking out their assistance or centers of influence. If you will learn to apply this formula, you will amass an incredible collection of influential people while simultaneously providing benefit to others. Approach every networking opportunity as a chance to contribute your experience and knowledge. Begin with the belief that every person you meet is an opportunity to help and be helped.

In 1989, my energetic and active father, at age 54, was diagnosed with esophageal cancer and told he had only 3 months to live. Before I proceed, I am happy to report that as of this writing my father is alive and well, courtesy of a positive attitude, good nutrition and good doctors. At the time I was a young, up and coming corporate executive looking to become a *master of the universe.* I was completely consumed with success and material possessions. I am embarrassed to say that often I looked to associate with people who could make me more successful. My mantra was, "What is in it for me?"

While we had many discussions during his treatments, one conversation resonates with me to this day. He cautioned me to stop pushing myself so hard to be a success at the expense of others. Instead, he advised, begin thinking about how you can make those around you more successful. Dedicate yourself to benefiting others by sharing your knowledge and good fortune ... let that be your gift. He said, "From this, wealth and peace of mind will find you no matter how long you live." What my father was saying, in essence, was to learn to become indispensable within my sphere of influence. When I processed his words, it was a breakthrough moment in my life.

If you follow my career or my teachings, you will note that this is a core belief of mine. In fact, when *Career* T.E.A.M. was recognized in 2001 by *Inc.* Magazine as one of the fastest growing privately held companies in America, I shared with *Inc.* that a key ingredient is to *become indispensable within your industry, company, department, work group, task force or team.* Connecting with fellow associates or customers and being able to distribute information and solutions quickly and efficiently is a prerequisite to upward mobility and promotion.

Bottom line: Climbing the ladder of success and finding and retaining your career calling require having the right relationships. The reality is that nobody achieves significant success in this world without a great deal of help and support from others. As a matter of necessity, we are all social beings.

In my company, I require that our leadership team meet every month to strategize on methods for building and maintaining relationships. We focus on 3 groups, what they want and why they want it:

1. Internal company relationships
2. Customer relationships
3. Industry partnership relationships

We know that our existence is reliant upon the ability to empower every member of our organization to make our vision a daily reality. We must have strong relationships between me, as the founder, the lead managers, implementation staff, entry level personnel, customers and subcontractors. Without this relationship focus and connection, our plans would never be properly executed and our business would fail. We support each other, recognize contribution and feel significant.

As a result, loyalty, an all but forgotten concept in today's fast moving global economy, is earned and cements individuals into a cohesive unit, a team. *Teams always outperform individuals.*

To build teamwork, I often question my key associates on their true motivations for deciding to share their unique and compelling contributions as a member of my company. I have the reputation for relentlessly pursuing people's true motivations, that is, what drives them to do the things they do. I find, when 2 people have an understanding of what each one truly wants, long lasting bonds are created. In business, this is essential for prosperity. The bottom line question we ask each potential associate is: *What do you really want and why do you want it?*

While technology and clever business phrases constantly change, I believe people remain basically the same in their needs, wants and values. We want respect, recognition, belonging and a feeling of importance. We want to be the best we can be, and we want to matter; finding your calling is the only way. Note: If you ever apply for a position with our company, be prepared to answer that question!

People do not only hire candidates that they like; that is a fallacy. People hire candidates who they believe will make their organization better and stronger. You must be able to communicate how you plan to make the organization stronger and if it is something you are truly passionate about, let your heart lead the way!

When I appeared as a guest on CNN for the first time, I began by sharing my extreme passion about the importance of career planning and life balance. The host, like many people, was looking for a quick solution or shortcut and asked me to define the *secret of success*. After a dramatic pause, I stunned the host who was probably expecting some long-winded, profound sounding business school answer by summing up the answer in a single word ... *contribution*. I explained that in order to develop key contacts and establish critical linkages—essential steps to attaining one's calling—you must develop the capacity to connect with potential mentors.

Potential mentors, like all of us, have busy schedules and likely will not partake in any meeting or conversation unless they understand how it helps *their* mission. Thus, your ultimate objective is to show them how investing time and energy in helping you realize your goal will assist them in moving closer to *their* agenda. You must first *contribute* in order to be worthy and deserving of another's time, effort or money. The key phrase is not "how can a contact help you," but rather, "how can you help them." Give to get!

In today's competitive job market, where a growing number of people are consultants or independent contractors and the average job tenure is less than 4 years, building relationships and connecting with others is a mandate. We each must develop our own *brand* and navigate our way through the maze of an ever evolving global economy. Loyalty is no longer based on seniority or prioritized by most companies (who must continually reinvent and re-structure to remain competitive), but rather loyalty exists in one's relationships. Personal loyalty and contribution to friends, partners and current and future customers are critical. Job security is no longer present in our economy and often the only surefire source of trust exists within your unique circle of contacts.

In the 21st century workplace, your network is the lifeblood of your career and speaks to your brand as an individual resource, which, as you are learning, exists to design and provide solutions.

The Importance of Mentors

> *"It doesn't matter how smart you are, what level of education you have, how much talent you have, or where you grew up . . . these things are irrelevant unless you understand that you cannot achieve your calling on your own . . . you must learn to cultivate resources and use the power of relationships. Show me a true success story and I will show you a person who has learned the skill of fostering and building relationships."*
>
> —Chris Kuselias

Let us begin the process of exploring the importance of mentors or, as some say, role models. Human beings are very much like chameleons. We take on the attitudes and behaviors of the people with whom we associate. One of my mentors is the famous businessman and investor, Warren Buffet, who said, "If you tell me who your heroes are, I can tell you how you're going to turn out in life." I thought about that statement and decided that Mr. Buffet was saying the same thing my now deceased grandmother used to tell us as children which was, "If you sleep with dogs, you will wake up with fleas."

The message is to choose your mentors wisely as they will have a profound effect on your development as a person and your ability to obtain your career calling. Expanding your base of contacts is one of the most overlooked but essential ingredients to career mastery. Quite simply, the more connections you have the more *leverage* you possess. Leverage provides options. But be very careful whom you select as a mentor. Mr. Buffet has been quoted as saying that he asks himself 3 questions concerning potential mentors or important people he is considering an association with:

1. Do I like them?
2. Do I trust them?
3. Do I respect them?

Personally, I look for 3 elements of trust when considering my mentors:

1. Are they like me and can I bond with them?
2. Have they assisted someone like me or in my position before?
3. Do I see them as an expert?

So what is a mentor? Well, the dictionary defines the word mentor as "a wise and trusted counselor or teacher." I have several mentors in my life who have been incredibly instrumental in my success and whom I constantly seek out for guidance, encouragement and support. In fact, I have even created a spreadsheet of my mentors in each important area of my life. I have mentors for my health and fitness goals, financial planning, relationship mastery, spiritual pursuits and, yes, my career aspirations.

Mentors Provide 3 Basic Benefits

> *"What if you were to interview one successful person (potential mentor) every month? Can you imagine the wisdom, knowledge and power you would obtain from these 12 new contacts each year? Their success leaves clues for you to discover and implement."*
>
> —Chris Kuselias

Mentors can assist us to clarify our mission, values and purpose. They can help filter out viable opportunities from dead ends. They can teach us to prioritize our most important tasks and activities and create a plan of action. They can also coach us to maintain balance in our lives while pursuing our career calling.

By studying the success and lifestyle of people who are more informed than we are, we expand our own horizons and create better opportunities. Mentoring promotes the exchange and sharing of information, knowledge, skills and wisdom faster than any other process available. Young athletes improve their skills by learning from mentors, young brokers learn their craft from mentors, young educators learn from experienced teachers and you can learn from mentors in your chosen career endeavor.

Here are 3 benefits:

1. Mentors provide us with the truth even when we do not want to hear it. They tell us what we *need* to hear and not what we *want* to hear. Their opinions provide valuable perspective and experience. Mentors can shortcut our learning curve and provide wisdom that would otherwise take us a lifetime to achieve.
2. Mentors improve our level of success and reduce our percentage of failures. Mentors simply know more about the subject than we do and can coach us to maintain a positive attitude in the face of adversity or challenge. They are our #1 cheerleader!
3. Mentors provide a realistic path to our outcome while teaching us the value of planning and preparation. A quality mentor knows the right mix of pressure and praise to extract the optimal effort from a protégé. Strong, focused mentor relationships ensure powerful outcomes.

Fast Fact

70% of all people earning over $100,000 obtained their position via networking!

5 Important Thoughts on Mentors

1. Select quality mentors for each area of your life where you require guidance and advice. Common areas include: career, fitness, financial, relationship (e.g, parenting), and spirituality
2. Create a "Personal Advisory Board" of mentors in each area of your life where you need to learn, grow and improve. Always be on the lookout for new mentors who can help shape or refine your perspective, attitude and habits while establishing short-cuts that will often save you months or years. The creation of my *dream team* was one of the best pieces of advice I have ever received and a critical factor in my personal and professional success!
3. Every successful person has mentors. A mentor will be your shortcut to prosperity, patience and perseverance. Mentors can be found in the strangest of places. You never can tell who or what

will evolve into a valuable mentor and, often times, mentors are discovered by complete accident.

4. Mentors don't need to be an actual person. A mentor can be in the form of a book, movie, CD, audio or any life changing activity, including a life changing illness (which happened to me!).

5. Set a goal to find one new mentor per quarter. That equates to 4 new mentors per year! Obtain new mentors through a carefully designed plan, which includes personal appointments (for example, lunches), email messages citing the benefit to them in being your mentor, new books in your field of interest, authors, speakers etc.

> *"Some people enter our lives and leave almost instantly. Others stay and forge such an impression on our heart and soul, we are changed forever."*
>
> —Author unknown

One of the biggest challenges people face is that their network is confined to friends and family, people who already know what you know and probably add little value to your knowledge base or wisdom. It is comfortable, but not necessarily profitable. You go to the same events, same parties and never really s-t-r-e-t-c-h your personal boundaries.

Throughout this book I will be coaching you to extend your circle of acquaintances and teaching strategies to make you comfortable when approaching new connections. Consider the words of master connector and networker, Keith Ferrazzi:

> *"I don't think of a network of people as a net, into which you wrangle contacts like a school of struggling cod. Again, it's like the Internet, an interconnecting series of links in which each link works collaboratively to strengthen and expand the overall community."*
>
> —Keith Ferrazzi, *Never Eat Alone*

How Finding Role Models Will Help You

One of the most profound discoveries I have ever made is that everything I have ever dreamed of wanting or achieving has most likely already been accomplished by another human being. I may design a modification to a solution or invent a new widget, but chances are some other person has already pioneered in this area through blood, sweat and tears. All I need to do is study their efforts and techniques and incorporate my own individuality to the process, any process, and I can most likely save years, even decades of time and energy while achieving a similar or better result. Successful achievement leaves traces like a motorboat leaves a wake. Often this research is available via the Internet, books, tapes, classes, seminars or workshops. Whether you seek to invent a cure for a disease, lose weight or increase your strength, start a business venture, raise capital, meet your ideal mate, improve your child's reading level or visit some obscure destination, someone else has already attempted or fulfilled your objective. Find them! ... Learn from them!

I want to introduce the importance of building quality relationships with those who can assist you in achieving your career calling. *Bottom line: Finding role models is critical to your success.* Understanding their thought processes, motivations and schedule are even more important. When you find a quality mentor, you should be analyzing these 4 things:

1. What do they focus on?
2. What do they think about?
3. What do they study and research?
4. How do they spend their time?

If you do not identify a quality role model or mentor in the critical areas that comprise each of our lives (including career!) you will not be your most successful self and will not fully experience your full potential! I attribute a huge portion of my personal and professional success to studying the habits of individuals who have achieved the status in a certain area of life that I also seek.

Do this right now! Create a list or spreadsheet of the kind of mentors you want and need in your life. Even if you do not know them personally, the key is to identify who can assist you. I have mentors for fitness, exercise, nutrition, financial planning, success in keeping a healthy marriage, parenting, meditation, business management and, of course, career planning. Do you?

Make a list of potential mentors in the key areas of your life. This process will identify where you may be missing key advisors so you can then devote your attention to the pursuit of creating a personal relationship with a subject matter expert in each critical area.

One other prediction: My guess is that you are having the biggest challenges in those areas where you have not yet identified a quality mentor.

Critical Area	Mentor or Role Models Name
Career Planning	
Business Management (If you own your own business)	
Diet and Nutrition	
Exercise Routine	
Financial Planning	
Meditation and Relaxation	
Parenting	
Relationship Management	
Spirituality	
Other? (Feel free to add your own category)	

Make sure you carve out dedicated time to meet with and continue to learn from your chosen mentors, your *dream team*. How many dream teams are you on where others see you as a source of inspiration or knowledge? Consider if you have built your career to the point where you are perceived an expert resource. What would have to happen for this to become a reality?

3 more thoughts on developing your personal and professional contacts:

1. The more expansive your network of contacts, the more leverage you possess (particularly when it comes to identifying roles that will lead you to your ultimate career calling!).
2. Remember first to attempt to provide a benefit to a mentor or contact before asking for a favor or benefit for yourself. This advice will assist you in building trust and credibility with mentors and professional contacts and create a foundation for mutually beneficial, long-term relationships.
3. Be passionate and committed to maintaining your most prized relationships. Be dedicated when it comes to things like birthday cards and letters of congratulations. You are never too busy to feed and nourish a great networking contact! It may sound corny, but remember the Golden Rule of Networking: *Be very quick to build connections and extremely slow to break them.*

Noted motivational speaker Zig Ziglar says: "You can have everything you want if you help enough other people get what they want. Everybody wants something. You just need to find out what they want and give it to them."

Eliminating Negative Influences

"People are often unreasonable, illogical, and self-centered; forgive them anyway. If you are kind, people may accuse you of selfish, ulterior motives; be kind anyway. If you are successful, you will win some false friends and some true friends; succeed anyway. If you are honest and frank, people may cheat you; be honest and frank anyway. What you spend years building, someone could destroy overnight; build anyway. If you find serenity and happiness, they may be jealous; be happy anyway. The good you do today, people will often forget tomorrow; do good anyway. Give the world your best anyway. You see, in the final analysis, it is between you and God; it was never between you and them anyway."
—Mother Teresa

Have you ever wondered why you hang around or associate with certain people? I have. For years, I used to engage in conversations or spend time with all kinds of folks, some of whom were draining my life energy without me even knowing or realizing it. One day, I decided to analyze who I was choosing to spend my most valuable asset with—my time—and I was consumed with the thought that many of my own limitations were the result of surrounding myself with negative thinkers, people who had not invested the time and energy to build themselves and—unbeknownst to me—were sapping my energy.

I am not suggesting it was their fault or that I was making excuses and blaming others. These were not necessarily bad folks; in fact some of them had many redeeming qualities, which is why they were a friend or associate. But when I really took the time to review each relationship and the foundation on which it was based, it dawned on me that certain interactions were downright unhealthy and often I was giving more than I was receiving.

Of course, I do not mean to suggest that you should only engage in relationships where you have something to gain, but simply that you honestly consider the true basis for the relationship. Does that person make you feel good about yourself? What is the foundation of your friendship? Do you still have the same interests or have you outgrown one another? Tough questions, but again, *your time is your most precious commodity*, so do not waste it!

Also, spending time with people who do not further your objectives in a positive way reduces the time you have in your busy life to meet new contacts and expand your horizons. I admit it is often more comfortable to continue to "hang out" with your current circle of friends, and often family contacts are inherited through marriage, but if you truly seek to explore the limits of your own enormous potential, limiting time spent in unproductive relationships is not something you should do, but rather something you *must* do!

While establishing new and better contacts is an important aspect of finding your calling, eliminating negative influences may be equally, if not more important. The people you hang around with do make a difference. Why would you choose to build relationships with people whom you don't trust, don't respect or don't like?

A Guide to Meeting Mentors

"Often, we cannot remember the 5 last presidents, the 5 last Oscar winning movies or name the top 5 Fortune 500 companies. Ask a person to name the top 5 people who have served as valuable mentors, role models or coaches in their life and presto! they will rattle off the names. We remember those who care about us and others will remember you if you show caring and appreciation of them."
—Chris Kuselias

The +, −, ? Exercise: Where Are You Now?

To clarify this point and assess your network, here is an interesting and informative exercise to evaluate your current spheres of influence, that is, who it is you choose to associate with and how they impact your life ... positively or negatively.

1. Make a list of the family members, friends, co-workers and other contacts with whom you interact most or with whom you typically spend the majority of your time.
2. Next, put a "+" next to each person who inspires, encourages or builds you up as a person, and put a "–" beside every person who is toxic—people who complain, spread rumors, act negatively, have a poor attitude, find the bad in people, whine, and criticize your dreams and aspirations. If you cannot determine which category to place the person in, put them under the ? category.
3. Make a commitment to reduce spending time with the people who have a "–" next to their name.

By following through on this exercise, you now have a blueprint as to which people in your life will truly help you to attain your goals and objectives and which people may be along for the ride.

The Best Strategies to Find Mentors

Question: Where are the places to go to meet people who can profoundly impact my life?

You may be thinking, Chris, this sounds groovy. I can now see the value of surrounding myself with quality people who can educate, inspire or inform me. I also agree with the importance of reducing or eliminating negative influences from my life. But how do I build a new circle of influential people who can support my newfound mission to obtain my unique and compelling skills and ultimately find my career calling? And why would these people want to help me?

Consider the words of William James, who said, "The deepest principle in human nature is the craving to be appreciated." People like to help others and be appreciated for their assistance!

I liken networking to building your own personal community of trusted advisors, who can also benefit in some way through your contributions. Often, people overlook obvious opportunities to create or expand their environment. For example:

- If you are currently employed, why not propose to your boss a plan that will require you to interact with new departments or individuals. A customer service rep can propose that the advertising department receive a presentation on the merits of customer service and how it can affect company promotional activities, brochures or their website.

[front]

Name _____

Title _____

Company _____

[back]

Notes (date you met, how you met, who referred you, key thoughts, follow-up tips, etc.):

_____

_____

_____

_____

_____

- If you graduated from an educational institution, no doubt they have an alumni group where you can share experiences and learn about several new industries or employers from people who, at one time, made the common decision to attend that institution.
- It is never too late to take a class or return to school and delve into a subject of particular interest, which may spark a connection to a new vocation or a part time job to supplement your current income.
- Volunteer! Many successful "connectors" started a new career by taking the 1st step of getting involved in an organization or group that promotes or shares a common interest. I have a friend who joined a fantasy sports league, became the league commissioner and started a website for other fantasy sports enthusiasts. He left his accounting job and gets paid to watch football on Sundays!

Let's First Build a Tree!

Connecting to mentors and building your network is like a muscle; the more you work it the larger it gets.

Beginning the process of itemizing contacts is the 1st step. Let me start by telling you that the Bureau of Labor Statistics estimates that the average American knows approximately 500 people. By knowing 500 people, you may have developed a bigger network of contacts and friends and a support system larger than you ever realized. Each of the 500 people you know has contact with 500 people of their own. The net result is (500 × 500 or 250,000) potential contacts. That many people would fill Yankee Stadium 5 times!

This exercise will serve to construct a visual depiction of your current centers of influence, people who have the potential to assist you. What I would recommend doing first is to develop what I call a tree diagram. Write your name on a blank piece of paper, and from that form little branches or clusters of your immediate family; then from that add your secondary family, until you get to your 3rd cousins. Next, list your friends or professionals or work associates, neighbors, your doctor, your dentist, people you've come to know, your former professors or teachers, the people who you've met through friends or a friend of a friend, and people you've met at social events. By creating this tree diagram, you'll find that you know a great many people.

Making contacts is crucial to your career success. I encourage you to network at all times. Taking advantage of obvious and not so obvious people connections is a positive step to ensuring career success. On a separate sheet of paper, list as many contacts as you can by name, occupation (field) and type of relationship. If possible, also include the method you will use to contact each individual.

To initiate this process, ask yourself the following questions:

Whom do you know?	
From your family?	Who is your attorney?
From your friends?	Who is your banker?
From your childhood?	Who is your doctor?
From your old job?	Who is your dentist?
From you school or college?	Who is your insurance agent?
From your civic activities?	Who is your realtor?
From your health club?	Who sold you your car?
From your church?	Who do you look up to?
From your PTA?	Who has a successful business?
From your neighborhood?	Who do the people you know, know?

Example:

Name	Occupation	Phone	Type of Relationship
Joe Smith	Teacher	555-0067	Friend of Bill Jones

Set a goal to increase your Contact List by one person per month. Remember to keep an active file! You can also complete this exercise by drawing a tree diagram and using the branches of the tree to reflect the different segments of contacts you know.

Now, as you stare at your tree diagram and analyze the specific professions and occupations of these people, you may find that your diagram can provide a lead for you to help get involved in the field or occupation of your choice. Then list specific occupations and job titles from your industry of preference.

Organizing Your Contact List

Each time you contact a person about a position, fill out a computerized index card and record the key information.

Finding your career calling can become a very competitive process. There is often a fine line between success and failure. But in terms of competition, everybody you meet who is relatively friendly may have many friends. But recognize that there are a lot of people looking for that same calling.

Understand that you can only expand your contact network by keeping track of the people you meet. Monitor your progress and record names, job titles and employer name, not on a napkin, but in an organized, professional manner. If you do not actively maintain and build your network of connections, you will most likely never find your true calling, with the strong possibility of working in a job that does not fulfill your passion or purpose.

Some do, but I never found it valuable to join unemployed networking groups. If you are between jobs, it simply does not make sense to attend "pity parties." Instead, associate with job givers—people who can hire—not folks who are without work.

All contacts are important in some way; the key is to figure out which are worth maintaining. If a person cannot directly hire you, they may refer 1 or 2 other names to you.

The Power of Asking

*" 'How come you never told us any of this?' the bosses in-
quired. 'How come you never asked?' the workers replied."*
Christopher Locke, *Gonzo Marketing*

I am constantly amazed at how many people are afraid or hesitant to ask
for something that they know will benefit them or their family. Have you
ever hear the saying, "The squeaky wheel gets the oil!" Asking for what
you want and deserve is not only your right, it is your obligation! Why?
Because asking for a person's assistance or for them to become one of your
key mentors is merely your attempt to obtain more knowledge. Here's a
useful acronym to remind you about asking:

Always
Seeking
Knowledge

So why do people stumble when they have an opportunity to ask? Essentially,
there are 3 reasons:

1. They have a belief system that says it's not right to ask.
2. They lack confidence.
3. They fear rejection.

The Bible says, "Ask and you shall receive, seek and you shall find, knock
and it shall be opened to you."

Defeating the Fear of Rejection

I must admit that at times I am a bit nervous when it comes to contacting
key individuals, not out of fear of rejection but out of concern that I will
not convey *my* contribution to them. Remember, true networking is the
process of finding creative ways to help *other* people be more successful.
What helps me to relax is to remind myself of the following:

*My decision to proceed is not one of success or failure, but rather between
choosing greatness (which requires risk) or accepting certain mediocrity and
the guilt associated with an inability to master my own emotions.*

There are 3 basic strategies for overcoming fear and anxiety associated
with contacting a potential mentor:

1. Acknowledge that it is perfectly normal to be anxious about the prospect of calling on a stranger. This is not a skill that comes naturally to most people; it is a learned behavior. Confidence is developed through experience, practice and rehearsal of your contribution and how it can be of mutual benefit to connect.
2. Understand that overcoming this fear through proper preparation and practice is absolutely essential to improving your technique and building a world class Rolodex.
3. Make a 100% commitment to improving your networking skills and making it part of your personal brand. Remember, 21st century superstars are master networkers and connectors!

Responding to Objections

Comment   I am too busy …

Reply   What is a better time to chat? Or Are you sure? I was told you were extremely helpful to passionate career seekers like me and your wisdom and knowledge was invaluable …

Comment   I am the wrong person …

Reply   May I please have the appropriate contact? Can I use your name as a referral?

Comment   Email or send me your resume

Reply   Will do. Can we also set a time and date for me to present myself in person?

Comment   We only hire experienced candidates …

Reply   Understood. But wouldn't you agree that passion can overcome perceived shortcomings? I promise not to waste your precious time.

Comment   We aren't looking for anyone right now …

Reply   Understood. As a key person in my chosen industry, can we spend a few minutes sharing information? It would be greatly appreciated.

I cannot overemphasize the importance of being persistent. Remember, you have value and are looking to solve problems. The people you are calling simply need to be made aware of what your contributions are and how you can help them! Do not be afraid or feel you are imposing. You have tremendous value and, unfortunately, the only way that a potential employer can learn about you is for you to make the connection.

The problem is that too many job seekers are unprofessional and have given legitimate seekers who have taken the time to learn the proper process a bad name, so many hiring authorities are skeptical and waste a lot of their time with unfocused career seekers. Show them you are focused and professional and they WILL talk with you!

Differentiating Yourself

It isn't enough to be at the right place at the right time, you must be the *right person* in the right place at the right time!

One of my favorite questions in life is: *"What is unique and compelling about you?"* Whether you are pitching a new product to a venture capitalist, trying to convince someone to date you, or attempting to get potential mentors to assist you in pursuit of your career calling, you must identify and be able to articulate your unique and compelling advantage. What *differentiates* you from others?

The most powerful way to differentiate your self is by mastering the use of language. The better your vocabulary, the faster you will achieve your objectives. Your vocabulary creates a first impression, helps you overcome obstacles, points out your sincerity and, above all, is the bond that creates lasting relationships. Whether you are speaking directly to a contact or using technology (email, etc.), word choice is powerful.

Contrary to opinion, you can improve your skills in this area. Many people make the excuse they were not born with, "the gift of gab" or lack charisma. Nonsense! It is simply a matter of committing to improving the way you describe yourself, your experiences and your contributions. I have found that charming people are simply those that are themselves and do not try to put on an act. Each of us is unique and compelling in some way; that uniqueness is your power.

As the Founder of *Career* T.E.A.M., I am proud of our accomplishments in building the nation's workforce, particularly in the area of assisting welfare recipients achieve self-sufficiency and become gainfully employed. Many of these folks come from incredibly challenging upbringings filled with abuse and neglect. We have worked in major cities across the country. Whenever we initiate a new training program, we always begin the 1st day by asking each attendee to write down 4 things about themselves, 3 that are true and one that is false. We call this exercise, "3 Truths and a Lie." We ask them to consider things that are unique and compelling, things that other people might find interesting. We are looking for a window into the person.

You would be amazed at the contributions folks have made or obstacles they have overcome but have not been afforded the chance to share with others. Often, their verbal skills are out of practice or they have forgotten their uniqueness. They are each required to stand in front of the group and share their list, which in itself requires a certain confidence.

But because they are talking about subjects they are intimately familiar with, their anxiety and nervousness is somewhat diminished. Classmates are asked to guess which 3 are true and which one is the lie or is a goal not yet attained. We have met chefs, hero's, foster parents, world travelers, artists, singers, poets, etc. This exercise sets the tone for one of the primary foundations of our conversion training:

> No matter who you are or where you come from or what hardships you have endured, we all have something unique and compelling to offer. We just have to identify what it is and communicate it to others!

But always remember to think before you speak! Remember the scene in the famous movie, *The Godfather,* when during a tense negotiating meeting with representatives from another powerful crime family (there was always the threat of gunfire!), Godfather Mob Boss Vito Corleone (played by Marlon Brando) slaps his son, Sonny Corleone (played by James Caan) for expressing his emotional opinion to the other family before thinking through the consequences. After the meeting is over, Vito chastises the volatile Sonny, by stating, "Never let anyone outside the family know what you are thinking." Remember: Never let your emotions control your dialogue; have a specific plan every time you meet with a potential new mentor. Often, people will ramble or let their emotions take over, but not you!

Do not be afraid to share aspects of your personal life with new contacts. I learned this valuable lesson when I was once attempting to negotiate a multi-million dollar contract to serve a large group of at risk youth with the Director of a large Washington, D.C.–based federal government agency. For months, I had attempted to get a meeting and had leveraged my connections and sent multiple letters and email messages creating a justification for the meeting. Finally, a breakthrough came as the timing of our program to assist the nation's youth coincided with this agency's priorities. The appointment was set 2 days before Christmas, not the ideal time but I knew I most likely wouldn't get a 2nd chance. After waiting in the lobby for 45 minutes, I was called into the office.

During the meeting, the dialogue was progressing but not at the pace or in the direction that I ideally wanted it to go. We were engaging in small talk and beginning to discuss our business, but I felt that something was missing. *There was no bonding occurring;* we were simply 2 people sizing each other up but without a connection toward a common objective. I began by sharing my passion for youth and how our program would benefit their mission (always give before your get!).

As I was talking, I noticed that my contact kept looking at the door of his office and into the reception area. Glancing over, I noticed an elderly looking woman sitting there who did not look like she belonged in a government office. I was tempted to continue but noticed that my contact seemed very distracted by his next visitor. My instincts told me to address the issue or my presentation might not get the attention I wanted. So I stopped my presentation and suggested that my contact greet his new visitor.

As it turns out, the visitor was my contact's mother, who had flown in from out of town to see her son, the well to do government director. Being extremely close to my mom and understanding his perspective, I suggested that we shorten our meeting so my contact could spend time with his mom, an obvious priority. His mom came into the room, we shared a few stories of my family values and childhood memories and our respective plans for the holiday. I was like one of the family!

My contact was so impressed with my sensitivity to the event and closeness to my own family, that we became friendly and established a business relationship that exceeded my wildest expectations. He later expressed that my professional attire and bottom line approach gave the impression of a "stick to business" mentality and masked my strong family beliefs and willingness to give "props" to moms. I shared that behind the large government building and button down shirt I assumed that he was probably stodgy. We were both wrong; the end result was we were awarded a contract to serve youth!

The lesson: Do not be afraid to let people in to meet the *real* you; it lets them know you are humble, honest and more than just a person with their hand out looking for assistance.

Here are a few suggestions to further give you a competitive edge:

1. Always keep good eye contact. Looking away makes you appear unconfident or sneaky.
2. Keep a reasonable distance and acknowledge your understanding with a confirmation (uh-huh or a nod)
3. Be relaxed and mirror the actions of your contact. If they sit, you sit. Also, never cross or fold your arms as this creates the appearance you are guarded. If your contact has their arms crossed or folded, they are most likely uncomfortable or in a defensive posture. Try to loosen up the conversation if this occurs.
4. Attempt to ease tension by physical contact meaning a handshake or by touching your contact's elbow, which is a bit more personable than a regular handshake. Ever watch a master politician glad hand a new group? They often (gently) grasp an elbow and acknowledge a new person. Hugs for first meetings are genuinely not recommended!
5. Always smile when you meet a new contact and an early compliment (if it is sincere) always helps! I remember a friend once recounting a story of his initial meeting with a powerful, elderly contact. In the influential contact's office for the first time, my friend, a bit nervous, tried to make small talk and offered a feeble attempt at a compliment by commenting how pretty the contact's daughter was from the photo on his credenza. Image my friend's embarrassment, when the contact said, "That isn't my daughter, young man, it is my new wife."
6. Focus on the other person's interests first and show genuine curiosity. Encourage your contact to discuss these interests and share their passions.

Best Strategies for Making Connections

AT THIS POINT YOU may be saying, "Well, Chris, that sounds great, and the information is very helpful. But I really have stage fright as far as how to actually go about contacting a potential employer or somebody else who can help me. I can do my own research on line, in a library or through company published information. And I can find a list of contact names. But when it comes to actually making the contact, I'm at a loss. I'm paralyzed with fear. I don't know exactly what to do." Many people have what I call paralysis by analysis, which means that they analyze too much and never take the action.

Without a plan, the process of developing a career contact network can be very difficult. But keep in mind that there are a number of different methods for contacting key individuals.

For example, when I made the decision to write this book, one of my immediate objectives was to meet and learn from a successful author in the business motivation category. I targeted Jeff Fox, a successful business-man, speaker and best- selling author of *How To Become A Rainmaker, How to Become CEO, How to Become a Great Boss, How to Become a Marketing Superstar, Don't Send A Resume, How to Make Big Money in Your Own Small Business,* and *The Dollarization Discipline.* When doing research to find out how to contact him, I discovered that he lived in my state.

Rather than call or email Jeff and ask for his assistance in helping me overcome obstacles (that no doubt consumed his precious time and en-ergy early on) or spend days trying to determine a person we both knew, I approached him with an opportunity to promote his published works in our company e-newsletter. I mentioned a couple other industry authors he would know who had also participated. In each issue, we would simply extract an excerpt from one of his books, include his photo and bio and presto, instant free publicity for Jeff to an audience of workforce profes-sionals around the country.

To initiate a dialogue with Jeff, I requested a luncheon (in his town with a choice of 2 specific dates) to meet and discuss the publicity offer. I closed my request by indicating that he might be helpful in guiding me in my new book offering. As it turns out, Jeff is a great guy and was helpful in terms of suggesting certain strategies: clearly a win–win scenario.

Here are a few hints and suggestions that I used:

1. Never make a cold call. Always begin by referencing a common person, event, educational experience, work experience, organization or award that creates a common bond. As my 1st boss used to say, "Cold calling is for suckers." I never, ever make cold calls; they are a waste of my time and do not work. I have the reputation for being able to make a connection with virtually any person I set my mind to meeting. My secret? While some people say I was born with the "gift of gab" or have the unique benefit of extensive negotiation training, you and I now know the true reason for my success … I always give before I ask for anything in return.

2. Another tip is to call people at unusual times. Busy people are more likely to answer their own phones when their assistants or receptionists are not in the office, meaning before 8 AM or after 6 PM. I know I do! Also, there isn't the competition for signatures or interruptions as most other staff has gone home.

3. Make warm calls! Begin by referencing a familiar reference (person, club, or institution) to establish a common bond and peak interest.

4. Indicate immediately how *they* will benefit from meeting *you*; your needs are secondary.

5. Be flexible with regard to a meeting time and date. Make it easy and convenient for the contact to say yes!

6. Do your homework! The Internet, via name search, provides instant access to information on your targeted connections; you are only a mouse click away!

For example, start by saying something like this. "I am currently in the process of exploring several career alternatives. But before making any final decisions regarding employment, I'm trying to benefit from the counsel or guidance of an experienced individual such as you. I've had a great deal of experience in the field of … Then list your field …

Next, you want to say something like, "I'm particularly interested in learning more about specific employment opportunities, the skills and responsibilities required, the advantages and disadvantages of the profession, as well as the future outlook in your field. Could you please take some time from your busy schedule to meet with me for 15 minutes and share your knowledge and perspectives?"

It is important to proactively build your connections in areas where you feel passion or purpose. Today's hobby is tomorrow's occupation. Here are 5 networking methods I recommend:

1. Meet new contacts for 15 minutes over a cup of coffee.
2. Use food to break the ice ... breakfast, lunch, an after work drink or even dinner
3. Share a hobby: play golf, workout or attend a sporting event. Find out your desired contact's interests in advance and show respect by selecting a venue that they feel comfortable with.
4. Conferences: If you are in a particular town and want to meet someone, why not invite them to a workshop or ask them to partake in lunch. Note: The American Society of Association Executives (ASAE) reports the meeting industry is an $83 billion market, with over $56 billion spent annually on seminars and conventions.
5. Have a dinner party! Invite a few guests who may benefit from knowing each other and, presto, instant connection.

Gaining an Appointment by Letter

Your Name
Your Address
Your City   ST   Zip

Date

Mr. Ray Green
Vice President
XYZ Enterprises, Incorporated
16 Glenn Road
Anywhere   ST   Zip

Dear Mr. Green:

I am exploring career opportunities in order to select a particular field or occupation. I thought it might be a good idea to obtain valuable insight from a more experienced individual like yourself.

I am particularly interested in learning about the responsibilities, skills, outlook and opportunities in (Name of field or industry).

I know you are extremely busy, but if you could provide me with 15 minutes of your time, you could really assist me in moving closer to my career goals.

I will be calling you or the secretary to determine your schedule, and, with your approval, solidify a mutually convenient time and date.

Should you wish to contact me in the meantime, please do not hesitate to call me at (insert your telephone number).

Sincerely,

Signature

Your Name

Note: Do not enclose your resume in a letter of this type because, if you do, you will look like a typical job seeker and that could turn the person off.

Gaining an Appointment by Telephone

Sell the appointment; do not ask for a job! Never talk about your need to find a job on the phone unless you can actually make and conclude the sale without seeing the prospect personally. Inexperienced career seekers, in their eagerness to get appointments with career mentors, often share their personal needs or hardships in the 1st couple sentences. If you do this you will ruin the opportunity with a potential mentor.

Your approach must break the preoccupation of the contact. Assume everyone you call on is busy and thinking about things unrelated to your career aspirations. Most people are completely involved in their own problems, work, family, health, business, or bills.

Try this approach: "I need about 2 minutes of your time. Is this a good time to talk?"

Remember:

1. You only have about 30 seconds at the outset of your discussion to get the prospect's complete and undivided attention
2. The first 25 words out of your mouth will set the tone for the rest of the conversation, so be prepared!
3. Be certain that you are speaking to the right person before making any attempt to set up an appointment

Improve Your Telephone Prospecting

There are 2 things you can do to improve the quality of your telephone prospecting.

1. The 1st is to stand up when you speak to the prospect. Standing will force you to project your voice and lends itself to more confidence. Sitting may lessen your enthusiasm.

2. The 2nd thing you can do is smile into the phone when you speak. The person on the other side may not see your face, but they will sense your enthusiasm if you "dial with a smile."

How to Obtain an Information Interview

1. Know the name of the person you are calling.
2. Confirm how the person prefers to be addressed. (Mr., Mrs., Miss, Ms., Dr., Etc.).
3. State how you got their name (referral source).
   a. Name (friend)
   b. Article in magazine
   c. From teacher or associate
4. State the purpose of your call (wish to meet personally to discuss opportunities.
5. Deliver your message.
   a. Refer to any previous letters sent, if appropriate.
6. Overcome objections.
   a. "I will be brief."
   b. "I know you are busy, would Tuesday be better?"
   c. "Should I contact your secretary?"
7. Close the presentation.
   a. Ask for a personal session (time and date).

Success Tip

In an information interview, it is rarely appropriate to ask for a job!

Networking (interviewing) is communicating . . .

> "A farmer went into his attorney's office wanting to file for a divorce from his wife. The attorney asked, 'May I help you?' to which the farmer replied, 'Yeah, I want to get one of those dayvorces.' The attorney said, 'Well, do you have any grounds? ' and the farmer said, 'Yeah, I got about 140 acres.' The attorney said, 'No, you don't understand. Do you have a case? ' and the farmer replied, 'No, I don't have a Case, but I do have a John Deere. ' And the attorney said, 'No, you really don't understand. I mean do you have a grudge?' And the farmer replied to that, 'I got a grudge. That's where I park my John Deere.' The attorney, still trying, asked, 'No,

sir, I mean do you have a suit?' The farmer replied, 'Yes, sir,
I got a suit. I wear it to church on Sundays.' The exasper-
ated and frustrated attorney said, 'Well, sir, does your wife
beat you up or anything? ' The farmer replied, 'No, sir. We
both get up about 4:40.' Finally, the attorney says, 'OK. Let
me put it this way. WHY DO YOU WANT A DIVORCE?'
And the farmer says, 'Well, I can never have a meaningful
conversation with her.'"

—Steven Covey, *The 8th Habit*

Communication is without question the most important skill in life. There are basically 4 modes of communication: reading, writing, speaking and listening. And most people spend ⅔ to ¾ of their waking hours doing those 4 things. The one that represents 40% to 50% of our communication time is listening; the other modes we have had the least training in.

Listening continuum:

1. Ignoring
2. Pretend listening (patronizing)
3. Selective listening
4. Attentive listening
5. Empathic listening

There are 2 ways to penetrate the hidden job market and arrange an information interview: via the telephone or via direct letter.

You can use the telephone to help you get the job you want and set up the information interview; many people have some form of phone fright, where they have a fear of picking up the telephone. Their hands get sweaty. They begin mumbling their words.

I teach people to avoid or overcome this problem through practice and by being prepared. The best way to guard against stumbling over the phone is to prepare a script or dialogue. And don't take anything for granted. Include everything from your name and how you're going to introduce the particular call to your background and accomplishments so that you don't appear unprofessional.

Also, preparing a script will keep you from omitting or forgetting important information you want to share with the person so that when you hang up you don't say, "Darn it. Why didn't I tell him about that accomplishment or my other accomplishment or my other activities?"

A basic phone script or outline should include the following information: The name of the person you're calling. And when you call them, don't be afraid to address them by Mr. or Mrs. Smith. And then ask them if they prefer or will allow you to call them by their first name. Tell them how you got their name, whether somebody referred you or you got their name out of an article or a magazine or from a former professor, teacher or friend. Tell them why you contacted them and how you got their name.

Clearly state why you're calling. There are 2 basic reasons for this; to either follow up on a previous letter that you sent them or to arrange a personal appointment. Now, because their time is valuable, tell them briefly why you feel your credentials will match the organization's needs or requirements.

If you previously sent an introductory or inquiry letter, simply restate the contents of what you sent to them in the previous letter, your specific talents and why you feel that a personal meeting would be better than just a phone conversation or having them refer you to the Personnel Department.

Remember, you want to learn more about the contact. You want to get inside their head and find out what makes them successful. And if you are successful and the person says, "Well, OK. Fine. I can meet you for 10 minutes either before or after work," make sure that you establish a specific appointment time and confirm the date. If they suggest meeting you at a restaurant, make sure you set a reservation, if needed. There would be nothing more embarrassing or unprofessional than to ask someone to meet you, have them agree to it and find the restaurant unable to accommodate you when you arrived.

If they tell you to meet in their office, make sure you have specific directions on how to get there. Or, hang up and call the receptionist or secretary for directions.

When all of these things have been accomplished, hang up the phone. My advice to you is: Don't make the call too long or the person will get bored. Don't waste the contact's valuable time by asking too many questions or you may turn them off.

Sample Telephone Script—"Cold Calling"

Below, you will find simulated challenges and strategies for those situations that require you to call an employer without the benefit of a referral or without knowing the name of the person who is responsible for hiring.

Challenge When the receptionist or another party answers ...

Strategy   Introduce yourself. Hello, my name is _____. May I please speak to the hiring authority/employment/personnel manager or (party you are calling)?

Challenge   The employment/personnel manager or your party is unavailable ...

Strategy   May I please have the name of the Employment/Personnel Manager? What would be a good time to reach him/her?

Challenge   There is no designated Employment/Personnel Manager ...

Strategy   In that case, who would I speak to about employment opportunities? Write down the name and title and then ask to speak with that person.

Challenge   If the Employment/Personnel Manager is available ...

Strategy   First, introduce yourself. Hello, my name is _____. I am interested in a position as (be specific). Do you have any openings for someone with my qualifications? (State your credentials). I have experience as ... I am skilled in ... My best qualities are ...

Challenge   If the company is not hiring ...

Strategy   May I leave a resume and fill out an application in the event that the situation changes?

Challenge   If the company is hiring ...

Strategy   Always ask for the interview. Would it be possible to come in for an interview? If yes, confirm the name of the individual, address, date, time etc.

Challenge   Final Comments ...

Strategy   Thank you for your time.

Before the call, rehearse your script and possible objections. Make sure that it sounds convincing. Role-play with another person, friend or family member. Talk into a tape recorder. Through practice and preparation, you'll improve your confidence and that will be displayed in the tone of voice you use in the telephone call. Once you have made the telephone call, it's important that you keep a record, an active file as to how each person may be able to help you.

Here are some rules to remember. Keep the phone call short and sweet. Try calling before the normal business hours of 9:00 to 5:00. Monday mornings are generally very busy and Friday afternoon people sometimes like to leave early and get ready for the weekend.

Try to be as professional as you can. Memorize your script so you don't sound like you're reading when you're on the phone. If you have a number of information interviews to conduct but 1 or 2 are most important to you, don't start with the one you want the most. Practice!

Remember names and titles. It's very embarrassing to stammer and say, "Uh, uh, yes, sir—ma'am. Yes. I forget the name, or, I'm not sure how to pronounce the name of the person I'm calling."

If you follow this advice, put together a strong outline, keep detailed records and monitor your progress, you should make the telephone call work to your advantage and alleviate some of that terrible fright and fear of using the telephone.

A typical call to a prospective information interview candidate may sound something like this.

"Hello, Mr. Jones. This is Chris Kuselias." "Yes, Chris. How can I help you?" *"Mr. Jones, Mr. Fred Johnson recommended that I call you. We haven't met yet, but Fred Johnson told me that you and he are old friends. And he and I have a mutually enjoyable relationship. He spoke very highly of you and recommended that if I were to give you a call, you may have a few minutes to talk to me about your industry. I'd like to gain your advice and opinions on some career options that I'm currently in the process of considering. And if you could spare a few minutes of your time to help me, that would be very beneficial to my career."*

At this point in time you may get lucky and the contact may say,

"Well, yes. OK, fine." He may recommend a date or he may say, "Well, I wish I could help you, but, Chris, I'm just a little too busy right now." At that point you might say, "Well, Fred Johnson told me that your schedule would be very difficult and he recommended that I ask if we could meet prior to 8:30 or after 5:00 or even in the evening or for lunch, if that's more convenient for you." The contact may say, "Well, all right. If you're that persistent—I usually get in very early in the morning or I stay late. If you can be here by 8:00 before work or meet me at 5:00 or 5:30 after work, we can spend a half-hour or so together."

Set a specific date and time, thank the contact, hang up the phone and record the information.

If your inquiry is answered by a secretary or receptionist, keep in mind that often these folks will screen calls for their bosses and it may be difficult for you to get an appointment. So, if you do get some resistance on the part of the receptionist or secretary, I would recommend something like this.

The secretary may answer by saying, "This is Mrs. Jackson's office." "Hello. This is Chris Kuselias. Is Mrs. Jackson there please?" The secretary or receptionist may say, "Well, she is in. But can I ask what this is in reference to or what is this regarding?" Sound familiar? "Well, yes. Joe Curtis, a good friend of Mrs. Jackson's, recommended that I call."

Under no instances are you to tell the secretary that you are seeking a job or they probably will not put you through. Your call is of a personal nature to obtain opinion.

In some cases, you may be rejected. They may just say, "I'm sorry. But my schedule won't permit me to help you right now. I'm just too busy." Your response could be, "Well, I understand what your job is and I can appreciate that. Is there another name you could give me or somebody else you recommend calling?" Gain some benefit. Try to get a referral to somebody else in the organization or to another person within the industry. They may provide another name. Try to find out what type of relationship the 2 people have if they do refer you elsewhere.

You now have a lead-in to call the person, a warm call. Cite the persons name and how the 2 know each other, on a certain committee together or had worked together, etc. You can always call the secretary back and say, "Your boss has given me permission to call another individual, but he didn't tell me what his affiliation or her affiliation with the other individual was. I didn't want to bother him or her because they seemed very busy. Can you help me?" In other words, keep digging for information. At all times write a thank you letter, whether or not they were directly helpful or just provided you with another referral. You never know. Maybe in the future you'll require their services or help again.

Lastly, remember that administrative assistants, secretaries or clerical office support people can either be a tremendous barrier or enormously helpful. Try to call before 8:00 or after 5:00. And at all times be courteous, kind and polite. Don't be overly persistent. Otherwise, you'll come off as a pest and that's not the impression you want to create.

The Information Interview

Let's talk now about penetrating the hidden or invisible career market with the information interview. By utilizing the information interview, you'll be more successful because you're learning to penetrate that hidden job market and you're not really asking the person who is helping you for a definite commitment. You're just asking for information. You're not putting the other person on the spot. However, it's important to go on an information interview as if it were a regular job interview.

What is an information interview?

An information interview is a practice meeting with a mentor that is used to acquire information to determine if their chosen career path could potentially be your career calling.

The information interview uses a carefully developed set of questions that you can ask of a person who earns a living in a field that you may have an interest in pursuing. The information interview can provide a great deal of information in a very short period of time.

Why should you conduct an information interview?

1. It can help you narrow your interests by giving you a chance to learn about specifics.
2. It can help you learn about openings and become more knowledgeable on employers within that industry.
3. It can help you "practice" your interviewing skills in a less stressful setting.
4. It can help you improve your self-confidence in dealing with other people and give you an advantage over other candidates.

Things to Notice in an Information Interview

1. Is it a formal or informal atmosphere?
2. How do these people dress? (suit, shoes, jewelry, hair, etc.)
3. What kind of hours do people work?
4. Do people seem friendly?
5. Can you see yourself in that environment?

Let's assume via letter, mail, telephone, or through a personal meeting you've been granted an information interview. Someone has agreed to sit down and talk with you about his or her company or industry.

Treat it like it was a real live interview. You'll want to dress properly and appropriately. Try finding out through the secretary or through your own network how people dress. If it's a conservative company, dress conservatively. If your contact tells you that the information interview will take place over lunch in a casual atmosphere or setting, dress accordingly.

Bring a couple of copies of your resume, just in case. Where appropriate, bring samples or demonstrations of your previous accomplishments. When you meet, be knowledgeable and prepared to show you have researched the industry. Think of yourself as a private investigator.

When you meet, the first thing you should ask for is their business card. Why? It will be a lot easier for you later to write a Thank You letter or additional letters in the future if you have the correct spelling, title of their name, address, etc. For example, many people who have met with me have a hard time spelling "Kuselias."

Now, when conducting an information interview, it's important to be a good listener. Many people don't have the skill of listening. Active listening is a difficult process. There are obstacles in your way when you're trying to listen intently to a contact share what is often detailed information.

First, people only listen to what they like to hear. Secondly, we all have an unconscious tendency to criticize the way a person speaks or delivers a message. You can become preoccupied with the person's dress or personal appearance or gestures or clothing and miss what they're really saying.

What's important is not the vehicle or how they present it, but their actual message. Try to get emotionally involved in the information interview. Don't be so concerned about preparing a response. Really listen to what the other person is saying. In reverse order, the 80/20 principal applies, only now you should only be doing 20% of the talking and you should get them to do about 80% of the talking.

Ask your contact open-ended questions that require them to answer your questions. Don't ever fake attention. And do not be afraid to ask for clarification if you don't understand something.

10 Information Interview Tips

1. Your dreams and needs are just as important as anyone else's. Do not view the people you talk to as more important that you are; they are just more experienced.
2. People enjoy being asked for advice, but do not waste their time—be prepared!
3. Keep in mind that the person you ask for information may also benefit from your meeting; for example, they may re-acquaint themselves with the person who referred you.
4. Choose reputable, successful people to talk with (for example, industry specialists)
5. Prepare "open-ended" questions that will make your contact talk about his or her field.

6. Decide what information you need and who can provide it.
7. Remember first impressions count, so maintain eye contact, take notes, and notice the way they dress.
8. Always begin by thanking the person and asking them how much time they have to spend with you. Remember, you want to make sure you get your most important questions answered! Hint: Do not exceed your agreed upon time!
9. If you do not understand something, ask them to clarify what they mean!
10. Do not ask for a job. Instead, try, "With what you know today, if you were in my shoes, what would you do to get hired in this field?"

Remember the 6 basic fact finders when questioning the person: who, when, where, what, how and why. I feel it's important to listen like a doctor; that is, probe, prod, stick, test and examine. The more information you obtain, the easier your decision to pursue. Question, clarify, lead and develop. Tell your contact what your objectives are. For example, "I am here to learn about the specific duties of a budget manager" (or whatever the position is). Ask them how they happened to choose the occupation. How did they get involved in this business? It's an excellent entry-level question to get both parties talking and at ease.

Second, ask them to describe their favorite aspect of the occupation. Ask them what they like best and least. Ask them what characteristics they find common to top performers in this type of work, and how they would describe a typical day. What does the average employee earn in the starting position? The list below is my suggested order.

20 Questions to Ask in the Information Interview

1. How did you happen to choose this occupation?
2. Describe your favorite aspect of this profession.
3. What do you like least about it?
4. What personal satisfaction do you receive from this occupation?
5. What characteristics do you find common to individuals who do this type of work?
6. How would you describe a typical day?
7. What does the average employee earn annually in a starting position?
8. What kind of personnel do you come in contact with on this job?

9. What part of this profession causes you to become angry or frustrated?
10. What is the potential for future opportunities?
11. What is your overall impression of this industry and the direction it is going?
12. What do you see as the objectives and values of this particular organization?
13. What specific qualifications are required to obtain an entry level position?
14. What kind of training is provided?
15. Can you give me the name(s) of any other individuals I may contact?
16. What individuals are responsible for the hiring process and steps one would need to take to be considered?
17. State your credentials and qualifications. Then ask: What other activities or organizations would I benefit from joining?
18. Do you know of any related resources (for example, seminars, books, magazines, annual reports) that could further enhance my knowledge of the industry?
19. Do you know of anyone else who may assist me in my pursuit of my calling?
20. Do you feel this is your career calling and what are your future plans?

End the session by thanking the individual for their time and summarize the points or facts learned in this information interview.

Under no circumstances should you ask a contact to disclose their personal salary figures. We've all heard horror stories about people who have asked, "Well, how much do you earn?" Instead, be generic. "What does the average employee earn in a starting position?" is a better question.

"What kind of person do you come in contact with in this type of job? Can you describe a particular on-the-job event or occurrence that produced a positive feeling?" Ask them what they like about it. What part of the profession causes them to feel angry or frustrated?

Be genuinely interested in their responses. And by all means, feel free to take notes. It will make them feel important when you write down and record what they have to say.

What is the promotion scale for future opportunities? What is their overall impression of the industry? Again, on a personal level, "What do you see as the objectives of this particular organization or personal satisfaction you receive from this occupation?" All of a sudden, you're becoming a professional interviewer.

When I designed this questionnaire, it was important for me to give you both perspectives of the interview process because I knew during the course of the information interview you would be acting as an interviewer yourself.

So now you are transitioning into discussing the actual position. "What qualifications are required to obtain an entry-level position? What kind of training does one receive in this job?" Also, can they provide the names of any individuals that you can contact that may be helpful to you in your job search campaign? And, by the way, "what individuals are responsible for the actual hiring once a person obtains the necessary qualifications?"

Continue by saying, "Well, Mr. or Mrs. Contact, you've helped me tremendously. Please describe the hiring steps and the requirements that need to be considered." If they are impressed with you, they will tell you. Then tell them your qualifications or qualities and credentials. Ask them in their opinion what other activities or organizations or groups you would benefit from joining that could help you get involved and learn more information that relates to this particular job or industry.

Ask them if they know any related sources, websites, seminars, tapes, books, magazines and Annual Reports that can further enhance your knowledge of the industry. Show them you have a real interest in gathering information and becoming a more valuable employee or potential employee.

Graciously thank them for their time, effort and energy and their responses. Insist on paying for lunch if it is a luncheon. Shake hands. And with business card in hand and your newfound competitive edge, it's time to assess and evaluate the results of your information interview and determine next steps to take. One such step might be to develop additional questions to ask during your next information interview.

The Information Interview: 25 Other Questions You Can Ask

1. What do you do in a typical day?
2. What kinds of problems do you deal with?
3. What kinds of decisions do you make?
4. How does this job fit into the overall organization/department?
5. How long have you been in this job?

6. How does your job affect your personal life?
7. What are you major responsibilities?
8. How did you enter this field?
9. How do you reach your current position?
10. Would you recommend it to others?
11. If so, what skills, education and experience are required?
12. What are typical entry-level jobs in your field?
13. Could someone with liberal arts, sociology, biology background obtain a position in this field?
14. What additional courses or work experience would you recommend?
15. What do you find most satisfying about your job? Most frustrating?
16. What are the toughest problems you face in this organization?
17. What other obligations, outside of normal work hours, go along with your job?
18. How many hours do you work during the average workweek?
19. What professional organizations do you belong to? Are you an active member?
20. Has your membership helped?
21. What changes are occurring in your field?
22. Is there a definite career path in your field/organization? Can you describe it?
23. What are the professional journals in your field? Which ones do you recommend?
24. Can you suggest anyone else whom I could contact for additional information?
25. If I become a viable applicant, whom can I contact in your organization, or in another firm?

Hint: Use the questions that are most relevant to your field!

A mini tape recorder is very helpful so that when you finish the information interview, you can immediately record your notes.

When assessing how the information interview went, what were the strongest skills of the employer or subject you talked with? What were their weaknesses? Was there a willingness there to help you out beyond this initial interview? How about a long-term relationship?

What about your performance? How did you do? How did you perform? How do you think the subject would describe you to another person after having met you? Do you think they would be willing to recommend you? Did they like you? Did you fulfill your goals and objectives?

If you want to distinguish yourself, by all means FOLLOW UP! I contend that 95% of all passion seekers fail to follow up correctly or on time. Email is acceptable; personal cards or letters are ideal. Use your follow up to confirm commitments and secure a next step or meeting. 3 keys:

1. Express appreciation for their time
2. Cite an interesting or humorous event from your meeting or discussion to build a bond
3. Confirm suggested next steps; be precise regarding time and date and reaffirm any other names or contacts referred

The most important point at this juncture is to determine your next action. The immediate action is to write a thank you letter. I have included samples so that you can choose which one is most applicable to your situation.

As an example: *Dear Mr. Smith, I appreciated the opportunity to talk with you on June 15. The information you shared with me on the company was excellent. I am excited about the possibility of applying my education, skills and talents in the positions we discussed. If I can supply you with any additional information, please let me know. I look forward to hearing from you soon. Sincerely, (sign your name)*

Sample Thank You Note

Name
Your Address
Your State, Zip

Date

Mr. Austin Dupont
MIS Director
Mayberry Hospital
Anywhere   ST   01234

Dear Mr. Austin:

I appreciated the opportunity to talk with you on (Date of Information Interview). The information you shared with me was excellent.

I am excited about the possibility of applying my educational skills and talents in the field and positions we discussed. If I can be of assistance to you, or if I can supply you with additional information, please let me know.

Thanks again for taking the time to talk with me.

Sincerely,

Signature

Your Name

Always remember to write a thank you letter to the person who has helped you so they receive it within 3 working days!

Sending a thank you is a very simple process; keep it short so it doesn't take a lot of the contact's time to read it. Get your name in front of them again, just as a reminder. It's the same thing if they invite you to visit their office, plant or home. And, lastly, try this one. "Your advice was most helpful in clarifying my questions on my career in the field and reinforced my belief that I possess the skills that can meet the needs of your company as an employee. Thanks so much for taking time out of busy schedule to meet with me."

It doesn't matter whether the note is typed or handwritten. Some people say that handwritten is a little more personal. Others cite that typewritten is much more professional. My personal preference is a typewritten letter with your own personal signature in ink. 80% of all job seekers will never send a thank you card, but you as a responsible professional, always do!

Remember that in an information interview there are 3 issues your contact is going to be considering. Number 1, "Why is this person here?" Number 2, they may be thinking, "Obviously the person is going to be looking for a job and information." They know what you're there for. "What can they do for me personally if I hire them or refer them? Or what can they do for the organization?" And, number 3, "What kind of person are they?"

Everything you do and say is going to impact their decision to assist you. Be honest. Don't lie. Don't appear to be irresponsible. Don't be arrogant. Certainly, don't be late. Obey any instructions or rules that you agreed to as to time or place. Have enthusiasm. And above all, be professional.

Remember that the follow-up letter is critical to your getting hired. It should be in their hands 3 days or less after you've met. Remind the person of your interest in getting involved in the company and again thank them.

Other tips for the information interview are as follows: If possible, see if you can obtain a position description or career track. Obviously, the person will not bring it with them to the information interview. But maybe you can agree to have them mail it out to you.

Every description will contain various duties, which will be very helpful to you with regard to accountability. It may also indicate the reporting structure. Who will be your immediate supervisor? Who will be your boss's boss? It should also detail for you the scope and responsibilities or duties of that particular job. It will list for you the personal requirements, such as educational background or special experience or special licenses that are required. By having this information before going on an actual interview, it will provide you with a definite competitive edge.

Be aware that the person who agrees to meet is going to be looking for a number of qualities. These include: your intelligence level, motivation and enthusiasm, how you communicate, how you feel about responsibility, your initiative and ability to work on a team. And, obviously, by setting up an information interview, you have taken the initiative. The ability to demonstrate energy and enthusiasm is something that 20% of career seekers master, and 80% do not!

Are you a flexible candidate? Do you have versatility? Are you a social person? Do you have good interpersonal skills? How well do you know yourself? Are you competitive? Are you goal-directed? Do you have a specific direction in mind or a singleness of purpose, which is so critical to career success? How clearly do you communicate? These areas are what people will be looking for and evaluating you on.

If you ask a contact to make a recommendation on your behalf and they feel confident that you are qualified in these areas, they will, most likely, advocate for you. Keep these thoughts in mind during the course of all your information interviews.

Searching for your career calling is challenging but fun! It takes a lot of energy and time and requires constant enthusiasm. Perhaps the best way to minimize the amount of frustration that you feel and to avoid procrastination is to keep a strict schedule and outline your appointments. Keep backup files on all your contacts; this list is like gold!

Information Interview Record Retention Form

Employer	Address	Phone	Contact Name	Letter/ Phone	Interest Expressed Yes/No	Follow-up Phone Interview?	Offer?	Salary

Because an effective career search campaign is not limited to only one strategy, you may utilize multiple approaches. The most effective career search campaign will involve a combination of different strategies and techniques. These will vary from person to person, field to field, occupation to occupation.

Thus far, you've learned to start with a broad range of career interests and narrow them down until you have a workable number of prospective employers. Of those that you have targeted, narrow this number down even further and research a few of them and then begin networking and researching them.

Contact these individuals via letter, phone or Internet and then conduct an information interview. Try to avoid mass mailings or traditional methods at all times. Target the hidden job market versus the traditional published job market. Every once in a while, there will be a good opportunity on an Internet job board or help wanted section.

Follow up on all your correspondence via the sample thank you letters or telephone examples I have included for you. Keep accurate records about whom you've contacted, what time and dates and what your next action will be. Remember to monitor your progress. And if your strategy is not producing the exact result you desire, change your technique until your career dreams become your daily reality.

Maintaining Key Relationships

It is absolutely essential to maintain an organized, up to date list of your key contacts and dedicate at least 2 hours per week in editing, updating or eliminating critical information. Just because you find your calling does not mean you neglect your network. Your needs will change. My strategy for keeping my list current is done via my email system. I have an "Address Book" which I divide into the following 3 categories:

1. Personal contacts
2. Professional contacts
3. Aspirational contacts (people I want to meet whose information I am compiling)

Every other month, I send all my professional and aspirational contacts an email press release on my activities. This includes new customers, new hires, training programs or conferences I attended, books I have read, useful articles, etc. I also personally call the top 20% of my professional contacts each month whether they are customers, partner organizations, suppliers or potential employees. This is typically a courtesy call but often results in a win-win opportunity.

To illustrate the importance of this activity, let me share with you a story.

I know an executive within Job Corps, a federally funded program designed to help youth ages 16–24 achieve a better life through training, job placement and retention. He is a respected leader; his performance and track record are tremendous. I have seen him speak and he is a consummate professional who obviously invests in relationships and creates a culture of support and recognition.

One of my objectives was to position our training solutions (many of the same techniques you are reading about) within the Job Corps industry, which serves about 60,000 new youth each year. Having him as a customer and a strong advocate would be beneficial.

When I first met with him, I immediately could see why he was so successful. I asked him what he felt was the basis for his success in a very difficult industry where often inner city youth were located to rural campuses away from their friends and family and asked to learn a whole new set of beliefs. Among other strong leadership activities, he told me he required his staff to read certain books and conduct reports on these books at regular staff meetings. He was, in essence, requiring his staff to build their knowledge base and learn managerial techniques at the same time, not as an obligation, but rather as a necessity to being the best Job Corps facility possible.

As a voracious reader, my personal learning library in my study has over 300 books on wellness. I sent him an email regarding a few book choices that my staff had reported on and which I felt would be beneficial to his team.

We immediately hit it off! He respected the fact that I understood his agenda and made a contribution to his team BEFORE asking for him to become a customer and purchase our training and materials. Today, he is not only a customer (and friend), he has been instrumental in helping our company establish credibility within the Job Corps system, resulting in several lucrative initiatives, which will provide tremendous benefit to the nation's youth served through Job Corps. He gets a regular call and is definitely in my top 20%!

In closing, the era in which we live offers the easiest and best time in history to build your network and connect to influential mentors who can assist you in the attainment of your career calling. The digital age and advent of the Internet allows for unprecedented connectivity to millions around the world, at the push of a button or click of your mouse. We are all connected with access to each other in ways never before possible. We can gain intelligence and knowledge about each other's needs, wants and desires in an instant. Passion and purpose can be cultivated and shared with developed communities of users with common interests or hobbies.

Some experts are even calling this the 'Social Revolution." There is no excuse for working in isolation or attempting to do it all on your own. Just be careful not to allow technology to replace your relationship building skills. Success, while advanced by technology, will always boil down to the ability to connect with key people and share a common vision or purpose.

Quoting Keith Ferrazzi, who some refer to as the ultimate networker from his book, *Never Eat Alone,* "Living a connected life leads one to take a different view. Life is less a quest than a quilt. We find meaning, love, and prosperity through the process of stitching together our bold attempts to help others find their own way in their lives. The relationships we weave become an exquisite and endless pattern."

As you have learned, the most successful technique for obtaining a great career is not to mass mail resumes, search job boards on the internet, read want ads or attend career fairs. Although sometimes successful, these methods fail in comparison to building your network through the information interview process. And remember: Only 20% of all career seekers utilize this approach. Seek out, contact and strategize with proven individuals in your field of interest.

Be persistent and innovative in coordinating a meeting to gain information on the industry or occupation. Be enthusiastic and demonstrate your knowledge of the job, company or industry. Obtain their buy-in that you have the passion for the occupation and seek their support in guiding and coaching you to a source or contact, which has the authority to offer you a position leading to your career calling. Build your power base of connections and your career will explode! Soon, you will be the one receiving calls to educate potential candidates on how to obtain their career calling!

Everything you will achieve is the result of quality mentors who have inspired your ideas, patterns and behaviors. If you want better results, commit to finding better mentors, whether it be in person, through books, tapes or webcasts. Make the decision to acquire the knowledge, wisdom and experience of the top people in your chosen career field and I promise you, you will find that special place referred to as your calling. None of us can do it alone; we are all in this quest together.

CHAPTER 9

Self-Promotion: Marketing the 21st Century's Most Unique Product ... You!

KEY QUESTION: HOW DO I PROMOTE MYSELF?

In this chapter, you will learn:

KEY TOPICS

- The Definition of Branding and Why It Is Essential
- Strategies for Marketing Your Unique Talents
- Packaging Yourself for Immediate Career Success

KEY MESSAGES

- In the 21st century workplace, you must promote yourself as a unique brand.
- Your personal brand is a work in progress, so constantly reinvent yourself!
- The best brands combine differentiation and relevance.
- Skills, experience and education are bricks in a wall, while your brand and personality represent the mortar.
- The resume is our personal advertisement and indicates who you are, what you know, what you have done, what you would like to do, and what you can do for an employer in the future.
- A resume is usually read for less than 30 seconds by an employer.
- 3 sections to the cover letter: Introductory paragraph (attract attention), the body (highlight your skills and get attention), the closing paragraph (ask for the interview).
- A first impression is often formulated in the first 12–30 seconds; you will never get a 2nd chance to make a good first impression.
- Dress for the calling you want and not for your current role.
- Be accurate and factual. The job application may forever be included in your personnel file.
- Obtain and complete the job application prior to the actual interview date.

> *"Regardless of age, regardless of position, regardless of the business we happen to be in, all of us need to understand the importance of branding. We are CEOs of our own companies: Me Inc. To be in business today, our most important job is to be head marketer for the brand called YOU."*
>
> —Tom Peters

The Definition of Branding and Why It Is Essential

BRANDING IS OFTEN THOUGHT of as something reserved for products or services. When I think of branding, I think of how one person *differentiates* themselves from another in the *careering* process.

What is a brand? Simply stated, a brand is the establishment of a reputation for a specific set of criteria. It is what people associate to your name, product or service. The "association" (image, feeling or belief) that a potential customer or hiring authority has to your brand is important to your success. For example, a song may remind you of a special person or time in your life. Simply hearing the song can evoke emotion or put you in a particular frame of mind.

To simplify, there are 3 stages to brand development:

1. Identifying your target audience (in this case, the person or people who can hire you or move you closer to your career calling)
2. Positioning your brand (in this case ... you!)
3. Activating your consumer (in this case, the employer or partner who may desire to try you out before they become loyal to your "brand")

To attain your career calling and be truly successful in the 21st century workplace, you must promote yourself as a brand. You must stand for something and effectively present your skills and talents. You must fully understand your own psyche and motivations (your personal brand) if you have any hope of discovering your unique place in the world.

Large organizations spend billions on PR machines designed to promote and shape their image. Think of the numerous examples like *Perdue Chicken, Hair Club For Men* or even *Trump*. While there may be mixed opinions on "The Donald," one thing is for certain—the man is a master at branding and self-promotion. While there are numerous real estate moguls all over the planet, if I asked you to name one, you most likely would name Trump. Did you know that there are far wealthier people in his industry? But clearly he is the most identifiable and well known. Why? Because he makes such a strong commitment to promoting himself and his brand. He knows the secret: If you don't promote yourself, nobody else will!

In my seminars, I often share with the audience that I am a huge fan of animal shows, especially exotic animals like tigers, lions, and sharks. I recount how when sharks swim and hunt there are straggler fish (called remoras) hanging around, seemingly attaching themselves to the shark. Clearly, if the shark wanted to, it could easily devour the Remora with its huge jaws, but no matter how many Remoras it ate, the shark would still be hungry and expend useless energy in the process. The point is that it is worth the effort and risk to seek bigger rewards—in this case, larger prey like seals or whales.

My question to you is this: Are you connecting with Remoras and building an insignificant brand (riding the coat tails of others) or are you targeting a brand and network that can propel you to greatness?

> *"As long as you are going to think anyway, think big."*
> —Donald Trump

When I founded *Career* T.E.A.M. in 1996, now a recognized brand in and workforce development, nobody had a clue what the company stood for. The organization needed name recognition and a plan to establish our brand, quickly. I knew we needed to make a splash within our industry and to our potential customers. My plan focused on identifying and capturing our unique and compelling contributions (our product and services) and educating our potential customers in a fun and creative way. I wanted them to *feel* innovation and performance when they heard the name, *Career* T.E.A.M.

Without a marketing budget (most start-up companies do not have one), I quickly organized a plan for "introducing us to the industry." I began by obtaining a list of the names and addresses of the top 1,000 potential customers who could benefit from our services. I purchased 1,000 lottery tickets and created a clever mailing campaign, which read: "You have a better chance of winning the lottery than achieving your goals without *Career* T.E.A.M." I inserted a lottery ticket in each envelope and mailed them out. Direct mail experts report that a 1–2% return is typical; we had over 30% call us back and say how impressed they were with our unique approach. Some called to say they could not accept our ticket but still appreciated our innovation. To this day, we still have customers from this initial campaign.

You need to distinguish yourself and create a buzz about you as a candidate. Your industry needs to perceive you as an innovative expert who promotes their contributions. Subsequent branding campaigns attracted the attention of newspapers, radio and television outlets. To this day, I author and mail out a press release every month to highlight our achievements and progression, always with the theme of innovation in mind.

I am often asked my opinion by various media outlets; "No comment" is not in my vocabulary. If you own your own business or seek to promote a cause, try this PR technique to build your brand: "I am a devoted follower of your newsletter, magazine, television show, etc ... I have a great story for you that I am confident your readers, customers, viewers, etc., will be passionately interested in." Always seek to find the innovative slant, the unique and compelling aspect that will attract attention. Find the top 3 aspects of your pitch and create an emotional bond with your contact. Remember, you have no more than 10 seconds to communicate your message or risk losing interest.

> *"Tell me quick and tell me true or else, my friend, the heck with you!"*
>
> —Sign outside the *Career* T.E.A.M.
> Marketing Department

In 2003, my brother Erik and I decided to pursue a lifelong career dream and cohost a national sports radio show. We worked hard on our audio demo and had one shot with the worldwide leader in sports, ESPN, located in Bristol, Connecticut. I knew that merely sending a demo tape to ESPN and waiting for a response would not yield the result we wanted, for 2 reasons: 1, we had no experience; and 2, because they received hundreds of unsolicited demo tapes per week. We needed a unique and compelling angle!

After researching the proper contact person, I mailed a CD demo of our work with a clever flyer that read: The Aarons, the Waners, the Dimaggios and now the *SportsBrothers*! I cited famous brothers in sports and included Erik and I in their category. I then called the lead radio producer (every night at 6:30 PM for a week, hanging up on his voice mail every time so he would not think I was a stalker) until one day he picked up the phone himself and I immediately said, "Sports talk is sounding repetitious; how about 2 highly accomplished brothers to revolutionize the industry with their natural chemistry and sibling rivalry?"

He loved my provocative opening line, passion and energy and invited us in for an informal interview. His office was filled with demo tapes from all over the world! He chose Erik and me to do a week-long audition and ultimately assisted in our hiring as full time radio hosts broadcasting to over 100 radio markets every weekday afternoon! I since have returned to my true calling at *Career* T.E.A.M., but as of this writing, Erik is still there living his!

The Importance of Self-Branding

Let's play a game. I will name a company and you tell me the 1st word that comes to mind. Ready? Here goes!

- Volvo ... Most likely you thought, Safety
- Nike ... Just Do It!
- Federal Express ... Absolutely, Positively Overnight
- Subway ... Most likely you thought of "Eat Fresh," the line from their popular advertising campaign.
- Maytag ... Most likely you thought of their appliances as "reliable."
- Do you like frozen waffles? Me too ... Leggo my_____! (Eggo!)

As you can see, the process of branding or associating certain words, phrases or visual images works and leaves an indelible impression on us. If you want to drive a Mercedes Benz or wear a Rolex watch, most likely you thought of "status." Pepsi ingrained in our heads that if you drink their soda you will suddenly "be young and have fun" as a member of the "new generation." For years, cigarette makers convinced the American public that smoking was a sophisticated, cool thing to do by positioning their product with celebrities and characters that we aspired to be like. Today, we know that the health risks outweigh the association, but the point is that "perception became reality."

Let me ask you to consider one more branding exercise; are you ready? Here goes. Go the nearest mirror and take a good look. What is the 1st picture or word that immediately comes to mind when we consider YOU as a brand? Is it easily identifiable? Would 10 people who know you all select a different word or is there a common, consistent brand or theme you project? Try this: Ask 10 family, friends or co-workers to provide the 1st slogan or word grouping that comes to mind when they hear your name (a.k.a. your brand). Are the answers consistent or are your qualities or slogan undefined or mixed into what we call "brand soup," meaning there are no defining characteristics or redeeming features that stand out.

How about a slogan to describe your philosophy? What do you stand for? What makes you unique and compelling when it comes to you as a candidate for hire?

Exercise: Create Your Own Personal Slogan:

Understand the world (including perspective employers, employment agencies, venture capitalists or bankers if you seek funding to start your own venture) will see *you* as a brand, which is, in essence, how you choose to consciously or subconsciously position yourself to others. Everything about you: dress, labels, choice of watch, hairstyle, resume, cover letter, briefcase, car you drive, makeup, vocabulary, eye contact, education, experience, references, etc., speaks to your personal identification, your *BRAND*. Advertisers spend millions, sometimes billions, on creating the appropriate identity or brand for the rest of the world to see.

Unlike soap detergent or cola, your DNA is unique; there is nobody else who shares your looks, thoughts, dreams, aspirations and experiences, which all fit into the contribution you are uniquely qualified to make. Obtaining your calling requires you to formulate your brand and ensure that the essential connections who make decisions about your future can easily identify what makes you unique and compelling.

If you are reading this book, most likely you are not yet where you want to be and have never had the concept of branding yourself presented to you in such direct fashion. Keep in mind that branding, like your happiness or satisfaction, is subject to change and modification. As you progress, your brand will become more sophisticated. Your values and desires may change over time. Everyone wants more, right? Politicians want a higher office, movie stars want more publicity, and salaried employees want a higher wage. The desire for upward mobility is universal.

What is the quickest way to get there? By establishing yourself as a definitive brand in a light most favorable to your desired career outcome.

Branding also sets the tone for your internal identity. Here is an example:

In one organization I coached, the receptionist was unhappy with her title and brand as the "person who answers the phone and forwards calls to more important people." She felt the perception was demeaning and created the wrong impression of her substantial talents and contributions to her company. The solution? She changed her title from "Receptionist" to the "Director of First Impressions"!

The lesson: Branding can change mindset!

5 Keys to Creating Your Brand

"Two essential ingredients for creating and achieving your career calling are the genuine belief in your entitlement plus self-branding."

—Chris Kuselias

When I was asked by my staff to share my unique value proposition (UVP), what some call my personal brand message, I shared the following:

"Chris Kuselias can be described as the world's most dynamic career consultant. His track record of industry innovations and passion for changing lives is an inspiration to all."

To truly change or establish yourself as a brand, here are 5 keys:

1. Make certain you have a clear and distinct understanding of who you are and what you want. It is important that you get in touch with your authentic self and have a congruent identity, one that both you and the world see as the same. Be deserving of success and feel truly worthy of attaining happiness. Be secure in the fact that you deserve a better life and your hard work and dedication entitle you to it! Why not you? Although easier for some than others to internalize, feeling an entitlement to success and the benefits to attaining your calling is a prerequisite to progression.

2. Be clear about your objectives and the credentials required to get there. Most candidates are hard-working, ambitious and team players; these are not unique credentials but rather expected contributions. An interview today is very similar to an ad agency pitching a new campaign to a prospective client. Put the employer in the moment; get them to feel emotional about your rise to success and the path you have taken to achieve the credentials worthy enough to be seated for the interview. You are ready; you are uniquely qualified!

3. Understand that your personal brand is ever evolving. I look back at some of my hairstyles, clothing choices and attitudes and realize that I have continually reinvented myself, at times to follow fashion trends or fads and at other times based on my age and view of the world. Regardless, when creating a brand for yourself, it is important to never forget your core competency. My focus has and will always be on positively impacting and empowering others and making a worthwhile contribution. Consider

Madonna and her brand, which some would define as cutting edge sexuality. Beginning in 1984, she began entertaining the world with "Like A Virgin," had us all "Vogue-ing" and now has begun to sell children's books. It is tough to argue that through this incredible metamorphosis, Madonna has maintained her core edginess, even as a cool mom in her 50s.

4. Begin by designing and reserving your own website: www.insertyournamehere.com. Having a website will force you to consolidate your unique and compelling attributes and capture the essence of what you offer to the world. This way, when you meet people and they do a quick Google search, they will see that you are a serious player.

5. Attend a minimum of 1–3 conferences per year in your industry or field of choice. It will cost you a few bucks, but you will create opportunities that sitting at home or surfing the net cannot compete with.

A Final Word on Personal Branding

In my current company, we have established a simple 5 point evaluation for determining if a candidate is a good fit for our organization. What we are really asking is: Would hiring them enhance our current brand?

Here are the 5 areas we focus on. Notice that personality and likability are important traits.

1. Do they have personality and are they likable?
2. Do they possess the necessary skills?
3. Do they have a good track record?
4. Do they understand our business and the future of our industry?
5. Do they comply with our commitment to a diverse workforce?

When considering the concept of branding, you will want to avoid the pitfalls that some of our large national companies encountered. Did you know that the following brands or slogans made international news?

1. KFC's "Finger Licking Good" is "eat your fingers off" in Chinese.
2. The Chevy Nova failed in Latin America because it translates into "No go."
3. The Ford Pinto had similar failings because it means "small male appendage" in Portuguese.
4. Coca-Cola was originally translated to mean "bite the tadpole" in Chinese.

Let's be sure that your personal brand (or if you decide to start your own firm and select a clever name) does not translate into something like "My product is lousy" or "Get the worst job of your Life" in another language.

While the subject of branding is large enough in scope that entire books have been authored on the subject, for your purposes, know that the best brands combine 2 important properties:

1. Differentiation   ... which I define as the degree to which you as a brand stand out in the eyes of an employer

2. Relevance   ... which I define as the degree to which a hiring authority believes your skills meet *their* needs

Your role is to present your unique and compelling contributions to a prospective hiring authority or source of capital. Be aware of both "differentiation" and "relevance" to the position, company and industry.

Strive to become a brand on the rise, one that inspires interest, loyalty and opportunities for your own personal growth. Finding your calling begins with a keen understanding of who you are, what you want and what makes you unique and compelling. This defines your brand!

Strategies for Marketing Your Unique Talents

Where the Opportunities Are

Even when you determine your passion and purpose and focus on a specific career, there is no single strategy that works 100% of the time to obtain the position.

Here are the 5 most effective strategies for finding a career (suggested % of time spent when job searching):

1. Building your network of influential contacts who alert you to an opportunity—60%
2. Utilizing staffing agencies or recruiters—20%
3. Responding to published opportunities on line or in print—10%
4. Researching and attending job fairs for leads—5%
5. Cold calling employers or sending out print or electronic mass mailings—5%

Today, almost ⅔ of all new opportunities are created by small businesses, those with 20 or fewer employees.

How People Find Jobs

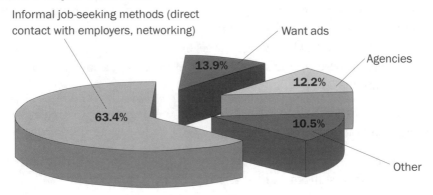

Informal job-seeking methods (direct contact with employers, networking)

Want ads

Agencies

13.9%

12.2%

63.4%

10.5%

Other

Where People Work

Hint: Many small businesses do not even have a Human Resources Department. Candidates should be targeting the highest ranking person, often the owner! Hint: Learn the techniques to target small businesses!

Why Traditional Methods Are Often Obsolete

> *"I just do not see where conformity makes a lot of sense."*
> —Chris Kuselias

Many people complete preschool, elementary school, and junior high school and, in many cases, graduate from high school. At that point in time, we have a decision to make. We either enter the working world or we decide to continue our education through vocational school (where we learn a specific trade or craft), community college, 4-year college and possibly graduate school. Incredibly, the skills of determining interest and then self-promotion (marketing oneself) are often not prioritized throughout the educational process.

The vast majority of career seekers feel unprepared to get any job, much less seek a career calling. They create a resume, post their accomplishments on multiple job boards and hope for the best. You may find yourself frustrated when you learn that less than 5% of all mass-mailed resume postings result in employment. The "hit" rate for internet-based job boards is just as dismal.

To improve my knowledge of how hiring authorities think and operate, I serve as a Director for one of the chapters of the Society for Human

Resources Management (SHRM). This experience has given me tremendous insight into the challenges faced by folks whose job it is to seek and procure talent. You may be surprised to hear that hiring authorities are frustrated with the lack of initiative and creativity exhibited by most candidates and constantly challenged by their company to become the "employer of choice."

> *"Do not play in someone else's universe ... define your own!"*
>
> —Chris Kuselias

Your 2 Options: The Hidden vs. the Published Market
To begin, there are 2 types of job markets. One is called the hidden job market and the other is called the published job market.

Let us begin with a review of the *published job market.* This source is comprised of Internet job boards, Want Ads, newspaper ads, and radio advertisements; these are media sources where employers will proactively seek employees. The published job market accounts for approximately 20% of all the jobs or one out of every 5 jobs.

The Internet
It is not an exaggeration to state that towards the end of the 20th century, the Internet essentially revolutionized career search. The Web continues to have a singular effect today on how candidates and recruiters interact and connect with each other. The advent of Internet based communications opened up information exchange beyond our wildest dreams and gave access to data once restricted to only those with specific, technical knowledge and special resources. Now with just a computer and a modem connected to the Internet, anyone and everyone has access, on a 24-hour-a-day, 7-day-a-week-basis, to virtually anything they may want or need to know.

Popular current job posting sites as of this writing (for more information, visit www.thecareerguarantee.com):

careerbuilder.com
craigslist.com
directemployers.com
employmentguide.com
hotjobs.com

monster.com

6figurejobs.com

Industry sites

There are also internet sites for virtually every career field, such as salesjobs.com, fashion-jobs.com, marketingjobs.com, etc. Please research your desired industry.

Employer sites

Finally, most employers today have their own websites, so make sure you visit them.

Web access today is a necessity—to send and receive information (via email) as well as to conduct research. The almost negligible cost of using the Internet is one of its most compelling features. Submitting your employment application materials electronically is a virtual click away.

Regardless of method, follow-up is the same: Obtain the name of a contact person and call or email a few days later to express your sincere interest and offer a concise statement indicating your qualifications. Find this contact name by visiting the company website and then playing detective with the receptionist to determine whom to contact.

The goal is to put your credentials in one screen's worth of content. This means including the essential data you need to attract attention at the beginning of your message. Your subject line has to motivate the recruiter to open your email; he or she may get hundreds of such messages daily so yours needs to stand out!

Be clever but still highly professional; present something that is intriguing and creative. Make sure that your email screen name is a variation of your name and not the handle you use for Internet dating or to correspond with cyber pals.

The main thing for you to remember when hunting online is that you follow recruiter directions, create a properly formatted resume, do your own follow-up and are relentless in pursuing your dream. The likelihood of you actually getting a job offer as a result of an Internet job board posting is still less than 5%, whereas we know for sure that about 80% of all new hires result from personal networking. So where do you think you should devote most of your time and efforts given these statistics? *Not* to the Internet job sites, but *to building personal relationships*. You can use the Internet for this purpose as well.

You can read headlines and scout out trade publications, follow the news, visit company websites, join and become familiar with the proceedings of various professional organizations and then contact the individuals mentioned. Tell them that you would like to speak with them FOR INFORMATIONAL PURPOSES (do not ever ask for a job). In this way, you will expand your scope and increase your chances to hear of career opportunities that are not advertised. Stay in touch by phone or email; send the person you met a relevant clipping or clever idea; connect them to someone else that they might be interested in knowing. You can even start an e-list group!

There is minimal success in an Internet career search. *The odds are against you,* because the competition is fierce and universal. Many ads are just a front for some commission-based recruiter's database. My opinion on Internet job search is it is a tool, but consider networking above all else as the most effective strategy to obtain your calling.

The Hidden Job Market

This is your key to entry into the hidden job market—to learn about new listings and changes within a company before the recruiters publicize their needs for new hires. You can gain a competitive edge, and be on the inside track so you can act on this information and suggest you are the person they need to meet even before they have advertised it!

80% of all the opportunities are found in the hidden job market. It takes inside information to hear about these jobs. The trick is to learn where those hidden jobs exist. I found that almost 80% of the people who are looking for a job will target those 20% published jobs, while only 20% or 2 out of every 10 people looking for a job are smart enough to penetrate the hidden job market and discover where the best leads exist.

If an employer has to advertise it signals they can't find a viable candidate from word of mouth or internal candidates and likely there is something questionable about that job.

The key is to gain inclusion in that 20% elite group, those who target the hidden job market. The reason why it's so challenging is because most people avoid critical reflection and don't know what really provides them with the greatest sense of happiness.

Hopefully you're mature enough to realize that no one position is perfect. No career will provide you with pleasure every single minute. You dictate your pleasure. B.C. Forbes stated, "Whether we find pleasure in our work or whether we find it a bore depends entirely upon our mental attitude towards it, not upon the task itself."

Think out of the Box

To outperform the competition, consider the following options:

1. Create an e-newsletter of your professional accomplishments and distribute to qualified hiring authorities or contacts. Include your career highlights, testimonials and the unique and compelling aspects (often called your unique selling proposition—USP). Keep it short and simple!

2. In the 21st century workplace, career seekers who desire to fulfill their passion and purpose have taken to using technology to create a competitive edge. In addition to the internet, e-newsletters and blogging, savvy career seekers are impressing hiring authorities with their own personal video calling card or CD bio. This format allows the employer to see and hear you on screen and further provides the ability to show you in action: presenting, selling, teaching, managing, etc. It is, in essence, a career movie starring you! This format is obviously more expensive and time consuming to produce, but for some, it has been the difference between success and failure.

5 Motivators to a Calling

Whether you use the hidden or published market, it is important to find out which values are most important to you as an individual. Get yourself motivated on the benefits of working. The top 5 requirements to motivate people to obtain their calling:

1. Economic security
2. Emotional security
3. Recognition
4. Self-expression
5. Self-respect

Question: Does your current position or target career provide your key values? If not, reconsider!

6 Helpful Hints

Measure your own personal *wants* and rank these motivators. Here are 6 helpful hints to assist you in finding your career calling. These steps include:

1. Target specific occupations, including the company, the location and advancement potential.
2. Determine the specific requirements for being hired.
3. Target specific contacts, which can assist you.
4. Target affiliated entities that can help you become more familiar with what an organization, such as trade journals, associations you can join, read the website and annual reports, etc.
5. Determine the hiring process. Who exactly is going to conduct the interviews? When are they going to be held? Where are they going to be held? What type of interview will it be?
6. Determine the key decision-maker. What individual or group will ultimately have the ability to say Yes or No regarding your employment? Is it an individual or a committee?

You must be like a detective and find these things out to win the game! Be willing to take risks and explore new possibilities. Meet new people. Those individuals who cultivate new contacts will be more successful than those who don't. Be unorthodox in your approach. Start at the top! Try letters of correspondence to the President or CEO. Here is one I received that worked!

> Dear Mr. Kuselias: I have read and acted on your strategies for finding my career calling. After spending time developing my professional credentials, I feel your organization may provide the ideal outlet for my unique contribution, ... assisting others with the courage and discipline needed to pursue their career dreams. If you are looking for a dedicated, focused and PASSIONATE associate to further your important vision, please have the appropriate member of your team contact me.

Be willing to volunteer your time to a particular industry in order to get your foot in the door. You may not be able to get paid for it, but in the long run it may pay off for you in the form of a position on the path to your true calling.

How a Vacancy Is Created

Companies fall into one of 4 hiring states:

1. *Necessity state:* Employer must hire; most competition for positions is here.
2. *Growth state:* Employer should hire or risk productivity loss.
3. *Luxury state:* No advertised jobs but good workers always wanted.
4. *Freeze state:* Not hiring; watch for turnaround and be first in line!

If they are actively hiring, an employment manager or business needs more staff. For the purposes of this example, let's call the employer Mr. Jones. Mr. Jones decides that he needs to add someone to the organization. So Mr. Jones develops a job description outlining the roles and responsibilities of the position. Then Mr. Jones seeks internal approval that "Yes, we do need to fill and create a job with these particular roles and responsibilities" and approval is obtained. The company will then put in their budget the money to pay the salary and benefits. Often, the Personnel Department has the responsibility for filling the position. The first place Personnel will look is within their own company, either by advertising in the company newspaper or by recruiting or broadcasting there is an opening. If no candidates emerge, Mr. Jones will then consider friends, family or other contacts. If this process doesn't produce a worthy candidate, Mr. Jones will then broaden the search outside the organization to include an executive search firm or employment agency. The search firm will utilize their own internal methodology, check their database, make cold calls to other related industries or companies and try to recruit a qualified person. The other tactic Mr. Jones can utilize is to advertise. Mr. Jones will discuss with the company Personnel Manager the particular characteristics sought. It is this discussion that serves as the basis for the Personnel Manager's advertising. Personnel will then write an advertisement, sometimes with the aid of an outside advertising agency.

The objective is to recruit a qualified candidate to fulfill the vacancy quickly, because, in the meantime, either the work is not getting done or the other co-workers are taking on more than their normal responsibilities. And that can lead to a morale problem. So, the pressure is not only on the Personnel Manager but also on Mr. Jones to fill the vacancy quickly.

I think it's important for you to understand how the process works because your focus will then be to convince them that you have the capabilities to solve that problem, to step in immediately and start assisting the organization and to take the burden off the other co-workers who have been doing double the work.

How the Personnel Department Works

Only about one to 5% of the people who contact the employer through the Personnel Department will gain an interview. Here is what happens to a response when it is received by the Personnel Department.

Mr. Jones wants no part of reviewing the hundreds and sometimes thousands of resumes that come in for the vacancy. They don't want the responsibility of screening resumes or trying to differentiate one from another. That's the job of Personnel. For example, a front line (for example, sales) manager who is responsible for generating significant television advertising revenues cannot afford to review a hundred resumes. That's the job of Personnel. That's what they get paid to do. Only in rare occasions will a front line manager bypass Personnel completely.

After reviewing candidates, the process is reduced to a workable number of applicants. Personnel will then begin screening process before recommending the top candidates for an interview with Mr. Jones; who will ultimately make the final decision.

It is important to realize that there are certain levels, most notably, Personnel, where they will look at your appearance, general attitude and qualifications and try to match up your accomplishments and credentials with the job description that Mr. Jones and the Personnel Manager collaborated on. And the candidate who best fulfills that description typically is offered the position.

If you are answering an advertisement in a trade journal or industry publication, it's important that you *mirror the wording of the advertisement.* Remember, the only purpose in responding to an advertisement is to get in the door, to get an interview. Your response, whether via telephone call or letter, should incorporate the wording that the advertisement cites. For example, if they're looking for a person who can type 50 words a minute, who is independent or has leadership capabilities and has 3 to 5 years of experience, it is important when you document you have fulfilled all of those specific requirements. The more, the better!

The Value of Career Coaches

Careering as an industry continues to expand. Finding an excellent coach local to you can be tricky. If you decide to pursue a career coach, be certain to ask the following:

1. What is your background?
2. What is your philosophy?
3. Where were you trained?
4. Do you practice client confidentiality?
5. Do you supply testimonials (ask for those similar to your situation)?
6. How do you measure success or failure?
7. What is the fee structure ($125 to 200 per hour is the standard range)?

Executive Recruiters and Search Firms

Executive recruiters or, as they're known to some people, headhunters can help you in a job search campaign. If you'd like to learn more, I recommend that you consult the *Directory of Executive Recruiters*, which lists all of the firms currently employed in that field.

I also recommend that if you're going to utilize a reputable search firm to help you obtain your career calling, you may want to put together a letter that sounds something like this.

Dear Mr. or Mrs. Recruiter,

Please review the enclosed resume with regards to any potential opportunities in the field (name the field that you have an interest in).

My expertise is ... (cite your value ... accounting, data entry, mergers & acquisitions, sales & marketing, systems integration, etc.)

My salary range is ... (be honest and respectful)

Attached is my resume for review and consideration ...

Always remember that it's important for you to present your desired salary level. If you're willing to relocate or you have any other special skills, also mention that in your cover letter. Close the letter and list your telephone number and address. It's important that your correspondence tells them if you're willing to relocate and your salary requirements.

Packaging Yourself for Immediate Career Success

R EMEMBER, DURING THE SELECTION process you are expected to convince or sell the interviewer on your ability. For this reason, I advise all candidates, regardless of profession, to become familiar with the basics and necessary elements of the selling process. Remember that the most important sale you will ever have to make is the job you do in selling yourself.

5 Keys to Selling Yourself

Simply put, career searching requires mastering sales techniques. If you do not obtain a basic understanding of how the exchange of goods and services for a fee works, you will restrict your ability to obtain your calling and most likely, lose significant leverage with regard to negotiating your salary and benefits.

To keep this simple, understand that your primary objective is not to convince, fool or impress the other party but rather, to transfer your passion and energy for the industry, field or occupation to the hiring authority. Selling is the process of transferring a common emotion (described as a benefit) from seller to buyer. This means you seek to use your words, appearance and documentation (resume, testimonials, application, etc.) to inspire the hiring authority that you are a quality candidate and that given the opportunity, this passion will translate into exceptional performance.

There are 5 sales steps associated with finding a qualified hiring authority. It is important to master each step if you seek to be your most successful self.

Remember, you represent the passionate (solution) to the employer's problem!

Step 1. Prospect Contact and meet new employers or hiring authorities

Step 2. Develop a contact network Use the Internet, telephone, letters, set up informal meetings and interviews to expand your mentors

Step 3. Qualify the employer Determine if the contact is an individual who can assist you, refer you or hire you directly

Step 4. Overcome objections/obstacles Be prepared to neutralize any concerns about your experience, education, skills or credentials

Step 5. Close Do not forget to ask for the position! If you believe the role fits within your career calling plan, aggressively pursue it. It was meant for you!

Your Essential Marketing Materials: Resume Time!

It is now time to itemize your marketing materials. While certain aspects of careering have changed dramatically (for example, Internet job boards, personality type assessments, etc.) certain aspects remain surprisingly similar. Much like a brochure or company website, the resume and cover letter represent your calling card; that is, how you create a first impression in print.

While in the past, the postal service served as the primary means of distribution (remember the dreaded mass mailed resume!), today career seekers use email and employer based websites to distribute their credentials. I am not a fan of mass-producing your credentials (either via print or internet) and strongly advise you to adopt a more targeted campaign aimed at specific employers or contacts.

One thing is clear: The creation of the resume serves the valuable purpose of inventorying your unique and compelling contributions. It is a summary of your brand and acts as your one page marketing campaign, a tradition still honored and recognized in the 21st century workplace.

One Candidate . . . One Page . . . One Shot!

> *Resumes don't get candidates hired . . . mainly they serve to screen people out!*

Now that you have determined your brand, interests, targeted your job aptitudes, researched opportunities in your area of interest, studied different markets or industries in terms of who is hiring and who is not, narrowed down specific employers, your next step is to inventory your credentials, so that you can talk intelligently about your past accomplishments and potential worth.

The creation of a resume is a task that most people dread, because it itemizes the sum total of your professional career in one document, typically on a single page! The end result produces 2 responses:

1. You get really excited and proud of your accomplishments when you see your finished resume.
2. Seeing your credentials reinforces the fact that you have not done your best work, have spent time in unfulfilling occupations and wasted precious time.

Let me remind you that it is not where you start but how you finish and regardless of how you initially feel about your professional summary to date, there is always the opportunity to improve yourself and build credentials that will provide a strong sense of accomplishment.

Fast Fact

Monster.com receives 1.6 million visitors a day to its website from job seekers.

So what is a resume? A resume is really a digest of your qualifications that inform the employer of 5 things:

1. Who you are
2. What you know
3. What you have done
4. What you would like to do
5. How you can benefit the employer

Think of yourself as an individual with unique qualifications. Portray yourself as a candidate who has a strong sense of self and stands above the competition.

Resumes should be brief and to the point, no more than 1 to 2 pages. Unless you have a specific long-term history, probably one page will suffice. Remember that you will never get the 2nd chance to make a good impression unless the interviewer interest in your resume. So, stand out.

If you take advantage of the hidden job market and develop a career contact network, one effective strategy is to have a friend of the interviewer or influential person write a personal note on your resume praising your abilities. The core of your resume is a list of facts, activities and experiences that summarize your accomplishments to this point in your life.

The very 1st step in putting together your resume involves making a complete list of all your achievements. After you have developed a list—and don't exclude anything from either your academic, job experience or personal life—edit those items that do not pertain to the targeted position. If it does not help your cause, leave it out!

A hiring authority is looking for 2 things:

1. Actual facts that indicate your qualifications: your education background, your employment history, social activities
2. Patterns reflecting different aspects of your character or skills: leadership ability, initiative, determination and actions of that nature

Highlight your most essential qualifications. For example, if the position requires strong leadership, tailor your resume to demonstrate those instances where you have been a leader.

From the information obtained in an information interview, learn what credentials top people in that organization exhibit on a consistent basis. Remember that question from the information interview? Once you know that, you can tailor your resume to the area most important to the employer.

An Overview of the Resume

Definition   By definition, the resume is the primary written vehicle of a productive and successful search.

You must develop your ultimate career objective in language that can be effectively communicated. It also requires you to assess your previous training, experience, skills, abilities, and other characteristics that qualify you for the position. In short, the resume must tell the employer what position you seek and what you have to offer.

Style   There are 3 types of resumes from which you can choose: the chronological, the functional, and the targeted. Hint: Let experienced people review your resume to make sure that it contains your best attributes. Focus on the most important accomplishments and be flawless in resume appearance.

What Employers Seek

1. The ability to become part of a team and have a great attitude
2. The ability to be flexible, versatile and to multi task
3. The ability to challenge previous ways of thinking and bring new, fresh ideas to the table

Regardless of your background, show your ability to take risks, set high standards, and behave professionally. *One top human resource director stated that when evaluating resumes, the number one requirement is a progression from jobs of lesser responsibility to jobs of greater responsibility, especially within the same organization.*

How to Begin

Through our previous exercises in critical reflection and goal setting, you should have a specific career target in mind and be able to identify an industry or employers of interest.

At this point, your resume should be a brainstorming effort. Start your momentum by writing down your name, address and phone number. Then jog your memory by identifying your objectives. Immediate goals may be one to 3 years; long-range goals may be 3 to 5 years or longer. List your previous professional experience, including any training you've had beneficial to the position sought. Include the names of companies and the specific responsibilities. List your specific talents and skills.

Update Your Resume on a Regular Basis

Remember, your resume is apt to change as your accomplishments, experiences, and knowledge level change. Update your resume on a regular basis and make sure that it is as current as possible.

Useful Resume Tips

Before being offered employment, you must convince the employer of your talents in 3 areas: yourself and your personality; your abilities and credentials; your potential, that is, your future worth to the company. Emphasize your strengths, downplay your weaknesses, and demonstrate your flexibility and versatility. Understand the employer's competition and their culture. Listen carefully, question intelligently, be aware and sensitive to the employers needs, and show persuasiveness. Your resume should introduce you as a creative problem solver, a person who is organized, persistent, and knows how to follow through.

> A resume should answer who you are, what you know, what you have done, what you would like to do, and what you can do for the employer.

Utilize numbers in your resume wherever possible. Quantify your achievements. For example, "Duties included coordination of entire sales team of 15 individuals with a budget responsibility of $10.2 million dollars." Wow! Those sentences seem to jump off the page at you. Consider … "Won the quarterly award from a total pool of 200 competitors" or "was responsible

"This resume deserves an award … for fiction!"

for opening 13 new client advertisers." Every role has a quantifiable aspect to it. How many boxes did you lift, millions did you manage, software programs did you install, how many words per minute do you type? Remember, the competition is successfully using this strategy ... you should as well!

Compile a list of image-building words even before you know how you're going to incorporate them. Don't be too flamboyant or flashy. Don't try to oversell or glorify a low-level job. Be honest and use your head. But don't be too timid or modest.

Recommended Phrases for Your Career Objective Section

> Achieved ...
> Attained ...
> Demonstrated ...
> Introduced ...
> Launched ...
> Proven performer in ...
> Significant experience in ...

Recommended Power Words to Command Respect

> Designed ...
> Eliminated ...
> Increased ...
> Improved ...
> Prevented ...
> Reduced ...

As I mentioned, be concise. Provide the interviewer only the bare materials or information to make them want to meet the person behind the resume. Entice them!

Basic Resume Format

1. Identification
   Name, address, telephone, email
2. Career objective
   Cite the job title you seek and skills you will use to perform
3. Education
   School and degree, year
   Emphasis and studies (List relevant courses)
   Grade Point Average (If it helps your cause)

4. Employment history
5. Achievements and honors (extra-curricular activities)
   Examples: dean's list, awards, special recognition, honor societies, clubs.
6. Personal interests (optional)
   Examples: traveling, reading, fitness, investment speculation
7. References (available upon request)

Notes

1. The 1st section is the *identification*. The identification is your name, your permanent and temporary addresses and phone numbers, including area codes, addresses, etc.

2. The 2nd category is called the *career objective*. Here you want to be specific. This may be the first place an employer looks. They want to know what your goals are. Avoid generic job objectives like "I would like to get into management" or "find a challenging position." Once you have decided on a particular occupation and employer, incorporate phraseology that corresponds with that occupation.

3. You can title this 3rd section Education or Educational History. List the name of the high school, trade school or college, grad school, the location, your degree or degrees, and a major or a minor, if applicable. Indicate areas of specialization or extensive course work, internships, or training courses, especially if it relates directly to the position for which you are applying. Seminars and specialty training that relate to the position sought should also be included.

> "Education is a progressive discovery of our own ignorance."
>
> —Will Durant

4. The 4th section of the resume is *employment history*. Indicate the name and location of the organizations that you worked for, the dates of your employment and the position, title and responsibilities. It is much better to spend more time on 1 or 2 positions that relate specifically to the job that you're applying for than to put down 5 or 6 non- related positions. Too many positions indicate a lack of focus or inability to maintain a job.

5. *Achievements* or *awards*

6. *Personal interests* is an optional section

7. The last section is the *references*. Many indicate they will are "available upon request." At this point, you won't actually need written references on your resume. Actively solicit former employers, teachers or colleagues as references. Depending upon the company, an employer may ask you to provide references in a 1ˢᵗ interview, while others will wait until the final hiring stages. Never include an individual as a reference without first obtaining permission.

Sample Resume

Please note that this is only an example. Your resume should be tailored to a specific industry and title. Try to keep your resume to 1 page!

I.M. Qualified
1234 Fifth Avenue
Anywhere   ST   01234
(205) 555-1111

CAREER OBJECTIVE: To obtain a challenging sales position in the medical field utilizing my education and experience.

EDUCATION: Whatsamatter College, Mayberry, California

- Bachelor of Science
- Double Major: Marketing and Computer Science
- Grade Point Average: 3.5, Dean's List Student
- Coursework Includes: Accounting, Public Speaking, Statistics, Money and Banking, Computer Finance

EXPERIENCE
(20xx–Present) Order Process—Internship Program
The Merrit Company, San Diego, California

- Responsible for entering new orders and correcting inquiries
- Achieved 100% accuracy levels for annual and random reviews
- Recipient of "Top Intern" award given for outstanding performance

(20xx–20xx)   Sales Representative
- The Athletic Store, Yurrika, Massachusetts
- Responsible for cash register entry and product shelving
- Utilized customer service skills to generate sales of athletic equipment to independent customers and distributors.

(20xx–20xx)   Teaching Assistant, English Department
Whatsamatter College, Mayberry, California

- Reviewed and evaluated homework for 20 freshman and sophomores
- Conducted and organized 30-minute study session

HONORS AND ACTIVITIES

Class Committee, Student Council; organized and planned class activities and fund raisers, 20xx

- Admission Office Tour Guide, Whatsamatter College, 20xx
- Senior Class Gift Committee Chairman, 20xx
- Financed 80% of education
- Varsity Soccer, 20xx

PERSONAL INTERESTS: Travel, attending learning seminars, reading, fitness

REFERENCES: Available upon request

As mentioned, there are 3 basic resume formats:

1. The 1st is called the *chronological* resume. The chronological format spells out job history from the most recent job backwards, with the most recent job having the most space and getting the most attention. Advantages of the chronological resume are it's easy to follow, it emphasizes continuity and career growth and highlights names of employers you've worked for. The disadvantages to this type of resume are if you have breaks in your work history, when you are changing your career direction or when an individual changes jobs quickly and frequently.

2. The 2nd type of resume is the *functional* resume. The functional resume is designed to emphasize your qualifications and not previous employers. This type of resume is useful for a person who has related experience in the position sought. The advantages to using the functional resume are that it gives considerable flexibility in your emphasis. It emphasizes skill areas that are marketable, in demand and relevant. It masks employment breaks or prior positions irrelevant to the position currently sought. The disadvantages to the functional resume are that it does not relate accomplishments to the specific employer. Many employers consider a candidate's prior affiliation when judging their accomplishments. Also, the same accomplishments may seem more

impressive if gained with an established company rather than a lesser-known company.

3. The 3rd resume format is the *targeted* format. The targeted resume format is designed with a specific job title in mind. It is not the type that you send out in an email, blast or mass mailing. It's tailored to that particular employer, so the actual name of the company may be referenced in the resume. You can use industry titles or buzzwords specific to that industry in this type of resume. The disadvantages to the targeted resume is that it's costly, when individually produced. It's very time-consuming if you are targeting more than one employer in a specific field and you need to weave in the names of specific people directly on the resume. It allows for less flexibility. However, the targeted resume can be the most productive in terms of specificity to a particular employer. In today's competitive job markets, I prefer the targeted resume. It is specific, not generic.

Resume Dos and Don'ts

Dos	Don'ts
Do use 1 to 2 page maximum unless special requirements	Don't include inaccurate information
Do verify accuracy of all information	Don't include any irrelevant information
Do use the "buzz words" from your field	Don't be too wordy (be concise)
Do select quality paper and print	Don't have any typos or spelling errors
Do select one of the 3 formats	Don't list specific salary requirements
Do be specific, not generic	Don't list many personal hobbies
Do start each sentence with action words such as:	Don't list references on your resume
Organized	
Assisted	
Developed	
Operated	
Programmed	
Designed	
Planned	
Analyzed	
Coordinated	

Resume Check List

Introduction	Appearance
Name, address, phone number(s), email_____	Margins correctly spaced
Career Objective	Easily readable
Prior Experience	Underlining and capitals
Employer name	Correct choice of style
Employer location	*Double-check*
Responsibilities	Eliminate typos
Achievements (numeric)	Check spelling
Job description	Verify punctuation
Job title	*Format*
Education	Consistent and accurate
Name of Institution	Logically organized
Degree(s)	Correctly spaced
Miscellaneous	*Miscellaneous*
Associations and memberships	Avoid abbreviations if possible
Awards and honors	Cite specific details and accomplishments
	Include updates
	Use short sentences with action verbs

The Cover Letter

The purpose of the cover letter is to introduce you to the employer, to spark an interest in your potential value to the employer and, ultimately, to get an interview. The cover letter should identify the specific position or type of position sought and should also illustrate your familiarity with the skills and training needed for effective performance. The cover letter should motivate the reader to want to meet you in person! The cover letter should be typed in standard business format on 8½-by-11 white bond paper and should include your name, address and date. It should not contain any spelling errors or typing errors and should be neat and grammatically correct. In all cases, it is important that your cover letter be addressed to a specific contact ("Dear Sir or Madam" is impersonal).

There are 3 sections to a cover letter:

1. *Introduction:* The opening paragraph should immediately attract attention. This can be done by using the name of a person who either referred you, referring to a specific job listing or by identifying a unique talking point about the particular organization.

For example, you may decide to get attention by referencing an article or fact a trade publication.

2. The *body* of the letter should point out your value and answer the employer's number one question, "Why should I hire you?" Use language that the employer is familiar with from their website, brochures, manuals, job descriptions and your own personal work experiences. Highlight and focus on the most relevant qualifications listed in your resume.

3. The *closing paragraph* is the action stage. Take the initiative and suggest arrangements for a specific interview time and date. You may want to suggest 2 or 3 dates. Your suggested meet date should never be more than 10 business days from the date of your letter. Close by thanking the employer for considering your letter and resume. You may want to type in the word "Enclosure" in the lower left-hand corner to indicate that your resume is included.

The cover letter should always be sent to the individual who has the authority to hire you or influence the decision. It should always be addressed to the person by first and last name. In your cover letter, tell your employer about yourself, who you are, what you have done, what job you would like, what you have to offer, discuss your potential and why you want to work for that organization.

Get The Employer's Attention

1. Keep it to one page.
2. Demonstrate your interest in a specific employer.
3. Demonstrate your interest in a particular position.
4. Reference any individuals who recommended the contact (get approval first).
5. Address it to the specific person and include their title.

Stimulate the Employer's Interest

1. Relate your abilities to the employer's requirements.
2. Emphasize your talents, skills and interest.
3. Describe why the employer should have an interest in you.
4. Emphasize your strengths and downplay your weaknesses.
5. Elaborate on the relevant qualifications in your resume.

Ask for an Interview!

1. Always ask for the interview.
2. Indicate that an interview will provide a better picture of your abilities.
3. Provide your availability (date, times).
4. Restate that you will contact the employer for an appointment.
5. Include your telephone number, address, and email address.

Hint: The better you do your homework on companies, the easier this will be.

Sample Cover Letter

Date

Mr. Ray Green
Vice President
XYZ Enterprises, Incorporated
16 Glen Road
City   ST   01234

Dear Mr. Green:

I am writing to introduce myself and to request your consideration for the position of _____. Enclosed, please find a copy of my resume.

Having studied the development of employers in your field, I believe I can help your organization meet its goals. My education and experience make me a positive contributor to your team.

If convenient, I would appreciate a personal appointment to present my qualifications and review my resume. I am available on [*date*] at [*time*] and on [*date*] at [*time*] and can be reached at [*telephone number*].

Sincerely,

Signature

Your Name

Address
City, State, Zip

Email

Enclosure or attachment if emailed

A Humorous Example

Just because the world has become more results focused and every individual is now seemingly forced to cost justify their own existence each year, doesn't mean we should lose touch with decency, courtesy and respect for others. Instead of working harder, many people have simply become numb to the paradigm shift where to compete, one must exert incredible energies just to keep up.

To illustrate the point of a career community gone bad, I found this sample cover letter amusing—I hope you agree!

Dear Employer:

Please consider me for any open position you have, today or at any time in the future. It is my career objective to find any good job with benefits and security. As for my approach, I pride myself on reading the want ads and sending out mass mailed resumes to numerous job boards. I cannot understand why these small-minded employers cannot spot my superior abilities from my basic, boring resume, which I always spel chek and personalize with, "To Whom It May Concern." Perhaps, you will be different.

As far as my credentials, I have spent an entire life in jobs that I didn't like and that I was generally overqualified for. This was primarily because I lacked discipline, wasn't really motivated and didn't push myself. You will be pleased to know that I have absolutely no plans to expand my expertise or focus in any one industry, as I am not sure what field I will find myself in next. As for continuing my education, not to worry: I have no plans to interfere with my nightly reality TV schedule.

As for experience, I have held several jobs, mostly because I took what was available, as I never spent the time to analyze what my true interests were or what kind of career was best for me. Because I still have no clue as to what my purpose or passion is, I am seeking a way to pay my bills and be able to say to my family and friends that I am working. While waiting to be laid off from your organization, maybe someone will miraculously discover my true hidden talents and put me on course to my ultimate destiny, whatever that may be. My friends, who all hate their jobs, told me that in this economy, its probably better to just stay in a job I despise and wait for someday to become one of the days of the week.

As for my prior performance, I was generally irresponsible and looked to cut corners whenever possible. I was respectful to my supervisors, who for the most part, were unappreciative of my hidden talents and often stole my brilliant ideas. I particularly enjoyed badmouthing the company and blaming the system or economy for my lack of success. For example, at my last job, I had a sign on my cubicle that read, "The only difference between this place and the Titanic was that they had a band." TGIF; Same *^#*@, Different Day; Another Day Another Dollar; and Life Sucks & Then You Die are my personal mottos.

With regard to my hobbies and extra-curricular activities, I enjoy my leisure time and escape my boring, mundane life by reading fiction or watching television. I would do more, but as a result of my lousy diet and lack of a regular exercise program, I barely have enough energy to make it through the day!

I am confident you can use a person with my ability—I am available to start immediately (or at least following my vacation). I promise you my most mediocre self!

Sincerely,

Joe or Jane Job Seeker

Dressing for Success

Tip!

When going to an interview, you may want to dress similar to the person who is hiring you because every company or organization or employer has a culture, whether it is conservative or flashy. If you have the opportunity to conduct an information interview prior to an actual interview, get the chance to walk into the building, go into their cafeteria, or just stand outside and see how people dress when they come out of work, do so. This investment in preparation will provide a competitive edge over the competition interviewing for the same position.

First impressions are extremely important. The interviewer or employer is going to see you before you have had an opportunity to open your mouth and discuss your qualifications. Many studies show that an opinion is formulated about candidates in the first 12 to 30 seconds. And in the first 12 or 30 seconds of a meeting, what happens? You walk in, maybe you shake hands, sit down. You probably haven't even had a chance to say Hello or "What a nice office you have here."

One of my material dreams when I was growing up was to drive a Jaguar. For some reason, I always admired the shape of the car, the sleek lines, the way it seemed to glide down the street and the fine wood inside the car. I loved everything about it. And I'd go to Jaguar dealerships in my old, clunky car with the bumper hanging off and it was always dirty because I couldn't afford the car wash. Kids would write "wash me" or obscene words on my car. The car was so run down I had a plastic milk crate stashed behind the driver's seat for support because the seat was broken and I didn't have the money to repair it. Sometimes when I hit bumps the milk crate would shift and I would fall completely backwards as the seat reclined!

I would occasionally drive up to this one particular Jaguar dealership in town, right up in front of the big glass showroom. The sophisticated sales-people would be sitting at their desks wouldn't even bother to greet me because they could tell I did not fit the profile of an individual who was interested in purchasing a Jaguar. I didn't look the part. I was just a dreamer, a tire-kicker.

Nonetheless, I would wander through the parking lot and dream about the car I'd pick out some day. I would picture myself selecting the color, the options and signing the contract and pulling out of the dealership knowing it was mine. Visualization is a powerful tool! And I vividly remember how upset and embarrassed I was to pull up in that old, clunky car and the fact that no one would bother to greet me. I would see other people pull up to the same dealership in other, flashier, expensive vehicles and immediately they would be greeted warmly and professionally. I vowed to buy my dream car someday! I even kept a picture in my wallet and in my success journal (a formal, leather bound scrap book which was a collection of photos of those things, accomplishments or possessions I craved).

Through these strategies, I had found my purpose, destination, taken action and achieved my career calling and I had been well compensated for my efforts. I remember going back to that same dealership one day for service. And as I pulled up in my Jaguar (not purchased from that dealership), the reaction was amazing. What a change! What a difference! When I pulled into their establishment, the salesmen seemed to jump to attention like there was an officer on deck! They greeted me warmly, offered me coffee, fresh bagels, brochures, a seat in their expensive lobby. "Could I help you?" They asked me my name, where I was from. I was the most important person on the world. And I chuckled at the importance of appearance and how much more attention I got as a result of pulling up in my new vehicle as opposed to my old former clunker.

What happened? I was basically the same person inside. But their perception of me had changed. Appearance and attitude matter! Here are 3 rules:

Rule #1   You will never get a 2nd chance to make a good 1st impression. Remember, the first impressions are lasting impressions.

- Target the type and style of dress your potential employer utilizes.
- Dress for the job you want and not for the job you currently have or recently had.

Rule #2   Hiring Authorities state that a first impression is often formulated in the first 12–30 seconds of an interview!

- Prior to the actual interview, practice feeling comfortable with your chosen interview attire by going out to dinner or wearing it in a public setting.
- Don't be stiff or uncomfortable or it will negatively impact your chances of getting hired.

Rule #3   If it comes down to spending a little less or a little more to look your best, spend the extra money; it will be worth it in the long run!

A Basic Outline

Tips
Dress in your best, most coordinated, and conservative attire.

1. Your outfit, suit or dress, should be a dark color, clean and pressed.
2. Be neat, cleaned, trimmed, and well groomed.
3. Jewelry, scents, and makeup should be on the conservative side.
4. Practice wearing new outfits before the actual interview.
5. Avoid fashion fads.
6. Dress for work, not to go out on the town.
7. Do not smoke for at least an hour before an interview, and NEVER smoke in your car on the way to the interview.

Remember ...
Inspect yourself before you leave for the interview and attend each session with a smile and enthusiasm.

1. Your first impressions are critical (opinions are formed in 12–30 seconds).
2. The interviewer will see you before you have an opportunity to discuss you qualifications. Look sharp.
3. Remember, if your appearance is not appreciated, you <u>will not</u> get the position!
4. Dress for the job you want, not the job you have or have had.
5. Look professional even as you park your car for the interview; you never know whose office you are parked in front of.

If you look good, you will feel good!

The Essential Wardrobe

Often, questions are raised as to how to dress for the job search process and, more specifically, what to wear to impress a potential employer. Of course, every person has individual style and may be sensitive to advice concerning professional attire or even what constitutes professional. However, be advised that impressions are often formulated by decision makers in the first 30 seconds of any meeting or interview. Do not take any chances! If you are unsure, the best suggestion is to visit the employer's location before your interview, observe what current employees are wearing and mirror their actions. Ideally, find out from an information interview.

See www.thecareerguarantee.com for more info and tips.

Suggestions for men

> Have 1 suit in a dark tone but not black (try to avoid polyester)
> Have 1 jacket in a dark tone (try to avoid the color black and polyester)
> Have at least 3 shirts (long sleeve): white, light blue, or a conservative stripe
> Have at least 2 ties: 1 multi-colored, 1 striped (try to avoid polyester)
> Have 1 pair of polished shoes, black is recommended, no scuff marks
>
> Note: If your interviewer does not require you to wear a shirt, tie, jacket or suit, it is still important to look neat clean and professional. Avoid wrinkled clothing!

Suggestions for women

> Have a jacket or blazer in preferably a dark color such as navy, black or gray
> Have 1 jacket or blazer (medium tones) such as deep tan, brownish or plaid
> Have 2 skirts (solid): black, small printed and beige tone
> Have 2 blouses: off white, floral and navy
> Have 2 pairs of shoes, preferably black pumps, brownish or beige
> Have 1 scarf (multi-colors)
> Have several pairs of hosiery in flesh tones or off black. Bring an extra pair with you in case of a run
>
> Note: If you have to substitute with a dress, consider wearing a jacket!

The Employment Application

So why do you have to fill out a job application? For starters, when you are accepted for a position, your employment application will remain in your personnel file forever. Employers keep records on everything that you do, starting with your acceptance into their organization, followed by your promotion scale, your medical history, your salary increases and any other important bits of information.

It is important that you be accurate and factual. There are horror stories about people who have included erroneous or untrue information. For example, when being considered for a promotion the employer found a falsified date or credential (somebody said they went to college and really didn't). Please, be honest because you never know when lies or untruths can come back to haunt you.

Hiring authorities place a great deal of importance on the job application. And some of them, quite frankly, have taken the time as part of their job description to design it. And they take great pride in the document. Perhaps they spent money with an advertising agency to help them formulate it and typeset it. So, take the time to do it correctly.

Job applications are more important to those of you who are just starting out in a career, returning to the work force, coming out of college or just starting in a career because you really don't have a track record or list of references that an employer can turn to for questioning or assistance on making a decision. So, oftentimes, an individual will be hired solely on the basis of their employment application and credentials, especially in entry-level or blue-collar type jobs.

4 Sections of the Employment Application

1. Number 1 is *personal data*. Employers will ask you for your name, how to get in touch with you, your address, phone number and if you're a citizen of the United States.
2. Secondly, an employer will solicit *employment information*—what you desire from the prospective employer. They may question ask you what position you seek, how soon you can start, if there is a shift choice, if you're interested in working part-time or full-time. They may also ask about you salary. If you're unclear on a salary level, put the initials TBD, which stands for "to be determined."
3. The next section is the *education and training* section. Here an employer will seek your track record from grammar school to

high school to college education or post-college education, to any business, correspondence or trade schools that you have attended. They may seek special achievements, whether it is academic, special talents, skills, tools or projects. If the position is of a technical nature, this information becomes all the more important.

4. The 4th section is *employment history*, which will require you to list current or previous employers and contact information. Applications can get quite specific in asking your previous supervisor's name and title if they seek a reference. They may even request your salary, when you started, were you promoted, why you left, what responsibilities you held. And they may ask you for 3 or 4 previous employers as references.

List those employers that you feel strongly or positively about and that are applicable to the position sought. Be accurate and factual. The final portion of the application will ask you to sign your name and confirm that all statements or claims made in the application or resume are truthful and complete. You may be asked to approve authorization to conduct any investigation in respect to examining your previous criminal or police record, if that's applicable, as well as any references that you may have cited.

Please review the application carefully, it may list specific contractual arrangements regarding employment benefits, additional compensation or at-will status.

Employer websites are getting more sophisticated every day. The use of screening tools, key word searches and other technology based pre-employment assessments are evolving as of this writing. Some of these tools are effective but my advice is to get to a decision maker and state your reasons for wanting to work with them. The employment application is a very important document and you should take proper care and attention and detail when filling it out.

There are 3 basic rules to consider when filling out an application for your ideal career.

1. Make sure you are in a location that allows you to have the proper frame of mind to fill out the application; be clear of any nervous thoughts, people looking over your shoulder and ensure you're in a comfortable writing position.
2. Make the employment application legible and pleasing to the reader. Employers like something they can understand and don't have to struggle to read.

3. Be accurate and factual. Include specific experience, credentials and qualifications and make them up-to-date.

10 Job Application Tips

1. Never underestimate the importance of the job application
2. Take the time to properly complete each job application you fill out
3. Take more than one copy in the event of a mistake.
4. Be legible and neat (type if possible)
5. Be accurate and factual (this form will forever be included in your personnel file)
6. If possible, obtain a copy of the job application prior to the actual interview date. Complete the application at your leisure and without the pressure of filling it out in an employer's lobby.
7. If possible, make a copy of the job application for your own records.
8. Always remember to sign your name!
9. Avoid citing specific salary demands. TBD (to be determined) or simply write "negotiable."
10. Your application is a reflection of you; demonstrate quality and commitment.

Let us now turn our attention to the interview ... your chance to shine!

CHAPTER 10

Lights, Camera, Action!
Mastering the Interview Process

KEY QUESTION: HOW DO I PRESENT MYSELF?

In this chapter, you will learn:

KEY TOPICS

- Successful Interviewing Strategies
- 5 Stages of the Interview Process
- How to Ask and Answer Difficult Interview Questions
- Assessing Your Performance: Post-Interview Activities

KEY MESSAGES

- Interviewing is an essential step to obtaining your career calling; it must be mastered!
- The first 30 seconds are the key to a successful interview.
- Although candidates often get nervous, the fact is that most interviews are very predictable and have an established format (greeting/small talk, 5–10 questions for you, 2–3 questions for the interviewer, ask for the position, thank the interviewer).
- Visualize interview success: Put yourself in a positive frame of mind by considering your relaxed state if you knew that you were going to be hired before the interview even took place.
- You are hired because of your strengths and eliminated because of your weaknesses.
- Interviewers decide emotionally and then justify logically; logic will make an employer think, but emotion will prompt an employer to act.
- Your primary competitor is often not another career seeker but your own lack of self-knowledge.
- Never respond with a specific salary figure; reply by asking 1) what a typical candidate with your skills and experience would earn or, 2) by inquiring as to what the position usually pays.
- You should be doing about 80% of the talking in your interviews; don't be shy!
- Ask for clarification and speak positively about former employers.
- Qualify your answers with numbers and facts.

The Ultimate Questions: What is your competitive advantage? Why are you the ideal candidate for the position?

Successful Interviewing Strategies

INTERVIEWING IS A NECESSARY step in the careering process.

Simply put, the interview process allows an interviewer a competitive forum to compare and contrast you to other candidates and you, the candidate, the opportunity to differentiate yourself from the competition.

When you are granted an interview, it becomes a contest; who will earn the right to the position by outperforming the other candidates? Competition does funny things to different people. Let me illustrate this by way of a humorous story …

2 close friends were outdoorsmen and enjoyed hiking. They were in the wilderness carrying backpacks and looking for a place to camp. As experienced outdoorsman, they had sophisticated gear and other necessities inside their packs. As they were looking for a place to camp, they heard a rustling in the woods behind them. To their horror, there was a 12-foot grizzly bear standing up on 2 legs and looking mighty hungry. There was no doubt they were now its prey and that it was going to charge.

Immediately they started running, carrying their backpacks, side by side; the grizzly bear in hot pursuit. Realizing the bear could ultimately outrun, out swim and out climb them, suddenly, 1 of the 2 friends stopped running, sat down on a rock, took off his backpack, pulled out a pair of running shoes and quickly began to put them on.

The other friend, who was now a few steps ahead of him, turned around and in a panic said, "What are you doing? Why are you sitting there? Don't even bother putting those track shoes on. You're never going to beat that bear." And the friend with the shoes looked up with an evil grin and said to his friend, "I don't have to beat the bear. I just have to beat you."

The lesson … The interview is a competitive process; play it to win! Before any interview, be prepared to discuss, "What is unique and compelling about me and my credentials?"

Very few people obtain their career calling in life without having to interview. All of your passion, purpose, power, preparation and research have targeted one thing: a successful interview. It's almost like practicing up for the big game or rehearsing for the opening night of a play. An interview is like a final examination. Your success will depend on how thoroughly you are prepared to handle the subject. And in this case, the subject is you.

When I attended law school I learned a valuable lesson; the majority of cases are won or lost BEFORE they actually go to trial, meaning true expertise is found in research and pre-planning. The same is true of interviewing. Your preparation and attention to detail before the actual question and answer session will dictate your success rate. How well you relate your skills, abilities, credentials, interests and, most importantly, *potential* to the needs of the prospective employer are critical. All of your education and previous experience has led up to this moment.

An interview is the occasion to *inventory* your personal values, educational skills, work experience, and interests. You must prove value and summarize the benefits you offer. The interview will typically last an hour or less, and involve an average of 12 questions. But its impact on your future career calling cannot be underestimated.

There is no getting around the fact that the interview process is a stress-filled process. Be careful not to develop such fear that you self-sabotage the interview!

To combat fear, I will train you to become fundamentally sound in your approach. Having a strong working knowledge of the process will ease your mind and allow you to channel your energy into your presentation as opposed to expending energy on suppressing your nerves. Prepare your answers in advance and get familiar with your motivations, because the questions in any interview are going to be about you. The more familiar you are your credentials, your abilities, your interests and your potential, the less nervous you are going to be. Together, we can learn to control as much of the process as possible.

Sometimes, there are factors outside your control. Examples include nepotism (where a company may hire a relative or friend) or requirements associated with racial or gender quotas. You may do your best work, but still not get the position for reasons outside your own performance. Remain confident in your skills and knowledge of the process, but it would be unrealistic to expect to get a yes every time you attend an interview. Remember, all you need is one yes. But don't be discouraged if there are many nos along the way. Good things are always worth waiting for. Use all interviews as learning experiences.

Just as there is no sure way to prepare for a final exam, championship sporting event or an opening night because of unknown variables, the interview process has its own variable, the interviewer. Interviewers, like each of us, have inherent bias, preferences and bad days. Most of my suggestions, techniques and strategies apply equally to interviews in business, technical fields, social services, non-profit organizations and educational sectors.

The good news is that interviewing does not vary that greatly among different fields or industries, unless you are being tested on specific technical or industry specific topics.

Definition of the Ideal Candidate

"As an interviewee, you are primarily a seller. The product you are selling is yourself, and the assets of the product are your experience, skills and personality. You communicate your experience and skills in your resume, but your personality comes across in the interview. It is your goal to arouse the interest of the interviewer in you. If you wait expectantly for questions and dutifully answer them, you have done nothing to distinguish yourself from the hundreds of others whom the interviewer will encounter."

—H. Anthony Medley, *Sweaty Palms:*
The Neglected Art of Being Interviewed

The 3-Purposes of the Interview

1. To provide the employer with information about you not already contained in your application, resume or cover letter.
2. To enable the interviewer to evaluate your personality, attitude, values, communication skills, motivations, interests in terms of the demands of the vacancy and their organization.
3. To enable you to obtain information about that particular employer. Many people approach an interview as if it were an interrogation. You are there to gather as much information as you can about the employer, just as they are there to gather as much information as they can about you. It is a mutually beneficial process.

Regardless of outcome, view every interview as an information-gathering session, a chance to learn and an opportunity to demonstrate your abilities. When confident in their abilities, successful athletes, actors and interviewers can hardly wait to get in that spotlight. You should have the same attitude.

5 Objectives of Any Interview

Remember, the interview process is a buyer/seller scenario. The interviewer has a problem and you are potential solution to that problem. Smart candidates obtain a definition of the ideal candidate for the open position and then do their best to convince the interviewer that you *are* that ideal candidate. More specifically, successful candidates should have these 5 objectives for any interview:

1. Create a favorable first impression.
2. Obtain a description of the ideal candidate sought by the employer.
3. Present yourself as the ideal candidate.
4. Overcome and neutralize any objections.
5. Get a 2nd interview or ideally, a formal job offer.

The Real Deal (What Employers Are Thinking ...)

Can this candidate do the job?

Does this candidate fit into our culture?

What is the risk of hiring this candidate?

Can we agree on compensation?

3 Areas That You Will Be Evaluated On

Before you will be considered for a position, you must convince the person of your talents in the following 3 ways:

1. Yourself and your personality
2. Your abilities and your credentials
3. Your potential worth to the company (What do you bring to the table?)

3 Keys to Interview Success

There are 3 keys to obtaining success in any interview process.

1. First, you need to plan and do research before pursuing an employer.
2. Become an industry specialist. Become knowledgeable about the employer's competitors. Learn the buzzwords for that particular industry or organization. It may sound obvious, but know what specific position is for hire, title and job description. Consider the interview forum itself. Is it going to be informal or formal; is it in an office or over lunch?
3. Strategize from the employer's point of view. Visualize yourself on the other side of the desk. Would you be impressed? What type of physical appearance do you think they're expecting or looking for? Is it a conservative employer or business casual atmosphere? Will they be impressed with your level of education and research effort?

Emphasize your employment strengths and downplay your weaknesses. *Remember, you are screened in because of your strengths and screened out because of your weaknesses.* Discuss your positive attributes and how it will benefit the employer. Remember to demonstrate your versatility. Through proper preparation, be in a position to answer any question, no matter how obscure. And that will impress the interviewer.

An Outline of the Interview Process

As an outline, consider the following steps to a successful interview:

1. Interview preparation (do your homework)
   Research the employer
   a. Review the website, obtain articles, annual reports, etc.
   b. Identify potential problems you can solve
   c. Formulate key questions/areas to discuss
2. Approach (strategy)
   a. The telephone approach
      - State your credentials (if you are currently employed, state your position)
      - State the reason for your call
      - Qualify the employer (are they the decision maker?)
      - Cite the benefits gained by hiring you
   b. The written approach
      - Cite the purpose of your letter (I want the offer !)
      - Review the benefits gained by the employer
      - Describe your method of contact (I was referred by …)
      - Transition to information gathering (ask for an information interview)
3. Learning the employer needs (long and short-term)
   a. Data gathering
      - Ask open and closed ended questions
      - Listen carefully to employer responses to your questions
      - Obtain operational and financial data (for example, organization chart)
      - Verify hiring criteria (what kind of person are they looking for?)
      - Determine future opportunities
      - Determine what would prevent you from being hired
      - Determine how you would fit in

    b. Assessment stage
- Organize the information you have obtained
- Evaluate the information
- Formulate your hiring strategy (if not already hired)

4. Your ultimate outcome (hire me please!)
    a. The process
- Restate employer objectives/goals as you understand them
- Obtain employer agreement to specific job objectives required
- Review the current condition/operations of the employer
- Obtain employer agreement that these conditions exist and are causing a problem (describe how you can solve this problem ...)
- Describe the general benefits to hiring you
- Describe the positive results gained by hiring you

    b. Close (confirm a response!)
    c. Action stage
- Summarize the reasons why the employer should hire you
- Restate the benefits of selecting you as an employee
- Summarize and restate your credentials/potential
- Demonstrate the monetary benefits to your being hired ($ saved, $ gained)
- Use effective closing techniques
- Overcome objections (if any)
- Ask for the position!

5. Post-interview (evaluate your performance)
    a. Etiquette and follow-up strategy
    b. Letter form/telephone (thank you letter and/or resignation techniques from current position)
    c. Neutralize problem areas

Interview Checklist

Here is a check list to test if you are ready: Have you mastered the ability to articulate your skills, researched the employer (including company websites or published information) and obtained a position description? Have you conducted an information interview with one or more employees in the company or in a similar industry? Do you know the major competitors of that particular company?

Befriend the Receptionist!

Make pleasant conversation with the receptionist and data-gather. It's always a good idea to research the individual who will be making a decision. If you are chatting with the receptionist as you're waiting in the lobby, you may mention the fact that you have an interview and cite the name. Maybe they will provide a clue about the interviewer. Can you tactfully inquire or come up with a comment or question that may provide you with some insight into the interviewer, such as, "How long has this person been with the company?" Or "Does he or she have a busy schedule today?" Or if you're clever, you can target questions designed to help you find out the employer's personal interests. Be creative.

On the way out the door, thank the receptionist for their courtesy and maybe even send a follow-up letter. You will be surprised how receptionists influence a decision (I always ask mine for their opinion!). Maybe they will add, "You know, that was such a nice man or woman who was in here. We could use a few more like them." That kind of endorsement can leave a very positive impression in the mind of any interviewer. It's the little things that make the difference.

The interview has two objectives:

1. To give the applicant a clear understanding of the position and responsibilities
2. To provide the interviewer an opportunity to develop information about the candidate's qualifications or credentials.

This is best obtained by the use of open-ended questions in a conversational setting. An open-ended question versus a closed-ended question

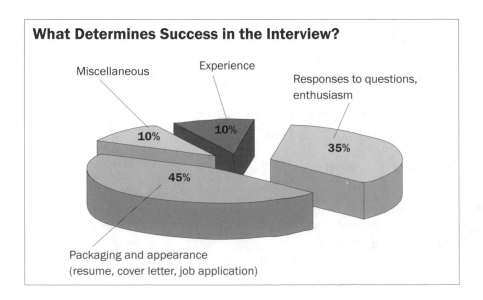

What Determines Success in the Interview?

Miscellaneous

Experience

Responses to questions, enthusiasm

10%

10%

35%

45%

Packaging and appearance
(resume, cover letter, job application)

differs in the following respect. "Do you want to work in marketing?" is a close-ended question. It prompts a single response. "How do you feel about working in marketing?" is an open-ended question, which invite additional conversation. Be prepared for both types of questions.

Here are the traits or qualifications most frequently sought in potential candidates:

- First of all is a candidate's ability to communicate. Can they organize their thoughts, their ideas and beliefs effectively and do they express those beliefs, thoughts and feelings clearly?
- Key traits include a willingness to accept responsibility, initiative, leadership skills, energy level, flexibility and versatility. Can you confront tough issues and deal with problems that may not have typical or normal solutions? Are you innovative? Can you present those thoughts or ideas in a persuasive way?

Do you know your own strengths and weaknesses? Can you handle competition? Do you have the capacity to compete with other people and not be afraid to have your performance measured? A recurring theme was how important it was for an individual to have goal-setting capabilities. That is why it's important that you articulate your long- and short-term career goals. It will give you a competitive edge. Consider these:

- Research the employer.
- Know the business of the firm interviewing you and their recent performance.
- Arrive ½ hour ahead of schedule (in the event you have to fill out an application. If not, 15 minutes should suffice.
- Bring an extra copy of your resume and references sheet.
- Make pleasant conversation with the hostess or receptionist (if applicable).
- If you must wait for the interviewer, be patient and review materials.
- Remember the name of the interviewer(s) (ask for a business card).
- Give a strong handshake and smile when meeting the interviewer.
- Be natural and try to relax by taking deep breaths.
- Bring a pen, notebook or briefcase.
- Speak slowly and quietly.
- Write down important points or topics.

- Do not chew gum, smoke, or tap your pen or feet.
- If asked to fill out an application, do so completely. Bring 2 pens of the same colored ink.
- Let the interviewer begin the conversation.
- Never interrupt or argue with the interviewer.
- Allow the interviewer to end the conversation before asking your prepared questions.
- Record what happened as quickly as possible following an interview.
- If applicable, thank the receptionist for his/her courtesy (by name).
- Send a thank you letter to the interviewer(s).

Dos and Don'ts of the Interview Process

Dos	Don'ts
Prepare prior to the interview	Be late to the interview
Be on time	Put down other people and previous employers
Be enthusiastic about the opportunity	Be dishonest or lie
Dress in appropriate attire	Discuss specific salary figures
Establish a rapport with the interviewer	Be pessimistic
Cite your accomplishments	Let the interviewer do all the talking
Ask well thought out questions	Bring friends to the interview
Take notes on important issues	Leave without an understanding of your chances
Send a thank you note	Forget to send a thank you note

Applicant Responsibilities

It is important to make sure that you take charge and direct the interview. Most people arrive at an interview with no plan, wait for the interviewer to direct the conversation and passively or nervously respond to the questions in a rehearsed fashion. Don't!

The successful career seeker takes control of the interview. If you're going to be successful, don't wait around to be asked what to do but, rather, you look for the opportunity to demonstrate your marketability and ability to contribute. Confidence will go a long way to helping you get an offer. Don't be indecisive. Both you and the employer have a list of responsibilities that an interview session is designed to showcase.

As an applicant, your responsibilities are to:

1. Highlight your background and capabilities, to demonstrate your achievements, to demonstrate a keen and sincere interest in the job
2. Reach a firm and complete understanding of what specifically the job responsibilities entail
3. Negotiate a successful benefit and salary package
4. Find out how interested that employer is in you by asking good questions
5. Convince the employer that you are the best candidate for the job

Interviewer Responsibilities

Interviewer responsibilities are to:

1. Make you feel comfortable so that they get a true sense of the person they're interviewing
2. Evaluate your credentials, your appearance and personality
3. Target a match between your qualifications and the opening
4. Obtain a firm, complete understanding of your goals and objectives
5. Make sure you understand specifically what responsibilities the job entails and what the benefits, salary and vacation policies are
6. Let you know of a time frame for a decision and determine your interest
7. Negotiate a fair salary package and determine if you are the best candidate

Visualize Success

Win over the employer and get them on your side. Propose, if you will, a partnership and try not to alienate yourself from the employer. Try to make them feel like you're already part of their team. You both have a similar or mutual interest. Establish a sense of camaraderie with the interviewer. As Abraham Lincoln said, "If you would win a man to your cause, first convince him that you are his sincere friend."

I like to think of an interview like a first date, where both parties are trying to impress each other. In relationships, the sooner you can break down those superficial barriers of trying to impress someone and get to your true essence, only then will you really know if you'll be comfortable with someone.

It's the same process in an interview. Try not to present an image of something you're not because if you successfully mislead the interviewer and get hired for a role that doesn't fit your true character, you and the company may both end up disappointed. Interviewers as professionals will do their best to break down those barriers. Let an interviewer know that you're at ease and you can be yourself so your interview is a comfortable setting and not like an uncomfortable first date.

What you do in the first 12 to 30 seconds of an interview will have a bearing on whether you're hired or given a, "Thank you, but we'll keep you in mind." If the first impression that you give to an employer is negative regarding attire, attitude or your personality, you run the risk of being eliminated before you have a chance to demonstrate your credentials. The sad fact is that employers are busy people and have a number of candidates to interview, so they like to screen people out as quickly as possible.

Be enthusiastic and look the interviewer directly in the eye. Studies show that if you don't look someone in the eye, it may suggest you are sneaky or less than honest. Don't be too cocky, conceited or abrasive. Don't be too egotistical or overly aggressive. Politely greet the secretary or clerical support who often will assess you before the interviewer.

Your resume, cover letter, phone conversations or information interview have resulted in an actual interview. Your potential employer first will want to know that you have done your homework and have an understanding of the company and the position. They will test that knowledge by asking specific questions such as, "What do you know about our company or organization?"

Demonstrate to the interviewer that you have done your homework on them as a person, their personality style, how long they have been with the organization, and the company itself. There's nothing more impressive to help your own cause than to show an interviewer that you took the time to find out something about *their* interests.

I remember one candidate who found out that the person who would be interviewing him had just celebrated a birthday the day before the actual interview. You can imagine how impressed the interviewer was when the applicant walked in, looked him right in the eye with a firm handshake and said, "Happy belated birthday."

Please review each interview situation carefully. But in a situation where you have found out that the person doing the interviewing has a particular hobby or interest, by all means try to take advantage of that in a clever but not phony way.

I'm going to take a moment here to talk about visualization. I'm a firm believer that if you visualize something in a positive sense prior to doing it, it can provide a competitive edge.

As a former marketing executive, I remember listening to a variety of self-help tapes that taught me to go into every sales call visualizing that I was going to get the sale and that the person was eager to meet me. Anticipate a positive outcome. Use the same strategy in your interviews.

Before your interview, close your eyes. Breathe deeply. Picture a successful interview. See yourself getting up in the morning professionally dressed, riding the train, bus or driving your car to an interview. Imagine what the building looks like. Imagine yourself being greeted by the receptionist and indicating that your interview is about to take place.

Visualize a firm, strong handshake, and following them confidently into their office. Visualize yourself sitting down, having a positive first 12 or 30 seconds with strong eye contact, a nice smile, confident and enthusiastic. Visualize your professional posture as you sit in your chair. Picture the interviewer asking the very same questions you anticipated. Observe yourself answering those questions professionally without fault. Visualize the interview ending on a positive note with your being hired. How does that feel?

Overcoming Nervousness!

Many of you are probably thinking, "Well, that sounds great, Chris, but I'm petrified to go on an interview. Visualization can help me, but I'm still nervous!"

How do you overcome nervousness? Let me ask you a question. If you were going into an interview situation and you knew in your heart you were 100% confident that you were the best candidate for the job, the most prepared, the most knowledgeable and you knew that the interviewer was going to offer you the position before you even went in the door, what would your attitude be while you were walking in? Would you be nervous? Not likely.

Perception can be reality. If you visualize a positive experience, chances are, more likely than not, you're going to have a positive interview. If you see yourself as nervous, getting nauseous, having a headache, sweating, botching the interview, stammering over your words, you're probably going to experience that.

You will become what you dream about and think about. In this case, focus on a positive interview and tell yourself that you're a great candidate.

"Did you need a break or do you want to continue the interview process?"

Self-talk is important! Before you walk in the door, give yourself a little pep talk before walking into the interview, and tell yourself, "I'm the best candidate for the position. This is a step in attaining my career calling. I'm a great employee. I'm a great worker. I am knowledgeable about the company, I know exactly what position is for hire and I know that my credentials and background will be unmatched by any of the competition."

Gear yourself up so that when you walk in the door and shake the interviewer's hand and look them right in the eye, they'll know right from the beginning that you are the right candidate for the position!

Interviewing Is a Selling Proposition

> *"Whatever you say to a prospect about your product or service, imagine that he is looking at you and saying, "so what?"*
>
> —Brian Tracy, *The Psychology of Selling*

Many people think that *sales* is a dirty word. Often, a salesperson conjures up the image of a pushy, sleazy person who will say anything to get you to part with your hard earned money. Although there are certainly "less than honest" salespeople who give the profession a bad name, there are an equal number of honorable individuals who understand that the essence of selling can be summarized by this: *Selling is a transference of feelings and emotions between 2 interested parties who seek a mutual gain.*

Interviewing is selling. When on an interview, you are simply sharing your enthusiasm for your ability to solve the challenges resulting from their vacancy.

Success Tip

The key is to get the interviewer emotionally involved in the process and to perceive your skills, values and abilities as a favorable solution to their challenge.

You and the interviewer are merely strategizing on the best way to solve the problems, (lost revenues, overworked staff, etc.) caused by the current vacancy or employees who are not as competent as you are. You are the consultant in possession of the experience, work ethic and a set of solution-oriented skills, which will make everybody's life easier. Get it? Got it? Good!

It is not enough to simply introduce the interviewer to your credentials (education, experience, accomplishments); you must clearly demonstrate *how* these valuable attributes will benefit the employer. The use of word stories and citing specific cost savings or revenue increases resulting from your contribution is the ideal method to win over an interviewer.

Earlier, I stressed the importance of starting any activity with the end in mind. Before any interview, have a plan for exactly what you want to occur. You should be asking yourself these 2 questions before every interview:

- "What would have to happen for you to make me a formal offer?"
- "What would you have to be convinced of to hire me today?"

Here is an important fact to help you realize that interviewing is a selling opportunity for you. *Interviewers buy benefits and solutions!* Features may arouse interest, but benefits arouse buying desire.

Make sure that you demonstrate to every interviewer solutions you bring to the table. People do not buy products; they buy solutions to their problems. They invest in ways to satisfy their current or future needs. Here are 5 recommended questions for you to ask the interviewer:

1. "Who currently occupies this position or function?"
2. "What are you currently doing now in this area?"
3. "How is that working for you?"
4. "What are your plans for the future in this area?"
5. "What would you have to be convinced of to offer me the position?"

In a way, you are like a detective. You are seeking clues that will result in a formal job offer. As you can appreciate, your body language is important in interviewing. According to Albert Mehrabian of UCLA, the message you convey in a negotiation is "55% body language, 38% tone of voice, and only 7% in the words that you use."

Reasons for Hiring or Not Hiring

The Ultimate Questions

What is your competitive advantage? Why are you the ideal candidate for the position?

In every interview (sale!), there is a *primary benefit* that the interviewer is seeking. This is the one thing that the person who can hire you must be convinced of before they offer you a position. Your responsibility is to uncover this primary benefit and then to convince the interviewer that they will enjoy this benefit if they hire you.

At the same time, there is a *primary objection* to every sale, the major reason that the customer will hesitate or decide not to buy. It is absolutely essential that you uncover this key objection and find a way to answer it to the customer's satisfaction.

If you discover several reasons why the company is looking for candidates such as yourself, focus your attention on the top 20% of the benefits that your prospect will enjoy, and convince him or her in a professional manner that they will obtain these benefits by hiring you. If you can successfully demonstrate that hiring you will help them realize these benefits faster than from any other candidate, the interview becomes much easier (and the position is yours!)

"We will be in touch," "we will let you know" and "let me think it over," are common put-offs. You want an answer now! If you have truly done your job of articulating your unique and compelling skills and contributions in a passionate and purposeful manner, there should be nothing to think over, unless the interviewer does not have the authority to make you a formal offer. If this does occur, you can immediately reply by saying, "Mr. Interviewer, at this moment you know *a great deal* about me as a candidate. From our discussion and your reasons for needing to fill this position, I am a perfect match for you. When can I start?" More on asking for the position later in this chapter …

When conducting seminars, I always make it a point to ask my audiences, "What percentage of an interviewer's decision is based on emotion, and what percentage is based on logic?" Almost everyone will say that interviewers are 50% emotional and 50% logical. But the correct answer is that hiring authorities are 100% emotional. Remember this: *Interviewers decide emotionally and then justify logically.*

3 Keys to Strategic Interviewing

1. *Present yourself as a unique and compelling candidate. Identify your unique selling proposition (USP).*
   Consider this story:

It Takes Your Breath Away

Some years ago, the distributors of Smirnoff vodka attempted to introduce Smirnoff to the market in the United States. They had little success. At that time, vodka was considered not only a foreign drink, but also a Russian foreign drink. The Cold War was a reality and Americans were not particularly favorable to any Russian products, especially in the form of liquor. The Smirnoff distributors spent an enormous amount of money attempting to position Smirnoff vodka as a superior choice to whiskey, scotch, gin, rum, and other liquors. But to no avail. Finally they identified the "unique selling feature" of Smirnoff: after drinking Smirnoff, no one could smell it on your breath. They instantly created an advertising campaign around this unique selling proposition (USP) with 2 lines: "Smirnoff! It takes your breath away" and "Smirnoff! It leaves you breathless." In no time at all, Smirnoff became a $50 million product, and eventually a $500 million product. It broke the market open for vodka sales, which are now well in excess of a billion dollars a year. By identifying the competitive advantage of a beverage that people could drink at lunch without folks back at the office knowing, they were able to create a great marketing success.

2. *Differentiate yourself from other candidates who seek the same position through the "Prove it" technique (Don't just say it … prove it with a fact or example to make your statement real!)*
   If you are in sales, document your sales record. If you drive a truck, cite your delivery record. If you were a teacher, quantify your ability to empower students. If you are a social worker,

recount stories of self-sufficiency or helping clients overcome barriers. If you are from an IT background, detail how you saved your previous employer money or improved revenues through your unique contributions.

3. *What is it that makes you superior to the other candidates? (Why you? Just being a "hard worker" or "team player" isn't enough!)* Many average candidates when confronted with the question, "Why should I hire you?" blurt out some rehearsed, uninspiring answer that derails the interview and results in a rejection. You need to inspire the person across the desk with a passionate, purposeful response that confirms you are a person in possession of the essential competitive edge … attitude! If you are not excited about describing your credentials and unique capabilities, then you are most likely confused, uncertain and lack confidence to be an A-list player.

How to Research Your Career Calling

Success Tip

In most instances, your primary major competitor is not another career seeker. It is ignorance. Employers simply do not know your services are available.

Here is a short list of 5 things you should consider and analyze:

1. What are the trends in your targeted industry?
2. Who exactly is your ideal employer partner? (Make a list of all the qualities and characteristics that your ideal employer would have).
3. Who will be your future employers? Project ahead 1, 3, 5 and 10 years. (Will you be working for a company or start your own firm?)
4. What other opportunities might there be for your skills? (Consultant, sub-contractor, part time employee)
5. Who or what is your primary competition? What benefits could the interviewer see in hiring another candidate? What are your shortcomings or weaknesses?

The 5 Interviewer Personality Types

There are 5 basic personality profiles that interviewers possess.

1. Laid Back Linda   Approximately 10% of interviewers have this profile. Traits include apathy, negativity, cynical attitude, distracted and sometime pre-occupied with their own challenges. By all means, do not get caught up in their toxicity, but rather focus on getting them excited about you joining their team.

2. For Certain Cindy   Approximately 10% of interviewers have this profile. Traits include having a clear understanding of what they want from an applicant, a keen knowledge of skills and abilities needed to fill the position and an inflexible approach to compensation and salary negotiation. "Take it or leave it" could be their motto.

3. Analytical Arnold   Approximately 25% of interviewers have this profile. Traits include a focus on quantifying value, detail, accuracy and being concise. If you cite an accomplishment on your resume or verbally communicate an achievement, document via statistics or numbers or else. These folks will catch your mistakes and hate typos! When thinking of this profile, think accountant, attorney, bean counter, engineer, banker, etc.

4. Friendly Frank   Approximately 25% of interviewers have this profile. Traits include a deep need to be liked and respected. Friendly and outgoing, these folks like to build a relationship with candidates because they believe that is the key to effective interviewing. Use personal stories vs. inundating them with facts and figures and be complimentary about their office and location. This style may procrastinate on a final decision, which can be frustrating.

5. Bottom Line Betty   Approximately 30% of interviewers have this profile. Traits include a very direct, almost impersonal approach to the interview process, where the outcome is more important than the person seeking the position. You may be viewed as a "resource" responsible for measurable tasks and duties vs. a human being with feelings and emotions. I advise you to be concise and don't mince words, get to the point and be respectful of their time, which they value tremendously. Think of them as a radio station ... WIIFM (what's in it for me?) should be their motto.

Great Listening = Great Interviewing!

> *"You have 2 ears and 1 mouth so listen twice as much as you talk"*
>
> —Sign on a *Career* T.E.A.M. door

If there is one skill that I would personally like to improve, it is the art of being a great listener. My problem is that I like to talk and when engaged in a conversation, often I am thinking about what I want to say next vs. truly hearing what the other person is really saying. While I have made significant progress, I still have a ways to go before I would categorize myself as an attentive listener.

You must become proficient at the art of listening to the interviewer and hearing the direct and subtle references or clues in their dialogue. Failure to do so will jeopardize your chances of success and create the impression that you are incapable of active listening or, in some cases, following direction. Listening is one of the most important competencies. Here are 5 keys to effective listening:

1. *Listen attentively, respond actively:* Be respectful to every interviewer you interact with; it is a privilege to be there. Let them begin the line of questioning. Listen without any attempt to interrupt, change the direction of the dialogue or dictate your own ideas. Understand before you attempt to be understood.

2. *Always remain patient in your responses:* When the interviewer concludes a point or line of questioning, make sure they are completely finished with their point. Before you respond, the strategy is to pause, wait a few seconds and then carefully articulate your answer. When you stop to think before you speak, you accomplish the following:
   - You ensure clarity in what the interviewer truly means and minimize the potentially embarrassing risk of interrupting the interviewer, who may simply be looking for the right word or organizing their thoughts.
   - You follow the old adage that, communicating takes places with the words, but acceptance of the candidate occurs during the silence.
   - By pausing, you communicate (non-verbally) that you are seriously contemplating their point before reacting. In so doing, you are demonstrating a respect for their opinion by carefully absorbing the impact of their thoughts.

3. *The person asking the questions is in control:* You should never be merely responding to questions, but rather engaged in an *active* dialogue with the interviewer. Ask questions if you do not understand! Never assume that you know what the interviewer

means or is thinking; this can be a fatal flaw. Rather, I suggest you tactfully ask, "How or what do you mean?" This question will force the interviewer to elaborate on the issue at hand and provide clarification. When you are talking at about 100 to 150 words per minute, an interviewer can process words at the rate of 600 words per minute. This means that the interviewer has ¾ of his or her time available to contemplate other thoughts while you are responding. Conversely, when you ask a question, 100% of the interviewer's attention will be focused on answering you. This is why you both should be asking questions, not just the interviewer.

4. *Repeat key information to the interviewer:* Using your own vocabulary, feed back what the interviewer just said to you in your own words. When you can repeat what an interviewer has said or may be thinking, you demonstrate that you were really paying attention.

5. *Use both open-ended and closed ended questions:* Whenever you ask a question beginning with *who, what, where, when, how, why, which,* you encourage the prospect to talk and give you more information. Examples include: "What is a typical day like? How do you feel about the direction of this organization?" Incorporate close-ended questions to bring the conversation to a conclusion. These are questions that can be answered by a yes or no. Examples include: "Are you ready to make a decision today? What 2 skills are most important to have for this job? When could I start?"

The 3 Types of Job Interviews

> *"How well we communicate is determined not by how well we say things but by how well we are understood."*
> —Andrew S. Grove

There are different types of interviews that you will be subjected to during the course of finding your ideal career.

1. The first type of interview is the *basic question-and-answer session.* Here, an interviewer will conduct your session in a very methodical, detailed and structured manner. They seek specific

information about your wants, objectives, skills, experience, education, capabilities and future potential. Make the interview more of a conversation than a one-sided question session conducted by the employer.

2. The next kind of interview, and the most common, is the *free-flowing interview*, where the interviewer usually begins with a question like "Tell me about yourself" and uses open-ended questions to gain insight.

    Depending upon the position, you may have multiple interviewers or successive interviews, where you'll meet a number of different people from that organization in the same day, usually in succession. You may be required to impress a Personnel Manager, then a front line manager, then maybe one of your future co-workers before acceptance. Maintain a high level of enthusiasm and energy for every session.

3. Some employers conduct a *group interview*, which sometimes is the most difficult and most stressful. My experience shows that only about 10 to 20% of all applicants will have to go through a group interview. But they can occur regardless position sought, from entry level to CEO.

Group interviews usually occur when a person will have to give presentations to a number of people and an employer wants to see how the candidate responds to multiple opinions. Questions are asked from 2 or 3 directions. It's important to maintain eye contact with each person. Sometimes employers will create a good guy/bad guy situation where 1 or 2 of the members will seemingly be on your side while the 3rd member will be put in there as a plant to try to distract you, disrupt you, throw you off, or try to see if you get flustered easily. ID the enemy! Determine what specific credentials are required and transfer your enthusiasm!

Regardless of format, the interviewer has a lot to lose if they select the wrong candidate. A great tip is at the end of your presentation, ask, "What is it about my particular credentials or qualities that would make you hire me?" The question will impress them, believe me, because they'll have to answer you and focus on your best attributes. You want them to verbalize your strengths, this question ensures that occurs. At the end of any interview the employer really has only 3 options: 1 is to hire you, 2 is to hire somebody else, and 3 is to do nothing or keep on interviewing. Try to find out at the end of your interview which 1 of the 3 choices the interviewer has made. And if you're not sure, try to reinforce your competitive edge; that is, what separates you from the other applicants. Help them make a decision, in your favor!

15 Most Cited Reasons for Rejecting Applicants

1. Poor personal appearance
2. No career purpose or goal
3. Lack of enthusiasm
4. Lack of confidence
5. Overemphasis on money
6. Failure to ask questions about the job
7. Lack of courtesy
8. Failure to look the interviewer in the eye
9. Limp handshake
10. Failure to research the employer
11. Indefinite response to questions
12. Sloppy resume
13. Cynical attitude
14. Inability to take criticism
15. Failure to express appreciation for interviewer's time

When talking with a number of professional recruiters, personnel managers and interviewers, I've found that:

> When an employer says No to you as far as a job opportunity is concerned, what he or she is really saying is "know,"that is, "I don't know enough about your potential" or "I am not convinced to the degree that I need to be about your potential."

Preparation is critical. You've heard many athletes, celebrities, actresses or actors talk about the importance of dress rehearsal or practice. Remember one thing: The excitement of the successful interview and career achievement in general is always preceded by unsensational job search preparation or practice.

Create an enthusiasm within your interviewer. Be a spark in their life and don't be afraid to communicate a bit of humor within an interview. But be careful because humor is a sensitive issue; it can backfire if misused.

I remember one interviewer was telling me a story where he was in an interview, and the woman interviewing him asked, "Well, how much money do you feel you need?" The candidate tried to be funny and responded,

"Well, how much do you have?" In this case, that type of humor did not work because the interviewer was an analytical, bottom line type of personality who didn't find it funny and didn't warm up to that type of response.

Employer Concerns

Remember that an interviewers fear of making a poor decision exceeds their desire of being applauded for hiring a good candidate. They are scared to make a bad hiring decision, make their life easy! Target a game plan to overcome some of their possible concerns, which are:

- If I hire this candidate and it doesn't work out, I'll be looked upon as a person who can't make the correct decision or evaluate talent.
- They are concerned that maybe you won't be able to do the job because your skills or experience level is deficient, yet they felt that you did such a good job interviewing that you could overcome that lack of experience.
- Interviewers also have a hidden fear that if you're accepted, you may take too long to become comfortable with your responsibilities and that the company will not profit from hiring you.
- They may have a concern that you won't get along with other people or that you'll be a loner or your personality, even though you have talent or experience, may conflict with your potential supervisors or co-workers.
- They may have a concern that you are a person who gets by doing just the minimum rather than striving to achieve maximum potential. They may fear that you won't put in a full day, or that you may be out sick a lot.
- They may be concerned about your commitment. They fear you may accept the position, but leave shortly thereafter because you have been being lured by another company, organization or recruiter.
- They fear you're a person who will always be looking for more money, that you'll constantly be pestering people for a raise, and that people will point to the interviewer as the person who hired you.
- They are concerned that you're the kind of person who doesn't take initiative and needs to be given constant orders, one who constantly needs a kick in the rear end.

10 Great Tips

"At Career T.E.A.M., we hire individuals who are seeking an outlet to demonstrate their passions. Ideally, they are on the cusp of finding it for the first time in their life, that is, where their heart and soul meets. When I personally interview them, I can immediately see this passion in their eyes, the spark surrounding their being is unmistakable. I can observe in these candidates a need to prove it to me. Why is this important? Because success is fleeting while greatness derived from a deep sense of calling endures over time. At Career T.E.A.M., we ideally seek candidates who are about to experience a career defining moment … This is one of the secrets to our incredible success.

—Chris Kuselias

1. Punctuality, smile, eye contact, firm handshake and proper introductory greeting
2. A quality application, resume and cover letter that cites relevant information
3. The inclusion of a clearly defined career objective
4. The Big 5: Attitude, enthusiasm, energy, confidence and dependability
5. The critical 4: listening skills, research, use of industry "buzz" words, persistence
6. An ability to communicate ideas clearly and effectively
7. The ability to organize and sell key points
8. Overall presentation and appearance
9. Desire to win the position and ability to ask for it
10. Closing techniques and comments

20 Areas You Will Be Evaluated On in an Interview

Ability to Communicate	Flexibility	Interpersonal skills
Appearance	High Energy	Leadership
Competitiveness	Honesty	Maturity
Confidence	Imagination	Optimism
Creativity	Initiative	Personality
Enthusiasm	Integrity	Punctuality
Experience	Interests	

Hint: Consider how you will be positively evaluated in each area.

5 Stages of the Interview

First Impression—Stage 1

Building Rapport (5–10 Minutes)

Usually this dialogue is "small talk" on the traffic, weather, local sports team, current events. This stage is designed to put both parties at ease. Remember, first impressions are extremely important!

Track Record—Stage 2

Question And Answer Session (20–30 Minutes)

Usually, the interviewer will ask 10–15 questions, which can be either open or closed ended. This stage is designed to determine your ability to handle the job and your future potential. Prepare for this stage by reviewing all possible questions and by practicing your responses. Remember to "prove it" and support your answers with documented examples.

Career Goals—Stage 3

Your Questions (10–20 Minutes)

Here is your chance to obtain any information not already covered. Remember, some employers state that it is the questions you ask and not your answers that provide best insight to your true potential. Prepare 3–5 questions for this stage.

Company Match—Stage 4

Evaluation (5–10 Minutes)

Does the position further your career calling? Can you see yourself working with this employer? Do you think they are excited about you working for them?

Summary—Stage 5

The Close (5–10 Minutes)

Use this stage to review your credentials, restate your interest and, ask for the position! One suggestion is to ask the interviewer, "How do we proceed?"

5 Essential Things Interviewers Look For

Here is a behind the scenes view of what the interviewer looks for:

1. In the 1st *impression* stage is the introduction, greeting, some small talk about traffic conditions, location, the weather, or maybe a sporting event. The interviewer is evaluating handshake, eye contact, appearance and dress, and your poise and ease in an unfamiliar social situation.

2. The 2nd stage is *track record*. At issue is your education, grades, work experience and level of responsibility. The interviewer will evaluate your intellectual abilities, special or general interests, reaction to authority, sensibility in terms of resources, time, energy and money, vitality, enthusiasm, willingness to follow directions and ability to motivate yourself and make things happen. An employer will consider your relationships, interests, extracurricular activities and hobbies, positive attitude and social awareness. Are you a good person and a good citizen?

3. The 3rd stage in the interviewer's perception is review of your *career goals*. The interviewer's targeted questions will lead you to disclose your immediate objectives, long-term objectives and interest in the company. It will also showcase your attitude about topics like relocation and other factors that may affect your performance. Here the interviewer seeks a realistic knowledge of your strengths and weaknesses, how prepared you are for this particular opportunity and your seriousness of purpose. Do you have a calling? Are you, in fact, career-oriented rather than just specific job-oriented? There's a big difference. Career-oriented people think long-term where job-oriented people think specific job only. Interviewers will target your knowledge of the company and whether your contributions are in line with your talents. Are you a dreamer or achiever? And most importantly, what are his or her company's chances to hire you at this stage?

4. The 4th stage is called the *company match*. Here you will discuss opportunities and how to fit in on both current and future projects. The interviewer will discuss the major issues and departments, the training programs and the educational or other benefits offered. The interviewer is specifically looking for informed and relevant questions that you ask, indications of your interest in the answers, and an appropriate interest in the salary or benefits offered.

5. The 5th and final stage of the perception portion is called the *summary*. During the final stages of an interview, you may be asked to provide further information on the application your references. Finally, the interviewer will tell you when you will be notified of a decision.

Assessing Your Interview Performance

During the course of an interview, there are certain aspects that you have to come away with a complete and thorough understanding of.

1. *Do you fully understand the duties?* Understand completely what the particular vacancy or opportunity involves. You've researched the employer, maybe done an information interview or two, and talked to people who do the job. Use the interview process to gain a clear understanding of the opportunity so that you can make a well-informed decision about whether you want to pursue your calling there.

2. *Can you see yourself pursuing your calling with this organization?* After doing your homework, information interview, meeting people in the lobby, and meeting the interviewer, is this where you want to pursue your calling. You have options. Are these the kind of people that you see yourself becoming socially active with? Do they share your values? Or are your goals or skills different to the point that you won't be comfortable?

3. *Is there a match?* Do you understand the role well enough to make a decision? The interview process should confirm that match. Use the interview as an opportunity to sell yourself and market your potential and capabilities. But also use it as an information-gathering session.

4. *What does the interviewer care about?* Remember to make the interviewer like you. Be interested in what they have to say. Have a smile on your face. Be enthusiastic. Remember their name. Listen intently when they're talking. Don't be afraid to take notes. Talk highly about other people or past employers. Don't talk negatively about your former employers or your former boss. And don't make excuses about your shortcomings. Talk in terms of *their* interest.

5. *Did you establish an emotional bond?* Be sincere and make the other person feel important, establishing a camaraderie and common bond. If they can see you as a cost effective value and they like you personally, that will go a long way to your acceptance.

Consider these questions:

1. Did I make a good first impression?
2. Did I talk enough?
3. Did I justify my statements with factual statements?

4. Which questions did I handle well?
5. Which questions did I handle poorly?
6. Was I confident?
7. How was my appearance?
8. Was I enthusiastic?
9. Would I have been impressed with me?
10. What will I do to improve my next interview?

Interview Rating Sheet

Add up your total score on the rating sheet below.

Name: _____

Date: _____

Part 1	Meeting and Greeting	5 Points
1. Smile (1 point)		
2. Eye contact (1 point)		
3. Shake hands firmly (1 point)		
4. Introduce yourself using the interviewer's name (1 point)		
5. Indicate what you are there for (1 point)		
Part 2	Poise	30 Points
1. Leans slightly forward (5 points)		
2. Appropriate hand gestures (5 points)		
3. Eye contact (10 points)		
4. Faces interviewer (10 points)		
Part 3	Answering Questions	30 Points
1. No mumbling (6 points)		
2. Complete answers (6 points)		
3. No slang (6 points)		
4. Keep professional (6 points)		
5. No tangents (6 points)		
Part 4	Asking Questions	30 Points
1. No mumbling (5 points)		
2. No slang (5 points)		
3. Complete sentences (10 points)		
4. Show interest in what you can contribute (10 points)		
Part 5	Closing the Interview	5 Points
1. Shake hands (1 point)		
2. Thank the interviewer, using his or her name (1 point)		
3. Restate your strengths (1 point)		
4. Ask for the job (1 point)		
5. Next step: ask when you will hear back (1 point)		

What is your score (out of 100)?

Performance Evaluation Sheet

This is a sample of a form an employer might use to evaluate your performance. Look it over to see what an employer expects and use it to rate your *own* performance on the job. This is your future report card!

	Excellent (5)	Above Average (4)	Average (3)	Below Average (2)	Poor (1)
Job Results					
Accuracy and quality					
Thoroughness					
Productivity (quantity output of meaningful work					
Job Knowledge					
Understands work procedures, methods and techniques					
Uses equipment and tools properly					
Learns and adapts to change					
Performs all parts of his or her job description					
Dependability					
Attendance record					
Follows directions carefully					
Maintains consistent and reliable work habits					
Works efficiently under pressure, meets deadlines					
Adheres to company policy, safety codes, rules, etc.					
Exercises sound judgment and decision-making skills					
Interpersonal Relationships					
Cooperates with co-workers and other staff members					
Demonstrates respect for and consideration of others					
Accepts constructive criticism					
Creates positive impressions inside and outside the company					
Initiative					
Strives to improve skills and abilities					
Finds creative ways to improve the way work is done					
Handles and resolves problems as they arise					
Assumes new responsibilities willingly					
Works well independently					

It is important to evaluate your performance and reflect on how you could improve your next opportunity. 5 questions to reflect on:

1. How well did the interview go?
2. How do you feel that you did in regards to some of the decisions you made during the interview and did you take any risks to distinguish yourself?
3. How well did you handle the interviewer's questions and did you ask and get answers to your most important questions?
4. What could you have done differently?
5. Did you accomplish all of your objectives?

Warning! Make Sure You Heard Right ...

One of the biggest frustrations career seekers endure is to accept a position based on a series of perceived promises only to find out that what they thought they heard the interviewer say or agree to is, in fact, much different once they start working.

Before you accept any position, do your best to make certain that the following issues are clearly understood by both parties (even to the extent of getting them in writing). This may include a written job description and duties, compensation plan clearly defined, and organization chart depicting your role on the team and authority to make decisions.

Keep in mind that while you can never guarantee that your duties, title, function or compensation won't change or be modified in the best interest of your employer (things move fast these days!), requesting clarification in the interview process will present you as a serious, professional candidate.

Here are the 3 biggest issues that, if not addressed, often result in stress and anxiety.

1. Salary and compensation do not equate to what was promised in the interview; career objectives tied to commissions or bonuses are modified (increased) making them more difficult to attain.
2. The job title or duties are radically different from what you understood: you wind up wearing more than one hat and your job responsibilities are much more involved than you were led to believe.
3. Your decision making capabilities are less than you were led to believe; you have less authority than you thought.

Sample Thank You for Interview Letter

Date

Interviewer's Name
Title
Company
Address

Dear _____:

I appreciated the opportunity to meet with you on (date). The information you shared with me about (company name) was excellent, and I am excited about the possibility of applying my education and experience to the position.

During our discussion, you indicated that you were looking for a candidate who (restate qualities sought by employer). I believe that I have the skills and confidence needed to make an immediate contribution.

If I can provide you with any additional information concerning my qualifications, please let me know. I look forward to hearing from you soon.

Sincerely,

Signature

Your letter should:

- Provide relevant information not already covered
- Refer to your previous accomplishments/experience
- Demonstrate that you are a viable candidate
- Reinforce your interest in the position
- Offer references and request a 2nd interview (if applicable)

How to Ask and Answer Difficult Interview Questions

THE PURPOSE OF THIS section is to provide strategies for answering the difficult questions. Depending upon the type of job, level of job or title of the interviewer, the actual questions may vary or be tailored toward a particular industry or occupation. The following should provide you with a solid foundation on which to build exceptional responses.

Because the interview process can create anxiety, it's always a good idea to practice these answers prior to attending an interview. By doing so, you'll establish a greater level of self-confidence, improve your performance in the interview and give yourself a better chance of getting a yes. These selected interview answers will provide a competitive edge.

Articulate your strengths in these areas:

1. Your personal background
2. Your achievements and accomplishments
3. Your employment history

Communicate to the interviewer that you are:

- A hard worker who likes to start early, and looks to do more than just the minimum required
- Your interview answers should demonstrate that this new opportunity will provide you with a strong sense of purpose, motivation and accomplishment
- If you are unsure about a question, ask for clarification!
- Always speak positively about former employers
- Be completely honest with all of your answers
- Turn questions about your weaknesses into answers of strengths
- Be prepared to answer questions about your long term goals
- Demonstrate flexibility and give examples of your ability to work with all types of people
- Demonstrate that you are a person who is organized and disciplined
- Use anecdotes or examples to illustrate your statements whenever possible
- Be poised, confident, and incorporate your personal experiences in your answers

Confidence is Key!

20 Most Frequently Asked Interview Questions

1. Tell me about yourself.
2. Have you ever done this type of work before?
3. Why have you chosen this particular industry?
4. Why do you want to leave your present job? Why did you leave your previous job?
5. Why are you interested in this particular organization?
6. Why should we hire you?
7. What interests you the most about this particular job?
8. Are you willing to relocate?
9. Who has had the greatest influence on your life?

10. What is your greatest strength?
11. What is your greatest weakness?
12. What would you like to be doing 5 years from now?
13. How would you describe your personality? How would others describe you?
14. What aspect of this job would interest you the least?
15. How do you feel about a male or female boss?
16. What type of people do you not like to work with?
17. Why have you changed jobs so frequently?
18. Why have you been out of work for so long?
19. Do you have plans to continue your education?
20. How do you tolerate coworkers with different goals, interests or ambitions?

Hint: Write out all the answers to these questions. Then, practice your answers aloud!

Many career seekers are terrified by the prospect of interviewing. The key to mastering anything new is preparation and familiarizing yourself with what will occur. Regarding the interview, this means reviewing the proper procedures. So, what are the most frequently asked questions in a typical interview session?

Tell me about yourself   In the majority of interviews, the 1st question is "Tell me about yourself." This question is what I call a "convince me" question. Begin the answer by expressing your interest and desire to contribute to the employer. Offer to share your credentials and your prior research. In your answer, you have 3 basic options:

1. To discuss your personal background
2. To discuss your educational accomplishments
3. To discuss your professional experience or work history

Begin with the most impressive and relevant aspect of your credentials. By doing so, you will establish an all-important first impression! If you choose, for example, work history, express your interest and desire to work for the employer and demonstrate your knowledge of their operations. Share how this contribution is your calling! State that you are a hard worker, that you come in early, are often the last to leave and are looking to do more than just the bare minimum required for the position. Tie in your previous experience to the position. If you do not have a strong work history, focus on your education. The key is to tie your strength to the position you are interviewing for.

Have you ever done this type of work before?   In this case, the employer needs to feel confident that you possess the necessary experience. Your response should include the fact that you are a flexible, versatile individual and demonstrate from your background or credentials that you can adapt quickly to new challenges. Document examples that confirm your assertions. Don't just say it, prove it!

Why have you chosen this particular industry?   In this instance, you have a perfect opportunity to share with the interviewer a true interest in the job, to demonstrate knowledge of the field or industry and then convince them of your capability to perform successfully. Convince the interviewer how this type of work will provide you with a strong sense of purpose, motivation and accomplishment. Another tip is to mention the specific functions of the role and industry that you are passionate about.

Why do you want to leave your current job or why did you leave your previous job?   Emphasize the fact that you decided on a career change because you realized that your previous job was not providing you with every benefit that you felt could be derived from your career. Also, mention that you want a position in which you can grow and demonstrate your potential talents. For example, "I would be more effective in a position like this one where my computer skills, team player mentality and customer service experience could be utilized." Provide specific examples of how these skills will be of benefit to the employer. Successful candidates always support claims of talent or skills with specific examples from prior experiences. By doing so, you develop credibility with an interviewer. Never speak negatively about your previous job or employer.

Why are you interested in working for this particular organization?   Be specific and remember, "Because I need a job" is not an unacceptable answer! It is important to emphasize the fact that you are interested in working for *this* employer and that you have done your homework, researched the industry and its competitors. This is your calling! It would be helpful to point out specific reasons why this particular employer is superior to some of the others. For example, "Your organization has introduced 14 new products in the last 3 years, while your competition has only introduced 2 new products" or "I prefer a more dynamic organization with a reputation for quality." The key is to support your reasons with facts and not just generic mumbo jumbo.

Tell me, why should we hire you?   "Why should we hire you?" is one of the most important questions any interviewer can ask you. This question is a direct opportunity for you to present your credentials, qualities, experiences and educational background. Make a statement like, "I have the capabilities to successfully do the job and my previous record of experience and education demonstrate that." Or, if you are just coming out of school or re-entering the job market, you may want to say something like, "I'm a quick study, a fast learner, for example." Or you may want to say something like, "I've done a great deal of preparation and planning to make sure that this is a field which matches all of my job requirements. I know that this particular organization and job function will provide me with all that I am looking for to be my most successful self. Because I am passionate about the duties, you as the employer will benefit." Note: More experienced candidates should focus on their maturity and judgment.

What interests you most about this particular job?   Or another way of saying it is, What's important to you in a job?

These 2 questions are a perfect opportunity to present to the interviewer what it is that you view as most interesting about the position. Is it the competitive nature that you possess? Is it the outlook that the website, company information or a particular article that you reference seemed to indicate? Is it the challenge of the position or the fact that a new division or product line has been introduced and you would like to help make that a success? Is it a team environment? The interviewer wants to make sure that your personal aptitudes and qualities are in sync with those that contribute to the progress of the employer's objectives. If they are, great, if not, you may become bored or discouraged and ultimately leave the job. Downplay the importance of salary or fringe benefits unless, of course, you're interviewing for a commission-based position and you want to show that you are motivated by accomplishment. For example, the more revenue you help to generate, the more the employer will benefit.

Are you willing to relocate?   This question is asked because the potential exists to move you to a different geographic location, if not immediately, then maybe in the future. If you say "No" to the question of relocation, there's a very good chance that you are diminishing your chances to be hired because they're probably looking for flexibility. The best answer is,

"Yes, for the right opportunity." Inquire as to potential duties, locations and type of programs or incentives for people who do relocate. Keep in mind that you might not be willing to relocate for entry-level but for a promotion to management, maybe yes.

Who has had the greatest influence on your life?   In this answer, only give one person's name. Try to have that individual be a person with authority, whether it is a former teacher, professor, a former boss or author of an article or book that you've read that was influential on your life. *Here they are looking for the qualities you relate to in a mentor.* The person you select often provides valuable insight into your character and also provides a reflection of your exposure to studying successful individuals in your chosen field. Employers are impressed with candidates who have the ambition to study the top minds or performers in their profession. Follow your selection with a short explanation as to why you feel they have been the most influential person, whether they taught you how to take risks, to live every day to its fullest or to focus and pursue your calling in life.

What is your greatest strength?   Or what have been your greatest accomplishments or achievements thus far? In any interview there are a few questions designed for you to sell yourself, and this is one of them. Interviewers categorize this as a "convince me" question. Before the interview, prepare 1 or 2 key qualities that you possess that you know from prior research to be the greatest demand for that particular job. Through questions, find out what traits are most sought after and tailor your presentation to those qualities. In other words, relate your greatest strength to the qualities needed to satisfy that position. If the employer is known for innovation, demonstrate that you are innovative. If they have a reputation for being conservative, follow suit. If they pride themselves on teamwork, discuss your ability to function within a group. State the quality or strength and then support your claim with your previous accomplishments. Be ready to cite 1 or 2 what I call "hero stories" that will make you attractive to your employer and be sure to make them as interesting as possible. Interviewers hate to be bored! If leadership is a sought after trait, consider people you have hired or led, an academic experience, training course or a committee you served on which demonstrates leadership.

What is your greatest weakness?   This is a trick question that has eliminated many qualified but unprepared applicants. The rule is to focus on the positive. Stay away from the negative. And never answer, "Well, I'm constantly late" or "I lack attention to detail" or "I'm afraid to be a leader." Common sense dictates everyone has his or her positives and negatives. Remember this golden rule: You are screened in because of your strengths and screened out because of your weaknesses. In your reply, substitute the word weakness for challenge and consider, "Well, it's true that everybody has their strengths and challenges. However, I feel that if I had to identify my biggest challenge, it would be an inability to tolerate other workers around me who were not as dedicated to the achievement of the organization's objectives. I am a dedicated team player who goes above and beyond the call and I expect the same from my co-workers." Then supplement with a word story.

For example, in the past maybe you've coached a fellow employee to become more focused, to be motivated or be in sync with the organization's objectives. Try, "In my previous job, I came across an individual who was unfocused and didn't seem particularly excited about working. And as a result, his or her performance was lacking. I immediately noticed it (thereby showing sensitivity and a keen awareness of your co-workers), but rather than tattle to management or chastise my fellow co-worker, (here you're showing your maturity), I called him or her aside quietly and tried to find out if it was a personal distraction and offered my assistance." (There you are demonstrating loyalty and good judgment). This strategy will go a long way to your being hired.

What would you like to be doing 5 years from now? This question provides the interviewer with useful information on your future objectives. Their exact thought process: Should we make an investment in this person or are they here for a pit stop? Remember, the employer may be investing thousands of dollars in your training, so they want to be certain of a return on their investment! Many an unprepared candidate has no idea where their career will lead them. They haven't done their homework with regard to upward mobility and have no clue about the progression schedule for outstanding talent. Interviewers want to know that you have a plan! Regardless of the job title for which you are applying, you should know what the next job title and duties would be if you were promoted. Know the career path! Highlight your plans to acquire the necessary skills for long-term growth within that organization. By doing so, you will demonstrate maturity, good preparation skills and a true knowledge of yourself and the company and its career path. That will go a long way to being accepted.

How would other people describe you? In this case, the interviewer is looking for clues to your personality. Inform the interviewer that you get along with co-workers, have achieved the respect of your subordinates, previous instructors or supervisors, and articulate that you work well with other people. Create a picture of positive self-esteem and an active social participant so that the employer senses that outside the confines of the job, your co-workers will respect you.

What particular aspect of this job do you think will interest you the least or you think you'll have the most problem with?   The strategy is to convert the question into an opportunity to sell yourself. Describe your passion for the field or industry and why you chose the occupation. Tell the interviewer that you recognize that some aspects are more exciting than others but that you're not afraid of detailed type of work. Add that the positives totally outweigh the negatives. It is a good practice to never admit any negative feelings about the job, no matter how much the interviewer coaxes you into doing so. If the interviewer tries to throw you or sway you by saying, "Well, you realize that this is a very difficult work schedule and sometimes there's a lot of overtime involved " or "Some of our customers are very difficult to handle" or "Sometimes the organization is very cutthroat," reply in a positive but honest manner. They may be just testing you.

How do you feel about either a male or female boss?   Many times an interviewer will ask you about having a boss who is the opposite sex than you are. Cite the fact that you get along well with male and female co-workers, subordinates and supervisors and cite specific references to support that statement. Tell the interviewer that you are not a person who discriminates and that you have had pleasant relationships with both male and female co-workers in the past.

What kind of people irritate you or do you not like to work with? Answer this question by citing that you do not tolerate irresponsible people, that you take your career seriously and prefer people with clear focus. Be very firm with this answer.

Why have you changed jobs so frequently?   If your resume indicates that you're a "job-hopper," it's important that you tailor your resume to exclude unrelated positions to help you appear more stable. One of the major reasons why applicants are rejected is because interviewers fear that the person is unfocused. Share why you are passionate about this field. The interviewer will appreciate your honesty and candor.

Why have you been out of work so long?   Take the offensive and address this concern before it becomes a negative issue. If you have gone back to school, raised a family or you took the time to change your career path completely and needed a training course or apprenticeship program, these are acceptable answers. If you have no acceptable answer or went through a tough time in your life, try this. "Well, quite frankly, I used this time period to really sit down and reexamine my personal goals and lifelong objectives. I have reached the conclusion that this particular job function and your particular company fit my goals and objectives for these reasons," and then list those reasons.

Do you have plans to continue your education? Many employers, especially large corporate employers, have education or tuition reimbursement programs. If you decide to go on for additional training and it relates to the job at hand, the employer may pay for a percentage of your tuition. A common concern is: "Will that help me or will they feel that if I go back for more education, it will distract me from my performance during the working hours?" The rule here is to do your homework and find out if it's a prerequisite to having the job. If you're already continuing your education, be honest and tell the employer that you don't feel that your class time will be a detriment to your job. Restate that you are a person who is organized and disciplined and your schooling definitely will not detract from your performance on the job. If you are taking continued education, stress to the employer or interviewer that this knowledge will help you because it will make you a more valuable asset to their organization.

Is it difficult for you to tolerate or put up with other co-workers or individuals who have different interests, goals or are less ambitious than you are? This question is a perfect opportunity for you to display the all-important flexibility and versatility that employers seek. Cite a specific word story or situation, which has demonstrated your diversity and ability to tolerate different interests. Interviewers recognize that you might not get along well with everybody in the organization. And that's OK as long as you can continue to do the job effectively. Consequently, you want to demonstrate an ability to persuade and influence others.

Do you have any questions for me? It is always regarded as professional to pull out a well-prepared sheet of 3–4 specific questions that were not covered during the course of your interview. Questions can help you and are an essential element of job-hunting etiquette. Regardless of how positively or negatively the interview itself may have gone, don't appear too lazy by not asking questions. The questions you ask will also demonstrate how intelligent you are. In fact, many hiring authorities believe it's not your answers that are important but the questions you ask that will really demonstrate how capable you are of doing the job. Intelligent questions convey to the interviewer preparation, seriousness of purpose, and a real sense of knowledge of the position.

Don't be afraid to ask about the incumbent, why the position is open, the training, how the career path will be changing in the future, new product lines or changes to the industry. Don't be afraid to ask the interviewer about their passion or how they got started within the company. In fact, if it's difficult to break the ice at the beginning of an interview, I counsel my clients to ask the person across from them, "Tell me, how did *you* get started with this organization? What's your background? What do you like most about the company?" Remember, the interview is a conversation, not an interrogation.

Many candidates report that when using my techniques, interviews sometimes ask, "Hey, who's conducting the interview here, me or you?" When that happens, I know you're on the offensive and showing passion for the role. At the end of the interview feel free to pull out your notes, sit back and fire away with your questions that clarify any open issues.

The 10 Best Questions to *Ask* Any Interviewer

1. How are employees evaluated and promoted?
2. Will I be able to see my specific work location?
3. How did you get started with this organization?
4. Can you describe your training program?
5. How did the opportunity become available?
6. What separates top performers from average employees?
7. What are the most important attributes that you look for when hiring?
8. What is the potential for advancement?
9. When will you be making a decision on this position?
10. *How do we proceed from here or is there anything we have discussed that would prohibit you from hiring me?* This is my personal favorite. It forces the interviewer to disclose any possible hesitancy, which you can then overcome.

Post Interview Activities

A FTER EVERY INTERVIEW, I suggest you analyze your performance in an effort to improve.

Criteria to Evaluate Before Taking a Job

As far as salary is concerned, avoid any mention of a specific figure. Let the interviewer be the first to name a salary figure. Be reasonable in terms of your demands. Research what people in that industry or organization earn. Remain open and flexible in regards to compensation.

If unsure, say, "I'm looking for a salary and benefit package commensurate with what a person of my experience, background, capabilities and potential would normally obtain" or "What would you normally pay somebody with my skills and background?" That way, they are forced to answer the question and you can decide if it's in your acceptable range.

In the course of your answers, the interviewer will determine your maturity level, initiative, if you work well as a team member, how flexible and adaptable you are, how conscientious you are and if you're a hard worker. They'll be looking at your honesty, sincerity, how disciplined a candidate you are, any emotional adjustment and, finally, your professionalism.

These factors influence their decision with regard to how generous they are concerning the salary and benefits package. Here is a summation of what you should evaluate before making a commitment. To begin, there are 3 primary categories typically associated with compensation, which include:

1. Salary (base, bonus, commissions, profit sharing, equity)
2. Benefits (medical, dental, disability insurance)
3. Savings Plan (401K, matching funds, stock options, equity positions)

Other Considerations

(Should not be minimized, as they add up!)

Advancement potential
Cell phone reimbursement
Child or day care
Company car or vehicle
Computer allowance

Counseling services
Equal opportunity employer
Expense account
Job location
Memberships/associations
Overtime
Parking privileges
Performance appraisal
Relocation reimbursement or allowance
Training
Travel requirements
Tuition reimbursement
Union or non-union
Vacation time

Evaluating A New Offer

Accepting or rejecting an offer is part emotion, part intellectual and part gut feeling. To assist you in the process of determining if an offer fits into your big picture plan for attaining your career calling, here is a list of questions:

- Can I fulfill these duties?
- Will I fit into this new culture?
- Is the commute reasonable?
- Is the organization stable?
- Is there an opportunity for growth?
- Is the compensation fair?
- What adjustments will I have to make?
- Does it fit into my overall career calling plan?

Resignation Letter

(Should you ever need it!)

Date

Name of Employer
Title
Company
Address

Dear _____:

This purpose of the letter is to inform you that I have made a decision to leave (name company). My last planned date of employment is _____. I have gained tremendous experience here, and have enjoyed working for you. This decision to change was reached only after thorough consideration.

I wish continued success to (name company). Please feel free to contact me after I leave if I can be of any further assistance.

Sincerely,

Signature

Your Name

The Exit Interview

You never know when you might cross paths with a former employer, supervisor or co-worker, especially if you remain in the same industry. No matter the circumstances leading to the change in your employment, always be professional!

Always remember to leave on positive terms. Be professional! No matter what the reason for leaving (fired, quit, downsized, etc.) you should always be cordial and classy. No slamming doors, throwing coffee in your former boss's face (yes, I have seen this!), harsh words about promised compensation, negative feedback on how you would have managed the place, etc.

Being professional means putting in a full day of work, even on your very last day, and not compromising your work ethic. Be sure to erase all of your computerized documents, including email, and when you leave for good, make sure you don't forget any personal items. Praise those individuals who have been helpful to you and make sure you assist your replacement (if applicable) to the very best of your abilities. Nothing less is acceptable. You never know when you will come in contact with your former employer, supervisors or co-workers.

If you are asked to do an exit interview, be positive, or if you find it difficult to do so, at the very least be neutral in your feedback. Employer bashing never helped anyone and usually causes more problems. The last 10 minutes is how people will always remember you, so be professional!

25 Hints on Being Successful Once You're Hired

1. Start on a positive note
2. Play the game!
3. Keep an open mind

4. Participate in social activities
5. Get along with others
6. Be aware of the power channels
7. Question your own efficiency
8. Be professional at all times
9. Stay away from complainers
10. Continue to challenge yourself
11. Gear up for your next promotion
12. Attend as much training as possible
13. Learn quickly who your real friends are
14. Be open minded to new responsibilities
15. Determine your role and responsibilities
16. Gravitate toward the stars in the organization
17. Dress for the position you want, not the job you have
18. Be respectful
19. Don't be a complainer
20. Plan your day each day
21. Be courteous and attentive
22. Be helpful and responsive
23. Respect your supervisors
24. Be confident yet reserved
25. Listen more that you talk

Note: Keep an active file of your achievements, build a network of contacts, set new goals and continuously move ahead!

I hope you found this information to be both helpful and informative. In fact, all of these interview based questions, with permission from employers, were taken directly from actual hiring authorities, including Personnel and Human Resource Departments.

Practice and it will be like having the answers to the test before you take the exam. All you need to do is prepare and rehearse. If you can answer (and ask) these questions intelligently, with poise and with confidence, and incorporate your own personal achievements into your answers, you are very likely to achieve your career calling!

What's Next ... Ensuring Success in the 21st Century Workplace

KEY QUESTION: HOW DO I *MAINTAIN* SUCCESS?

In this appendix, you will learn:

KEY TOPICS
- Taking Control of Your Future
- How to Dictate the Game: A Checklist for the 21st Century Superstar
- Recommended Sources for Additional Information
- How to Contact the Author

KEY MESSAGES
- The pursuit of your career calling is a process, not a destination.
- You are never too old to start a new career; at the age of 40, over half of your working life is ahead of you!
- Consistency is a sign of maturity, do not let the process get you too emotionally high or low.
- It is often easier to get hired if you are employed than in you are unemployed.
- Become an opportunity magnet: Study your industry for innovation, new developments, new offerings, and technological advancements; also review the competition and future outlook.
- Become a solutions broker: Continually grow as a person and improve your value as a contributor.
- The average person changes jobs about every 3 years and will hold more than 15 jobs; create a plan to ensure that every action moves you closer to your calling!
- Develop a personal learning library collection of motivational and self-improvement materials.
- Monitor your progress: If your plan for attaining your career calling is not producing the results you seek, alter your strategy and modify your actions.
- Remember, it's not lonely at the top; it's crowded at the bottom!
- Visit www.thecareerguarantee.com for additional resources and strategies.

I have decided to replace the common (and unfortunately unpopular) saying of life @*&%#$ and then you die, with my own mantra ... Life is amazing, and then your legacy lives on!

Taking Control of Your Future

"I know not what your destiny will be, but one thing I know: the only ones among you who will be truly happy are those who have sought and found how to serve."

—Albert Schweitzer

Dictate the Game!

One of the essential points I would like to leave with you is the importance of taking control of your professional activities. Be proactive. Create; don't simply respond. Hopefully, I have provided you with a glimpse into my own life and what has worked for my family and the thousands of clients served through these principles.

Football is the most popular sport in America today. One of the sports innovators, Bill Walsh, best known as former coach of the multiple world champion San Francisco 49ers, actually scripted the first 20–25 plays of every game on his clip board. He was the first professional coach to do this. It was his philosophy and proactive mentality that instead of reacting to the game events, he would seize control of the contest by dictating what went on during the game. Today, every team in the National Football League scripts their plays in an attempt to control the events on the field.

The message: Script your life and don't be dictated to when it comes to your career activities! Do not be directed by the economy or by industries in demand; instead, focus on exactly what you want and it will come to you.

What is important is not that you have finished this book, but that you will actually apply what you have learned to pursue your god given greatness. You now have a blueprint for exploring and finding your unique and compelling career calling. With these newfound principles and techniques, this change from working for a living to contributing to your calling can be swift and powerful. Reading the words is important but taking action is the key! Recall one of my favorite Chinese proverbs:

I hear and I forget.
I see and I remember.
I do and I understand.

Please reflect carefully on the following 5 questions:

1. Will you have found your unique and compelling contribution or will you simply fade into mediocrity?
2. Will you have given more than you have received in your one shot at life?
3. What individuals or organizations will benefit from your professional talents?
4. Will you become a mentor; what person or entrepreneur can benefit from your expertise?
5. What will be your legacy and how do you want to be remembered?

Living Your Purpose

> *"For all sad words of tongue and pen, the saddest of these, it might have been!"*
>
> —John Greenleaf Whittier

For me, those 5 questions guide my actions and everyday thoughts. If I am not moving closer to my purpose and passion then I am simply moving farther away. It is important to condense your purpose, write it down (I carry mine in my wallet) and refer to it each and every day. Here is my latest version:

> *"My purpose is to inspire and empower others to find their career calling and achieve a life filled with balance and happiness. I assist others to fulfill their dreams through my speeches, workshops, radio and television appearances and practical personal growth books. I believe we are all born to do something extraordinary; my life's work is to make certain this occurs for every person or organization with whom I interface."*

Stop and take the time to write yours!

Your career and everything you do should be an expression of your purpose. I do not wish for you to end up like many, wandering generalities unsure of their purpose or passion and working in a job without a clue as to why they are doing it. Be mindful of the "Is this all there is?" syndrome. As you have learned, it is important, almost essential to have felt a yearning or a void, a sense of emptiness that will motivate you to pursue your rightful place in the world, a place where you can exhibit your unique and compelling gifts and contributions. Without a strong enough motivation, often we are complacent and miss an opportunity for greatness.

Your objective is not to accumulate "stuff" to validate your success. If you want a possession, make sure your motives are because you truly want it and not because you feel it will validate your accomplishments to others. Trust me, most people don't really care. Gradually people come to the realization that collecting material things is unfulfilling.

At some level we all hunger for greater purpose and meaning in our lives. We need to feel in our heart and souls that we matter, that we are making a difference to others, that we are leaving the world a better place. It is an empty feeling to merely take, to exist; there is so much more to life.

Adopting a belief system that puts passion and purpose first provides an opportunity to inspire others, by leaving your mark and contributions in a positive, unforgettable way. Be memorable, be unforgettable!

6 Reasons People Fail in Their Quest

> "If a man is called to be a street sweeper, he should sweep streets even as Michelangelo painted, or Beethoven composed music, or Shakespeare wrote poetry. He should sweep streets so well that all the host of heaven and earth will pause and say; here lived a great street sweeper who did his job well."
>
> —Dr. Martin Luther King

Pride in a job well done is a key ingredient to career success and happiness. Regardless of where you are in the cycles of obtaining career passion and purpose (finding your calling), you MUST always give your best to the job at hand. Here are 6 reasons why many people fail in their quest ... beware!

1. *Negative attitude:* Be careful of your negative self-talk and self-defeating beliefs about your potential. You have learned to control your thought process and expect success!
2. *Lack of persistence:* You have been exposed to countless examples of individuals who have overcome hardship and obstacles to

achieve their calling; simply commit to avoiding excuses and see roadblocks as adventures to be conquered.

3. *No enthusiasm:* Get excited! Regardless of economic indicators, there has never been a better time in history to pursue your individual career calling. There are innovations and inventions creating incredible opportunities for great careers where you can contribute and demonstrate your unique and compelling skills and abilities.

4. *Disorganized approach:* Start with the end in mind and direct all of your energies, resources and contacts to that objective. You have learned the systematic process of getting in touch with your authentic self and mastering the 5P's ... *Passion-Purpose-Power-Profit-Peace of Mind!*

5. *An inability to handle objections:* You have learned to anticipate challenging questions and how to effectively answer them with conviction and specific examples. Nobody obtains their career calling without overcoming obstacles; expect them and use them as an opportunity to learn!

6. *Failure to seek help or ask for the position:* You have learned to expect success and more importantly, to deserve it! It is your destiny; do not let a little discomfort or shyness prevent you from asking for what you truly want and deserve!

Here is a fun story, one that takes a humorous view of persistence, dedication and a "no matter what" approach to obtaining a position:

> The CIA had an opening for an assassin. After all the background checks, interviews and testing were completed, they identified 3 candidates ... 2 men and a woman.
>
> For the final exam, the CIA recruitment officer took one of the men to a large metal door and handed him a gun. "We must be confident that you are able to follow your instructions, no matter what the circumstances. Inside this room, you will find your wife sitting in a chair. Kill her," the CIA recruitment officer said. "You cannot be serious, I could never shoot my own wife," said the candidate. The CIA recruitment officer said, "Then you are not the right man for this job. Take your wife and go home."
>
> The 2nd male candidate was provided the same instructions. He took the gun and went into the room. All was quiet for a few minutes. Then the male candidate came out with tears in his eyes. "I tried, but I cannot kill my wife." The recruitment officer said, "You do not have what it takes for this job. Take your wife and go home."

Finally it was the female candidate's turn. She was given similar instructions to kill her husband. She took the gun and went into the room. Shots were heard, one after another. Then screaming, banging, crashing on the walls of the room. After a few minutes, everything was quiet. The door slowly opened and there stood the woman.

She wiped the sweat from her brow. "This gun is loaded with blanks," she said. "I had to beat him to death with the chair. When do I start?"

This example is extreme and meant to be humorous, but it illustrates the importance of persistence, overcoming objections, distinguishing yourself, using ingenuity and above all ... asking for the position!

Commit to Lifelong Learning

"If the rate of change on the outside exceeds the rate of change on the inside, the end is near."
—Jack Welch, former chairman
and CEO of General Electric

It is my hope that the www.thecareerguarantee.com website becomes an essential resource in your family's personal learning library. It is a valuable source of inspiration and knowledge for the serious career seeker. I strongly recommend that your family creates what I call a *personal learning library* in your home. This should include beneficial websites, books, articles, tapes and anything that furthers or supports your family mission. In our home, we have an area in our den and all family members, including the kids, regularly contribute to this evolving library of positive messages and helpful resources. If you don't have one already, start one today!

Success in life and the attainment of your career calling require you to behave and act in accordance with your authentic self, that is, your *true identity*. You have learned that incredibly, you can alter and control your own internal identity, which is a mirror of your belief systems and associations to events that have occurred throughout your life.

Your true identity should be unique and compelling and through your career calling, you should aspire to contribute your gifts to others for the betterment of society.

Seek out quality mentors and strive to become a quality mentor for others. Be a person others seek out for guidance and wisdom regarding mastering this increasingly complex and confusing game called life. Differentiate yourself and strive to become what my mom calls "an angel on earth."

Be unconventional; that is, do not follow the path of least resistance or follow the crowd but rather carve out your own niche, your own special place in society. Work hard to rid yourself of fear, uncertainty and doubt that restrict your progress and erode your confidence and self-esteem. Tap into that inner reservoir of talent, creativity and contribution to solve problems and challenges of others. Create new systems, inspire your peers, develop new solutions and invent new products and services that enrich lives.

Every day is an opportunity to further your purpose and enhance your passion. Be mindful of the 5 P's (passion, purpose, power, profit and peace of mind), which are essential to achieving true balance and happiness. Here are my suggestions for lifelong learning and living the life of your dreams:

See the Bigger Picture In the scheme of time, we are all here for but a brief moment. That does not mean we cannot strive to become significant. Come to grips with your place on earth, in your community, in your family, in your employment and in your own heart. Avoid the limiting beliefs of others who have fallen prey to the trappings of materialism or other external reward systems. Serve a higher power, whatever that higher power is for you. Push your own boundaries and you will find that you have a gift for others to expand their own horizons as well.

Be Accountable for Every Action You Take We are all imperfect beings on a journey of self-knowledge and contribution. You will make mistakes and bad decisions; if you are not you are most likely playing it safe and not testing your full capabilities. Convert each defeat or failure into a learning experience that results in progress. Push yourself! As indicated, we are only using about 10% of our mental capacity. Strive to achieve larger accomplishments to impact more people through your thoughts, words and actions.

Be a Mentor and Role Model By pursuing your career calling, you become an automatic role model to others who are stuck in a negative cycle or repeating destructive patterns or behavior. Share your newfound knowledge of the process and educate others and their families on what it takes to achieve true balance and happiness. Share the secrets of your success! Make certain that each and every day, your presence raises the expectations and performance of those with whom you interact.

Adopt the philosophy that you are a "success celebrity," and that meeting you is a privilege. People want to study you, mirror your actions and achieve similar results. You are a person of influence; use this gift wisely!

Live With Integrity Be a class act under all circumstances and eliminate pettiness, jealousy or envy from your life. Set standards based on your own personal thermostat and not by artificial measures or others' beliefs. Every champion record holder knows that to attain a state of grace and excellence, one must create their own targets in order to further their calling. Raising my standards has been a catalyst for massive change and success in both my personal and professional life.

If you adopt these belief systems and live by these standards, you will find more people want to be with you, do business with you, interact with you and seek your friendship. We can all use more quality friends! Select your associates and friends carefully; as you grow personally you will often find that your interests and dialogue may require a change in your relationships.

Checklist for the 21ˢᵗ Century Superstar

> *"Don't give them what they want; give them what they never believed was possible."*
>
> —Orson Welles

With all the changes brought about by the emerging global economy, increasing frequency of career changes and mandate to control and manage one's own career, here are my thoughts regarding what makes a superstar in this new era.

1. *Smart, educated and informed* (21ˢᵗ century superstars understand you can have more degrees than a thermometer, but if you do not remain informed on your industry, employer, department or product/solutions ...)
2. *Technologically proficient* (21ˢᵗ century superstars save time by investing in their knowledge of technology and the incredible value provided by the Internet)
3. *Articulate* (21ˢᵗ century superstars practice or join groups, for example, Toastmasters, to master the ability to speak in public, or at least to large groups)
4. *The ability to be decisive and not afraid to make decisions* (21ˢᵗ century superstars can be wrong more often than they are right, but they learn from each decision and keep swinging!)

5. *A willingness to take risks* (21st century superstars understand and live by the concept of no risk, no reward!)

6. *Act on conviction* (21st century superstars establish moral and ethical principles and stick to them!)

7. *Hard working and driven* (there is no end game or finish line, 21st century superstars understand that continuous improvement is the critical competency!)

8. *An abundance of physical, mental and emotional energy* (21st century superstars schedule time each and every day to feed their body, mind and spirit with beneficial exercise, wisdom and enlightenment!)

9. *A sincere and caring interest in people* (technologies become obsolete, machinery breaks, patents expire, but 21st century superstars understand that people will always be the common element to all business)

10. *The ability to anticipate the future* (21st century superstars always remain a step ahead!)

How to Dictate the Game: A Checklist for the 21st Century Superstar

IN STUDS TERKEL'S BOOK, *Working,* a phone receptionist from Chicago was quoted as saying, "I don't know what I'd like to do. That's what hurts the most. That's why I can't quit the job. I really don't know what talents I may have and I don't know where to go to find out."

Maybe you shared these feelings prior to reading this book. But if you gave your sincere attention and commitment to the text and corresponding exercises, I am quite confident that this will no longer be the case. So, congratulations! You have achieved your goal to finish what you started. And as the saying goes, "You've come a long way, baby."

You have been an active participant, are educated on the process and should be commended for sticking with it. Quoting Thomas Jefferson, "What we learn to do we learn by doing."

This book was designed to help you obtain your unique career calling. After reading it, you are now familiar with the tools and have "learned by doing" the strategies that will be helpful for the rest of your career. These techniques are time tested and produce results. They can work for you if you will make the decision to dedicate yourself and follow through. Armed with a competitive edge and useful tools, it is time to get busy!

One of my favorite sayings is, "It's what you do after you know it all that counts." You now know what to do, so go do it! Because each of us is truly a unique and compelling being, formulating a career path is a do-it-yourself activity and will take a great deal of effort to solidify each job as you move closer to your ultimate destination. How much effort you put into careering will have a direct correlation to how successful you are in finding your ideal role.

> *"The quality of a person's life is in direct proportion to their commitment to excellence regardless of their chosen field of endeavor."*
>
> —Vince Lombardi

The level of the role that you target is also going to have an effect on the amount of time you need to land that position. The more prestigious the position, the more time it's going to take you to find and secure it. It is easier to find an entry-level job simply because there are more of them and the skills required are less demanding. So persevere. The swift do not always win the race; sometimes the winners are those individuals who keep on running.

You have learned that it is advisable not to quit your current position until you have discovered one more suited to your talents. It is easier to get hired if you are employed than if you are unemployed. The perception on the part of some employers is that if you don't have a job, there may be something wrong with you. So try to conduct your search while you're still working and have a steady means of income. It will make things easier and put less financial pressure on you.

10 Career Success Rules to Live By

1. Remember that finding your career calling is a full time job.
2. Aim high but have reasonable expectations about your time frame.
3. You must enjoy your career or you will ultimately stop doing it.
4. If you don't have a career goal, you will most likely wind up working for someone who does.
5. Avoid fear and procrastination by identifying a specific career goal and reducing large job search activities to smaller tasks.

6. Start with the end in mind and have no regrets; remember the rocking chair scenario!
7. Your choices and actions, not fate, will determine your career destiny.
8. It is easier to find a new career while still employed; never quit until you've found a new career.
9. Spare no expense in your career search campaign. Remember: *Good things don't come cheap and cheap things are rarely good.*
10. To find your career calling be the most prepared; qualifications and intelligence are often secondary to preparation and dedication.

5 Career Axioms to Live By

1. Career success equals knowledge, desire, commitment and dedication.
2. You should target the decision maker who has the ability to hire you and demonstrate that you have problem solving talents that will help their organization achieve their goals.
3. Great careers may come to those who wait, but only those careers not wanted by those who hustle.
4. Career seekers: It isn't lonely at the top … it is crowded at the bottom!
5. The road to career success is always under construction; keep the faith!

There is never a perfect time, nor are circumstances ever ideal to obtain your ideal career; sometimes you just have to start! There will be costs to finding your calling, including: technology costs, telephone costs, postage, traveling costs and wardrobe. Be frugal, but not cheap! If you appear cheap or cut corners, that will show when you go to meet your employer. Don't sacrifice or be anything less than 100% professional because taking time to spend money now will pay big dividends in the future. If you spend an extra dollar here or there or are concerned about funds, think about the millions you'll earn over the course of your career.

For example, if you start at age 20 and retire at 60 (work for 40 years) and average, say, $50,000 a year, that's $2 million dollars earned over the course of your lifetime! With that perspective, a few dollars here or there shouldn't matter to you. If you're going to buy that one suit or dress for the interview, make it count. You deserve a professional resume. If you need to make a long distance telephone call to a mentor or buy lunch for an employer, do it!

With the tools that you now have at your disposal, I know that with effort you can find your ideal career. It will be challenging, but as a long-term thinker seeker, you know that good things take effort. Quoting again the great Vince Lombardi, "The difference between a successful person and others is not a lack of strength, not a lack of knowledge, but, rather, a lack of will."

By finishing this book, you should be congratulated on achieving that goal. You are ahead of 90% of all career seekers who talk the talk, but do not walk the walk. You have a competitive edge; now use it! Many people say that they found a great career after having completed less than half the book because a word, example or exercise created a breakthrough in their thought process.

It truly is the little things that make the difference. In today's 21st century workplace, people will be forced to change jobs and industries at a record pace, while many will start their own venture. That is why it is essential to take action and plan for the long term. This is a marathon, not a sprint! And please don't put the book on the bottom shelf or give it away because there will most likely is another day in the future when you may need to refresh your memory on the enclosed strategies.

I strongly recommend that you periodically go back to the "hot buttons" and refresh your memory, even after you have found what today you consider your career calling. Tomorrow your priorities could change. Remember: change is inevitable; progress is not!

Strive to continually educate yourself and be open to new ideas. Malcolm Forbes, at one time one of the world's richest men, said, "Education's purpose is to replace an empty mind with an open one."

Maybe you read this book because a decision to find a better career was made by you or, for many of the individuals who are unfortunate out there, it was made for you. So many of you have in your mind that this will never happen again or it could never possibly happen to you. I recommend that you remain ever alert and keep your options open. Maintain contacts with these friends and former employers through social events, letters or what have you. Give them a call once in a while just to keep in touch. Keep your credentials updated at all times.

Build your network and expand your connections. If you attended an educational institution, stay active in your alumni association. Keep track of the people that you meet through trade organizations or committees because you never know when you're going to need these people for support and guidance.

As I have told you, there are many different ways to adopt these tools and incorporate these concepts. Ultimately 10 people can get 10 different ideas from these concepts. But remember one thing. If your particular plan is not working, simply change your approach. Modify your actions. That is why I have included so many different variations of strategies, because what works for one career seeker might not be as successful for another. Your *Career DNA* is unique!

You should now be motivated to establish a long-term career plan and seek to derive incredible passion and energy from your chosen occupation. I want you to thoroughly enjoy the process of self-discovery. Do not achieve to be happy; happily achieve your objectives! And be confident that you now have the tools to achieve those goals.

Go back and review those particular components of the program that were confusing or you felt you might need more help on and use them as reinforcement. Use these materials before going into an information interview or an actual interview setting to assist you and to help build your confidence. Commit yourself to constantly being a lifetime achiever. As I mentioned earlier, be a personal growth stock and not a career seeker whose assets are on the decline. Become "Me, Inc!"

Be able to articulate your unique and compelling strengths and learn to create a desire for your talents. Make your strength your knowledge of yourself and your thorough preparation. If you have an audio player in your car, invest in positive messages and training programs rather than listening to music or news.

Give yourself a monthly credential review. Constantly review your accomplishments. If you join a new group or committee, keep an active computerized file, and keep updating your accomplishments. I personally keep a file in my desk drawer in my office at home and every month I update my credentials. Otherwise, I would forget all my accomplishments.

My message is to do it now! When you observe an opportunity, don't procrastinate. Do it right now! Of the 3 types of job seekers, the drifters, the dreamers and the doers, live in the last category. Be a doer! I want you to *do* the best you can and achieve your full potential. So, use all your resources.

The message is this. Constantly try to grow. Improve your worth. Don't become stagnant. As Albert Einstein said, "Try not to become a man of success but, rather, to become a man of value."

And remember, sometimes the most negative or hopeless situations can provide you with a great opportunity. When the chips are down and you think you're really out of it, that's when sometimes people can take more chances that they never would have taken, had they not run into such a challenge. How many times have you heard about very successful men or women who were down to their last nickel, who had gone bankrupt a number of times and had taken that one last step, that risk and forced themselves to do well and went on to greatness? Keep getting up!

You will never be a loser unless you admit you're a loser. As Josephus Daniels proclaimed, "Defeat never comes to any man until he admits it." And as Samuel Johnson said, "Life affords no higher pleasure than that of surmounting difficulties, passing from one step of success to another and forming new wishes and seeing them gratified."

Remember the old saying, "You have 2 ears and 1 mouth. So listen twice as much as you talk." When starting a new career, be reserved. Take in the sights. Learn the employer's culture. See who the people in power are. Find out which people you can trust. Look for those people in a position of authority whom you'll have to impress. Once you find out who the key players are in the organization, learn what their particular objectives are and tailor your performance to coincide with their objectives. In other words, mirror the goals of the people who make up the power structure. And, more importantly, through your own methodology, let them know that you are mirroring their goals, either by memo form or just by your day-to-day performance.

Careering isn't always fair. Be aware that at certain times in your career you may truly be the best person for a job or for a promotion but, because of politics, friends or relatives of the people who are above you or who are your management, that may result in your not getting the position. You're not always going to win against the boss's son or daughter or son-in-law. My advice is to focus on your needs; there are always options. Use social activities like company picnics, sports, dining out or parties, to get to know your peers on a non-professional level.

Your outlook is now bright and you should feel energized by your new-found knowledge and potential. You have the competitive edge! Your dreams will become reality. Quoting Eleanor Roosevelt, "The future belongs to those who believe in the beauty of their dreams."

As mentioned earlier, most people change occupations several times during their lives. Job changes usually occur more frequently when career seekers are young. Generally, men tend to remain in occupations longer than women, college graduates longer than people with less education, full-time workers longer than people who are part-time workers, and self-employed people longer than individuals who collect wages or a salary. If you do decide to change careers, always leave a job on positive terms. You never know when you will need a good reference or recommendation. Leaving a job can be emotionally difficult. But, again, focus on the positive aspects of your new status.

Go to work with a smile on your face. And remember to be loyal to your employer. That doesn't mean loyal to the degree that you can never leave if things aren't working out your way or you're unhappy. But whether you are in a position 1 day, 2 days, 10 years, 20 years, be loyal to your employer. They deserve your best until you leave!

If you have an entrepreneurial drive, be smart and surround yourself with quality mentors. Starting a new business is difficult, but if you have a passion for your product or service, you have the essential ingredient already. If you decide that a franchise is where your career calling lies, do your homework and obtain testimonials from other franchise owners. At the risk of sounding sappy or like I am preaching, be sure to act polite and decent to every person who assists you, coaches you or inspires you. In most cases, you can get what you want by using these 4 expressions:

1 word: "Please"
2 words: "Thank-you"
3 words: "I love you"
4 words: "How may I help?"

If unclear on any aspect, I strongly urge you to review until you feel comfortable. Your career and life are that important. Do this until the career that you dream about becomes your daily reality. I am confident that you can find your career calling and, by doing so, will experience health, happiness and success in your life.

I will leave you with one of my favorite poems on the subject of contribution …

> "For man must live his life on earth
> Where hate and sin and wrong abound
> Tis here the soul must prove its worth
> Tis here the strength of it is found
> And he has justified his birth
> Who plants one rose on barren ground"
>
> —Edgar Guest

Find your passion, achieve your purpose, yield your power, realize your profit and attain what we all seek ... peace of mind. By following this *Master Career Formula* you will leave a positive legacy and know in your heart and soul you mattered.

Recommended Sources for Additional Information

HERE IS A PARTIAL list of books and authors I recommend for the serious career seeker.

Think and Grow Rich, Napoleon Hill, New York: Fawcett Crest, 1960

The Success Principles, Jack Canfield, HarperCollins Publishers, 2005

The One Minute Millionaire, Mark Victor Hansen and Robert G. Allen, Harmony Books, 2002

Do What You Are, 3rd edition, Paul Tieger and Susan Barron-Tieger Little, Brown, 2001

See You at the Top, Zig Ziglar, New York: Pelican, 2000

E-Myth Mastery: The Seven Essential Disciplines for Building a World Class Company, Michael Geber, New York: Harper Business, 2004

The One Minute Manager, Kenneth Blanchard and Spencer Johnson, New York: Berkley Books, 1983

Good To Great: Why Some Companies Make the Leap ... and Others Don't, Jim Collins. New York: HarperCollins, 2001

Body for Life: 12 Weeks to Mental and Spiritual Strength, Bill Phillips, New York: HarperCollins, 1999

The Millionaire Next Door and *The Millionaire Mind,* Thomas J. Stanley, Ph.D. Andrews McMeel Publishing, 2000

The Tipping Point, Blink, and *Outliers,* Malcolm Gladwell. Little, Brown and Company, 2006–2008

Getting Things Done: The Art of Stress-Free Productivity, David Allen, New York: Viking, 2001

Mavericks at Work, William C. Taylor & Polly Labarre, Harper Collins Publishers, 2006

Create Your Own Future, Brian Tracy, John Wiley & Sons, 2002

The Sales Bible, Jeffrey Gitomer, John Wiley & Sons, 2003

Never Eat Alone, Keith Ferrazzi, Amazon, 2005

Please visit www.thecareerguarantee.com for other great books, suggested career websites, useful career webinars and seminars, and other valuable information such as entrepreneurial references; some of them are free!

Please feel free to write to me if you feel I can be of service to you or if you learn of a new or interesting twist to the careering process. Through the website and publications, *I plan on awarding prizes for the most creative methods used to obtain one's career calling.* Upcoming projects include: solutions to starting your own business, managing your time wisely, and achieving peak physical and mental health.

As always, my focus is on positive contribution and assisting people to be enthusiastic, long-term learners. My goal remains to teach individuals to be healthy in mind and body and control their own destinies. Remember, constant and never ending improvement is the key! God bless you and let's keep in touch.

How to Contact the Author

CHRISTOPHER J. KUSELIAS AND his associates at thecareerguaran-tee.com offer a variety of programs based on the concepts and ideas in this book. Formats include keynote speeches, 1–3 day seminars, career coaching and organizational improvement programs. For more information, please call 800-237-8562 or email info@thecareerguarantee.com.